CULTURAL PROPERTY

While nations, societies, and individuals have always been engaged with both the tangible and intangible aspects of cultural objects, such as archaeological artifacts, artworks, and historical documents, the twenty-first century is seeing a significant shift in the law, ethics, and public policy that have long characterized this field. This book offers a comprehensive analysis of recent developments concerning cultural property. It identifies the underlying forces that drive these changes, focusing on the new political balance between source countries and market countries, the strengthening of cross-border lawmaking and law enforcement, the growing impact of provenance research and due diligence as legal, professional, and ethical norms, and the transformative role of digital databases. The book sets out normative principles for designing a better synergy of the hard-law and soft-law mechanisms that govern cultural property policy and markets. It proposes a property theory of ownership and custody of cultural objects and outlines a model of "new cultural internationalism" to promote cross-border collaboration on cultural heritage, including new restitution frameworks.

AMNON LEHAVI is the provost, Atara Kaufman Professor of Law, and former dean of the Harry Radzyner Law School at Reichman University. He serves as a national correspondent at UNIDROIT (the International Institute for the Unification of Private Law) and an adjunct professor at Luiss University. Prof. Lehavi served as co-president of the Law Schools Global League. His previous books published by Cambridge University Press include *Property Law in a Globalizing World* (2019) and *The Construction of Property: Norms, Institutions, Challenges* (2013).

CULTURAL PROPERTY

Law, Policy, and Markets

AMNON LEHAVI

Reichman University

CAMBRIDGE
UNIVERSITY PRESS

Shaftesbury Road, Cambridge CB2 8EA, United Kingdom

One Liberty Plaza, 20th Floor, New York, NY 10006, USA

477 Williamstown Road, Port Melbourne, VIC 3207, Australia

314–321, 3rd Floor, Plot 3, Splendor Forum, Jasola District Centre,
New Delhi – 110025, India

103 Penang Road, #05–06/07, Visioncrest Commercial, Singapore 238467

Cambridge University Press is part of Cambridge University Press & Assessment,
a department of the University of Cambridge.

We share the University's mission to contribute to society through the pursuit of
education, learning and research at the highest international levels of excellence.

www.cambridge.org
Information on this title: www.cambridge.org/9781009449380

DOI: 10.1017/9781009449403

First published 2026

A catalogue record for this publication is available from the British Library

*A Cataloging-in-Publication data record for this book is available from the
Library of Congress*

ISBN 978-1-009-44937-3 Hardback
ISBN 978-1-009-44938-0 Paperback

Cambridge University Press & Assessment has no responsibility for the persistence
or accuracy of URLs for external or third-party internet websites referred to in this
publication and does not guarantee that any content on such websites is, or will
remain, accurate or appropriate.

For EU product safety concerns, contact us at Calle de José Abascal,
56, 1°, 28003 Madrid, Spain, or email eugpsr@cambridge.org

CONTENTS

FIGURES

ACKNOWLEDGMENTS

My interest in cultural property law grew as I was working on my previous book published by Cambridge University Press, titled *Property Law in a Globalizing World* (2019). In that book, I sought to offer a taxonomy of different types of assets and examine how their legal governance is affected by extralegal forces of globalization. Alongside land, intellectual property, and digital assets, I explored various types of chattels, and it was then that I began to realize how unique and fascinating the world of cultural objects is. What started out as an examination of a subset of chattels soon developed into a full-fledged academic passion for cultural property, and I have never looked back.

I am grateful to many colleagues and friends who share this enthusiasm. In March 2022, I hosted an international conference at Reichman University, my academic home, titled *Due Diligence, Digital Databases, and Cultural Property Law & Policy*. I had the pleasure of bringing together an exceptional group of colleagues, including Manlio Frigo, Giuditta Giardini, Corinne Hershkovitch, Vincent Michel, Marc-André Renold, Marina Schneider, Isabelle Tassignon and Matthias Weller.

I am also privileged to have been part of two incredible scholarly groups working on particular challenges in cultural property. One is the Working Group on "Private Art Collections – Orphan Objects," organized by the International Institute for the Unification of Private Law (UNIDROIT) in Rome and led by Marina Schneider, UNIDROIT's Principal Legal Officer. I had the pleasure of working alongside colleagues such as Eric Cottier, Patty Gerstenblith, Corinne Hershkovitch, Joanna van der Lande, Keun-Gwan Lee, Marc-André Renold, Jorge Sánchez Cordero, Marcílio Toscano Franca Filho, Till Vere-Hodge, and Anna Veneziano. The second group, led by Matthias Weller, the Alfried Krupp von Bohlen and Halbach Professor for Civil Law, Art, and Cultural Property Protection Law at the University of Bonn, was asked by the German federal government's Commissioner for Culture and Media to prepare a study on the restitution of Nazi-looted art. The study, titled *Stärkung der Beratenden*

Kommission ("Strengthening the Advisory Commission"), was published in April 2024. It was a privilege to collaborate with outstanding colleagues: Niv Goldberg, Alexander Herman, Antoinette Maget Dominicé, Franz-Stephan Meissel, Dan Michman, Mayo Moran, Felix Uhlmann, Lars van Vliet, and Charlotte Woodhead.

I have also greatly benefited from teaching, since 2023, as an adjunct professor at Luiss University in Rome alongside my dear colleagues, Christian Iaione and Elena De Nictolis. Working on cultural property law and policy in Italy, and specifically in the Eternal City of Rome, is, well, exactly as inspiring as it sounds. I am indebted to many other colleagues and friends, including Roberto Caso, Deborah Gerhardt, Michele Graziadei, Sefy Hendler, Raz Samira, Lior Zemer, and Dina Zilber.

Finally, my deepest gratitude goes to my family: my late father, Rami Lehavi, my mother, Aya Lehavi, my brother Avner Lehavi, my sister Shlomit Lehavi, and, above all, my incredible life partner, Sharon Aronson Lehavi, and our wonderful daughter, Lia. This book is dedicated to them.

~

Introduction

On September 17, 2022, a ceremony was held in Rome to celebrate the return of a group of three terracotta sculptures, dated to around 300 BCE, known as *Orpheus and the Sirens*. The sculptures, which depict a seated man and two mythical Sirens, were returned to Italy from the J. Paul Getty Museum in Los Angeles, where they had been on display since being purchased in 1976 by J. Paul Getty Sr. from a private Swiss bank for the sum of 550,000 U.S. dollars.[1]

The Getty Museum agreed to return the sculptures, without the need for formal proceedings, after it was presented evidence following a joint investigation conducted by the Carabinieri Command for the Protection of Cultural Heritage and the Antiquities Trafficking Unit at the Manhattan District Attorney's Office – two agencies whose work will be examined in this book – indicating that the sculptures had been illegally excavated in the early 1970s in southern Italy from a tomb in a town near Taranto in the region of Puglia, before being smuggled out of the country.[2]

The ceremony took place at the Museum for Rescued Art (Museo dell'Arte Salvata), which was inaugurated in June 2022 in a cavernous hall originally built during the Roman Empire as part of the Baths of Diocletian and now affiliated with the National Roman Museum (Museo Nazionale Romano).[3] The Museo dell'Arte Salvata displays recently recovered cultural items in Rome for a limited time before assigning them to the permanent collection of a museum geographically closest to the site of their probable origin, following a long-standing policy of the

---

[1] Elisabetta Povoledo, *From L.A. to Rome, Three Ancient Scupltures Get Hero's Welcome*, N.Y. TIMES, Sept. 17, 2022.

[2] *Id.*; Claire Voon, *The Getty Institute Will Return a Set of Illegally Excavated Life-Size Statues to Italy*, THE ART NEWSPAPER, Aug. 11, 2022.

[3] *See* the website of Museo Nazionale Romano (National Roman Museum), *Museo dell'Arte Salvata*, www.turismoroma.it/en/places/museo-nazionale-romano-museo-dell%E2%80%99arte-salvata (last visited Feb. 1, 2025).

Italian Ministry of Culture.[4] In the case of *Orpheus and the Sirens*, after being displayed at the Museo dell'Arte Salvata for a period of about six months, the sculptures were transferred in March 2023 to the National Archaeological Museum of Taranto (Museo Archeologico Nazionale di Taranto – MArTA), where they now form part of the museum's permanent collection. MArTA celebrated the arrival of *Orpheus and the Sirens* by holding a special exhibition.[5]

I visited the Museo dell'Arte Salvata in October 2022. Above the entrance to the museum, a banner was hung. It featured a photo of the head of Orpheus and the text: "*Il ritorno di Orfeo in patria*" ("The return of Orpheus to the homeland"). Orpheus and the Sirens, facing each other, were placed on a platform in the center of the hall – where the photo that serves as the cover image of this book was taken. Behind the display, a large screen showed videos documenting the efforts of the Carabinieri and other Italian agencies to protect the nation's cultural heritage. Throughout the hall, various artifacts were displayed, including items from a collection of 142 purloined antiquities seized by the Antiquities Trafficking Unit in New York and returned to Italy in the summer of 2022 (forty-eight of which were recovered from the collection of Michael H. Steinhardt).[6]

***

We live in a time witnessing an influx of interest and dramatic changes in the field of cultural property. While nations, societies, and individuals have always been engaged with both the tangible and intangible aspects of cultural objects, such as archaeological artifacts, artworks, and historical documents, considered "on religious or secular grounds … as being of importance for archaeology, prehistory, ethnology, history, literature, art

---

[4] Elisabetta Povoledo, *In Rome, a New Museum for Recovered Treasures before They Return Home*, N.Y. TIMES, July 17, 2022.

[5] Museo Archeologico Nazionale di Taranto (MArTA), *Orpheus and the Sirens Exhibition at MArTA in Taranto*, https://museotaranto.cultura.gov.it/en/orpheus-and-the-sirens-exhibition-at-marta-in-taranto/ (last visited Feb. 1, 2025). *See also* Cesare Bechis, *Il ritorno a casa di "Orfeo e le Sirene," il ministro Sangiuliano: "Queste opere rappresentano la bellezza,"* CORRIERE DELLA SERA, Apr. 5, 2023 (It.) (reporting on the exhibition's opening).

[6] Tom Mashberg, *New York Returns 142 Looted Artifacts to Italy*, N.Y. TIMES, July 20, 2022. Following a joint investigation of the Carabinieri and the Antiquities Trafficking Unit, hedge-fund pioneer Michael H. Steinhardt surrendered 180 items he had bought from dealer Robert Hecht and that turned out to be stolen and illegally placed on the market. *See also* Paolo Conti, *Arte, tornano a casa le opere rubate all'Italia e finite nei musei Usa,* CORRIERE DELLA SERA, Sept. 4, 2022 (It.) (reporting on the six-month operation held by the Antiquities Trafficking Unit).

or science,"[7] the twenty-first century is seeing a significant shift in the legal, ethical, public policy, and professional paradigms that have long characterized this field. Moreover, the heightened focus on cultural property today extends far beyond industry "insiders" such as museums, auction houses, collectors, and other professionals. It also comes from political actors, civil society organizations, and the public at large, as reflected in the widespread media coverage of cultural property issues around the globe.

This book offers a comprehensive analysis of recent developments concerning cultural property. It identifies the underlying forces that drive these changes, focusing on the new political balance between source countries and market countries, the strengthening of cross-border lawmaking and law enforcement, the rising importance of provenance research and due diligence as legal, professional, and ethical norms, and the transformative role of digital databases. The book then sets out normative principles for designing a better synergy of "hard-law" and "soft-law" mechanisms that govern cultural property policy and markets. It proposes a property theory of ownership and custody of cultural objects, and outlines a vision of "new cultural internationalism" to promote cross-border collaboration on cultural heritage, including new models of restitution.

Two key normative principles guide the analysis of law, policy, and markets for cultural property throughout the book.

First, the various drivers of change in the world of cultural property point to a dynamic interplay between the recent development of national and cross-border "hard-law" instruments pertaining to cultural property and the political, professional, reputational, and technological changes that are gradually moving cultural property away from its formerly dominant features of political imbalance, opacity, and secrecy toward becoming a field that is increasingly typified by at least a certain degree of transparency and accountability. This latter trend affects countries, communities, cultural institutions, collectors, and other key actors, often through decentralized but persistent processes.

Thus, as the book illustrates, the growing duty – whether legally binding or professionally and ethically expected – to engage in due diligence while dealing with cultural property and the increasingly important role

---

[7] Council of Europe, Convention on Offences Relating to Cultural Property (CETS No. 221), signed on May 19, 2017, Ch. 1, art. 2, §2a (defining the term further, based on the formal designation of objects "by any Party to this Convention or to the 1970 UNESCO Convention on the Means of Prohibiting and Preventing the Illicit Import, Export and Transfer of Ownership of Cultural Property," while also enumerating various categories of cultural property).

of provenance research, significantly attributable to the nonbinding 1998 Washington Principles on Nazi-Confiscated Art[8] – with digital, interactive databases of cultural property playing a key role in supporting these trends – attest to the dynamic interplay between law, policy, and markets. This is especially evident when political, professional, and ethical developments are consolidated over time to create a form of "soft-law jurisprudence" that can influence formal lawmaking and law enforcement processes. Thus, alongside international conventions that employ public international law and private international law tools, other legal avenues, particularly criminal law and law enforcement, are increasingly harnessed to address real-time issues, such as illegal excavations and illicit cross-border trade. The strong collaboration between U.S. and Italian law enforcement agencies described above exemplifies this approach.

At the same time, current ethical and moral deliberations about addressing past wrongs in the context of cultural property – whenever formal legal proceedings are not accessible, either because a past action was not deemed illegal at the time but is currently viewed as illegitimate or otherwise troubling or because the window for formal legal action is now closed owing to rules and doctrines such as statutes of limitations, the good-faith purchaser doctrine, or acquisitive prescription – are increasingly typified by what I term "legalistic ethical reasoning."

This approach implies that normative concepts such as wrongfulness, attribution, and scale of remedies, which are not detached from jurisprudential deliberations about legal liability and its consequences, play an important role in the soft-law jurisprudence that emerged in the context of restitution committees set up in certain European countries to implement the 1998 Washington Principles' call for a "just and fair solution" to address Holocaust-era dispossessions. Moreover, such legalistic ethical reasoning can also play a significant role in other contexts, as can be seen in France's evolving approach to the restitution of colonial-era objects to African countries.

The book, therefore, delves into the complex interface between national and international hard-law instruments and soft-law concepts and mechanisms that may develop over time as a result of gradual but persistent political, professional, and ethical shifts in the field of cultural property.

Second, reconsidering the concepts of "cultural nationalism" and "cultural internationalism," which emerged in the literature to depict

---

[8] U.S. Department of State, *Washington Conference Principles on Nazi-Confiscated Art* (Dec. 3, 1998), www.state.gov/washington-conference-principles-on-nazi-confiscated-art/ (hereinafter: "1998 Washington Principles").

competing interests and arguments put forward in the context of cultural property, this book advances a normative approach of "new cultural internationalism."

As explained in the book, the concept of new cultural internationalism seeks to facilitate collaboration between countries, cultural institutions, and other actors – including those in both source countries and destination countries – while granting the various stakeholders a "safety net" that promotes better-balanced bargaining power, mutual trust, and prospects for long-term cooperation in designing a legal future for governing past treasures.

In turn, such an approach may also view potential claimants, such as source nations demanding the return of artifacts taken from them many decades or centuries ago, as bearing certain duties as global custodians of such cultural artifacts, even if the claim for their return is based on the objects' local/territorial origin or significance. In other words, a normative design for restitution in an era of new cultural internationalism must consider the rights and duties of all relevant stakeholders.

What this means is that there is no inherent contradiction or tension between protecting the "national" and the "international" or "universal" values of cultural objects and cultural heritage. Once nation-states, and source nations in particular, are assured that their domestic laws and policies – from patrimony laws to rules on the export of cultural objects – are more effectively protected across borders through both international legal norms and practical measures of enforcement, they can and should commit to their role as global custodians of culture. As such, nation-states should be accountable, at least to some degree, not only to intergovernmental organizations or other countries but, even more importantly, to the decentralized global audience.

The concept of custodianship, and its relation to a normative theory of new cultural internationalism, also serves as a basis for a general theory of ownership and custody of cultural objects held by cultural institutions. It argues that, alongside in rem rights, cultural institutions also have certain in rem duties, including toward the decentralized global audience that may attach value to these objects. Thus, museums should provide, inter alia, basic digital access to images and other information about items in their collections, recognizing the cross-border value of culture.[9]

***

---

[9] *See* Chapter 5, Section 5.4.

The book is structured as follows. The first part identifies four types of factors driving the fundamental changes in the world of cultural property over the past few decades – the new balance between nationalism and internationalism; the evolution of national and cross-border lawmaking and law enforcement; the growing importance of provenance research and due diligence as legal, professional, and social norms; and the transformative role of digital databases.

Chapter 1 analyzes the new balance of power emerging in the world of cultural property between source countries and market countries. It begins with a case study of the Benin Bronzes and the recent measures of "cultural diplomacy" employed between Nigeria, as the source territory of these objects, and governments and cultural institutions located in Western countries. It then explores cases where cross-border collaboration takes place to address real-time or recent acts of illegal excavation, looting, and smuggling of cultural objects across national borders. With these in mind, the chapter introduces the concept of new cultural internationalism, suggesting that these changing dynamics should not be seen as leading to "isolationism" or a backlash against globalization. This is particularly true as the cross-border nature of cultural property markets is probably more dominant than ever before, though it now bears more complex and multidirectional traits compared to the traditional categorical division into source countries and market countries.

Chapter 2 portrays the changing legal landscape addressing the legality – or lack thereof – of the cross-border movement and trade of cultural property. It starts by identifying the key features of legal divergence across national legal systems, concerning both private law and public law aspects, and discusses how this disparity poses a challenge for dealing not only with past actions but also with the current features of the global market for cultural objects. It then provides an overview of the evolution of international institutions and legal norms related to cultural property, such as the 1970 UNESCO Convention on the Means of Prohibiting and Preventing the Illicit Import, Export and Transfer of Ownership of Cultural Property,[10] which focuses on public international law, and the 1995 UNIDROIT Convention on Stolen or Illegally Exported Cultural Objects,[11] which introduces a key dimension of private international law.

---

[10] United Nations Educational, Scientific and Cultural Organization (UNESCO), Convention on the Means of Prohibiting and Preventing the Illicit Import, Export and Transfer of Ownership of Cultural Property, Nov. 14, 1970, 823 U.N.T.S. 231.

[11] UNIDROIT Convention on Stolen or Illegally Exported Cultural Objects, June 24, 1995, 2421 U.N.T.S. 457.

This chapter demonstrates how new legal avenues are being pursued to address the gaps created by the traditional system of international conventions, specifically through the introduction of criminal law and law enforcement measures, including regional and bilateral collaborations. It highlights, respectively, the role of the European Union and bilateral mechanisms to which U.S. federal and state agencies are a party. The chapter then introduces how "legalistic ethical reasoning" may operate in scenarios where hard-law claims are unavailable, such as in cases involving cultural property dispossessed during the Nazi era.

Chapter 3 observes the stark contrast between long-standing practices of market opacity and secrecy in the field of cultural property and current legal, professional, reputational, and ethical trends that promote a requirement to engage in due diligence in dealing with cultural property. It then highlights the changing role and scope of provenance research, which has evolved from a highly selective focus on an object's "career highlights" to promote its value to the task of identifying potential "dark holes" in the chain of title and possession of an item since its creation or discovery. This changing paradigm can be largely attributed to the renewed interest, as of the 1990s, in the history of items that may have been involuntarily lost by their Jewish owners during the Nazi era. This chapter shows how the professionalization and systematization of provenance research, while taking different forms across various jurisdictions in Europe and beyond, may prove essential for promoting provenance research on the history of other cultural items, such as colonial-era objects.

Chapter 4 offers a first-of-its-kind taxonomy of different types of cultural property databases that are being developed and expanded at an increasing rate by a multitude of private and public entities. It explains how such digital databases may facilitate a legal, public-policy, and professional shift in designing law, policy, and markets for cultural property. The chapter begins with a study of the recently launched Digital Benin project, and then offers an overview of (1) international and national databases for crime detection, such as INTERPOL's Stolen Works of Art Database; (2) private databases offering due diligence services, such as the Art Loss Register (ALR); (3) theme-specific databases on Nazi-looted assets and colonial contexts; and (4) academic and professional databases for provenance research, such as the Louvre's open-access digital database, which was launched in 2021 and features more than 500,000 objects from the museum's collections, or the Getty Provenance Index, which provides access to about 2.5 million items. The chapter seeks to demonstrate that digital databases on cultural property can (1) facilitate fact-finding in specific disputes; (2) serve as a professional or even legal benchmark for abiding by due diligence and similar norms; (3) enable information-sharing as a basis for "just and fair solutions" in the context of Nazi-looted artifacts, "colonial contexts," and other circumstances that address past wrongs; and (4) promote a general value of transparency in a field previously dominated by opacity and secrecy.

The second part of the book offers a normative blueprint for designing the legal future of cultural property – anchored in the concept of new cultural internationalism – while considering the interface between legally binding norms and soft-law instruments, professional norms, ethical considerations, and other forces that impact the actions and motives of the various stakeholders.

Chapter 5 seeks to identify the normative foundations of a property theory of ownership and custody of cultural objects. It begins by examining the case study of the current legislative, administrative, and judicial framework in Italy, which aims to grant cultural institutions an essentially eternal right to control the reproduction and use of images of their cultural holdings. It then addresses the redefinition of a "museum" adopted in 2022 by the International Council of Museums (ICOM), and the implications this may have for the role of cultural institutions. The chapter then seeks to delineate the contours of a property theory of cultural objects and the corresponding sets of in rem rights and in rem duties that should apply to cultural institutions as both proprietors and custodians, by reconsidering the role of "placeness" of cultural institutions and their collections. In particular, a theory of ownership and custody of cultural objects held by cultural institutions should refer to the link between culture and space in considering the mirror-image questions that have been at the center of legal, professional, and public attention, namely: does a cultural institution have an in rem right to appropriate the value components of cultural objects, such as by limiting or prohibiting others from using or reproducing images of items in its collection; and, conversely, does a cultural institution have an in rem duty, as a custodian of culture, to actively make accessible to the public images and other information on items in its collections?

Chapter 6 aims to construct a future-looking theoretical framework for handling cultural objects for which questions of past illegality and/or illegitimacy arise, but where a potential claimant – whether an individual, community, or source nation – is unable to pursue formal legal proceedings against the current possessor, and the relevant law enforcement agencies cannot equally pursue criminal, administrative, or public law proceedings.

Accordingly, the chapter seeks to identify normative principles for dealing with the issue of "restitution" (broadly defined) that operates outside the realm of hard-law norms and institutions. It starts by examining the key aspects of the institutional/procedural and normative principles of the restitution committees established in certain European countries and tasked with the development and implementation of "just and fair solutions" to address Holocaust-era wrongful dispossessions. It then considers whether "just and fair solutions" can be devised for other contexts and, if so, how legalistic ethical reasoning could be adapted for these settings. The focus then shifts to the case study of France and its complex approach to the restitution of colonial-era objects to African source countries. The chapter then examines the various remedial mechanisms that are in operation, or that can be developed, to apply such normative principles to broader contexts of addressing past wrongs, including long-term loans, digital restitution, and the establishment of cross-border trusts to enable the joint custody and stewardship of collections. The chapter, and the book, conclude by addressing the role of such a normative blueprint, aligned with the concept of new cultural internationalism, in moving toward the convergence of law, policy, and markets for cultural property.

PART I

Drivers of Change in the World
of Cultural Property

1

Changing Winds in the Cross-Border
Politics of Cultural Property

1.1   The Benin Bronzes and Beyond

In the summer of 2022, the governments of Germany and Nigeria signed a "Joint Declaration" on the transfer of ownership of 1,130 cultural artifacts that had been part of the collections of German public museums for many decades.[1] While the Joint Declaration itself is nonbinding, it indicates a strong tentative commitment by both the government and twenty public museums and institutions in Germany that hold these pieces to enter into specific agreements with the National Commission for Museums and Monuments (NCMM) in Nigeria.[2]

These items form a significant part of the "Benin Bronzes" – thousands of bronze, brass, ivory, and wooden artifacts that were looted, as a punitive measure, by the British army in 1897 from the royal palace of what was then the Kingdom of Benin, located in present-day southern Nigeria. These artifacts subsequently ended up in museums and collections, mostly in Western countries.[3] According to the digital database "Digital Benin," launched in late 2022 and discussed in Chapter 4, information has been collected, as of early 2025, about 5,285 Benin objects held in 136 museums and other institutions across twenty countries.[4]

---

[1] Joint Declaration on the Return of Benin Bronzes and Bilateral Museum Cooperation between the Federal Republic of Germany and the Federal Republic of Nigeria, signed on July 1, 2022, https://kulturstaatsminister.de/fileadmin/user_upload/Downloads/Aufarbeiten/2022-07-01-Joint-Declaration-Benin-Bronzes.pdf (hereinafter: "Germany–Nigeria Joint Declaration").

[2] *Id.* art. 4. For an analysis of the Germany–Nigeria Joint Declaration, *see* Alexander Herman, *Benin Bronzes: Germany–Nigeria Joint Declaration*, 27 ART ANTIQUITY & L. 159 (2022).

[3] John Henry Merryman, *Introduction, in* IMPERIALISM, ART AND RESTITUTION 1, 6–7 (John Henry Merryman ed., 2006); David Frum, *Who Do the Benin Bronzes Belong To?* THE ATLANTIC, Oct. 2023, at 60.

[4] Digital Benin, *About*, https://digitalbenin.org/ (last visited Feb. 1, 2025). *See* further details in Chapter 4, Section 4.1.

The Germany–Nigeria Joint Declaration, described as heralding a "new era in cultural diplomacy,"[5] is a milestone in a process that is also impacting other countries and institutions. It vividly illustrates the changing winds in the cross-border politics of cultural property, including in relation to previously unsuccessful campaigns by African countries to reclaim cultural objects that had been taken from the continent, and their respective territories, during the colonial era.[6]

Jesus College at the University of Cambridge was the first institution to return a Benin Bronze item to Nigeria in 2021.[7] In the summer of 2022, both the University of Cambridge and the University of Oxford announced their intention to return their entire collections of Benin Bronzes to Nigeria, comprising 116 and 97 items, respectively.[8] Later that year, the British Charities Commission, which regulates decisions by such nonprofit organizations, approved this measure.[9] The Horniman Museum in London also announced in 2022 that it would hand over ownership of its seventy-two Benin items.[10] However, in contrast to Germany, the British government has not yet committed to returning items, including around 900 pieces that are part of the permanent collection of the British Museum,[11] and would thus require a legislative amendment to enable such a return.[12]

In October 2022, the Smithsonian Institution in Washington, D.C., returned twenty-nine Benin Bronzes to the NCMM in a ceremony held in the Smithsonian's National Museum of African Art,[13] and several other

---

[5] Gareth Harris, *"The Benin Bronzes Are Returning Home:" Germany and Nigeria Sign Historic Restitution Agreement*, THE ART NEWSPAPER, July 4, 2022 (quoting Nigeria's ambassador to Germany, Yusuf Tuggar).

[6] For more on the failure of these previous campaigns, which had been initiated during the 1950s and 1960s, *see* BÉNÉDICTE SAVOY, AFRIKAS KAMPF UM SEINE KUNST: GESCHICHTE EINER POSTKOLONIALEN NIEDERLAGE (2021) (Ger.).

[7] Nadia Khomani, *Cambridge College to Be First in the UK to Return Looted Benin Bronze*, THE GUARDIAN, Oct. 15, 2021.

[8] Craig Simpson, *Oxbridge Agrees to Return Looted Benin Bronzes to Africa*, THE TELEGRAPH, July 29, 2022.

[9] Craig Simpson, *University of Cambridge Given Go-Ahead to Return Its Benin Bronzes to Nigeria*, THE TELEGRAPH, Dec. 12, 2022.

[10] Emma Gregg, *The Story of Nigeria's Stolen Benin Bronzes, and the London Museum Returning Them*, NATIONAL GEOGRAPHIC, Sept. 17, 2022.

[11] *Id.*

[12] For the complex legal situation concerning the British Museum and other national museums in Britain, *see* Alexander Herman, *Museums, Restitution and the New Charities Act*, 27 ART ANTIQUITY & L. 193, 193 (2022).

[13] Smithsonian Institution, Press Release, *Smithsonian Returns 29 Benin Bronzes to the National Commission for Museums and Monuments in Nigeria* (Oct. 11, 2022), www.si .edu/newsdesk/releases/smithsonian-returns-29-benin-bronzes-national-commission-museums-and-monuments.

museums in the United States have followed suit.[14] The key role of France
in dealing with objects amassed during the colonial period, mostly from
Africa, is discussed in Chapter 6.[15]

Under most of these agreements, not all items are immediately and
indefinitely returned to Africa, meaning that, alongside the transfer of
ownership, museums that hitherto possessed the Benin Bronzes would be
able to maintain and exhibit some of them through long-term loan agreements and other arrangements. Thus, for example, while the signing of the
Germany–Nigeria Joint Declaration was followed by the physical return of
twenty items by Germany's foreign minister in a ceremony held in Nigeria
in December 2022,[16] the specific agreements between German museums
and the NCMM typically include permission to retain a considerable
number of items in German museums. These arrangements acknowledge
the underlying ownership while offering a new context for exhibiting the
Benin Bronzes, as seen, for example, at the Rautenstrauch-Joest-Museum
in Cologne[17] and at the Ethnological Museum in the Humboldt Forum in
Berlin (see Figure 1.1).[18]

A somewhat unexpected turn of events – at least from the perspective
of Western governments and museums – occurred in March 2023, when
the president of Nigeria published a formal decree in the country's Official
Gazette recognizing the traditional Oba of Benin Kingdom's ownership
of the Benin Bronzes and vesting in him the custody and management of
the objects.[19]

The Nigerian government's decision, which applies retroactively to all
returns already made as well as future returns of Benin Bronzes, has been

---

[14] Hannah McGivern, *Trove of Benin Bronzes in U.S. Museums Collections Repatriated to Nigeria*, THE ART NEWSPAPER, Oct. 11, 2022.

[15] *See* Chapter 6, Section 6.2.

[16] Gareth Harris, *Germany Kicks off Major Benin Bronze Restitution with Return of 20 Artefacts to Nigeria*, THE ART NEWSPAPER, Dec. 22, 2022.

[17] Gareth Harris, *Cologne Museum to Transfer 92-Strong Benin Bronze Collection Back to Nigeria*, THE ART NEWSPAPER, Dec. 10, 2022.

[18] *See* Humboldt Forum, *Benin Bronzes*, www.humboldtforum.org/en/temporaere-neukonzeption-der-benin-sammlung/ (last visited Feb. 1, 2025). For the underlying concept of the Humboldt Forum, inaugurated in September 2021, which includes the collections of the Ethnological Museum and the Asian Art Museum of the Staatliche Museen zu Berlin (National Museums in Berlin), *see* HUMBOLDT FORUM, (POST) COLONIALISM AND CULTURAL HERITAGE: INTERNATIONAL DEBATES AT THE HUMBOLDT FORUM (2021).

[19] Notice of Presidential Declaration – On the Recognition of Ownership, and an Order Vesting Custody and Management of Repatriated Looted Benin Artefacts in the Oba of Benin Kingdom, Order No. 1 (2023) 110:57 O.G. A245-247 (Nigeria) (hereinafter: "2023 Decree").

Figure 1.1 Uhunmwun elao, memorial head of a queen mother (iyoba). Nigeria, Benin Kingdom, sixteenth century.

Source: Ethnological Museum, Humboldt Forum, Berlin. © Staatliche Museen zu Berlin, Ethnologisches Museum/Pierre Adenis.

met with mixed reactions from Western governments and museums. Many of them have expressed the concern that, as well as the problem that lies in the transfer of the ownership of the Benin Bronzes to the private hands of the Oba, rather than maintaining public ownership under the government or the NCMM, this unilateral act could also adversely impact the preservation, accessibility, and exhibition of these items.[20] This concern is particularly pronounced because, prior to the 2023 decree, the Nigerian government and NCMM had set up the EMOWAA Trust, tasked with developing a new cultural institution, the Edo Museum of West African Art,[21] which is designated to serve as the new home of many of the Benin Bronzes.[22]

While the government of Nigeria announced in March 2023 that it would build a royal museum in Benin City, on behalf of the Oba and his court, to display many of the items, this was not immediately followed by concrete plans.[23] The resulting uncertainty prompted the University of Cambridge to announce in May 2023 that it would delay the return of the items in its possession.[24]

In contrast, in May 2024, the Swedish ambassador to Nigeria announced their government's decision to return thirty-nine Benin Bronzes during a courtesy visit to the Oba of Benin, Ewuare II, at his palace in the ancient City of Benin, thereby coming to terms with the Oba's legal entitlement.[25] Similarly, in July 2024, the University of Iowa Museum of Art returned two Benin objects to the Oba of Benin rather than the government, becoming the first U.S. museum to do so.[26]

---

[20] Gareth Harris, *Nigeria Transfers Ownership of Benin Bronzes to Royal Ruler – Confusing European Museums' Plans to Return Artefacts*, THE ART NEWSPAPER, Apr. 26, 2023.

[21] *See* Museum of West African Art, *About*, https://wearemowaa.org/our-story/ (last visited Feb. 1, 2025).

[22] Alex Marshall, *Who Owns the Benin Bronzes? The Answer Just Got More Complicated*, N.Y. TIMES, June 4, 2023. In November 2024, the Museum of West African Art Institute inaugurated the first building within the planned campus in Benin City. Catherine Hickley, *Benin City Museum Opens First Part of Planned Campus*, THE ART NEWSPAPER, Nov. 4, 2024.

[23] Marshall, *supra* note 22.

[24] Macdonald Dzirutwe, *Return of Benin Bronzes Delayed after Nigerian President's Decree*, REUTERS, May 10, 2023. This position was met with criticism in Nigeria, despite internal divisions, with the director of the Museum of West African Art calling "for a new focus, based on realities on the ground rather than romantic notions of the West." Philip Ihenaco, *Benin Bronzes: Whose Restitution Is This, Anyway?* THE ART NEWSPAPER, May 31, 2023.

[25] Usman A. Bello, *Sweden to Return 39 Artefacts to Oba of Benin Palace*, DAILY TRUST (Nigeria), May 15, 2024.

[26] Gareth Harris, *Iowa Museum Becomes First in the U.S. to Return Looted Benin Bronzes to Royal Ruler*, THE ART NEWSPAPER, July 18, 2024.

It remains to be seen how the case of the Benin Bronzes will unfold over the course of time, but it is likely to have broader implications and lessons for addressing the cross-border aspects of cultural property. Moreover, while the restitution or return of cultural artifacts to African countries, or other former colonies,[27] has been framed as part of an effort to "right colonial wrongs,"[28] and is accordingly part of a broader inquiry and initiatives concerning collections that have a "colonial context,"[29] key developments and intricate normative considerations about cultural property extend beyond the colonial past or other historic events, such as those concerning Nazi-looted artifacts.[30]

In fact, the complex ways in which the changing cross-border political dynamics become embedded in the operation of global markets for cultural property, professional and ethical norms pertaining thereto, and the myriad of "hard-law" and "soft-law" national and supranational instruments are vividly manifested in the meeting of present challenges concerning cultural property. In other words, the rebalancing of cross-border political power, national public policy, markets, and law currently unfolding around the globe is proving crucial not only for addressing past events but, to an even greater extent, for engaging in cross-border action in real time.

Thus, as illustrated in the introduction to the book, Italy is playing a dominant role in reclaiming cultural items that have been stolen or illegally excavated from its territory over the past few decades and which then found their way, through a chain of intermediaries, to museums and collections in other countries.

---

[27] The term "return" is generally used to describe the physical transfer of cultural items back to the source country from where they were removed *before* the implementation of international conventions, while the term "restitution" refers to the returning of items that had been illegally removed from a country *after* it had ratified one of the international conventions on the matter. *See* PIERRE LOSSON, THE RETURN OF CULTURAL HERITAGE TO LATIN AMERICA: NATIONALISM, POLICY, AND POLITICS IN COLOMBIA, MEXICO, AND PERU 2–3 (2022).

[28] Harris, *supra* note 5.

[29] For example, on March 13, 2019, German government institutions at the federal, state, and local levels agreed on the "Framework Principles for Dealing with Collections from Colonial Contexts" (an English version of the text is available at www.auswaertiges-amt.de/resource/blob/2210152/b2731f8b59210c77c68177cdcd3d03de/190412-stm-m-sammlungsgut-kolonial-kontext-en-data.pdf and consequently established a joint platform, titled *A German Contact Point for Collections from Colonial Contexts* (available at www.cp3c .org/). The Netherlands is following a similar path. *See* Catherine Hickley, *Forging Ahead with Historic Restitution Plans, Dutch Museums Will Launch €4.5m Project to Develop a Practical Guide on Colonial Collections*, THE ART NEWSPAPER, Mar. 10, 2021.

[30] *See* Chapter 6 for a detailed analysis of the institutional and normative features concerning Nazi-looted assets.

The Italian government and its special law enforcement unit dedicated to this task – the Carabinieri Command for the Protection of Cultural Heritage[31] – are increasingly working with governments and law enforcement agencies in other countries to take action against theft, unlawful excavations, and illegal trafficking of cultural items, and to return such items to Italy, in most cases to the state itself, given its patrimony laws regarding antiquities.[32] These efforts have been aided to a large extent by Italy's collaboration with two designated agencies in the United States: the federal Homeland Security Investigations (HSI) Department of Cultural Property, Art, and Antiquities Smuggling[33] and the New York State Antiquities Trafficking Unit, operating within the Manhattan District Attorney's Office.[34] The collaboration between HSI, the Antiquities Trafficking Unit, and the Carabinieri will be discussed further in Chapter 2, in the context of bilateral mechanisms for law enforcement collaboration that combines both civil and criminal proceedings. However, it should be viewed at the outset as reflecting and further reinforcing the changing *Zeitgeist* in the cross-border spheres of politics, markets, and ethics concerning cultural property. As the title of a 2022 *New York Times* report suggests, "For U.S. Museums with Looted Art, the Indiana Jones Era Is Over,"[35] reflecting not only legal measures but also a broader political change.

This also means that, in many cases, once reliable information about potential acts of unlawful excavation, illegal export, theft, or other wrongdoing is exposed and becomes publicly known, cultural institutions and their respective home countries may surrender objects without exhausting legal proceedings in order to mitigate the professional and reputational damage they may suffer by being associated with such illicit cross-border actions. As noted in the introduction to the book, in the context of *Orpheus and the Sirens*, the J. Paul Getty Museum agreed to return the artifacts to Italy upon receiving the investigation's results, in stark contrast to the years-long dispute between Italy and the Metropolitan Museum of Art

---

[31] *See generally*, LAURIE RUSH & LUISA BENEDETTINI MILLINGTON, THE CARABINIERI COMMAND FOR THE PROTECTION OF CULTURAL PROPERTY: SAVING THE WORLD'S HERITAGE (2015).

[32] Arianna Visconti, *Fighting Cultural Property Trafficking: The Italian Criminal Law Framework and Its Forthcoming Reform*, 26 ART ANTIQUITY & L. 317, 322–25 (2021).

[33] Homeland Security Investigations (HSI), *Cultural Property, Art, and Antiquities Smuggling*, www.dhs.gov/hsi/investigate/cpaa-smuggling (last visited Feb. 1, 2025).

[34] Manhattan District Attorney's Office, *Antiquities Trafficking*, https://manhattanda.org/category/antiquities-trafficking/ (last visited Feb. 1, 2025).

[35] Graham Bowley, *For U.S. Museums with Looted Art, the Indiana Jones Era Is Over*, N.Y. TIMES, Dec. 13, 2022.

in New York over the Euphronios Krater, looted in 1971 from a tomb in Italy and sold a year later to the museum for a then-unprecedented sum of 1 million dollars, and returned to Italy only in 2008.[36] This does not mean, of course, that cultural institutions in market nations, such as the United States, will always yield to purely political or reputational pressure. Chapter 2 will discuss three high-profile disputes concerning the J. Paul Getty Trust, the Cleveland Museum of Art, and the Art Institute of Chicago.[37] But the influx of cases concerning the exposure of cross-border acts such as illicit excavations, illegal export/import, theft, or title "whitewashing" should be attributed not only to more effective law enforcement but also to major changes in the cross-border politics of culture.

The importance of the changing dynamics between "source countries" and "market countries" is also evident in other parts of the world.[38] This is due to the fact that acts of theft, pillage, and illegal excavations of art and antiquities are taking place across all continents, and in some regions their occurrence seems to have accelerated over the past few years. This is particularly the case in source countries that are in the midst of war, civil unrest, or the collapse of the rule of law, such as Iraq, Syria, Yemen, Libya, and elsewhere.[39] Such situations are exploited by local and international smuggling rings, organized crime, and terrorist groups, with the existence of a vibrant global illicit antiquities market[40] and online platforms for

---

[36] Tom Mashberg, *Vase, Thought to Be Looted, Is Seized from Met*, N.Y. TIMES, Aug. 1, 2017 (depicting this case, alongside the 2017 seizure of another ancient vase from the museum that had also been looted in Italy in the 1970s). The Metropolitan Museum has also engaged more recently in returns of items that turned out to have been looted, without the need to pursue formal legal measures against it. *See* Graham Bowley & Tom Mashberg, *The Met Will Return 16 Ancient Treasures Tied to Looting*, N.Y. TIMES, Dec. 15, 2023 (returns made to Cambodia and Thailand).

[37] *See* Chapter 2, Sections 2.2.3 and 2.3.2.

[38] For more on the concepts of "source nations" and "market nations," *see* MARA WANTUCH-THOLE, CULTURAL PROPERTY IN CROSS-BORDER LITIGATION: TURNING RIGHTS INTO CLAIMS 21–22 (2015) (noting, however, that many countries, such as Australia or China, can be typified as both source nations and market nations).

[39] The "market" for looting may also flourish in countries experiencing extreme poverty and insecurity, motivating certain residents who are in economic duress to take part in such activities. SIMON MACKENZIE ET AL., TRAFFICKING CULTURE: NEW DIRECTIONS IN RESEARCHING THE GLOBAL MARKET IN ILLICIT ANTIQUITIES 3–5 (2020); ZEYNEP BOZ, FIGHTING THE ILLICIT TRAFFICKING OF CULTURAL PROPERTY: A TOOLKIT FOR EUROPEAN JUDICIARY AND LAW ENFORCEMENT 67–75 (2018).

[40] Clooney Foundation for Justice, *Conflict Antiquities: The Need for Prosecuting Participants in the Illegal Antiquities Trade for Complicity in International Crimes and Terrorism Financing* (June 8, 2022), https://cfj.org/the-docket-projects/looted-antiquities/need-for-prosecutions/.

illicit trade in such objects,[41] further fueling conflicts in these areas. Unlike in colonial times, the forces driving this illicit market are more much dispersed and globalized, and the sums of money that can be made, especially by brokers and sellers who engage in the "whitewashing" of items prior to their sale to museums or collectors, pose a significant challenge to the protection of cultural property.

At the same time, illicit trade in cultural property has increasingly become, especially since the beginning of the twenty-first century, a matter of genuine global concern. Accordingly, international organizations are seeking to better protect source countries against the tangible and intangible losses incurred through such illicit cross-border actions.[42] In 2003, the U.N. Security Council adopted Resolution 1483,[43] "stressing the need for respect for the archaeological, historical, cultural, and religious heritage of Iraq,"[44] and accordingly decided that:

> All Member States shall take appropriate steps to facilitate the safe return to Iraqi institutions of Iraqi cultural property and other items of archaeological, historical, rare scientific, and religious importance illegally removed from the Iraq National Museum, the National Library, and other locations in Iraq ... including by establishing a prohibition on trade in or transfer of such items and items with respect to which reasonable suspicion exits that they have been illegally removed.[45]

This process, by which the world's most prominent international organization engages directly with cross-border cultural property and calls on all member states to act within their own boundaries, culminated in Security Council Resolution 2347 of 2017,[46] which "deplores and condemns the unlawful destruction of cultural heritage ... as well as the looting and smuggling of cultural property from archaeological sites, museums, libraries, archives, and other sites, in the context of armed conflicts, notably by terrorist groups."[47] Resolution 2347 "calls upon Member States, in order to prevent and counter trafficking of cultural property illegally

---

[41] See, e.g., Katie A. Paul, *Facebook Is the Biggest Marketplace of Illegal Antiquities*, MEDIUM, July 3, 2019.

[42] Ana Filipa Vrdoljak, *Introduction*, in THE 1970 UNESCO AND 1995 UNIDROIT CONVENTIONS ON STOLEN OR ILLEGALLY TRANSFERRED CULTURAL PROPERTY: A COMMENTARY 3, 17 (Ana Filipa Vrdoljak, Andrzej Jakubowski & Alessandro Chechi eds., 2024).

[43] S.C. Res. 1483 (May 22, 2003).

[44] *Id.* Preamble.

[45] *Id.* para. 7.

[46] S.C. Res. 2347 (Mar. 24, 2017).

[47] *Id.* para. 1.

appropriated and exported in the context of armed conflicts, notably by terrorist groups, to consider adopting the following measures, in relation to such cultural property" and provides a detailed list of measures.[48]

Beyond their significance as instruments of international law, these decisions also seem to reflect a new approach to the cross-border political dynamics concerning cultural property. In many cases, these changing winds have been internalized within market nations, motivating law enforcement agencies to act and collaborate with each other without necessarily being pressured to do so by source countries, thereby gaining professional and reputational prestige. Perhaps the most notable example is the New York Antiquities Trafficking Unit, led by Assistant District Attorney Matthew Bogdanos.[49] The Antiquities Trafficking Unit reported in September 2024 that since its establishment it had "recovered more than 5,700 antiquities valued at more than $450 million, and returned more than 4,600 to more than twenty-five countries."[50]

In a high-profile case in 2019, the Antiquities Trafficking Unit was granted a search warrant and seized an Egyptian gold coffin from the Metropolitan Museum of Art after it was revealed that the museum had bought it for 4 million dollars from sellers who were at the top of a global smuggling ring. This ring looted the coffin from an archaeological site in Egypt during the Arab Spring protests in 2011 and then forged provenance documents to facilitate the sale to the museum.[51]

The investigation of this smuggling ring also led to a May 2022 warrant against Jean-Luc Martinez, former director of the Louvre Museum in Paris, who was investigated in France on charges of complicity in fraud and money laundering for allegedly ignoring warning signs about archaeological items sold to the Louvre Abu Dhabi Museum (which is jointly governed by the government of Abu Dhabi and the Louvre) and approving the 2016 purchase

---

[48] *Id.* para. 17. Paragraph 17 then details ten different measures, including civil, administrative, and criminal ones.

[49] For a profile of the Antiquities Trafficking Unit, *see* Ariel Sabar, *The Tomb Raiders of the Upper East Side: Inside the Manhattan DA's Antiquities Trafficking Unit*, THE ATLANTIC, Nov. 23, 2021.

[50] Manhattan District Attorney's Office, *D.A. Bragg Announces Return of 14 Antiquities to the People of Türkiye*, Sept. 12, 2024, https://manhattanda.org/d-a-bragg-announces-return-of-14-antiquities-to-the-people-of-turkiye/. *See also* Benjamin Sutton, *US Authorities Return Antiquities Valued at $10M to India*, THE ART NEWSPAPER, Nov. 15, 2024 (reporting on the return of 1,440 artifacts to India in November 2024).

[51] Elaine Velie, *NY District Attorney's Office Seizes Allegedly Looted Antiquities from the Met*, HYPERALLERGIC, June 1, 2022, https://hyperallergic.com/737317/district-attorneys-office-seizes-allegedly-looted-antiquities-from-the-met/.

for 8 million euros of a granite stele depicting the pharaoh Tutankhamun, along with six other items, all smuggled out of Egypt amid the chaos of the Arab Spring.[52] The same cross-border investigation led, in June 2022, to another search warrant and seizure of artifacts from the Metropolitan Museum of Art, this time of five smuggled Egyptian antiquities purchased by the museum for 3 million dollars from the same sellers.[53] The museum surrendered these items without contest, unlike in previous cases.

In 2021, Iraq reclaimed 17,000 artifacts that had been looted from the country over the past few decades and ended up in the United States – 12,000 artifacts purchased by the Museum of the Bible in Washington and 5,000 artifacts donated by a private collector to Cornell University.[54]

This return was due mainly to an investigation conducted by the U.S. federal law enforcement agencies, led by the Department of Justice, which also fined Hobby Lobby – the private corporation that controls the Museum of the Bible – 3 million dollars for failing to exercise due diligence in its acquisitions. According to the Iraqi minister of culture, this repatriation "restores not just the tablets, but the confidence of the Iraqi people by enhancing and supporting the Iraqi identity in these difficult times."[55] Therefore, the implementation of the 2003 U.N. Security Council Resolution 1483 by domestic law enforcement efforts undertaken within the United States is aligned with a new cross-border approach shared by many market and source countries.

These dynamics are increasingly typifying other cultural property conflicts around the world. In June 2024, the governments of Germany and Cyprus signed an agreement to return sixty antiquities, including twenty-four ecclesiastical relics, that were looted after the Turkish invasion of Northern Cyprus in 1974 by a smuggling ring led by Turkish antiquities dealer Aydin Dikmen. Although the thousands of artifacts looted by Dikmen were seized in 1997, in 2004 the government of Cyprus had to embark on a lengthy legal process against Dikmen in the German courts

---

[52] Aurelien Breeden, *Former Head of Louvre Is Charged in Artifact Trafficking Case*, N.Y. TIMES, May 26, 2022. In February 2023, an appeals court in Paris announced it would maintain the charges against Mr. Martinez and French curator Jean-Francois Charnier, overruling a recommendation made in November 2022 by the French prosecutor to drop the charges. Devorah Lauter, *With Charges Upheld in Louvre Trafficking Case, Should Major Institutions Reconsider Acquisitions of Egyptian Antiquities?* ARTNEWS, Feb. 14, 2023.

[53] Vincent Noce, *Egyptian Antiquities Connected to International Trafficking Ring Seized from Metropolitan Museum in New York*, THE ART NEWSPAPER, June 1, 2022.

[54] Jane Arraf, *Iraq Reclaims 17,000 Looted Artifacts, Its Biggest-Ever Repatriation*, N.Y. TIMES, Aug. 3, 2021.

[55] *Id.* (quoting the Iraqi minister of culture, tourism, and antiquities, Hassan Nadhem).

regarding 316 relics of Cypriot origin, with partial restitution ordered only in 2013 and again in 2015.[56] The current repatriation, by intergovernmental agreement, serves as yet another landmark case in which "cultural diplomacy" is playing an increasingly important role alongside legal action.

Therefore, in all of these cases, cross-border law enforcement cannot be divorced from a new geopolitical discourse – one that seeks to offer a new balance between market countries and source countries. However, as the next section suggests, this discourse should refrain from a simplistic division between "international" and "national" concepts. Instead, it offers a new perspective on the cross-border nature of culture – one that combines political, ethical, economic, and legal aspects.

1.2   Introducing the Concept of "New Cultural Internationalism"

Throughout history, cultural property has been a realm characterized by a complex relationship between the local/national creation, control, and meaning of antiquities, artworks, and other objects, and international/global actions and cultural perspectives. This section seeks to reconsider the concepts of "cultural nationalism" and "cultural internationalism" that have emerged in the literature by pointing out historical and normative problems in drawing lines between these allegedly competing concepts. Instead, it proposes a new approach: "new cultural internationalism."

Particularly since the demise of colonialism in the mid twentieth century, the debate over the possession and control of cultural objects between source countries and market/destination countries, and their "universal" or "encyclopedic" museums,[57] has relied on various arguments. Alongside questions regarding the protection of specific items or collections, given the limited resources some countries of origin may have for preserving or displaying items in comparison to such museums, the debate has dealt, inter alia, with the need to identify the stakeholders of cultural heritage and to consider the link between culture and political identity.[58]

In a prominent article, John Henry Merryman characterizes this debate as being embedded in two different ways of thinking about cultural

---

[56] Gina Agapiou, *60 Looted Cyprus Antiquities to Be Returned*, CYPRUS MAIL, June 11, 2024.

[57] For more on the concept of the "universal" or "encyclopedic" museum, *see* James Cuno, *View from the Universal Museum, in* IMPERIALISM, ART AND RESTITUTION 15 (John Henry Merryman ed., 2006).

[58] For an overview of this debate, *see* LOSSON, *supra* note 27, at 5–10.

property: "cultural internationalism" versus "cultural nationalism."[59] While the former approach focuses on the "cultural heritage of all mankind," a term that appears in the Preamble to the 1954 Hague Convention for the Protection of Cultural Property in the Event of Armed Conflict and its two protocols,[60] the latter emphasizes the interests of states in their "national cultural heritage," an approach supported by later international instruments such as the 1970 UNESCO Convention on the Means of Prohibiting and Preventing the Illicit Import, Export and Transfer of Ownership of Cultural Property.[61]

However, the framing of the debate along these lines – and, accordingly, the juxtaposition of these two concepts – is susceptible to both historical inconsistencies and normative ambiguities.

Even when considering the concept of "art imperialism," which refers to a situation in which a dominant country or military force uses its power to take control over cultural items in other territories, various modi operandi have been at play, with potentially diverging normative implications.[62] The longest-standing and most troubling strategy has been one of aggression, institutionalized during the period of the Roman Empire and later practiced by various forces, from the looting by Napoléon's army of archaeological artifacts, artworks, and manuscripts and their transportation to the Louvre, National Library, and other French institutions to the mass plunder of art and other items from Jews by the Third Reich. Alongside the desire for the art itself, the looting of enemy property has also played a role of "political triumphalism" – boasting about the success of the conquering force while humiliating the enemy.[63]

---

[59] John Henry Merryman, *Two Ways of Thinking about Cultural Property*, 80 Am. J. Int'l L. 851 (1986).

[60] Convention for the Protection of Cultural Property in the Event of Armed Conflict, May 14, 1954, TIAS 09-313.1, 249 U.N.T.S. 215 (hereinafter: "1954 Hague Convention"); Protocol to the Convention for the Protection of Cultural Property in the Event of Armed Conflict, May 14, 1954, 249 U.N.T.S. 358; Second Protocol to the Hague Convention of 1954 for the Protection of Cultural Property in the Event of Armed Conflict, Mar. 26, 1999, 2253 U.N.T.S. 172.

[61] United Nations Educational, Scientific and Cultural Organization (UNESCO), Convention on the Means of Prohibiting and Preventing the Illicit Import, Export, and Transfer of Ownership of Cultural Property, Nov. 14, 1970, 823 U.N.T.S. 231, Preamble ("it is incumbent upon every State to protect the cultural property existing within its territory") (hereinafter: "1970 UNESCO Convention").

[62] John Henry Merryman, *Introduction*, in IMPERIALISM, ART AND RESTITUTION 1, 3–10 (John Henry Merryman ed., 2006) (hereinafter: "Merryman, Introduction").

[63] *Id.* at 3–8.

Alongside pure aggression, world powers and other dominant countries have historically gained control over cultural property in other territories by employing various strategies, such as "opportunism."[64] Perhaps the best-known example is the approximately one half of the Parthenon Marbles, taken from the Acropolis in Athens by Lord Elgin between 1801 and 1805 during the rule of the Ottoman Empire, based on a highly dubious Ottoman letter of permission, and later sold to the British Museum in 1816. The debate over the legality and morality of this act has been lingering between Britain and Greece for nearly two hundred years, since Greece gained independence in 1831, and has come to a head over the past few decades.[65] Another strategy was that of "partage," in which a foreign archaeological team and the source nation would divide artifacts found during excavations – a practice now considered obsolete around the globe.[66]

What are we to make of these historical, now generally illegitimate, strategies for amassing cultural property? Did they represent a "national" or "international" approach when they were practiced? Can the current practice of "universal museums" be detached from their past and, if so, what must they do to be more genuinely international? Moreover, did the acquisition practices that typified many American museums during the 1960s and 1970s represent a "universal" approach?[67]

At the other end, one may ask whether source nations always have a superior claim about recovering cultural items, regardless of the specific circumstances under which these items entered the collections of cultural institutions in other countries, the conditions under which they have been kept, and the meaning that these cultural items have acquired for a decentralized global audience. Should cultural objects be viewed simply as an extension of the national territory from which they originated?

To understand some of the internal inconsistencies of the current framing of the "nationalist vs. internationalist" debate and the need to look beyond this dichotomy to move forward with the cross-border governance of cultural property, one can go back to 1815 – the same year Lord

---

[64] *Id.* at 8–9.

[65] For recent academic studies of this dispute, *see* ALEXANDER HERMAN, THE PARTHENON MARBLES DISPUTE: HERITAGE, LAW, POLITICS (2023); CATHERINE TITI, THE PARTHENON MARBLES AND INTERNATIONAL LAW (2023); David Rudenstine, *Trophies for the Empire: The Epic Dispute between Greece and England over the Parthenon Sculptures in the British Museum*, 39 CARDOZO ARTS & ENT. L.J. 377 (2021).

[66] Merryman, Introduction, *supra* note 62, at 9.

[67] *See* text accompanying *infra* notes 78–79.

Elgin petitioned Parliament to approve the sale of the Parthenon Marbles to the British Museum.[68]

The Congress of Vienna, convened after the defeat of Napoléon's army, dealt specifically with the fate of the plundered works of art, manuscripts, and archives that were taken back to France.[69] As Ana Filipa Vrdoljak notes, "[t]he 1815 Congress of Vienna witnessed the earliest articulation of the first rationale for the restitution of cultural property in modern international law, that is the restoration of the 'sacred' link between people, territory and cultural objects."[70] Despite differences among the various delegations, the overriding principle that emerged from the Congress of Vienna was the territorial link between the cultural object and its place of origin. More broadly, this period also saw the rise of national cultural patrimony and national museums.[71]

Yet, somewhat ironically, although the Louvre and other museums in France were seized by the Allied forces to allow for the restitution of objects, it was the Louvre itself and other "encyclopedic" or "universal" museums in Paris that served as the benchmark for the establishment and curation of museums in Europe and North America.[72] For Britain, the evolution of the British Museum, and later of the South Kensington Museum (now the Victoria and Albert Museum) following the 1851 Great Exhibition in London, as well as other cultural institutions, sought to establish a British cultural identity not confined to artifacts from the British islands but rather reflective of a colonial empire that prided itself on its vast collections of non-European objects.[73]

More generally, while international rules began to develop in the late nineteenth century to protect cultural heritage during armed conflicts, these protections, as I show in Chapter 2, were not applied with equal force to most non-European countries. Consider that out of

---

[68] HERMAN, *supra* note 65, at 54.

[69] The Congress of Vienna was initially convened in September 1814. The Final Act of the Congress of Vienna, which is a collection of over 100 treaties, was signed on June 9, 1815, nine days before Napoléon's defeat in the Battle of Waterloo. For the Final Act of the Congress of Vienna, *see* UNESCO, Austrian National Commission, *Final Document of the Congress of Vienna*, www.unesco.at/en/communication/documentary-eritage/memory-of-the-world-in-austria/final-document-of-the-congress-of-vienna-1815 (last visited Feb. 1, 2025).

[70] Ana Filipa Vrdoljak, INTERNATIONAL LAW, MUSEUMS AND THE RETURN OF CULTURAL OBJECTS 23 (2006).

[71] *Id.* at 26.

[72] *Id.* at 24.

[73] *Id.* at 53–56.

the twenty-six countries that participated in the 1899 Hague Peace Conference, only four were from outside of Europe or the United States: China, Mexico, Persia, and Siam.[74] This means, for example, that at the same time that Britain was signing the 1899 Hague Convention[75] and the 1907 Hague Convention,[76] British museums were receiving cultural objects looted during war from various parts of the world[77] – including the Benin Bronzes, taken in 1897.

Therefore, to the extent that encyclopedic or universal museums assumed the role of promoting "cultural internationalism," one may be left to wonder what their exact vision of "internationalism" entailed. This query extends beyond their ethical and professional perceptions during the colonial era, but also later, during the "Indiana Jones Era" that typified numerous Western museums well into the second half of the twentieth century,[78] and specifically U.S. museums, including university museums, which competed over the "very best" objects.[79]

At the same time, it is important to consider the ways in which some national governments have claimed exclusivity over the right to repossess and control cultural items, regardless of the specific circumstances under which such items made their way across national borders, their history prior to the establishment of the current nation-state, or their role in the cultural heritage of nonstate actors, such as indigenous communities, groups of ethnic or religious origin, and individuals.[80]

---

[74] General Report of the United States Commission, *Peace Conference at the Hague 1899* (July 31, 1899), available at the Yale Law School Avalon Project website: https://avalon .law.yale.edu/19th_century/hag99-04.asp#:~:text=On%20the%20following%20day%20 the,Great%20Britain%20and%20Ireland%2C%20Greece%2C%20 (last visited Feb. 1, 2025).

[75] Convention (II) with Respect to the Laws and Customs of War on Land, July 29, 1899, 32 Stat. 1803, 1 Bevans 247 (hereinafter: "1899 Hague Convention").

[76] Convention (IV) Respecting the Laws and Customs of War on Land, Oct. 18, 1907, 36 Stat. 2277, 1 Bevans 631 (hereinafter: "1907 Hague Convention").

[77] VRDOLJAK, *supra* note 70, at 67–71 (noting that the South Kensington Museum had received spoils of war).

[78] *See supra* note 35.

[79] Stephanie M. Lee, *The Little Museum's Big Score*, THE CHRONICLE OF HIGHER EDUCATION, Aug. 23, 2023 (exploring the collecting practices of the Michael C. Carlos Museum at Emory University, especially after a 1999 special gift of 10 million dollars by the Carlos family that "would turbocharge the ancient Greek and Roman Collection" – with the instructions then given to the museum's curator "to look for not the best, but the very best").

[80] Ana Filipa Vrdoljak & Francesco Francioni, *Introduction, in* THE OXFORD HANDBOOK OF INTERNATIONAL CULTURAL HERITAGE LAW 1, 5–9 (Francesco Francioni & Ana Filipa Vrdoljak eds., 2020) (addressing the growing role of nonstate actors such as communities, civil society groups, and corporations in the field of cultural heritage).

As Pierre Losson demonstrates, Latin American governments such as those in Colombia, Mexico, and Peru have used return claims as a tool of nationalist politics, one that often seeks to reinvent history for current political purposes, promoting an "ideology that seeks to imagine a community of belonging that the state, as a political organization, claims to embody."[81] As part of the appropriation of pre-Colombian cultural heritage, high-profile claims for the return of cultural objects emerged as "new instruments of nation-building for states in a crisis of legitimacy through the performance of a nationalist ideology."[82] Moreover, once return claims are understood as performative discourses in the service of this ideology, it turns out that "whether a claimed object actually returns is relatively irrelevant. What matters is that it is claimed."[83] This also means that the cultural juxtaposition of "nationalism" and "internationalism" may too often result in a deadlock.

What can be done to move this discourse forward so that the "international" and "national" aspects are not seen as mutually exclusive, but rather as complementary? I suggest that a better – though very far from perfect – political balance between source nations and market nations may facilitate the advancement of a new approach of "new cultural internationalism." This perspective could serve not only to address past disputes more effectively but also, even more importantly, to aid in the design of future-looking legal, professional, and ethical cross-border tools.

The concept of "new cultural internationalism" starts by emphasizing the importance of "place."[84] The physical presence and location of a cultural object entail significant tangible and intangible values. These features are instrumental in understanding the original context within which an item was created or discovered, thus tying it to the concept of "provenience" and the specific trajectory of the item through time and space – its "provenance."[85]

---

[81] LOSSON, *supra* note 27, at 11.

[82] *Id.* at 14, 55–66.

[83] *Id.* at 90.

[84] In Chapter 5, I address the concept of "place" in more detail in the context of cultural institutions and their possession of items. *See, generally,* Sophie Forgan, *Building the Museum: Knowledge, Conflict, and the Power of Place*, 96(4) FOCUS – ISIS 572 (2005); MUSEUMS & PLACE (Kerstin Smeds & Ann Davis eds., 2019); Kai Yin & William Nitzky, *Openness and Fluidity of Place: A Practical Dilemma for Ecomuseums in China*, 74 MUSEUM INT'L 30 (2022).

[85] For the origins of these two concepts, *see* Patty Gerstenblith, *Provenience and Provenance Intersecting with International Law in the Market for Antiquities*, 45 N.C. J. INT'L L. 457, 461–69 (2020). *See* Chapter 3 for the development of the term "provenance" as carrying an ever-increasing weight, both legally and professionally.

Accordingly, a source nation, being the collective political entity within whose boundaries an object was created or discovered – even if the current nation-state and its boundaries were formally established after the creation or discovery of the specific item – should play a prominent role in revealing and documenting the item's history, identifying the stakeholders who contributed to its value over time, and preserving both its tangible and intangible qualities.

This means, inter alia, that in fulfilling their unique role source countries should be broadly legitimized in establishing patrimony laws, such as rules that grant the nation-state the exclusive authority to conduct or supervise archaeological excavations within its territory and further institute a blanket property rule by which all discovered items are claimed as state property.[86] The same also holds true for other types of national cultural heritage laws, which address issues such as the protection of monuments and historical sites, national collections that may be subject to rules of inalienability, or the conditions for allowing the export or import of cultural objects.[87]

Moreover, under the 1970 UNESCO Convention, the very definition of "cultural property" relies prominently on the designation of items as such by nation-states and on the mechanisms they establish to delineate the scope of their national interests in these objects. As outlined in Article 1, "For the purposes of this Convention, the term 'cultural property' means property which, on religious or secular grounds, is specifically designated *by each State* as being of importance for archaeology, prehistory, history, literature, art or science and which belongs to the following categories."[88]

This does not mean, however, that the power and authority of the source nation – or of a country that has otherwise designated an item in its legitimate control or possession as "important" – should be oblivious to the cross-border value that is attributed to such items outside of its territory.

---

[86] For a discussion of such patrimony laws, *see* Chapter 2, Section 2.1.3.

[87] The UNESCO Database of National Cultural Heritage Laws, launched in 2005, provides information about such national laws. *See* UNESCO, *UNESCO Database of National Cultural Heritage Laws Updated* (Apr. 20, 2023), www.unesco.org/en/articles/unesco-database-national-cultural-heritage-laws-updated.

[88] 1970 UNESCO Convention, *supra* note 61, art. 1 (my emphasis). For the drafting history and interpretation of Article 1, *see* Janet Blake, *Article 1 of the 1970 UNESCO Convention: Definition of "Cultural Property,"* in THE 1970 UNESCO AND 1995 UNIDROIT CONVENTIONS ON STOLEN OR ILLEGALLY TRANSFERRED CULTURAL PROPERTY: A COMMENTARY 53 (Ana Filipa Vrdoljak, Andrzej Jakubowski & Alessandro Chechi eds., 2024).

Chapter 5 outlines a property theory of ownership and custody of cultural objects by cultural institutions, such as museums. It argues that, alongside in rem rights, cultural institutions also have certain in rem duties, including toward the decentralized global audience that may attach value to these objects. Thus, museums should provide, inter alia, basic digital access to images and other information about items in their collections, recognizing the cross-border value of culture.[89]

Accountability associated with ownership, possession, and control of such items should also extend to nation-states in both their patrimonial and regulatory capacities. Once source nations are able to more effectively protect their core legitimate interests as a matter of both cross-border legal norms and practical political power, they should abstain from an "isolationist" approach and recognize that they have to be accountable not only to intergovernmental organizations or other nation-states but, even more importantly, to the decentralized global audience. The concept of the "cultural heritage of all mankind," referred to in the 1954 Hague Convention,[90] can and should be reinforced alongside the concept of national heritage, *because* of the changing winds of cross-border politics, and *because* source nations can promote culture without yielding to the use of brute force or opportunism by other nation-states.

This new way of thinking, which aims to create a synergy, rather than an inherent conflict, between the national and international/global values and benefits embedded in preserving and promoting human culture, which I dub "new cultural internationalism," may also be supported by the definition of "cultural objects" in Article 2 of the 1995 UNIDROIT Convention: "For the purposes of this Convention, cultural objects are those which, on religious or secular grounds, are of importance for archaeology, prehistory, history, literature, art or science and belong to one of the categories listed in the Annex to this Convention."[91]

A notable difference between the definition of "cultural objects" in Article 2 of the 1995 UNIDROIT Convention and "cultural property" in Article 1 of the 1970 UNESCO Convention is that the newer definition in the 1995 UNIDROIT Convention omits the words "by each State"; hence, the Annex to the 1995 UNIDROIT Convention details eleven types of objects that apply across borders, thereby creating a common

---

[89] *See* Chapter 5, Section 5.4.
[90] *See* text accompanying *supra* note 60.
[91] UNIDROIT Convention on Stolen or Illegally Exported Cultural Objects, Jun. 24, 1995, 2421 U.N.T.S. 457, art. 2 (hereinafter: "1995 UNIDROIT Convention").

denominator for defining – and, accordingly, protecting – cultural objects that "are of importance." Beyond the formal implications of this new type of definition, and the ways in which it reflects the drafting history of Article 2 of the 1995 UNIDROIT Convention,[92] this reconceptualization of cultural objects also carries significant ethical, symbolic, and even political weight. It seeks to emphasize that cultural objects "are of importance" not only to specific nation-states but also to human society. It does so without derogating from the protections that are awarded to nation-states when cultural objects are stolen or illegally exported from their territory. In fact, as Chapter 2 shows, the 1995 UNIDROIT Convention provides more effective protection to source countries compared to the 1970 UNESCO Convention, not only because of the self-executing nature of the convention that establishes operative rules for the return of cultural objects but also because it expands the scope of protection to source nations, such as by stipulating in Article 3(2) of the 1995 UNIDROIT Convention that: "For the purposes of this Convention, a cultural object which has been unlawfully excavated or lawfully excavated but unlawfully retained shall be considered stolen, when consistent with the law of the State where the excavation took place."[93]

What this means is that there is no inherent contradiction or tension between protecting the "national" and the "international" "universal" values of cultural objects and cultural heritage. Once nation-states, and source nations in particular, are assured that their domestic laws and policies – from patrimony laws to rules on the export of cultural objects – are more effectively protected across borders through both international legal norms and practical measures of enforcement, they can and should commit to their role as *global custodians* of culture.

The concept of "new cultural internationalism" therefore seeks to promote not only more effective mechanisms for the resolution of past disputes[94] but also a future-looking approach aimed at fostering

---

[92] *See* Janet Blake, *Article 2 of the 1995 UNIDROIT Convention: Definition of "Cultural Objects,"* in THE 1970 UNESCO AND 1995 UNIDROIT CONVENTIONS ON STOLEN OR ILLEGALLY TRANSFERRED CULTURAL PROPERTY: A COMMENTARY 526 (Ana Filipa Vrdoljak, Andrzej Jakubowski & Alessandro Chechi eds., 2024).

[93] 1995 UNIDROIT Convention, *supra* note 91, art. 3(2).

[94] *See* Carsten Stahn, CONFRONTING COLONIAL OBJECTS: HISTORIES, LEGACIES, AND ACCESS TO CULTURE vi–vii (2023) (depicting previous and present political campaigns for the return of colonial objects, and suggesting that restitution or return should not be considered the "gold standard" for all objects; rather, placing the emphasis on "the need to search forms of consent in relation to ownership, presentation, or conservation, based on the nature of the objects, structural injustice, and contemporary relations."

cross-border collaboration between countries, their cultural institutions, and the global audience.

Returning to the nearly-200-year debate between Britain and Greece over the Parthenon Marbles, it seems the political pendulum is now swinging toward Greece – not as a matter of formal law but as one of politics and public opinion. In a 2022 interview, the British Museum's deputy director called for a "Parthenon partnership" to resolve the conflict.[95] Whether this will happen remains to be seen but, if it does, and the new cross-border political reality brings about the long-overdue resolution of this conflict, it would be fair to hold Greece accountable as a custodian of the *global* heritage of the treasures of the Parthenon.

As the following chapters show, such a new normative approach can be advanced by combining international and national lawmaking and law enforcement mechanisms (Chapter 2), norms and practices concerning provenance research and the exercise of due diligence (Chapter 3), and the transformative role of digital databases as promoting both transparency in dealing with cultural property and accessibility to cultural items for a global audience (Chapter 4). Accordingly, the new cultural internationalism serves as a benchmark for the normative blueprint outlined in Part II of the book, which proposes a property theory of ownership and custody of cultural objects (Chapter 5), and a graduated approach to questions of wrongfulness, attribution, and remedies in resolving past disputes and streamlining new modes of cross-border collaboration and restitution (Chapter 6).

---

[95] *See* Sarah Bexter & Liam Kelly, *Elgin Marbles: "Partnership" Raises Hope of Deal for First Return to Greece in 200 Years*, THE SUNDAY TIMES, July 30, 2022; Naomi Clarke, *British Museum Executive Calls for "Parthenon Partnership" over Elgin Marbles*, INDEPENDENT, July 31, 2022.

Lawmaking, Law Enforcement, and "Legalistic Ethical Reasoning"

2.1 Legal Divergence in a Global, High-End Market for Cultural Objects

Chapter 1 analyzed the changing cross-border political and reputational dynamics concerning cultural property. This chapter delves into the legal landscape governing the legality – or lack thereof – of the cross-border movement and trade of cultural property.

Prior to a discussion about the evolution of international institutions and legal norms (Section 2.2), regional and bilateral collaboration in law enforcement (Section 2.3), and "legalistic" ethical reasoning for the return of cultural items for which "hard-law" claims may not be available (Section 2.4), Section 2.1 outlines the key features of the legal divergence across national legal systems and describes how this disparity poses a challenge in addressing not only past actions typified by the use of power or opportunism but also the current dynamics of the global market for cultural objects.

2.1.1 The Market for Cultural Property: An Introductory Note

Chapter 3 will explore some of the features of the global market for cultural property and, particularly, the gradual – though very far from complete – transition from long-established practices marked by opacity and secrecy to professional and legal norms that embrace transparency and accountability, driven mainly by the rise of provenance research and the duty of due diligence.

For the purposes of this chapter's analysis, it is sufficient to underscore the major gap between the legal divergence among national legal systems regarding the substantive and procedural rules concerning the protection of the chain of title in cultural objects and the global nature of the market, as well as the vast amounts of money that are stake when disputes arise over cultural property.

As noted in Chapter 1, buyers around the globe – including some of the world's most prominent cultural institutions – have been competing, especially since the second half of the twentieth century, for the "very best" cultural items,[1] and are accordingly paying ever-increasing amounts for archaeological artifacts, works of fine art, ethnographic items, and so forth.

For instance, while the 1 million dollars paid in 1972 by the Metropolitan Museum of Art for the *Euphronios Krater* was considered record-breaking at the time,[2] this figure has since been easily surpassed by acquisitions of archaeological artifacts, such as those made by the Louvre Abu Dhabi and the Metropolitan Museum of Art involving Egyptian items that were later revealed to have been the result of illicit excavations carried out during the chaos of the Arab Spring protests.[3]

Despite the increasing scrutiny over the provenance of many archaeological items and the fact that, in some cases, auction houses or private sellers may withdraw such items from sale,[4] the global market for archaeological artifacts remains active and continues to generate substantial revenue. Between 2015 and 2020, numerous archaeological items sold in auctions fetched millions of dollars from museums and private collectors, including an Assyrian stone relief from the ninth century BCE, which Christie's sold in 2019 to an anonymous buyer for 31 million U.S. dollars[5] – the second most expensive archaeological artifact ever sold at an auction.[6]

This trend is even more pronounced in the fine art market. The year 2022 was record setting, with Sotheby's reporting sales totaling 6.2 billion

---

[1] *See* Chapter 1, text accompanying notes 78–79.

[2] *Id.* text accompanying note 36.

[3] *Id.* text accompanying note 51.

[4] *See, e.g.,* Carlie Porterfield, *Christie's Withdraws Four Ancient Greek Vases amid Concerns about Their Provenance and Connection to Disgraced Antiquities Dealers*, THE ART NEWSPAPER, Apr. 10, 2024.

[5] Mia Forbes, *11 Most Expensive Auction Results in Ancient Art in the Last 5 Years*, THE COLLECTOR, Oct. 18, 2020, www.thecollector.com/ancient-art-auction-results/ (reporting that the relief "had been personally owned by Sir Austen Henry Layard, the archaeologist responsible for the discovery of the huge palace in Nimrod").

[6] The highest price paid for an archaeological item at an auction was for *The Guennol Lioness*, a 5,000-year-old limestone figure from Mesopotamia – reportedly found at a site near Baghdad, acquired in 1948 by Alastair and Edith Martin, and sold in 2007 through Sotheby's to a private collector for over 57 million dollars. *Lion Sculpture Gets Record Price*, BBC NEWS, Dec. 6, 2007.

dollars for auctions and private transactions in this category alone, out of its total sales of 8.4 billion.[7] According to the 2024 Art Market Report, annual global art market sales increased from 39.5 billion dollars in 2009 to 65 billion in 2023 (with some fluctuations, and peaks registered for 2014, 2018, and 2022).[8]

Moreover, the art market has become more global, with an increasing share of high-end buyers of cultural property coming from places such as Russia, China, and the Gulf States.[9] Consequently, the number of jurisdictions that could become implicated in legal disputes over title to items has expanded, encompassing museums and collectors also in emerging "market countries."

A high-profile example that encapsulates the current features of the art market with regard to the sums of money at stake, the origin countries of high-end buyers, the potential legal implications across multiple jurisdictions, and the thick web of cross-border political interests is the case of *Salvator Mundi* ("Savior of the World"). The painting was sold at a November 2017 Christie's auction as an authenticated work by Leonardo da Vinci for 450 million dollars – the highest price ever paid for an artwork – to an anonymous buyer, later identified as a proxy for the Crown Prince of Saudi Arabia, Mohammed bin Salman.[10] Long believed to be a copy or the work of Leonardo's studio, the painting was acquired in 2005 by a consortium of art dealers for under 10,000 dollars. It was then heavily restored and presented at an exhibition at the National Gallery in London, after it was reassessed by a group of experts as the work of Leonardo himself. In 2013, the painting was sold for 80 million dollars to Swiss art dealer Yves Bouvier, who immediately resold it for 127.5 million dollars to his client, Russian billionaire Dmitry Rybolovlev. Rybolovlev later accused Bouvier of swindling him out of nearly 1 billion dollars in this and other art deals, and the

---

[7] Anny Shaw, *"An Absolute Art Market Record": Christie's Posts $8.4bn in Sales for 2022,* The Art Newspaper, Dec. 19, 2022.

[8] Art Basel & UBS, Global Art Market Report 21 (2024), https://theartmarket .artbasel.com/download/The-Art-Basel-and-UBS-Art-Market-Report-2024.pdf.

[9] Mia Castagnone, *China's Growing Stature in the Art Market Fosters Well-Informed Collectors, Demand for Advisory Services from Banks,* South China Morning Post, Apr. 1, 2024.

[10] Julia Michalska & Anna Somers Cocks, *Saudi Arabia's Crown Prince Revealed as Buyer of $450m Leonardo and Loan Confirmed to Louvre Abu Dhabi,* The Art Newspaper, Dec. 7, 2017.

two were involved in worldwide criminal and civil proceedings[11] until finally settling in 2023.[12]

A month after *Salvator Mundi* was sold at the Christie's auction, the Louvre Abu Dhabi announced that it would display the work, but a scheduled unveiling in September 2018 was canceled without explanation, and the painting's whereabouts have remained a mystery ever since. According to a 2021 documentary, the painting was intended to be displayed at the Louvre in Paris in its special Leonardo exhibition that opened in October 2020. This plan was canceled, however, after a scientific examination by the Louvre's team of experts concluded that Leonardo had "only contributed" to the *Salvator Mundi* and that its "authenticity" could not be confirmed, with the French government denying requests by Saudi officials that the painting be exhibited at the Louvre show next to the *Mona Lisa* as an undisputed work of Leonardo.[13] According to an August 2024 report, *Salvator Mundi* is currently in storage in Geneva, with plans to feature it as a permanent exhibit in a new museum to be built in Saudi Arabia.[14]

Whether and how the *Salvator Mundi* will be displayed to the public – and with what artistic attribution – remains to be seen. However, this case highlights the significant shifts taking place in the cultural property market. These changes encompass not only the vast amounts of money that are being spent in the art and antiquities market but also the fact that the identity of buyers and the designated venues for exhibiting high-value cultural items no longer conform to a simple West–East (or North–South) divide. The Louvre Abu Dhabi, designated to display the *Salvator Mundi* on loan from the Saudi Crown Prince, considers itself "a universal museum in the Arab world," seeking to "bring different cultures to shine fresh light on these common stories of humanity, beyond individual

---

[11] Nina dos Santos, *$1B Feud Involving Leonardo's "Salvator Mundi" Reveals Dark Side of the Art World*, CNN, May 30, 2021; Vincent Noce, *Billionaire Battle Rages on as Geneva Court Overturns Dismissal of Dmitry Rybolovlev's Fraud Case against Art Dealer Yves Bouvier*, THE ART NEWSPAPER, July 28, 2022.

[12] Eileen Kinsella, *The Sprawling Legal Dispute between Yves Bouvier and Dmitry Rybolovlev Is Finally Over*, ARTNET, Dec. 11, 2023, https://news.artnet.com/art-world/yves-bouvier-rybolovlev-dispute-settled-2406832.

[13] Sarah Cascone, *The Saudi Crown Prince Refused to Lend the "Salvator Mundi" to the Louvre Because the Museum Disputed Its Authenticity, a New Film Says*, ARTNET NEWS, Apr. 7, 2021. The film, titled *The Savior for Sale: The Story of the Salvator Mundi* (Zadig productions/FTV, 2021), was directed by Antoine Vitkin.

[14] Jonathan Rugman, *Power, Oil and a $450m Painting – Insiders on the Rise of Saudi's Crown Prince*, BBC, Aug. 19, 2024.

civilisations, times or places."[15] Yet, along with the expanding scope of market nations, alongside source nations, comes a widening gap between the global market and the divergence of legal norms.

2.1.2   Divergence in Substantive and Procedural Private Law Doctrines

As this section shows, a key challenge that has traditionally hindered efforts to protect the chain of title in cultural objects and to remedy past violations – such as illegal or illegitimate transfers of possession, especially in cases of cross-border "relocations" – is the long-standing, significant disparities among national legal systems, and the corresponding absence of binding international norms for identifying, protecting, and enforcing the chain of title in cultural property items.

Cultural objects are usually considered by national legal systems as belonging to the broader category of "movables," "goods," "personal property," or "chattels" – as corporeal movable assets are often defined within various national legal systems.[16] This classification means that the legal regime that applies to cultural objects in property law disputes traditionally follows the rules pertaining to movables, unless cultural objects are specifically distinguished as a self-standing category (such as in the case of patrimony laws concerning archaeological items, discussed in Section 2.1.3).[17]

Property law doctrines on movables have exhibited significant divergence among legal systems, spanning beyond the civil law/common law divide. This disparity has posed challenges for various attempts at supranational approximation or harmonization of norms, despite the increasingly regional and global nature of markets for goods.[18] Thus, numerous attempts to harmonize the rules on security interests in movable assets at the level of the European Union have yet to come to fruition, despite the potential ill-effects on the EU's "internal market."[19]

---

[15] Louvre Abu Dhabi, *About Us*, www.louvreabudhabi.ae/en/about-us/our-story (last visited Feb. 1, 2025).

[16] These terms are generally, although not perfectly, interchangeable. *See, e.g.*, SJEF VAN ERP & BRAM AKKERMANS, CASES, MATERIALS AND TEXT ON PROPERTY LAW 193–206, 212–13 (2012).

[17] For state patrimony laws, *see infra* Section 2.1.3.

[18] *See, generally*, AMNON LEHAVI, PROPERTY LAW IN A GLOBALIZING WORLD 126–71 (2019).

[19] *See, e.g.*, ULRICH DROBNIG & OLE BÖGER, PROPRIETARY SECURITY IN MOVABLE ASSETS: PRINCIPLES OF EUROPEAN LAW (2014); DIVERGENCES OF PROPERTY LAW, AN OBSTACLE TO THE INTERNAL MARKET? (Ulrich Drobnig, Heck J. Snijders & Erik-Jan Zippro eds., 2006).

Disparities in national property laws on movables have proven particularly prominent in doctrines that address problems with the chain of title or possession – the very types of issues often at the heart of cross-border disputes over cultural property. Alongside the broad distinction between legal systems that embrace the principle of *nemo dat quod non habet* ("he who does not have cannot give"), which favors the original owner over subsequent buyers/possessors, and those systems that protect "good-faith purchasers," at least after a certain period,[20] the landscape of property doctrines is highly complex, transcending well beyond a common law/civil law taxonomy.

Two recent global comparative studies demonstrate the broad scope of divergence in the substantive rules that apply to disputes involving parties that do not have contractual privity among themselves but which assert simultaneous, conflicting claims of rights or priorities to the same movable asset, with such a "legal accident" resulting from wrongdoing by yet other parties.[21]

In 2017, Giuseppe Dari-Mattiacci and Carmine Guerriero published a database of 126 legal systems, examining the differences between national legal doctrines pertaining to various types of proprietary disputes that implicate a breach of the chain of title or possession.[22] One such comparative analysis explores the national rules concerning the purchase of a stolen movable good. The database's indicators gauge the number of years after which the buyer may acquire ownership, if at all, through either a private sale, public market, auction, or purchase from a professional seller.[23] Another set of variables addresses the purchase of a movable good that was embezzled, that is, unlawfully traded by someone entrusted to hold or use the good for a specific purpose (such as a bailee). As with the variables in the case of theft, national law indicators gauge the number of years after which the buyer, if ever, acquires ownership of an embezzled good purchased via private sale, public market, auction, or professional seller.[24]

---

[20] Dan Klerman & Anja Shortland, *The Transformation of the Art Market: Law, Norms, and Institutions*, 23 THEORETICAL INQ. L. 219, 222–23 (2022).

[21] Menachem Mautner, *"The Eternal Triangles of the Law": Toward a Theory of Priorities in Conflicts Involving Remote Parties*, 90 MICH. L. REV. 95 (1991).

[22] Giuseppe Dari-Mattiacci & Carmine Guerriero, *A Novel Dataset on Horizontal Property Rights in 126 Jurisdictions*, 11 DATA IN BRIEF 557 (2017) (hereinafter: "Dari-Mattiacci & Guerriero, A Novel Dataset"). The online version of this database is available at www.sciencedirect.com/science/article/pii/S2352340917300811?via%3Dihub (last visited Feb. 1, 2025).

[23] Dari-Mattiacci & Guerriero, A Novel Dataset, *supra* note 22.

[24] *See* the summary of variables at *id.*, 560, Table 2.

The differences between national systems for these two sets of variables are significant and cut across the common law and civil law traditions. According to the study, under U.S. law – determined at the state level – the original owner almost always prevails over a subsequent buyer in each one of these scenarios (theft and embezzlement/entrustment).[25] In England, the purchaser would prevail over the original owner after a period of six years in the case of theft (based on the general provisions of the Limitation Act 1980),[26] and a good-faith buyer would, under certain circumstances, prevail over the original owner in the case of a purchase from an agent to whom the owner voluntarily surrendered possession of the good (including in the case of embezzlement).[27]

Differences also exist within the civil law system, in which the protection of a good-faith purchaser as an exception to the *nemo dat* rule is more pervasive. For example, in Germany, the purchaser would prevail over the original owner after a period of ten years in the case of theft, and would triumph as a good-faith buyer immediately in the case of embezzlement.[28] In comparison, in France, a good-faith buyer would prevail over the original owner after a period of three years in both theft and embezzlement/entrustment scenarios.[29]

In his 2023 book, Yun-chien Chang presents a hand-coded dataset on the good-faith purchase doctrine from 246 jurisdictions around the world, revealing at least twenty-one variants of this doctrine – from a strict application of the *nemo dat* rule to broad and immediate protection of good-faith purchasers, with many interim doctrines positioned along this spectrum.[30] Thus, even among the twelve countries that can be depicted as following a universal *nemo dat* rule (the "Type A" group), nine countries allow good-faith possessors to acquire ownership of the goods, after a certain period of time, through the doctrine of acquisitive prescription.[31]

---

[25] *Id.* at 561, Appendix A, Supplementary Material.

[26] Limitation Act 1980, s. 3 (U.K.).

[27] Dari-Mattiacci and Guerriero, A Novel Dataset, *supra* note 22, at 561, Appendix A, Supplementary Material; *see also* DUNCAN SHEEHAN, THE PRINCIPLES OF PERSONAL PROPERTY LAW 60–66 (2017).

[28] Dari-Mattiacci and Guerriero, A Novel Dataset, *supra* note 22, at 561, Appendix A, Supplementary Material.

[29] *Id.*

[30] YUN-CHIEN CHANG, PROPERTY LAW: COMPARATIVE, EMPIRICAL, AND ECONOMIC ANALYSES 259–61 (2023).

[31] *Id.* at 262–63. The doctrine of acquisitive prescription (often termed "adverse possession" in common law countries) exists in some version in 175 of the 202 jurisdictions surveyed in Chang's study. *Id.* at 125–26.

Also, while most common law countries adhere to the *nemo dat* rule in the case of theft, these jurisdictions may stipulate different rules for nonstolen goods – such as goods embezzled and sold by persons to whom they were entrusted (the "entrustment rule") or, in cases of a voidable title, where the seller's title has not yet been voided at the time of the sale but becomes void later (the "voidable title rule").[32]

Differences across legal systems in governing proprietary disputes involving chain of title or possession issues are manifested not only in the substantive principles of granting priority to a certain party based on economic, social policy, or cultural considerations[33] but also in procedural or evidentiary doctrines that may be equally critical for resolving a dispute.

This is particularly true for rules pertaining to the statute of limitations, which may bar an actionable claim from being brought before a court and adjudicated on the merits of the case.[34] Such divergences may exist with regards not only to the general time period set for such limitations, but also the types of circumstances under which the clock starts – or, rather, stops – running.[35]

For instance, while the statute of limitations in New York State is three years – seemingly, at first glance, similar to the time period after which protection is given to a good-faith purchaser in France – the New York statute of limitations does not begin until the original owner locates the object, identifies its current possessor, and makes a request for its return.[36] Practically, this means that the ability to bring a case for conversion and replevin, or a similar remedy, in property conflicts that involve a breach of the chain of title is much more favorable to claimants in New York than in jurisdictions where the three-year limitation starts from the date of the

---

[32] *Id.* at 262–65.

[33] Compare Chang, *id.* at 260 (arguing that "optimizing the incentive schemes" of the different parties "is difficult, and efficiency-minded lawmakers emphasize different aspects of the incentive scheme. The doctrine, thus, diverges") with Giuseppe Dari-Mattiacci & Carmine Guerriero, *Law and Culture: A Theory of Comparative Variation in Bona Fide Purchase Rules*, 35 OXFORD J. LEGAL STUD. 543, 563–73 (2015) (arguing that the existence of a "culture of self-reliance" in a certain jurisdiction is the key determinant of the variations in the good-faith purchaser doctrines).

[34] Marc-André Renold, *Legal Obstacles to Claims for the Restitution of Looted Art*, 19 YB. PRIVATE INT'L L. 247, 254–55 (2017/2018) (illustrating such differences, even among the different states across the United States).

[35] Klerman & Shortland, *supra* note 20, at 221–22.

[36] *See, e.g.*, Solomon R. Guggenheim Foundation v. Lubell, 569 N.E.2d 425, 429 (N.Y. 1991) (reasoning that, "until demand is made and refused, possession of the stolen property by the good-faith purchaser for value is not considered wrongful" for purposes of New York's statute of limitations).

wrongful or contested action, such as the theft or purchase of the item by the current possessor.[37]

Other doctrines in certain jurisdictions may also prove crucial in deciding the fate of legal claims for returning movables, including cultural items. For example, New York State, which is more lenient toward claimants than other jurisdictions regarding the statute of limitations, applies a counterbalancing equitable doctrine of "laches," by which an original owner who fails to search diligently for a stolen object or does not make a demand in a timely fashion after identifying the current possessor may be denied recovery, even if the statute of limitations has not yet elapsed.[38]

In the 2021 case of *Republic of Turkey v. Christie's, Inc.*,[39] the U.S. District Court for the Southern District of New York, applying New York State law, dismissed Turkey's claim against Christie's and the collector Michael H. Steinhardt to recover an Anatolian marble female idol. Turkey argued that the idol had been unlawfully excavated and smuggled out sometime after 1906, when it enacted a decree establishing its patrimony over archaeological items found in its territory. The District Court held that, even if Turkey were able to establish ownership over the item under its patrimony law, "the trial record readily establishes that Turkey slept on its rights, which bars recovery under the doctrine of laches."[40]

In 2023, the Court of Appeals (Second Circuit) affirmed the District Court's ruling on the issue of laches,[41] reasoning that, based on the factual record, "Turkey should have been aware of its potential claim in the 1990s."[42] It further held that by initiating the proceedings only in 2017 Turkey had prejudiced the defendants' rights, also compounded by the death, during that interim period, of former possessors of the object who could have served as key witnesses.[43] Reasoning that the "application of laches also requires a fact-intensive inquiry into the reasonable diligence

---

[37] Klerman & Shortland, *supra* note 20, at 221–22.

[38] *Id.*

[39] Republic of Turkey v. Christie's, Inc., No. 17-cv-3086 (AJN), 2021 WL 4060357 (S.D.N.Y. Sept. 7, 2021).

[40] *Id.* at *1.

[41] Republic of Turkey v. Christie's, Inc., 62 F.4th 64 (2d Cir. 2023). It should be noted, however, that, while the Second Circuit affirmed the ruling on the doctrine of laches, it disputed the District Court's legal test for the required burden of proof placed on the claimant to establish its right of ownership over the object, had the case been decided on its merits. This did not change the outcome of the case, which was dismissed due to the doctrine of laches. *Id.* at 70–71.

[42] *Id.* at 72.

[43] *Id.* at 73.

of both parties,"[44] the Second Circuit concluded that, while the current possessor of the object took actions to investigate the object's provenance, Turkey failed "to act for over twenty-five years," such that the balance of diligence worked in favor of the defendants.[45]

Given the legal divergence on both substantive and procedural matters across different jurisdictions, any proprietary conflict over a movable that involves parties from more than one jurisdiction – as is often the case in the context of cultural property – raises "conflict of laws" issues that may prove crucial for a decision on the case.[46] In fact, applying rules for conflict of laws adds another layer of legal disparity and complexity. This is because, unlike disputes over immovable assets, which typically follow the rule of *lex rei situs* (the place where the asset is located) for both jurisdiction and applicable law,[47] different legal systems adopt various rules for conflict of laws concerning movable assets. Some jurisdictions follow the *lex situs* of the asset at the time of the buyer's acquisition of the good, while other countries embrace the *lex originis* (country of origin in which the theft or other wrongful dispossession from the original owner took place), and yet other jurisdictions employ a multifactor test to identify the "law of the closest connection."[48]

The "law of the closest connection" approach is currently adopted in most U.S. jurisdictions.[49] For instance, in the case of *Bakalar v. Vavra*,[50] the U.S. Court of Appeals (Second Circuit) applied an "interest analysis" to determine whether to apply New York law or, rather, Swiss law in a dispute involving a painting by Egon Schiele that was allegedly dispossessed from its Jewish owner in Austria during the Nazi era, later sold to a Swiss gallery, and eventually found its way to New York, where it was sold to the current possessor. The court decided to apply New York law, holding that "New York has a compelling interest in the application of its law" owing to the concern that the alleged "'events and omissions' made New York a 'marketplace for stolen goods' and, more particularly, for

---

[44] *Id.* at 73–74.

[45] *Id.* at 74.

[46] Renold, *supra* note 34, at 252–54.

[47] SJEF VAN ERP, *Lex Rei Sitae: The Territorial Side of Classical Property Law, in* REGULATORY PROPERTY RIGHTS: THE TRANSFORMING NOTION OF PROPERTY IN TRANSNATIONAL BUSINESS REGULATION 59–81 (Christian Godt ed., 2016).

[48] For an analysis of these different conflict-of-laws rules in the context of cultural property, *see* MARA WANTUCH-THOLE, CULTURAL PROPERTY IN CROSS-BORDER LITIGATION: TURNING RIGHTS INTO CLAIMS 234–51 (2015).

[49] Klerman & Shortland, *supra* note 20, at 222–24.

[50] Bakalar v. Vavra, 619 F.3d 136 (2d Cir. 2010).

stolen artwork, which was of special concern," whereas "[b]y contrast, the resolution of an ownership dispute in the Drawing between parties who otherwise have no connection to Switzerland does not implicate any Swiss interest simply because the Drawing passed through there."[51] Obviously, a court located in another country may have weighed the various interests at stake differently when deciding which law to apply under such circumstances.

Moreover, the potential complexity and uncertainty resulting from the varying rules on conflict of laws, and the underlying divergence in substantive rules for proprietary conflicts over movables – particularly cultural property – are also prevalent in countries that otherwise have an expansive approach toward applying their jurisdiction to disputes, as is the case with the United States.[52]

For example, in its 2022 decision in *Cassirer v. Thyssen-Bornemisza Collection Foundation*,[53] the U.S. Supreme Court addressed which law should apply to a dispute over the ownership of a painting by Camille Pissarro, *Rue Saint-Honoré in the Afternoon. Effect of Rain* (1897) (Figure 2.1).

The parties to the case were the heirs of Lilly Cassirer, who was forced to surrender the painting to the Nazis in order to obtain an exit visa from Germany, and the possessor of the painting, a Spanish foundation created and controlled by the Kingdom of Spain that had purchased the artwork in the early 1990s and had been displaying it in its museum in Madrid. The U.S. District Court established its jurisdiction over the case, invoking an exception to the principle of sovereign immunity under the Foreign Sovereign Immunities Act of 1976.[54] However, in selecting the applicable law, the court relied on a federal common law rule that mandated the use of Spanish property law. Consequently, the District Court ruled in favor of the foundation based on the Spanish doctrine of good-faith acquisition and possession under Article 1955 of the Spanish Civil Code, which grants title to movable goods after "three years of uninterrupted possession in good faith."[55] The Court of Appeals (Ninth Circuit) affirmed the ruling, but the U.S. Supreme Court vacated and remanded the decision, holding that the choice-of-law rule should have mirrored the one that would

---

[51] *Id*. at 144.

[52] Klerman & Shortland, *supra* note 20, at 222–24.

[53] Cassirer v. Thyssen-Bornemisza Collection Foundation, 142 S.Ct. 1502 (2022) (hereinafter: "Cassirer, USSC").

[54] The Foreign Sovereign Immunities Act of 1976 (FSIA), 28 U.S.C. §1602 et seq.

[55] Cassirer v. Thyssen-Bornemisza Collection Foundation, Case No. CV 05-3459-JFW (Ex), 2019 WL 13240413 (C.D. Cal., 2019) *19.

Figure 2.1 Camille Pissarro, *Rue Saint-Honoré in the Afternoon. Effect of Rain* (1897).
Source: By permission of Museo Nacional Thyssen-Bornemisza, Madrid.

have been used in a comparable litigation in a state court against a private defendant – in this case, California's choice-of-law rule.[56] Following this decision, the case was returned to the Court of Appeals (Ninth Circuit).[57]

---

[56] Cassirer, USSC, *supra* note 53, at 1508–9.
[57] Cassirer v. Thyssen-Bornemisza Collection Foundation, 69 F.4th 554 (9th Cir. 2023).

The Court of Appeals identified California's choice-of-law rule as following a "comparative impairment analysis," the third step of the three-pronged "governmental interest approach." However, finding no guidance as to how this rule should be applied to a property dispute, it decided to certify the following question to the California Supreme Court:

> Whether, under a comparative impairment analysis, California's or Spain's interest is more impaired if California's rule that a person may not acquire title to a stolen item of personal property (because a thief cannot pass good title, and California has not adopted the doctrine of adverse possession for personal property), were subordinated to Spain's rule that a person may obtain title to stolen property by adverse possession.[58]

The California Supreme Court declined to answer the certified question, leaving the Court of Appeals "to determine, whether under the California choice-of-law test, Spain's laws or California's laws apply to determine title to the Painting."[59] Examining the "circumstances of the present case,"[60] the Court of Appeals concluded in 2024, based on its own interpretation of the three-step analysis of California's choice-of-law test, and particularly the third prong of a "comparative impairment analysis," that the balance favored applying Spanish law in this case. The Spanish foundation therefore won good title to the painting, based on the U.S. federal Court of Appeals' interpretation of a U.S. state's conflict-of-laws doctrine, which happened to favor the application of Spanish law, based on the "circumstances of the present case." That said, in March 2025, the U.S. Supreme Court granted a writ of certiorari, vacated the 2024 judgment and remanded the case to the Court of Appeals to review the potential application to this case of a specific amendment to California's Code of Civil Procedure enacted by the state legislature in response to the 2024 judgment – and according to which California substantive law shall apply to claims that concern works of fine art unlawfully taken or stolen during the Holocaust era.[61]

This case demonstrates the genuine legal complexity of coming up with a common ground for resolving property disputes over cultural property,

---

[58] *Id.* at 571.
[59] Cassirer v. Thyssen-Bornemisza Collection Foundation, 89 F.4th 1226, 1234 (9th Cir. 2024).
[60] *Id.* at 1237.
[61] *See* Cassirer v. Thyssen-Bornemisza Collection Foundation, 145 S.Ct. 1331 (Mem) (2025), referring to Assem. Bill 2867, 2023–2024 Reg. Sess. (Cal. 2024) that amended §338 of the Code of Civil Procedure. *See also* Martha Lufkin, *US Supreme Court Reopens Lawsuit over Nazi-Looted Pissarro Painting*, THE ART NEWSPAPER, Mar. 18, 2025.

especially those that involve parties across national borders. The divergence in substantive and procedural doctrines pertaining to property conflicts that deal with the chain of title or possession, as well as the myriad rules on the choice of law, may apply not only across different countries but also within a given jurisdiction. The lack of international legal standards on both property doctrine and the choice of law, even within regional organizations, such as the European Union,[62] poses a major obstacle to advancing common, clear, and workable legal standards of conduct for the global cultural property market.

2.1.3   Incongruence between Private Law Doctrines and Public Policy

Moving from general property doctrines and choice-of-law rules on movables to their specific application in the case of cultural property reveals a further layer of complexity and fragmentation. Each country establishes its own public policy on cultural heritage based on political, historical, social, and other considerations – a process that makes sense and should be defended normatively. However, within the same jurisdiction, one can often identify incongruence between national public policy (and, consequently, public law rules on cultural property) and the normative tenets of private law doctrines on movables and their application to cultural property. This internal inconsistency between private law doctrines on movables and public law rules about cultural property and national heritage can result in a "mixed message" to actors in that jurisdiction.

For example, Italy is a country that grants immediate protection to a good-faith purchaser of a stolen or embezzled good, including a cultural object.[63] In comparison to other jurisdictions, Italy is considered to provide the strongest protections to such buyers.[64] This means that at the level of private law policy and doctrine, the Italian legal system endorses free trade, alienability of assets, and relatively little scrutiny of buyers operating in the market.

---

[62] For example, Regulation (EC) No 864/2007 of the European Parliament and of the Council of 11 July 2007 on the Law Applicable to Non-contractual Obligations (Rome II), 2007 O.J. (L 40) 199, which addresses the law applicable to noncontractual obligations, is seen as not applying to property law or to proprietary remedies that seek to vindicate the claimant's right of ownership. *See* WANTUCH-THOLE, *supra* note 48, at 234–39.

[63] Civil Code (*Codice Civile*), art. 1153 (It.).

[64] CHANG, *supra* note 30, at 268 (listing Italy among the four states that grant the "strongest good-faith purchase protection").

At the same time, Italian public law rules on cultural property, promulgated at least since the early twentieth century, point to a very different balance of interests, one that generally puts national concerns ahead of private interests, including with regard to the principle of free circulation of objects.[65] Whereas during the nineteenth century the prevalence of a liberal ideology that advocated the inviolability of private property blocked legislative attempts to constrain the transportation and sale of privately owned cultural property,[66] public policy shifted with the approval of Law no. 364 in 1909,[67] commonly known as the "Rosadi–Rava Law" (after the surnames of its two initiators).[68] This law established a set of fundamental principles that promoted the state's national interests in cultural heritage, including a public ownership (patrimony) rule for all archaeological finds.[69] These principles are accompanied by restrictive measures aimed at keeping certain types of cultural objects in the country, which may also apply to privately owned items, including artwork and archaeological artifacts that were excavated before the patrimony rule went into effect.[70]

Thus, under the Code of the Cultural and Landscape Heritage (CCLH),[71] adopted in 2004 and since amended (including for the purpose of incorporating EU directives),[72] the permanent export of protected "cultural property," as defined in Article 10, is forbidden.[73]

According to Article 10(1) of the CCLH, "cultural property consists in immovable and movable things belonging to the State, the Regions, other territorial government bodies, as well as any other public body and institution, and to private non-profit associations, which possess artistic,

---

[65] See Alberto Frigerio, *The New Italian Law on the Exportation of Cultural Goods and Its Relationship with EU Regulations*, 24 ART ANTIQUITY & L. 263, 263–64 (2019) (discussing the changing attitudes toward the balance between the public interest in preserving control over cultural heritage items and the market interests in promoting trade throughout the evolution of Italian legislation on the protection of cultural property since the early twentieth century).

[66] *Id.* at 262–63.

[67] Legge 20 giugno 1909, n. 364 (It.) (hereinafter: "Rosadi–Rava Law").

[68] Frigerio, *supra* note 65, at 264.

[69] Rosadi–Rava Law, *supra* note 67, art. 15.

[70] Frigerio, *supra* note 65, at 263–64.

[71] Decreto legislativo 22 gennaio 2004, n. 42., G.U. Feb. 24, 2004, n. 45 (It.), as amended, www.normattiva.it/uri-res/N2Ls?urn:nir:stato:decreto.legislativo:2004;42 (hereinafter "CCLH"). *See* English translation of the 2004 CCLH (without later amendments) at https://whc.unesco.org/document/155711?.

[72] Arianna Visconti, *Fighting Cultural Property Trafficking: The Italian Criminal Law Framework and Its Forthcoming Reform*, 26 ART ANTIQUITY & L. 317, 320 (2021).

[73] CCLH, *supra* note 71, art. 65.

historical, archaeological or ethno-anthropological interest,"[74] based on a "verification of cultural interest" undertaken by the Ministry of Culture under the code's Article 12.[75] Article 10(2) applies the classification of "cultural property" automatically to all collections of museums, picture galleries, art galleries, and other exhibition venues, as well as to archives and book collections of libraries belonging to the state, the regions, and other governmental bodies, unless such items are specifically exempted from this category.[76] Importantly, according to Article 10(3) of the CCLH, the definition of cultural property, and the corresponding prohibition on its permanent export, also applies to privately owned cultural objects for which the Ministry of Culture has made a specific "declaration of cultural interest" under Article 13(1) of the CCLH.[77]

Moreover, even for privately owned cultural items that do not fall under Article 10(3) of the CCLH, the export of an item may require the owner to obtain a "certificate of free circulation" from the superintendent export office.[78] On this point, however, the provisions of the CCLH were amended in 2017 by the "Law on Competition,"[79] to ease at least some of the regulatory requirements imposed on the Italian art market. According to this recent amendment, cultural items created by living artists, or produced not more than seventy years ago by deceased artists, do not require a certificate of free exportation. This also applies to works that were created over seventy years ago but whose estimated market value is less than 13,500 euros (with the owner required to present a self-certification of the value to the office).[80] That said, Italy maintains a highly restrictive public law regime on the export and trade of cultural items, in contrast to otherwise market-friendly provisions that apply in the realm of private law doctrine.

The United States presents something of a mirror image to that of Italy in the way that private law doctrines on proprietary disputes involving movables diverge from public law rules on cultural items.

As discussed above, state law across the United States generally embraces the *nemo dat* principle for movables, including cultural items,

---

[74] *Id.* art. 10(1).

[75] *Id.* art. 12.

[76] *Id.* arts. 10(2), 13(2).

[77] *Id.* art. 13(1).

[78] The superintendent (*Soprintendenza*) export offices are regional organs of the Ministry of Culture, whose primary responsibility is to identify and protect cultural goods in their jurisdiction. Frigerio, *supra* note 65, at 265.

[79] Legge 4 agosto 2017, n. 124, G.U. Aug. 14, 2017, n. 189 (It.).

[80] Frigerio, *supra* note 65, at 264–67.

alongside rules on jurisdiction and time periods for submitting claims. These rules grant original owners strong protection vis-à-vis subsequent purchasers or possessors, despite the potential hindrances to the market for arts and antiquities.[81]

At the same time, U.S. patrimony law concerning antiquities is relatively limited, applying only to antiquities found in federal or state lands,[82] or to Native American items,[83] but it generally allows for private ownership of archaeological items discovered on private land, with the landowner's consent.[84] Moreover, the United States is one of the few countries that does not impose general limits on the export or import of cultural property as a self-standing category, meaning that cultural items are treated like other goods, including for customs and border control purposes.[85]

Particular limits on the export or import of cultural items in the United States are mostly introduced as part of bilateral agreements with other countries, based on Article 9 of the 1970 UNESCO Convention on the Means of Prohibiting and Preventing the Illicit Import, Export and Transfer of Ownership of Cultural Property, which allows state parties "whose cultural property is in jeopardy from pillage of archaeological or ethnological materials" to call upon other countries to collaborate in order to "carry out the necessary measures, including the control of exports and imports and international commerce in the specific materials concerned."[86] The United States has entered into such agreements following requests from other countries, but it has not imposed a universal ban on the import of cultural goods whenever it is not explicitly authorized by the source country.[87]

---

[81] *See* text accompanying *supra* notes 20–32.

[82] This principle was first established in the Antiquities Act of 1906 (16 U.S.C. §§431–33m).

[83] Archaeological Resources and Protection Act of 1979 (16 U.S.C. §§470 aa–mm).

[84] For an overview of the rules that apply to ownership over archaeological finds, based on the type of land or the type of artifact found (such as in the case of Native American heritage), *see* Patty Gerstenblith, *The Legal Framework for the Prosecution of Crimes Involving Archaeological Objects*, 64(2) U.S. ATTORNEYS' BULLETIN 5, 13–15 (2016).

[85] *See* WANTUCH-THOLE, *supra* note 48, at 56–57.

[86] United Nations Educational, Scientific and Cultural Organization (UNESCO), Convention on the Means of Prohibiting and Preventing the Illicit Import, Export, and Transfer of Ownership of Cultural Property, Nov. 14, 1970, 823 U.N.T.S. 231, art. 9 (hereinafter: "1970 UNESCO Convention").

[87] Patty Gerstenblith, *Provenience and Provenance Intersecting with International Law in the Market for Antiquities*, 45 N.C. J. INT'L L. 457, 471–72 (2020). For a current list and timelines of the Article 9 bilateral agreements to which the United States is a party, *see infra* note 283.

A different type of specific limit, placed on exports, concerns Native American cultural items. The Safeguard Tribal Objects of Patrimony Act of 2021, approved in December 2022,[88] imposes a flat prohibition on the export of certain items and establishes an "export certification" system for other Native American cultural items.[89] Such limits on the export or import of cultural objects remain, however, an exception to the promarket approach toward cultural property.

According to a 2022 study by the U.S. Department of the Treasury, the relatively lenient rules regarding the type and scope of cultural objects that can enter the market, the key role of private stakeholders such as sellers, intermediaries, financiers, and buyers, and the fact that the U.S. share of the global art market is the largest in the world (accounting for 42 percent, or 21.3 billion dollars in 2020),[90] have contributed to a broad perception of the American art market as "unregulated."[91] This has had implications for the standards of behavior that apply to various actors, including highly reputable cultural institutions such as museums. Moreover, for many decades, the traditions of American museum collecting have been characterized by a sense of "swashbuckling"; in the 1960s and 1970s, "some museum curators embraced the chase for prized artifacts as if it were a big hunting game," often turning a blind eye to potential problems in the chain of title or to other factors that might call the legitimacy of transactions into question.[92] This was also the case with certain university museums that "turned a blind eye" to dubious circumstances.[93]

U.S. public policy and regulation on cultural property, at least until recently, seems therefore to have diverged from other principles guiding private law doctrines on protecting the chain of title and guarding against the unauthorized circulation of goods. This created a form of dissonance with regard to the standards of behavior required in practice from U.S. market actors, a disparity that has cross-border implications owing to the U.S. dominance in the global market for cultural items.

---

[88] The Safeguard Tribal Objects of Patrimony Act of 2021, H.R. 2930.

[89] *Id.* Sect. 5.

[90] U.S. DEPARTMENT OF THE TREASURY, STUDY OF THE FACILITATION OF MONEY LAUNDERING AND TERROR FINANCE THROUGH THE TRADE IN WORKS OF ART 2 (2022), https://home.treasury.gov/system/files/136/Treasury_Study_WoA.pdf.

[91] *Id.* at 31.

[92] Graham Bowley, *For U.S. Museums with Looted Art, the Indiana Jones Era Is Over,* N.Y. TIMES, Dec. 13, 2022.

[93] Stephanie M. Lee, *The Little Museum's Big Score,* CHRONICLE OF HIGHER EDUCATION, Aug. 23, 2023 (reporting on the Michael C. Carlos Museum at Emory University's collecting history of Greek and Roman artifacts).

However, as the following sections demonstrate, this jurisprudential disparity may gradually narrow owing to the growth in cross-border law enforcement actions to which countries such as the United States and Italy are parties, and the impact of criminal and civil proceedings concerning the patrimony of foreign states. Moreover, a growing number of jurisdictions are promulgating specific rules for cultural property within the context of private law, distinguishing them from the general doctrines concerning movables. This may allow for a better public/private law congruence.

2.2 Evolution – and Limits – of International Institutions and Legal Norms

2.2.1 Instruments of Public International Law and Private International Law

The first international instruments aimed at cross-border protection of cultural property were created in the context of armed conflicts. Dating back to the 1648 Peace Treaty of Westphalia, the 1815 Congress of Vienna,[94] and, later, the 1899 Hague Convention[95] and the 1907 Hague Convention,[96] numerous bilateral or multilateral treaties required states to abstain from the destruction of cultural sites or the looting of enemy property.[97] However, the two Hague Conventions failed to protect immovable and movable cultural property during the First World War,[98]

---

[94] For a discussion of the 1815 Congress of Vienna, *see* Chapter 1, text accompanying notes 69–71.

[95] Convention (II) with Respect to the Laws and Customs of War on Land, July 29, 1899, 32 Stat. 1803, 1 Bevans 247 (hereinafter: "1899 Hague Convention"). For an analysis of the provisions in the 1899 Hague Convention that address the unnecessary destruction of enemy property and, more vaguely, the protection of religious or artistic sites, *see* Matthew Smart, *An Issue of Monumental Proportions: The Necessary Changes to Be Made before International Cultural Heritage Laws Will Protect Immovable Cultural Property*, 91 Chi.-Kent L. Rev. 759, 772–74 (2016).

[96] Convention (IV) Respecting the Laws and Customs of War on Land, Oct. 18, 1907, 36 Stat. 2277, 1 Bevans 631 (hereinafter: "1907 Hague Convention"). *See* Smart, *supra* note 95, at 774–75 (noting that alongside the adoption of many of the provisions of the 1899 Hague Convention, the 1907 Hague Convention adds in its Article 27 the explicit duty to protect historic monuments during armed attacks, in addition to the duty to do so after military occupation).

[97] Zeynep Boz, Fighting the Illicit Trafficking of Cultural Property: A Toolkit for European Judiciary and Law Enforcement 1, 18 (2018).

[98] Smart, *supra* note 95, at 775 (attributing this mostly to the introduction of a new weapon: aerial bombardments).

a failure that was even more evident during the plunder of cultural property by Nazi Germany.[99]

Following the Second World War, the most prominent international instrument concerning the protection of cultural property during times of war was signed: the 1954 Hague Convention for the Protection of Cultural Property in the Event of Armed Conflict and its two protocols,[100] which prohibit, inter alia, the "theft, pillage or misappropriation" of cultural property.[101] Over the years, the 1954 Hague Convention was supplemented by instruments aimed at enabling the cross-border return of artifacts looted during wartime, such as the 2019 Resolution of the European Parliament.[102]

That said, the restitution of wartime-looted artifacts continues to encounter numerous difficulties. This is due especially to the insufficient legal framework concerning private law, private international law, and civil procedural aspects pertaining to illegally obtained artifacts – which means that private individuals and other nonstate entities often lack the procedural and substantive legal tools to claim restitution from the current possessors of the looted artifacts.[103]

As this section illustrates, the gaps between the scope of public international law norms and the rules that govern private law, private international law, and civil procedure are similarly prevalent for the restitution of artifacts lost, stolen, or illegally exported/imported outside the context of war.

These gaps are evident in the 1970 UNESCO Convention,[104] accepted or ratified as of early 2025 by 147 states.[105] The 1970 UNESCO Convention does not include a unified definition of "cultural property." Under

---

[99] *See infra* Section 2.4.

[100] Convention for the Protection of Cultural Property in the Event of Armed Conflict, May 14, 1954, 249 U.N.T.S. 215 (hereinafter: "1954 Hague Convention"); Protocol to the Convention for the Protection of Cultural Property in the Event of Armed Conflict, May 14, 1954, 249 U.N.T.S. 358 (hereinafter: "1954 First Protocol"); Second Protocol to the Hague Convention of 1954 for the Protection of Cultural Property in the Event of Armed Conflict, Mar. 26, 1999, 2253 U.N.T.S. 172 (hereinafter: "1999 Second Protocol").

[101] 1954 Hague Convention, *supra* note 100, art. 4(3).

[102] Resolution of the European Parliament of 17 January 2019 on Cross-Border Restitution Claims of Works of Art and Cultural Goods Looted in Armed Conflicts and Wars, 2019 O.J. (C 411) 125, §§M30–31.

[103] *Id.* §§J, M3.

[104] 1970 UNESCO Convention, *supra* note 86.

[105] UNESCO, *Fight Illicit Trafficking (1970 Convention), States Parties*, www.unesco.org/en/legal-affairs/convention-means-prohibiting-and-preventing-illicit-import-export-and-transfer-ownership-cultural?hub=416#item-2 (last visited Feb. 1, 2025).

Article 1, an asset is classified as cultural property if it is "specifically designated *by each State* as being of importance for archaeology, prehistory, history, literature, art or science," and it must also fall within one of the eleven general categories listed in Article 1.[106]

Accordingly, each member state must designate and publicize in its national laws the types of assets it wishes to protect as cultural property. Moreover, the 1970 UNESCO Convention places the main onus on potential source states to set the terms for exporting cultural artifacts, such that a cross-border transfer that violates the norms established by the source state would be considered illicit. However, in the absence of specific norms promulgated by the state of origin, the cross-border transfer of artifacts is not per se prohibited. According to Article 6, states of origin are called upon to "introduce an appropriate certificate in which the exporting state would specify that the export of the cultural property in question is authorized"[107] and "to prohibit the exportation of cultural property from their territory unless accompanied by the above-mentioned export certificate."[108]

Article 8 goes further by requiring states, with regard to the prohibition referred to in Article 6(b), to "impose penalties *or* administrative sanctions on any person responsible for infringing the prohibitions,"[109] but it does not entail specific requirements for doing so. As shown in Section 2.2.2, the lack of criminal sanctions that can be enforced across borders can prove to be a major detriment to the ability of source nations to protect their cultural property against such trafficking.

This is especially evident given that the duties imposed on destination states under the 1970 UNESCO Convention are much narrower. Most importantly, a state's duty to return a cultural artifact to the state of origin arises only when the cultural property has been stolen from a "museum or a religious or secular public monument or similar institution" and upon the specific request of the state of origin to the destination state, made through "diplomatic offices."[110] According to Article 7(b)(i) of the 1970 UNESCO Convention, the destination country is also required to take real-time measures to prohibit the import of such a stolen item,[111] and

---

[106] 1970 UNESCO Convention, *supra* note 86, art. 1 (my emphasis).
[107] *Id.* art. 6(a).
[108] *Id.* art. 6(b).
[109] *Id.* art. 8 (my emphasis). *See* further discussion of Article 8 in Section 2.2.2.
[110] *Id.* art. 7(b)(ii).
[111] *Id.* art. 7(b)(i).

Article 8, concerning the duty to impose penal or administrative sanctions, would apply to the enforcement of such an import prohibition.[112]

However, the convention *does not* impose a general duty on destination countries to prohibit the import of cultural property whenever a cultural item crosses borders without an appropriate export license, outside of the specific circumstances of Article 7(b). As Section 2.3 will show, such reciprocal export/import duties are increasingly embraced in regional and bilateral instruments and modes of law enforcement,[113] but this is not the case with the 1970 UNESCO Convention.

Moreover, even for the limited subset of stolen cultural artifacts that mandate cross-border return, the 1970 UNESCO Convention does not establish clear, unified rules as to the conditions under which the buyer or current possessor of the artifact should be compensated for restitution. While Article 7(b)(ii) provides that the "requesting State shall pay just compensation to an innocent purchaser or to a person who has valid title to that property,"[114] it does not specify the standards for identifying the buyer or current possessor as an "innocent purchaser," leaving room for disparity owing to substantial differences between national legal systems, as discussed in Section 2.1.[115]

Additionally, the 1970 UNESCO Convention does not include any rule on the time limit for claims, which means that, as each state party implements the convention (because the convention is not self-executing), states may apply their domestic limitation periods, leading to further legal disparity.[116]

Furthermore, the 1970 UNESCO Convention applies only to states. It does not grant standing to nonstate claimants, such as a privately owned museum from which an artifact, classified as "cultural property" under the respective national laws, has been stolen.[117]

---

[112] *Id.* art. 8.

[113] *See infra* Section 2.3.1.

[114] 1970 UNESCO Convention, *supra* note 86, art. 7(b)(ii).

[115] *See* Section 2.1.2, text accompanying *supra* notes 22–33.

[116] Wantuch-Thole, *supra* note 48, at 188–89; *See also* Section 2.1.2, text accompanying *supra* notes 34–45.

[117] *But see* Stephen K. Urice & Gideon A. Levy, *Article 7(b)(ii) of the UNESCO Convention: Cooperation for the Return of Cultural Property, in* The 1970 UNESCO and 1995 UNIDROIT Conventions on Stolen or Illegally Transferred Cultural Property: A Commentary 245, 255 (Ana Filipa Vrdoljak, Andrzej Jakubowski & Alessandro Chechi eds., 2024) (arguing that "we find no evidence that the government of a State Party, under whose laws a non-governmental museum is organized and operated, could not pursue a claim on behalf of the museum").

The 1970 UNESCO Convention therefore lacks cross-border private law, private international law, or civil procedure mechanisms that govern the respective rights and duties of the parties – especially nonstate parties – making restitution under this convention an impractical pursuit.[118]

To remedy these institutional and legal deficiencies, a different strategy was adopted in the 1995 UNIDROIT Convention on Stolen or Illegally Exported Cultural Objects.[119] This convention seeks to apply a private international law approach to aid in the "fight against illicit trade in cultural objects," by "establishing common, minimal legal rules for the restitution and return of cultural objects between Contracting States."[120] In so doing, it aims to improve the prospects of returning illegally exported or stolen cultural artifacts. That said, it should be noted that the 1995 UNIDROIT Convention has been ratified by a smaller number of states – fifty-five, as of early 2025 – most of which are source nations, such that its global scope is more limited than the 1970 UNESCO Convention.[121]

The 1995 UNIDROIT Convention creates a uniform definition of cultural objects, unlike the 1970 UNESCO Convention. Explicitly applying to "claims of an international character,"[122] the 1995 UNIDROIT Convention is self-executing and addresses the prospective substantive and procedural rights of distant parties, whether public or private, in a cross-border dispute.[123]

As for the illegal export of cultural objects, the 1995 UNIDROIT Convention provides that a court or another competent authority in the

---

[118] Marina Schneider, *The 1995 UNIDROIT Convention: An Indispensable Complement to the 1970 UNESCO Convention and an Inspiration for the 2014/60/EU Directive*, 2016 SANTANDER ART & CULTURE L. REV. 149, 152–54 (2016) (identifying these weaknesses of the 1970 UNESCO Convention and recounting an initiative to adopt a protocol to the convention that would cover crucial issues of private international law, which was ultimately abandoned).

[119] UNIDROIT Convention on Stolen or Illegally Exported Cultural Objects, June 24, 1995, 2421 U.N.T.S. 457 (hereinafter: "1995 UNIDROIT Convention").

[120] *Id.* Preamble, para. 4.

[121] *See* UNIDROIT, *UNIDROIT Convention on Stolen or Illegally Exported Cultural Objects (Rome, 1995) – States Parties*, www.unidroit.org/instruments/cultural-property/1995-convention/status/ (last visited Feb. 1, 2025).

[122] 1995 UNIDROIT Convention, *supra* note 119, art. 1.

[123] *See* Elina Moustaira, *Article 1 of the 1995 UNIDROIT Convention: Claims of an International Character*, in THE 1970 UNESCO AND 1995 UNIDROIT CONVENTIONS ON STOLEN OR ILLEGALLY TRANSFERRED CULTURAL PROPERTY: A COMMENTARY 514, 519 (Ana Filipa Vrdoljak, Andrzej Jakubowski & Alessandro Chechi eds., 2024) (explaining that, "unlike the 1970 Convention, the UNIDROIT Convention allows only the reservations expressly stated within it. This way, a uniform law may be created").

destination state must order the return of the object if the state of origin establishes that the removal of the object from its territory violated the provisions of its domestic law on exporting cultural artifacts, and that such an act "significantly impairs" the physical preservation or integrity of the object, the preservation of information of a scientific or historical character, or the traditional or ritual use of the object.[124] In such cases, the possessor of the object, who acquired it after its illegal export and "neither knew nor ought reasonably to have known at the time of acquisition that the object had been illegally exported" (thus placing the onus of proof on the possessor), is entitled to "fair and reasonable compensation" by the requesting state.[125]

In the case of a stolen object, the 1995 UNIDROIT Convention provides that the possessor of a cultural object that has been stolen shall return it,[126] while subjecting the claimant to certain time periods for filing a claim for restitution.[127] Article 4(1) stipulates that "[t]he possessor of a stolen cultural object required to return it shall be entitled, at the time of its restitution, to payment of fair and reasonable compensation provided that the possessor neither knew nor ought reasonably to have known that the object was stolen and can prove that it exercised *due diligence* when acquiring the object."[128]

The term "due diligence," which does not appear in the 1970 UNESCO Convention, was chosen as a distinctive legal benchmark in order to avoid the ambiguity and legal disparity among national legal systems over the more commonly used legal concept of "good faith."[129] This choice of legal terminology reflects the broad aspiration of the 1995 UNIDROIT Convention to bridge the gaps between public international law and private international law. The term "due diligence," aimed at creating a common applicable legal standard for handling "claims of an international

---

[124] 1995 UNIDROIT Convention, *supra* note 119, art. 5(3).

[125] *Id.* art. 6(1). Article 6(2) then provides: "In determining whether the possessor knew or ought reasonably to have known that the cultural object had been illegally exported, regard shall be had to the circumstances of the acquisition, including the absence of an export certificate required under the law of the requesting State." *Id.* art. 6(2).

[126] *Id.* art. 3(1).

[127] "Any claim for restitution shall be brought within a period of three years from the time when the claimant knew the location of the cultural object and the identity of its possessor, and in any case within a period of fifty years from the time of the theft." *Id.* art. 3(3).

[128] *Id.* art. 4(1) (my emphasis).

[129] Schneider, *supra* note 118, at 154–55. *See also* ASPER TAŞDELEN, THE RETURN OF CULTURAL ARTEFACTS: HARD AND SOFT LAW APPROACHES 77–87 (2016); JOHN SPRANKLING, THE INTERNATIONAL LAW OF PROPERTY 55–56 (2014).

character"[130] that may involve both public and private parties, is analyzed in detail in Chapter 3.

Another key supranational instrument, the European Union's 2014 Council Directive on the Return of Cultural Objects Unlawfully Removed from the Territory of a Member State,[131] seeks to complement public international (here, EU-level) norms with certain rules pertaining to private law and civil procedure in order to facilitate the cross-border return of "unlawfully removed" cultural artifacts among EU Member States.[132] Providing in Article 3 that "cultural objects which have been unlawfully removed from the territory of a Member State shall be returned in accordance with the procedure and in the circumstances provided for in this Directive," the 2014 EU Directive focuses on interstate claims for restitution of cultural objects defined by a Member State as "national treasures" and removed from the territory of the Member State in breach of its national provisions on national treasures or the 2009 Council Regulation on the Export of Cultural Goods.[133] It does not address private claims for cross-border restitution based on the ownership of the claimant, which are covered by Article 7(4) of Regulation (EU) No 1215/2012, which addresses civil and commercial matters generally.[134]

The 2014 EU Directive aims to improve the deficiencies of the previous European directive on the matter, Council Directive 93/7/EEC,[135] which had limited success in combating illegal trade in cultural goods.[136] The 2014 EU Directive applies to artifacts identified as "national treasures"

---

[130] *See* text accompanying *supra* note 122.

[131] Directive 2014/60/EU of the European Parliament and of the Council of 15 May 2014 on the Return of Cultural Objects Unlawfully Removed from the Territory of a Member State (Recast), 2014 O.J. (L 159) 1 (hereinafter: "2014 EU Directive").

[132] Schneider, *supra* note 118, at 160–61.

[133] According to Article 2(2) of the 2014 EU Directive, the term "unlawfully removed from the territory of a Member State" means: "(a) removed from the territory of a Member State in breach of its rules on the protection of national treasures or in breach of Regulation (EC) No 116/2009; or (b) not returned at the end of a period of lawful temporary removal or any breach of another condition governing such temporary removal." *See* further discussion of the 2014 EU Directive and the Council Regulation 116/2009 of 18 December 2008 on the Export of Cultural Goods, 2009 O.J. (L 39) 1 (hereinafter: "2009 EU Export Regulation") in Section 2.3.1.

[134] Regulation 1215/2012 of the European Parliament and of the Council of 12 December 2012 on Jurisdiction and the Recognition and Enforcement of Judgments in Civil and Commercial Matters, 2012 O.J. (L 351) 1.

[135] Council Directive 93/7/EEC of 15 March 1993 on the Return of Cultural Objects Unlawfully Removed from the Territory of a Member State, 1993 O.J. (L 74) 74 (hereinafter: "1993 Directive").

[136] Schneider, *supra* note 118, at 160.

by each Member State,[137] without imposing the additional requirements for such designations that were included in the 1993 Directive, which had proven burdensome.[138]

Focusing on restitution claims between a requesting Member State (i.e., the country of origin) and a requested Member State (i.e., the country where the artifact is currently located) that are submitted to the court in the requested Member State, the 2014 EU Directive addresses issues of civil procedure and private law that may be particularly prone to legal disparity among Member States – while in many respects aligning with the relevant provisions of the 1995 UNIDROIT Convention. It thus sets a timeline for submitting a claim, which must be made within three years of the requesting Member State becoming aware of the location of the cultural object and the identity of its possessor.[139]

As for the right of the current possessor of the cultural object to compensation from the requesting Member State in the case of restitution, the 2014 EU Directive uses the normative benchmark of requiring the possessor to exercise "due care and attention" in acquiring the object.[140]

While the 1993 Directive used this term without providing any criteria for determining "due care and attention" – leaving it to the interpretation of the national court with jurisdiction over the claim and thus perpetuating legal divergence among Member States – the 2014 EU Directive offers a nonexhaustive list of considerations for assessing "due care and attention."

This list is taken almost verbatim from the list of criteria used to define the term "due diligence" in Article 4 of the 1995 UNIDROIT Convention in cases involving stolen property.[141] Accordingly, Article 10 of the 2014 EU Directive also considers "the documentation on the object's provenance" and, specifically, whether "the possessor consulted any accessible register of stolen cultural objects and any relevant information which he could reasonably have obtained."[142]

---

[137] This is done pursuant to Article 36 of the Treaty on the Functioning of the European Union (TFEU), which allows Member States to place certain limits on exports within the internal market. Consolidated Version of the Treaty on the Functioning of the European Union, Oct. 26, 2012, 2012 O.J. (C 326) 47, art. 36 (hereinafter: "TFEU").

[138] Schneider, *supra* note 118, at 160.

[139] 2014 EU Directive, *supra* note 131, art. 8. Article 8 also provides that such proceedings shall not be brought, in any event, more than thirty years after the unlawful removal of the object from the territory of the requesting Member State, or within an extended period of up to seventy-five years for certain categories of protected cultural objects. *Id.*

[140] *Id.* art. 10.

[141] 1995 UNIDROIT Convention, *supra* note 119, art. 5(3).

[142] 2014 EU Directive, *supra* note 131, art. 10.

Although the 1995 UNIDROIT Convention is currently binding on only fifty-five countries, most of which are not major "market nations" for stolen or illegally removed cultural artifacts, and the 2014 EU Directive applies only within the twenty-seven EU Member States, the broader cross-border impact of consolidating legal provisions should not be underestimated. These provisions may govern the rights and duties of parties in cultural property disputes, and aim to bridge the existing gaps between public international law and private international law in order to streamline the protection of cultural property.

The effect of these more recent international instruments is manifested in at least three ways. First, creating new terminology such as "due diligence" (1995 UNIDROIT Convention) or "due care and attention" (2014 EU Directive) in the context of cultural property may inspire, or even have a mutually reinforcing impact on, the development of doctrines in national law, cross-border soft-law provisions, and professional or ethical norms. This point is demonstrated in Chapter 3.[143]

Second, the development of supranational instruments that are at least conscious of the need to bridge gaps between public international law and private international law – even if the solutions that such instruments provide are not always sufficient – may serve as a benchmark for evaluating the efficacy of previous (e.g., the 1970 UNESCO Convention) and subsequent hard-law instruments that deal with issues pertaining to the cross-border protection of cultural heritage, such as the 2001 UNESCO Convention on the Protection of the Underwater Cultural Heritage.[144]

Third, and probably most importantly, because the 1970 UNESCO Convention, 1995 UNIDROIT Convention, and 2014 EU Directive primarily deal retrospectively with illicit acts that have already occurred – i.e., acts of theft, illegal export, and the trafficking of cultural property across

---

[143] *See* Chapter 3, Section 3.3.

[144] UNESCO, Convention on the Protection of Underwater Cultural Heritage, Nov. 2, 2001, 2562 U.N.T.S. 45694 (entered into force on Jan. 2, 2009) (hereinafter: "UCHC"). *See* Patrizia Vigni, *The 1970 UNESCO and 1995 UNIDROIT Conventions and the UNCLOS and the 2001 Underwater Cultural Heritage Convention*, in The 1970 UNESCO and 1995 UNIDROIT Conventions on Stolen or Illegally Transferred Cultural Property: A Commentary 762, 780 (Ana Filipa Vrdoljak, Andrzej Jakubowski & Alessandro Chechi eds., 2024) (arguing that, in spite of "patent discrepancies between the 1970 UNESCO and 1995 UNIDROIT Conventions and the [2001] UCHC, these international instruments seem to share the common goal of preserving cultural heritage" such that in order "to accomplish this common goal, the 1970 and 1995 Conventions should be applied as instrumental rules to implement the general principles emerging from the holistic approach of the UCHC").

borders – and may thus encounter numerous difficulties in remedying such illicit acts ex post, these instruments raise awareness of the need to engage in real-time cross-border action.

This means that alongside ex post remedies of public international law and private international law, another set of tools must be employed to better protect cultural property across national borders: criminal law – and consequently criminal law enforcement – alongside other modes of law enforcement, including real-time information sharing, customs control, and civil forfeiture.[145] The next section discusses the growing role of criminal law, while Section 2.3 will address law enforcement.

2.2.2 Criminal Law: From the UNESCO Convention to the Nicosia Convention

As noted in the previous section, the ability of public international law norms to remedy in retrospect cases of illicit trafficking of cultural property, and even more so to prevent such actions in real-time through cross-border law enforcement, has proven somewhat limited. This has led to a growing focus on the ability of additional legal instruments and operative modes of law enforcement to protect against the trafficking of cultural property, particularly as such illicit actions continue to take place on a massive scale through cross-border smuggling rings.[146]

In particular, the limited role of current public international law in this area has led to increasing calls to broaden the scope of criminal law for the protection of cultural property, and to do so in a way that would apply in both source nations and market nations. Beyond the general deterrence effect that criminal law sanctions may carry, their importance may lie in leveraging the more effective mechanisms of criminal sanctions and law enforcement actions, especially in dealing with cross-border offenses. As Stefano Manacorda and Arianna Visconti note, "adopting criminal sanctions in domestic jurisdictions would have the additional positive effect of facilitating judicial and police cooperation. Some of the most important cooperation instruments, and especially those that

---

[145] For the differences between civil forfeiture and criminal forfeiture in the United States, and the relevance of each type of asset forfeiture for the recovery of cultural property, *see* Stefan D. Cassella, *Recovering Stolen Art and Antiquities under the Forfeiture Laws: Who Is Entitled to the Property When There Are Conflicting Claims*, 45 N.C. J. INT'L L. 393 (2020).

[146] *See* Chapter 1, Section 1.1.

provide for extradition, are based on double criminality."[147] This section reviews recent developments in the international arena. Section 2.3 will explore how regional and bilateral collaboration in this area is becoming an increasingly effective tool.

In the context of the 1970 UNESCO Convention, Article 8 states that parties "undertake to impose penalties or administrative sanctions on any person responsible for infringing the prohibitions referred to under Articles 6(b) and 7(b) above."[148] Beyond the fact that countries can opt solely for administrative sanctions, even in cases where criminal sanctions are imposed, the requirements under Article 8 apply only to adding a criminal law component to export controls that a country had already decided to enforce as a source country (Article 6(b)). In the case of destination countries, Article 8 applies only to prohibitions against the importation of items "stolen from a museum or a religious or secular public monument or similar institution" in another country (Article 7(b)) – representing a very narrow subset of the cases in which cultural goods are illicitly trafficked across national borders.

Moreover, while countries are, of course, free to criminalize other actions related to cultural property in their domestic law, outside the scope of their commitments under Article 8 of the 1970 UNESCO Convention – and many countries did so well before 1970 – such criminal law norms are very often nonreciprocal, in the sense that they focus on protecting cultural property in the state's capacity as a source country (including through the introduction of criminal sanctions as part of its patrimony laws or export restrictions) without criminalizing the importation of items that violate another country's domestic law.

This is particularly the case with countries, such as Italy and Spain, that had comprehensive cultural heritage laws, including criminal sanctions, before the ratification of the 1970 UNESCO Convention. However, such rules have focused almost entirely on protecting their own cultural property. But this has also been the case with countries like China and Egypt, which adopted cultural heritage laws in preparation for – or following their adoption of – the 1970 UNESCO Convention.[149]

---

[147] Stefano Manacorda & Arianna Visconti, *Article 8 of the 1970 UNESCO Convention: Penalties or Administrative Actions, in* THE 1970 UNESCO AND 1995 UNIDROIT CONVENTIONS ON STOLEN OR ILLEGALLY TRANSFERRED CULTURAL PROPERTY: A COMMENTARY 262, 267 (Ana Filipa Vrdoljak, Andrzej Jakubowski & Alessandro Chechi eds., 2024).

[148] 1970 UNESCO Convention, *supra* note 86, art. 8.

[149] Manacorda & Visconti, *supra* note 147, at 277.

Moreover, in many cases, market countries explicitly allow for the import of certain categories of cultural property, even when the respective source countries prohibit the export of these items. Courts in market countries are often reluctant to enforce such foreign legislation.[150] Courts and law enforcement agencies in such market countries would regularly base their unwillingness to intervene in favor of source countries on the traditional "principle of territoriality," which is a corollary of each state's independence and equality in international law and by which "the public law of a foreign state shall be exercised only on the territory of the state which enacted it."[151]

This inherent imbalance has somewhat changed over the past few decades – not only in the context of regional or bilateral legal instruments or agreements, which will be analyzed in Section 2.3, but also through more recent domestic legislation addressing cultural property. A prominent example is Germany's 2016 Act on the Protection of Cultural Property,[152] which includes, alongside a system of export bans and controls, a detailed list of import prohibitions and controls,[153] with both sets of provisions supported by a system of criminal and administrative sanctions.[154] However, this gap continues to pose a challenge to effective collaboration against cross-border illicit trafficking that addresses the specific complexities of cultural property.[155]

That said, cross-border collaboration in criminal law enforcement can rely on the application of more general criminal law provisions, which

[150] Michele Graziadei & Barbara Pasa, *The Single European Market and Cultural Heritage: The Protection of National Treasures in Europe*, in CULTURAL HERITAGE IN THE EUROPEAN UNION: THE PROTECTION OF NATIONAL TREASURES IN EUROPE 79, 83–84 (Andrzej Jakubowski et al. eds., 2019).

[151] WANTUCH-THOLE, *supra* note 48, at 272.

[152] Gesetz zum Schutz von Kulturgut (Kulturgutschutzgesetz) [Cultural Property Protection Act], July 31, 2016, Federal Law Gazette [BGBl] Pt. I, at 1914 (hereinafter: "2016 Act" or "KGSG"). An English translation of the KGSG is available at www.gesetze-im-internet.de/englisch_kgsg/englisch_kgsg.html.

[153] *Id.* §31 ("unlawful export of cultural property"), §32 ("unlawful import of cultural property"), §83 ("criminal provisions"), §84 ("provisions on administrative fines"), and §85 ("confiscation and extended forfeiture").

[154] Manacorda & Visconti, *supra* note 147, at 278–79 (referring to such provisions in the KGSG, as well as to the laws of countries such as Canada and Australia that represent a more balanced approach to export and import).

[155] For some of these complexities in the context of cross-border law enforcement, *see* European Commission, *Communication from the Commission to the European Parliament, The Council, The European Economic and Social Committee and the Committee of the Regions*, Dec. 13, 2022, COM(2022) 800, §2, https://eur-lex.europa.eu/legal-content/EN/TXT/?uri=CELEX%3A52022DC0800 (hereinafter: "EU Action Plan").

exist across practically all legal systems, whenever there are specific violations of these laws in the context of cultural property. This is particularly
the case with various property crimes, such as the theft of cultural items,
or for offenses such as forgery (namely, the illegal imitation of cultural
goods or the use of forged documents in this context).

A third and important category that has been increasingly recognized
as falling under the general scope of criminal law – one that is recognized and enforced across national legal systems and can therefore also be
addressed by cross-border law enforcement collaboration – is the offense
of looting, namely, "the removal of ancient relics from archaeological sites
and old buildings."[156]

The 1970 UNESCO Convention does not explicitly address the issue
of such looting or illegal excavations from archaeological sites or similar
locations.[157] The 1995 UNIDROIT Convention does so, in Article 3(2),
which states: "For purposes of this Convention, a cultural object which
has been unlawfully excavated or lawfully excavated but unlawfully
retained shall be considered stolen, when consistent with the law of the
State where the excavation took place."[158] This provision was fiercely
debated during the drafting process of the 1995 UNIDROIT Convention.
It was strongly supported by countries rich in archaeological sites that
are vulnerable to such illicit actions and opposed by others, with the delegations of the United States, Japan, Austria, and UNESCO proposing its
deletion.[159] Ultimately, the provision was included in the final version of
the convention by a majority vote (with some delegates suggesting during the debates that this inclusion might deter some opposing countries
from joining the convention).[160]

Following the adoption of Article 3(2) as part of the 1995 UNIDROIT
Convention, and in order to facilitate its implementation in favor

---

[156] Europol, *Crime Areas, Cultural Goods Crime*, www.europol.europa.eu/crime-areas-
and-statistics/crime-areas/illicit-trafficking-in-cultural-goods-including-antiquities-
and-works-of-art#:~:text=Cultural%20goods%20crime%20is%20one,organised%20
criminal%20groups%20every%20year (last visited Feb. 1, 2025) (identifying three "typi-
cal" cultural goods crimes of "theft," "looting," and "forgery").

[157] Schneider, *supra* note 118, at 154.

[158] 1995 UNIDROIT Convention, *supra* note 119, art. 3(2).

[159] Alicja Jagielska-Burduk & Derek Fincham, *Article 3 of the UNIDROIT Convention: Claims
for Restitution of Stolen Cultural Objects, in* THE 1970 UNESCO AND 1995 UNIDROIT
CONVENTIONS ON STOLEN OR ILLEGALLY TRANSFERRED CULTURAL PROPERTY:
A COMMENTARY 545, 549–50 (Ana Filipa Vrdoljak, Andrzej Jakubowski & Alessandro
Chechi eds., 2024).

[160] John H. Merryman, *The UNIDROIT Convention: Three Significant Departures from the
Urtext*, 5 INT'L J. CULTURAL PROPERTY 11, 14 (1996).

of source countries, in 2011 UNSECO and UNIDROIT published the Model Provisions on State Ownership of Undiscovered Cultural Objects.[161] These provisions state that "undiscovered Cultural Objects are owned by the State, provided there is no prior existing ownership" (Provision 3) and that "cultural objects excavated contrary to the law or licitly excavated but illicitly retained are deemed to be stolen objects" (Provision 4).[162] However, such model provisions, even when adopted into the legislation of source countries (and such provisions already existed in some form in patrimony laws enacted prior to these model provisions), can only be useful if they are recognized by other states, namely by the destination states to which such illicitly excavated archaeological artifacts are trafficked.[163] Importantly, while most market countries have not joined the 1995 UNIDROIT Convention[164] – regardless of whether their reason for abstaining has been the incorporation of Article 3(2) – legal systems in these market countries have come to recognize both the civil and criminal force of such provisions in patrimony laws.

A key decision in this regard was the 2003 ruling by the U.S. Court of Appeals (Second Circuit) in *United States v. Schultz*.[165] The court upheld the conviction of a New York art dealer of a conspiracy to receive Egyptian antiquities that had been smuggled out of Egypt in violation of its 1983 patrimony law (known as "Law 117," which declares all antiquities found in Egypt after 1983 to be the property of the Egyptian government).[166] The court ruled that this conduct amounted to a violation of the U.S. National Stolen Property Act (NSPA),[167] by which

> [w]hoever receives, possesses, conceals, stores, barters, sells, or disposes of any goods ... of the value of $5,000 or more ... which have crossed a State or United States boundary after being stolen, unlawfully converted, or taken, knowing the same to have been stolen, unlawfully converted, or taken ... [s]hall be fined under this title or imprisoned not more than ten years, or both.[168]

---

[161] UNESCO–UNIDROIT Model Provisions on State Ownership of Undiscovered Cultural Objects (adopted 2011), CLT-2011/ CONF.208/ COM.17/5, www.unidroit.org/ instruments/cultural-property/2012-model-provisions/.

[162] *Id.* provisions 3–4.

[163] Jagielska-Burduk & Fincham, *supra* note 159, at 550.

[164] *See* text accompanying *supra* note 121.

[165] U.S. v. Schultz, 333 F. 3d 393 (2d Cir. 2002).

[166] For the relevant provisions of the Egyptian "117 Law," *see* id. at 399–400.

[167] National Stolen Property Act (NSPA), 18 U.S.C. §§2314–2315.

[168] *Id.* §2315.

The court held that "Schultz's actions violated the NSPA if the antiquities he conspired to receive in the United States belonged to someone who did not give consent for Schultz (or his agent) to take them. That 'someone' is the nation of Egypt,"[169] and, accordingly, that "the NSPA applies to property that is stolen in violation of a foreign patrimony law."[170]

Following *U.S. v. Schultz* and judicial decisions in other countries – including those that upheld the civil law aspects of property rights granted to a state under a patrimony law concerning undiscovered or illegally excavated archaeological items[171] – the looting of such archaeological artifacts is now considered an offense falling under the "double criminality" principle, and can therefore be enforced by cross-border criminal law enforcement measures.

Accordingly, international criminal law enforcement and special operations focus on these three offenses, alongside related crimes. As noted by the European Commission (whose work with other EU bodies on this matter will be addressed in more detail in Section 2.3):

> The three main illegal activities associated with trafficking in cultural goods are (1.) theft and robbery, (2.) looting (the illicit removal of ancient relics from archaeological sites, buildings or monuments), and (3.) forgery of cultural goods. Related crimes include fraud, disposal of stolen goods (fencing), smuggling or corruption. Beyond trafficking, criminals can abuse even legally acquired cultural goods, for money laundering, sanctions evasions, tax evasion or terrorism financing.[172]

Accordingly, INTERPOL, Europol, and other international and national law enforcement agencies (including customs authorities) are increasingly engaging in joint operations. In 2016, these bodies launched the annual global Operation Pandora, which, as of 2023, has led to hundreds of arrests and to the recovery of over 150,000 cultural items across national borders.[173] In these and other law enforcement activities,

---

[169] U.S. v. Schultz, *supra* note 165, at 399.

[170] *Id.* at 410.

[171] *See* Government of the Islamic Republic of Iran v. The Barakat Galleries Ltd [2007] EWCA Civ. 1374 (U.K.).

[172] EU Action Plan, *supra* note 155, at 1–2.

[173] Europol, *A Total of 52 Arrests in Operation across 28 Countries Targeting Trafficking in Cultural Goods* (Mar. 9, 2022), www.europol.europa.eu/media-press/newsroom/news/total-of-52-arrests-in-operation-across-28-countries-targeting-trafficking-in-cultural-goods (reporting on Operation Pandora VI, held in 2021); INTERPOL, *International Art Trafficking Operation Leads to 60 Arrests and over 11,000 Objects Recovered* (May 4, 2023), www.interpol.int/en/News-and-Events/News/2023/International-art-trafficking-operation-leads-to-60-arrests-and-over-11-000-objects-recovered (reporting

INTERPOL has been utilizing its Stolen Works of Art Database and ID-Art, its mobile app, which are analyzed in Chapter 4 along with other cultural property databases.

A further development in criminal law enforcement has been the growing linkage between cultural property trafficking and the cross-border battle against organized crime and terrorism.[174]

While the 2000 United Nations Convention against Transnational Organized Crime (UNTOC),[175] which has 192 parties as of early 2025,[176] does not specifically address cultural property, it could potentially do so if member states classify offenses related to cultural property trafficking as "serious crimes" under Article 2(b) of UNTOC.[177] Such a proposal was put forward by the 2015 UNESCO Operational Guidelines, which were adopted by consensus at the meeting of the parties to the 1970 UNESCO Convention,[178] although this proposal has not yet come to fruition.[179] Undoubtedly, once cultural property offenses (including looting) fall within the province of UNTOC, this will facilitate the various modes of international cooperation under the convention.[180]

Cross-border law enforcement also targets the illicit trafficking of cultural property used to finance the activities of terrorist organizations.

---

on Operation Pandora VII, held in 2022); EU Action Plan, *supra* note 155, at 1 (reporting on the aggregate results of Operation Pandora between 2016 and 2022).

[174] *See* text accompanying *supra* note 172.

[175] United Nations Convention against Transnational Organized Crime, and the Protocols Thereto, Nov. 15, 2000, 2225 U.N.T.S. 209 (entered into force on Sept. 29, 2003) (hereinafter: "UNTOC").

[176] U.N. Office on Drugs and Crime, *Signatories to the United States Convention against Transnational Organized Crime*, www.unodc.org/unodc/en/treaties/CTOC/signatures .html (last visited Feb. 1, 2025).

[177] UNTOC, *supra* note 175, art. 2(b) (defining a "serious crime" as "a conduct constituting an offence punishable by a maximum deprivation of liberty of at least four years or a more serious penalty"). Article 3(1) of UNTOC provides that "This Convention shall apply, except as otherwise stated herein, to the prevention, investigation and prosecution of … (b) Serious crime as defined in article 2 of this Convention; where the offence is transnational in nature and involves an organized criminal group."

[178] UNESCO, OPERATIONAL GUIDELINES FOR THE IMPLEMENTATION OF THE CONVENTION ON THE MEANS OF PROHIBITING AND PREVENTING THE ILLICIT IMPORT, EXPORT AND TRANSFER OF OWNERSHIP OF CULTURAL PROPERTY (2015), para. 66, C70/15/3.MSP/OperationalGuidelines/EN, https://unesdoc.unesco.org/ ark:/48223/pf0000388413.

[179] Manacorda & Visconti, *supra* note 147, at 268.

[180] UNITED NATIONS OFFICE ON DRUGS AND CRIME (UNODC), DIGEST OF CASES: INTERNATIONAL COOPERATION IN CRIMINAL MATTERS INVOLVING THE UNITED NATIONS CONVENTION AGAINST TRANSNATIONAL ORGANIZED CRIME AS A LEGAL BASIS (2021).

Chapter 1 examined the significance of Security Council Resolution 2347 of 2017,[181] which "deplores and condemns the unlawful destruction of cultural heritage ... as well as the looting and smuggling of cultural property from archaeological sites, museums, libraries, archives, and other sites, in the context of armed conflicts, notably by terrorist groups."[182] The resolution then calls upon member states to take specific actions to increase international collaboration against such terrorist groups by employing criminal law mechanisms in addition to military force.[183]

Increasing concern over the potentially growing links between the illicit trafficking of cultural property and the cross-border activities of organized crime and terrorist groups has also bolstered support for the creation of a binding international convention specifically addressing the criminal law aspects of illicit actions in cultural property. Thus, while a previous attempt undertaken by the Council of Europe in the mid-1980s to adopt the European Convention on Offences Relating to Cultural Property failed owing to the inability to secure the minimum number of ratifications required for the convention to enter into force,[184] a more recent initiative succeeded. The Nicosia Convention on Offences Relating to Cultural Property,[185] signed in May 2017 and open for signature also by countries that are not members of the Council of Europe, entered into force on April 1, 2022, upon attaining the required five ratifications. As of early 2025, the Nicosia Convention has been ratified by five European countries – Cyprus, Greece, Hungary, Italy, and Latvia – as well as Mexico.[186]

While the number of states parties to the Nicosia Convention would obviously have to increase over time to facilitate effective collaboration in criminal law enforcement on a global scale, the convention already serves as a benchmark by being "the only international treaty specifically dealing with the criminalisation of the illicit trafficking of cultural property."[187]

---

[181] S.C. Res. 2347 (Mar. 24, 2017).

[182] *Id.* para. 1.

[183] *See* Chapter 1, text accompanying notes 42–48.

[184] Manacorda & Visconti, *supra* note 147, at 271.

[185] Council of Europe Convention on Offences relating to Cultural Property, adopted on May 3, 2017 (Council of Europe Treaty Series (CETS) no. 221) (hereinafter: "Nicosia Convention").

[186] Seven other countries have signed the Nicosia Convention but have not yet ratified it. Council of Europe, *Chart of Signatures and Ratifications of Treaty 221*, www.coe.int/en/web/conventions/full-List?module=signatures-by-treaty&treatynum=221 (last visited Feb. 1, 2025).

[187] EU Action Plan, *supra* note 155, at 11.

Importantly, the Nicosia Convention includes an offense of "illegal exportation" in Article 6,[188] as well as an offense of "illegal importation" in Article 5. These would apply not only to cases of theft or illegal excavations but also to violations of the source country's export laws,[189] thereby extending the future scope of criminal sanctions and cross-border law enforcement.[190]

Moreover, as noted by the European Commission in its 2022 Action Plan against Trafficking in Cultural Goods – addressed in Section 2.3 – the Nicosia Convention is important for cross-border criminal law enforcement for yet another reason. A major impediment to comprehensive cross-border intelligence gathering is that "there is neither a uniform data collection methodology, nor a uniform categorisation of cultural goods related crimes."[191] The detailed catalog of cultural property crimes set out in the Nicosia Convention contains guidance on categories of crimes that member states' authorities can use to facilitate uniform categorization, thereby improving the prospects of effective cross-border enforcement.[192]

2.2.3   *The European Court of Human Rights Steps In:* Getty v. Italy *(2024)*

The previous analysis examined the evolution of the web of cross-border legal norms pertaining to cultural property, and particularly, the often complex and somewhat ambiguous interplay between domestic law and international law; public international law and private international law; civil law, administrative law, and criminal law; and the various law enforcement mechanisms that operate, in real-time or ex post facto, to combat the cross-border illicit trafficking of cultural property.

---

[188] Nicosia Convention, *supra* note 184, art. 6(1) ("Each Party shall ensure that the exportation of movable cultural property, if the exportation is prohibited or carried out without authorisation pursuant to its domestic law, constitutes a criminal offence under its domestic law, when committed intentionally").

[189] *Id.* art. 5(1) ("Each Party shall ensure that, when committed intentionally, the importation of movable cultural property, the importation of which is prohibited pursuant to its domestic law on the grounds that it has been … (c) exported in violation of the law of the State that has classified, defined or specifically designated such cultural property in accordance with Article 2 of this Convention, constitutes a criminal offence under its domestic law where the offender knew that the cultural property had been stolen, excavated or exported in violation of the law of that other State").

[190] EU Action Plan, *supra* note 155, at 11.

[191] *Id.*

[192] *Id.*

In May 2024, the European Court of Human Rights – arguably the world's most prominent supranational court addressing human rights, with influence extending well beyond its formal applicability to the members of the Council of Europe that are part of the European Convention on Human Rights[193] – issued its decision in the case of *The J. Paul Getty Trust and Others v. Italy*.[194] This decision introduced an additional key layer of international legal norms concerning cultural property.

This section analyzes the *Getty v. Italy* decision and its broader implications for the current supranational legal order governing the cross-border movement of cultural items, as well as the respective rights and duties of different parties, from source countries to leading market actors.

Beyond the novelty of the court's reasoning in its conclusion, by which the 2018 confiscation order issued by Italian authorities for the sculpture *Victorious Youth* – which has been in the possession of the Getty Museum in Los Angeles since 1978 – does not constitute a violation of the right to the "protection of property" under Article 1 of Protocol no. 1 to the Human Rights Convention,[195] this decision should also be read in light of three aspects that underlie the ways in which the human rights analysis is embedded in the particular landscape of cultural property law.

First, in identifying the Italian confiscation order of a cultural item that was illegally exported from Italy under its domestic laws as representing the promotion of a "public interest" or "general interest" for the purposes of Article 1, the court relies not only on the national interest of Italy but also on the growing international recognition of the importance of cultural property. This includes recognition by instruments

---

[193] European Convention for the Protection of Human Rights and Fundamental Freedoms, opened for signature Nov. 4, 1950, Eur. TS No. 5, 213 U.N.T.S. 221 (hereinafter: "the Human Rights Convention"). For a list of the signatory parties to the Human Rights Convention and, particularly, Protocol No. 1 to the European Convention for the Protection of Human Rights and Fundamental Freedoms, Mar. 20, 1952, E.T.S. 9 (hereinafter: "Protocol One of the Human Rights Convention"), *see* European Court of Human Rights, *European Convention on Human Rights*, www.echr.coe.int/european-convention-on-human-rights (last visited Feb. 1, 2025).

[194] App. No. 35271/19 (May 2, 2024), https://hudoc.echr.coe.int/eng?i=001-233381 (hereinafter: "Getty v. Italy").

[195] Article 1 reads: "Every natural or legal person is entitled to the peaceful enjoyment of his possessions. No one shall be deprived of his possessions except in the public interest and subject to the conditions provided for by law and by the general principles of international law. The preceding provisions shall not, however, in any way impair the right of a State to enforce such laws as it deems necessary to control the use of property in accordance with the general interest or to secure the payment of taxes or other contributions or penalties." Protocol One of the Human Rights Convention, *supra* note 193, art 1.

that do not directly apply to the United States government or to parties in its territory.

Second, the analysis of the "fair balance" between the public interest of the source country and the proprietary interest of the possessor of the cultural item cannot be derived simply from previous precedents of the court regarding the protection of property for other types of assets (such as land). Instead, this analysis must take into account the specific attributes of cultural items and the array of domestic and international norms, with their unique combination of civil, administrative, and penal aspects.

Third, the analysis of a "fair balance" or the "proportionality" of the measures taken by the respondent country does not view the possessor of the cultural item as a "passive" burdened party. On the contrary, the possessor must show that it acted "with the necessary diligence"[196] to evaluate the strength of its proprietary claim under the Human Rights Convention. This notion, advanced by the court, is tied to the increasing general duty imposed on parties involved in cultural property transactions to exercise diligence and engage in provenance research, as discussed in Chapter 4.

To briefly set the scene: in 1964, an ancient Greek bronze statue of a young man, later to be known as the *Victorious Youth* (Figure 2.2), was discovered in the waters off Pedaso on the Adriatic Coast by Italian fishermen, who took it to the port of Fano. The fishermen sold the statue to a group of four men, and it was kept in the house of one of them before being sold to other unknown parties in 1965, after which its whereabouts became unknown.[197] The four men were charged with receiving and handling stolen goods in connection with the theft of an archaeological object belonging to the state, pursuant to Section 67 of the then-in-force patrimony law, Law no. 1089 of June 1, 1939.

The four men, who argued that the vendor had assured them that the statue had been found in Yugoslav waters, were ultimately acquitted of the criminal charges in 1970 owing to a lack of "direct and convincing evidence of the origin and location of the discovery of the statue in Italian territorial waters," and, accordingly, of the crimes with which they had been charged.[198]

The statue reappeared in Munich, Germany, on the premises of a German art dealer, who acted on behalf of a company registered in Liechtenstein, the alleged owner of the statue. In 1973, an official of the

---

[196] Getty v. Italy, *supra* note 194, at para. 379.
[197] *Id.* para. 6.
[198] *Id.* paras. 10–14.

Figure 2.2   Statue of a victorious youth; Unknown; Greece; 300–100 BCE.
Source: The J. Paul Getty Museum. Made available under the Creative Commons CC0
1.0 Universal Public Domain Dedication. www.getty.edu/art/collection/object/103QSX.

Italian Ministry of the Interior wrote to the Munich criminal police, informing them of the circumstances in which the statue had been exported and stating that it was in the hands of the art dealer. Criminal charges against the art dealer were discontinued due to lack of evidence. The following year, an Italian magistrate opened an investigation into the "unlawful exportation" of a cultural object under Section 66 of Law 1089 of 1939, but the Munich public prosecutor's office dismissed the Italian authorities' request to seize the statue and discontinued its investigation against the art dealer. In 1976, the Italian authorities discontinued their own investigation, on the grounds that the perpetrators of the unlawful export remained unknown.[199]

While the statue was in Germany, the J. Paul Getty Trust entered into negotiations with the art dealer, acting as a representative of the Liechtenstein company, for the purchase of the statue. In August 1972, J. Paul Getty Sr. made a tentative offer of 3.5 million dollars and requested a copy of the Italian court decisions in the criminal proceedings concerning the circumstances of the statue's discovery. Following correspondence between the parties, and based on representations made by the vendor asserting that it held good title to the statue, the J. Paul Getty Trust purchased the statue in July 1977 for 3.95 million dollars through a contract concluded in the United Kingdom. The statue entered the United States in August 1977 through the port of Boston and arrived at the Getty Villa in California in March 1978, where it has been displayed ever since.[200]

In December 1977, the Italian customs authorities, through INTERPOL, sent a request for investigation, which was forwarded to the U.S. Customs Service in Washington, D.C., and then to a special agent in Los Angeles. The agent issued a report in January 1978, concluding that the statue's entry into U.S. territory did not appear to have violated U.S. customs law. This investigation was closed in 1984.[201]

During that time, an Italian magistrate in Gubbio opened a new investigation into the unlawful exportation of a cultural object. Following lengthy proceedings – which ran parallel to unsuccessful diplomatic efforts by Italy to recover the statue from the J. Paul Getty Trust – a preliminary investigations judge at the Pesaro District Court issued a confiscation order in 2010. However, this order was annulled by upper Italian courts in 2015 owing to the lack of an adequate public hearing.[202]

---

[199] *Id.* paras. 15–22.
[200] *Id.* paras. 23–38.
[201] *Id.* paras. 40–44.
[202] *Id.* paras. 45–85.

In June 2018, a second confiscation order was issued by the Pesaro District Court. Regarding the establishment of the facts, the Pesaro judge concluded that the discovery of the statue had occurred in Italian territorial waters, based on statements made in December 1977 by the captains of the two boats, who indicated that the discovery was made a few miles off the coast. Moreover, even if the discovery had occurred outside territorial waters, the judge determined that the Italian state had acquired ownership of the statue as it was discovered by an Italian-flagged vessel and therefore within Italian territory, in accordance with Article 4 of the Italian Navigation Code.[203] The confiscation order was based on the provision of Article 174 of the CCLH:

Article 174: Unlawful exportation

1. Whoever transfers abroad objects of artistic, historical, archaeological, ethno-anthropological, bibliographic, documentary or archival interest, as well as those referred to in Article 11 § 1 (f), (g) and (h), without a certificate of free circulation or export license, shall be sentenced to one to four years' imprisonment or a fine between EUR 258 and EUR 5,165.

   …

3. The judge shall order confiscation of the objects unless they belong to a person not involved in the criminal offence. Confiscation shall be carried out in accordance with the provisions of customs law relating to smuggled goods.[204]

The Pesaro judge further held that, even if the trust had not committed any criminal offense, it was not a "person not involved in the criminal offence" (as per Article 174 §3 of the CCLH), that is, someone who, at the time of the purchase had no knowledge – through no fault of their own – of the object's illicit origin and had not profited from it in any way. In particular, the Pesaro judge found that the J. Paul Getty Trust had been negligent in purchasing the statue without a proper and independent inquiry into the legitimacy of the previous transfers under Italian law, relying instead merely on the representations and legal assessments provided by the vendor's lawyers.[205]

The confiscation order was upheld in a final decision by the Italian Court of Cassation in January 2019.[206] The Court of Cassation ruled that the

---

[203] *Id.* paras. 86–91.

[204] CCLH, *supra* note 71, art. 174.

[205] Getty v. Italy, *supra* note 194, at para. 91.

[206] Corte di Cassazione Penale, Third Section, Jan. 2, 2019 (hearing held on Nov. 30, 2018), judgment no. 22, www.ambientediritto.it/giurisprudenza/corte-di-cassazione-penale-sez-3-02-01-2019-sentenza-n-22/ (It.). The references to the decision of the Court of Cassation in this paragraph are based on Getty v. Italy, *supra* note 194.

confiscation order under Article 174 of the CCLH "is not a penalty" but has instead "'primarily a recovery purpose' ... apt to be pursued also with respect to persons not involved in the commission of the offense ... since it was aimed at ensuring respect of the public interest violated by an unlawful export by way of restoring the 'original public control' over the object."[207]

As for the relevance of whether the J. Paul Getty Trust had been negligent or acted in bad faith when it purchased the statue, the Court of Cassation held that the term "person not involved in the criminal offence" in Article 174 §3, as interpreted by relevant domestic case law, considers whether "the 'addressee' of the measure had cooperated in the commission of the offense of unlawful exportation or whether, negligently or in bad faith, it had 'consciously benefited' from its commission and, consequently, had purchased or acquired the object despite knowledge of the offense."[208] The Court of Cassation observed that the Pesaro judge's assessment of the trust's bad faith or negligence in the matter was reasonable, and clarified that a confiscation order could still be imposed even if the proceedings did not lead to a criminal conviction because the relevant offense was time-barred.[209]

Following the Court of Cassation's decision, the Pesaro public prosecutor's office sent a letter of international request in July 2019 to the U.S. authorities for enforcement of the confiscation measure, pursuant to the Treaty of Mutual Assistance in Criminal Matters between the United States and Italy (hereinafter: "U.S.–Italy Treaty"),[210] alongside the Agreement on Mutual Legal Assistance between the European Union and the United States,[211] and UNTOC.[212] At the time of submitting the application to the European Court of Human Rights, the Office of the U.S. Attorney General had not yet decided whether to certify the request under the U.S.–Italy Treaty and submit it to a competent domestic court;[213] however, the European Court of Human Rights addressed the application, holding that the trust had already been "sufficiently affected by the contested measure."[214]

---

[207] Getty v. Italy, *supra* note 194, para. 95.
[208] *Id.* para. 96.
[209] *Id.* paras. 97–98.
[210] Treaty between the United States of America and the Italian Republic on Mutual Assistance in Criminal Matters, signed Nov. 9, 1982 (entered into force Nov. 13, 1985), T.I.A.S. 85-1113.
[211] Agreement on Mutual Legal Assistance between the European Union and the United States of America, July 19, 2003, O.J. (L 181) 34.
[212] UNTOC, *supra* note 175.
[213] Getty v. Italy, *supra* note 194, paras. 104–5.
[214] *Id.* paras. 224–31.

The European Court of Human Rights reviewed the array of domestic, bilateral, regional, and international legal sources that apply directly to the case, as well as those legal sources that serve to identify the broader trends in domestic and cross-border protection of cultural property.

In so doing, the court examined, inter alia, Article 9 of the Italian Constitution;[215] Law no. 1089 of 1939 (which was in force when the statue was found), later replaced by Legislative Decree no. 490 of 1999, and subsequently by the 2004 CCLH;[216] Article 826 of the Civil Code, which regulates the inalienable patrimony of the state, provinces, and municipalities;[217] and the Italian Navigation Code,[218] as well as other laws, presidential decrees, and court cases – particularly those involving the term "not involved in a criminal offense" as introduced by case law even prior to the 2004 CCLH.[219]

The court then looked at the various cross-border legal instruments. These include, inter alia, the international instruments regulating judicial cooperation between the United States and Italy;[220] the international law of the sea;[221] the 1970 UNESCO Convention (ratified by the United States only in 1983);[222] the 1995 UNIDROIT Convention (neither signed nor ratified by the United States);[223] the 2001 UNESCO Convention;[224] the Nicosia Convention on Offences Relating to Cultural Property (neither signed nor ratified by the United States);[225] and EU instruments on the export and import of cultural property, discussed in Section 2.3, to which the United States is obviously not a party.

Turning to the analysis of the applicable rule under Article 1 of Protocol no. 1 of the Human Rights Convention, the court noted that "the present case concerns a very particular issue, namely the protection of cultural heritage and the recovery of an unlawfully exported cultural object

---

[215] Art. 9 Costituzione [Cost.] (It.). For a discussion of Article 9 of the Italian Constitution, *see* Chapter 5, Section 5.2.

[216] CCLH, *supra* note 71.

[217] Art. 826 CC (It).

[218] *See* text accompanying *supra* note 203.

[219] Getty v. Italy, *supra* note 194, at paras. 122–30.

[220] *See* text accompanying *supra* notes 210–13.

[221] Getty v. Italy, *supra* note 194, at paras. 141–48.

[222] *See supra* note 105 for a list of states parties and dates of ratification of the 1970 UNESCO Convention.

[223] *See supra* note 121 for a list of states parties and dates of ratification of the 1995 UNIDROIT Convention.

[224] *See supra* note 144.

[225] *See* text accompanying *supra* notes 185–86.

through a measure that, although adopted within criminal proceedings, has civil effects."[226] Per the court, alongside domestic law, "similar measures aimed at recovering unlawfully exported cultural objects have been progressively regulated under international law,"[227] even if some do not apply directly to all parties, such that:

> In the light of the above, the Court considers that, irrespective of the applicable rule under Article 1 of Protocol No. 1, the justification for the interference at issue in the present case must be assessed by taking into account that, due to the unique and irreplaceable nature of cultural objects, States enjoy a wide margin of appreciation where cultural heritage issues are concerned.[228]

The court held that "the legal basis for the contested measure was sufficiently clear, foreseeable and compatible with the rule of law,"[229] in the "general interest of the community,"[230] and that "the legitimacy of the purpose of protecting cultural heritage is further demonstrated by the subsequent developments in the international and European legal framework."[231]

In examining whether the measure was "proportionate" to the aim pursued, such that there was a "fair balance" struck between the state's public interest and the applicant's proprietary interest,[232] the court looked at the conduct of the parties. It concluded that Italy's actions cannot be deemed inadequate, given the complexity and uncertainty it faced, and that it "operated in a legal vacuum, as there were no binding international legal instruments in force at the time in which the Statue was exported and purchased by the applicant which would have allowed it to recover it or, at the very least, to obtain the full cooperation of the foreign domestic authorities."[233]

Importantly, as part of proportionality analysis, the court also examined the behavior of the applicant, holding that the "standard of diligence laid down by Italian law was sufficiently clear and foreseeable," that "the nature of the transaction justified a high standard of diligence in the present case," and that "similar standards are nowadays enshrined in Article 4

---

[226] Getty v. Italy, *supra* note 194, at para. 278.
[227] *Id*. para. 279.
[228] *Id*. para. 280.
[229] *Id*. para. 325.
[230] *Id*. para. 340.
[231] *Id*. para. 341.
[232] *Id*. para. 374.
[233] *Id*. para. 400.

of the 1995 UNIDROIT Convention."[234] The court further held, based on the domestic court's findings, which were made after taking the applicant's arguments into account, that "the Trust's representatives had, at the very least, very weighty reasons to doubt the Statue's legitimate provenance."[235] However, while "the Trust's representatives had a clear duty to take all the steps that could reasonably be expected of them to investigate the Statue's legitimate provenance before purchasing it … they did not carry out a careful and objective assessment of the Statue's provenance."[236]

The court held, accordingly, that the assessment made by the Italian domestic authorities, according to which the trust's representatives "were, at the very least, negligent, if not in bad faith," cannot be seen as "arbitrary or manifestly unreasonable."[237] It thus reached the following conclusion:

> In light of the above findings, and taking into account that the State has a wide margin of discretion as to what is "in accordance with the general interest", particularly where cultural heritage issues are concerned, the strong consensus in international and European law with regard to the need to protect cultural objects from unlawful exportation and to return them to their country of origin, the applicant's negligent conduct, as well as the very exceptional legal vacuum in which the domestic authorities found themselves in the present case, the Court concludes that they did not overstep their margin of appreciation. Accordingly, the Court finds that there has been no violation of Article 1 of Protocol No. 1.[238]

It remains to be seen if the U.S. authorities will enforce the Italian confiscation order, but the *Getty v. Italy* case can already be seen as having a substantial impact on international legal norms.

2.3   Regional and Bilateral Collaboration in Law Enforcement

As Section 2.2 showed, while the international landscape of legal norms on cultural property has developed significantly over the past few decades, the practical effect of these legal instruments remains somewhat constrained, particularly regarding the two key international conventions in this area: the 1970 UNESCO Convention and the 1995 UNIDROIT Convention. This limitation arises, inter alia, because the scope of binding duties on market countries to prevent the import of illicitly trafficked

---

[234] *Id.* paras. 380–81.
[235] *Id.* para. 385.
[236] *Id.* paras. 387–88.
[237] *Id.* para. 390.
[238] *Id.* paras. 408–9 (internal citations and references omitted).

cultural goods is limited, under the 1970 UNESCO Convention, to a small subset of cases detailed in Article 7(b), and does not apply to illegal exports per se,[239] while the 1995 UNIDROIT Convention, which includes more affirmative duties, was not signed by most market countries.[240]

That said, many of the loopholes in cross-border lawmaking and law enforcement may be more effectively addressed through regional or bilateral collaboration between states. This section looks at two examples: the European Union's initiatives and bilateral measures taken by the United States.

2.3.1 European Union: Export/Import Controls and Action Plan against Trafficking

While the competences of the European Union are limited by its founding treaties – such that, for example, the EU does not have direct competence over criminal law, requiring Member States to introduce criminal sanctions through national legislation[241] – the EU's capacity to act is substantial in dealing with licit and illicit cross-border movement of goods. This competence has proven instrumental in consolidating reciprocal norms on the export and import of cultural property within the EU and establishing rules on export to/import from other countries.

As for the export of cultural property outside of the borders of the EU's internal market, a Council Regulation on cultural property was adopted as early as 1992.[242] It was then amended and replaced, without substantial changes, by the current 2009 EU Export Regulation.[243] Under Article 1 of the 2009 EU Export Regulation,[244] the term "cultural goods" refers to the items listed in Annex I, which includes fifteen categories of objects as well as criteria based on age and financial value.[245] Under Article 2(1), "[t]he export of cultural goods outside the customs territory of the Community shall be subject to the presentation of an export licence."[246] These uniform

---

[239] *See* text accompanying *supra* notes 110–18.

[240] *See* text accompanying *supra* notes 119–30.

[241] Manacorda & Visconti, *supra* note 147, at 274 (referring to Article 83 of the TFEU, *supra* note 137).

[242] Council Regulation (EEC) 3911/92 of 9 December 1992 on the Export of Cultural Goods, 1992 O.J. (L 395) 1.

[243] 2009 EU Export Regulation, *supra* note 133.

[244] *Id.* art. 1.

[245] *Id.* Annex I.

[246] *Id.* art. 2(1).

rules do not apply to objects that are defined by each Member State as "national treasures." In such cases, control over these items would be governed by the national laws of the Member State (meaning that their movement would also be restricted within the boundaries of the internal market, as discussed below).[247]

The 2014 EU Directive,[248] discussed in Section 2.2,[249] deals specifically with these "national treasures," which, according to Article 36 of the Treaty on the Functioning of the European Union (TFEU),[250] constitute an exception to the principle of the free movement of goods within the EU's internal market. Articles 1 to 3 of the 2014 EU Directive provide as follows:

Article 1
The Directive applies to the return of cultural objects classified or defined by a Member State as being among national treasures, as referred to in point (1) of Article 2, which have been unlawfully removed from the Territory of that Member State.

Article 2
For the purposes of this Directive, the following definitions apply:

(1) "cultural object" means an object which is classified or defined by a Member State, before or after its unlawful removal from the territory of that Member State, as being among the "national treasures possessing artistic, historic or archaeological value" under national legislation or administrative procedures within the meaning of Article 36 TFEU;
(2) "unlawfully removed from the territory of a Member State" means:

   (a) removed from the territory of a Member State in breach of its rules on the protection of national treasures or in breach of Regulation (EC) No 116/2009 [the 2009 EU Export Regulation];

   …

Article 3
Cultural objects which have been unlawfully removed from the territory of a Member State shall be returned in accordance with the procedure and in the circumstances provided for in this Directive.

The 2014 EU Directive therefore establishes a robust, reciprocal system for protecting Member States' "national treasures" within the European Union. Cooperation between the Member States on this

---

[247] *Id.* arts. 2(2)–(3).
[248] 2014 EU Directive, *supra* note 131.
[249] *See* text accompanying *supra* notes 131–42.
[250] For Article 36 of the TFEU, *see supra* note 137.

matter is facilitated through the Internal Market Information (IMI) system, introduced in 2016, which enables authorities to rapidly exchange information.[251]

Moreover, the fact that Article 36 of the TFEU and Article 1 of the 2014 EU Directive do not provide a definition for a "national treasure," leaving the determination to each Member State, and the fact that under Article 2(1) of the 2014 EU Directive a Member State can classify a cultural object as a "national treasure" even after the item's removal from its territory show that the "glue that holds the States together in protecting their cultural heritage is therefore attentive and active trust."[252] It is a system of reciprocal commitments that is achievable on a regional scale.

The third prong of EU regional lawmaking concerning the protection of cultural property addresses the import of cultural items from outside the European Union. With the 2019 EU Import Regulation,[253] the European Union took a major step in closing the gap between export control and import control – an issue highlighted in Section 2.2 in the context of the 1970 UNESCO Convention and the 1995 UNIDROIT Convention.[254] The 2019 EU Import Regulation achieves this by prohibiting, in Article 3(1), the introduction of cultural goods "which were removed from the territory of the country where they were created or discovered in breach of the laws and regulations of that country,"[255] if they belong to one of the categories listed in Part A of the Annex.[256]

Furthermore, Article 3(2) of the 2019 EU Import Regulation stipulates that the import of cultural goods listed in Part B of the Annex is permitted only if the importer obtains an import license from the country of origin according to the terms of Article 4.[257] Similarly, the import of cultural goods listed in Part C of the Annex is permitted only if the importer submits an "importer statement" providing proof that it is abiding by the laws of the source country, as specified in the terms set out in Article 5 of the regulation.[258]

---

[251] *See* Graziadei & Pasa, *supra* note 150, at 93.

[252] *Id*. at 92.

[253] Regulation (EU) 2019/880 of the European Parliament and of the Council of 17 April 2019 on the Introduction and the Import of Cultural Goods, O.J. (L 151) 1 (hereinafter: "2019 EU Import Regulation").

[254] *See* Section 2.2.1, text accompanying *supra* notes 110–30.

[255] 2019 EU Import Regulation, *supra* note 253, art. 3(1).

[256] *Id*. Annex, Part A.

[257] *See*, respectively, *id*. art. 3(2)(a); Annex, Part B; art. 4.

[258] *See*, respectively, *id*. art. 3(2)(b); Annex, Part C; art. 5.

According to Article 1(2) of the 2019 EU Import Regulation, it "does not apply to cultural goods which were created or discovered in the customs territory of the Union."[259] This means that the regulation does not cover the reimport of cultural property created or discovered within the European Union – including, for that matter, a cultural object that was illegally excavated in an EU Member State (e.g., Italy), subsequently illegally exported to a country outside of the EU (e.g., the United States), and then "reimported" into a country within the Single European Market (SEM).[260]

While the limits on the import of cultural items coming into the SEM from third countries under the 2019 EU Import Regulation may be seen as the "other side of the coin" of the restrictions on the export of cultural items outside of the SEM under the 2009 EU Export Regulation,[261] the connection is far from straightforward. This is evident in the loopholes that exist within the framework of the 1970 UNESCO Convention and the 1995 UNIDROIT Convention.[262] The decision by the European Union to adopt such a reciprocal approach toward the protection of cultural heritage from other source countries is thus a globally oriented policy decision, made possible by EU-level regional lawmaking tools.[263]

Importantly, according to the 2019 EU Import Regulation and the accompanying 2021 regulation that implements the 2019 Import Regulation (the "2021 Implementing Regulation"),[264] the system of import licenses and importer statements will rely on the introduction of a centralized electronic system. As outlined in Article 8 of the 2019 EU Import Regulation[265] and Chapter V of the 2021 Implementing Regulation,[266] the rules on

---

[259] *Id.* art. 1(2).

[260] Robert Peters, *Preventing Trafficking in Cultural Property: Import and Export Provisions as Two Sides of the Same Coin*, 5 SANTANDER ART & CULTURE L. REV. 95, 104 (2019).

[261] *Id.* at 105–6.

[262] *See* Section 2.2.1, text accompanying *supra* notes 110–30.

[263] *See* Tamás Szabados, *The EU Regulation on the Import of Cultural Goods: A Paradigm Shift in EU Cultural Property Legislation?* 18 CROATIAN YB. EUR. L. & POL. 1, 18 (2022) (noting that the "EU Import Regulation unilaterally puts trust in third countries, more precisely in the export legislation of third countries and their authorities issuing export certificates and other documents").

[264] Commission Implementing Regulation (EU) 2021/1079 of 24 June 2021 Laying Down Detailed Rules for Implementing Certain Provisions of Regulation (EU) 2019/880 of the European Parliament and of the Council on the Introduction and the Import of Cultural Goods [2021] O.J. (L 234) 67 (hereinafter: "2021 Implementing Regulation").

[265] 2019 EU Import Regulation, *supra* note 253, art. 8.

[266] 2021 Implementing Regulation, *supra* note 264, Ch. V.

import licenses and importer statements enter into force when the electronic system becomes operational – or, at the latest, on June 28, 2025.[267] The means that the new substantive rules on the control of cultural property imports are both formally and practically tied to the introduction of this law enforcement system.

This inherent link between substantive rules and law enforcement mechanisms carries broader implications. The European Union's ability to advance efforts against the illicit trafficking of cultural property relies, to a large extent, on close collaboration between law enforcement agencies in Member States, and particularly on the ability to harness the work of organizations such as Europol or permanent instruments like EMPACT (European Multidisciplinary Platform Against Criminal Threats) to enforce legal rules on cultural property.[268]

Of particular interest is the EU Action Plan against Trafficking in Cultural Goods, published in December 2022 by the European Commission.[269] This plan includes a detailed analysis of the "complex phenomenon" of trafficking in cultural goods,[270] and sets out "four strategic objectives for an effective and comprehensive response: (I) Improving prevention and detection of crimes by market participants and cultural heritage institutions; (II) Strengthening law enforcement and judicial capabilities; (III) Boosting international cooperation; (IV) Gaining the support of other key stakeholders to protect cultural goods from crime."[271]

Specifically, referring to the centralized electronic system for import controls, the EU Action Plan against Trafficking in Cultural Goods states:

---

[267] 2019 EU Import Regulation, *supra* note 253, art. 16(2)(b). *See also* Fred Clark & Abi Meho (Boodle Hatfield), *Incoming New EU Import Regulation on Cultural Goods: A Summary & Analysis of the Key Issues and Market Concerns* (Apr. 25, 2024), www.boodlehatfield.com/articles/incoming-new-eu-import-regulation-on-cultural-goods-a-summary-analysis-of-the-key-issues-and-market-concerns/.

[268] Europol, *Cultural Goods Crime*, www.europol.europa.eu/crime-areas-and-statistics/crime-areas/illicit-trafficking-in-cultural-goods-including-antiquities-and-works-of-art (last visited Feb. 1, 2025); Europol, *EU Policy Cycle – EMPACT: EMPACT 2022+ Fighting Crime Together*, www.europol.europa.eu/crime-areas-and-statistics/empact (last visited Feb. 1, 2025) (listing, within "Priorities 2022–2025," a priority to "disrupt criminal networks involved in … illegal trade of cultural property").

[269] EU Action Plan, *supra* note 155.

[270] *Id.* at 1–2.

[271] *Id.* at 3.

It is paperless, and will ensure the interconnection between relevant customs, cultural authorities, and existing databases. Moreover, it has the potential to reduce cases of document forgery, and eliminates the need to verify the authenticity of paper licences. The Commission is also considering a future extension of this system to export licences under Regulation (EC) 116/2009 [2019 EU Export Regulation].[272]

Therefore, one of the key actions that the European Commission plans to take as part of the EU Action Plan is to "explore the extension of the electronic system for regulating the import of cultural goods to handle the export of cultural goods, through a feasibility study."[273]

The EU Action Plan further notes that "the owners and managers of public and private collections can take voluntary measures to protect themselves better from property crimes." One key action is to keep up-to-date inventories and databases of collected cultural goods using "available tools recommended by law enforcement authorities, such as the International Council of Museums' (ICOM) Object-ID."[274] Moreover, reporting property crimes to law enforcement authorities helps to ensure that "cultural goods appear in national stolen art databases and Interpol's Stolen Works of Art Database."[275] Accordingly, the European Commission plans to act with "the aim of helping Member States establish *sales registries* to improve traceability of cultural goods," and encourages Member States to take "measures to *ensure that public and private collections duly register their possessions in databases and report property crimes* cases to law enforcement, with help from internationally agreed standards and tools (such as the Object ID standard or Interpol's Stolen Works of Art Database)."[276] The issue of cultural property digital databases and their instrumental role in promoting domestic and cross-border law enforcement – as well as other objectives related to cultural property – are explored in detail in Chapter 4.

2.3.2   *The Growing (Over?)Reach of U.S. Law Enforcement*

2.3.2.1   Federal and State Law in Action

As the previous sections have demonstrated, the United States holds a unique position within the international legal landscape of norms

---

[272] *Id.* at 4.
[273] *Id.* at 7.
[274] *Id.* at 5.
[275] *Id.*
[276] *Id.* at 7–8 (emphasis in the original).

pertaining to cultural property. On the one hand, private law rules in various U.S. states – particularly substantive rules applying the *nemo dat* principle and procedural rules concerning time limits for submitting civil court claims – have proven quite favorable to claimants. This includes source countries making proprietary claims based on patrimony laws for the restitution of illegally excavated archaeological items.[277]

Moreover, in the context of Holocaust-era assets – discussed in Section 2.4 – the United States has gone further in facilitating court claims by introducing federal legislation, the Holocaust Expropriated Art Recovery (HEAR) Act of 2016.[278] The HEAR Act grants, with certain exceptions, an extended timeframe for heirs of persons dispossessed during the period between 1933 and 1945 to submit claims that would otherwise have been time-barred. This makes the United States arguably the only major legal system where such civil court claims are still possible.

At the same time, the United States has likely been the most prominent "market country" for cultural property, especially in the decades following the end of the Second World War. U.S. cultural institutions and private collectors have been the most prominent buyers at auctions and private sales of cultural property, often asking few – if any – questions about the provenance of the items.[279] Moreover, as noted earlier in this chapter, the United States has not imposed general-scope limits on the export or import of cultural property, even after ratifying the 1970 UNESCO Convention, and it has yet to join the 1995 UNIDROIT Convention.[280]

That said, over the past few decades, the United States has been utilizing more law enforcement mechanisms, on both the federal and state levels, with some of the law enforcement agencies promoting what may be termed "legal creativity," especially in criminal law proceedings. As this section shows, while this contemporary law enforcement engagement has been rooted in bilateral agreements and collaborations with source countries, U.S. law enforcement agencies are taking it a step further, initiating their own investigations – some of which are now being contested in courts.

A starting point for analyzing the current modes of operation of U.S. law enforcement authorities is Article 9 of the 1970 UNESCO Convention, which allows state parties "whose cultural property is in jeopardy from

---

[277] *See* Section 2.1.2, text accompanying *supra* notes 25–61.
[278] Public Law No. 114-308, 130 Stat. 1524 (hereinafter: "2016 HEAR Act").
[279] *See* Chapter 1, text accompanying notes 78–79.
[280] *See* Section 2.1.3, text accompanying *supra* notes 81–93; Section 2.2.1, text accompanying *supra* notes 104–21.

pillage of archaeological or ethnological materials" to call upon other countries to collaborate in order to "carry out the necessary measures, including the control of exports and imports and international commerce in the specific materials concerned."[281] While the United States – unlike some other parties to this convention – has not imposed a general ban on the import of cultural property whenever its export was unauthorized by another member state, it has entered into a series of bilateral collaboration agreements with source countries under Article 9.[282] As of early 2025, the United States is party to bilateral collaboration agreements with thirty-two countries.[283]

As far as U.S. federal law enforcement of these bilateral agreements is concerned, based on the provisions of the 1983 Convention on Cultural Property Implementation Act (CPIA),[284] along with various U.S. customs statutes,[285] the key federal law enforcement agency involved in working together with law enforcement agencies in other countries and conducting criminal investigations in this area is the Department of Cultural Property, Art, and Antiquities Smuggling of Homeland Security Investigations (HSI) – a division of U.S. Immigration and Customs Enforcement.[286]

In addition, U.S. federal bodies, including the Department of Justice, engage in criminal proceedings in cultural property offenses that can be applied to general-scope federal offenses, such as those falling under the provisions of the NSPA,[287] as was the case in *United States v. Schultz*.[288] Working in collaboration with law enforcement agencies in countries that are parties to the bilateral agreements under Article 9 of the 1970 UNESCO Convention, or in other criminal cross-border investigations, as well as with U.S. state-level agencies – most prominently, the New

---

[281] 1970 UNESCO Convention, *supra* note 86, art. 9.

[282] Gerstenblith, *supra* note 87, at 471–72.

[283] For a current list and timelines of the Article 9 bilateral agreements to which the United States is a party, *see* U.S. Department of State, Bureau of Educational and Cultural Affairs, *Current Agreements and Import Restrictions*, https://eca.state.gov/cultural-heritage-center/cultural-property/current-agreements-and-import-restrictions (last visited Feb. 1, 2025).

[284] Pub. L. 97-446, codified as 19 U.S.C. §§2601–13 (hereinafter: "CPIA").

[285] For an analysis of these statutes, and the availability of civil and administrative remedies, alongside criminal ones, especially when U.S. customs laws are breached, *see* Cassella, *supra* note 145.

[286] Homeland Security Investigations (HSI), *Cultural Property, Art, and Antiquities Smuggling*, www.dhs.gov/hsi/investigate/cpaa-smuggling (last visited Feb. 1, 2025).

[287] *See* NSPA, *supra* note 167.

[288] *See* text accompanying *supra* notes 165–70.

York State Antiquities Trafficking Unit, discussed below – U.S. law enforcement has led to the restitution of thousands of cultural items to other countries.[289]

As noted in the book's introduction, which discussed the return of *Orpheus and the Sirens*, and the pending case of the *Victorious Youth* discussed in Section 2.2.3, the bilateral collaboration between U.S. law enforcement agencies and the Carabinieri Command for the Protection of Cultural Heritage has been particularly fruitful, leading to the return of a vast number of cultural objects to Italy over the last few years. In May 2024 alone, approximately 600 antiquities, valued at 65 million dollars, were returned to Italy.[290] According to an annual report published by the Carabinieri, over 500 items were restituted in the year 2023,[291] following multiple restitutions in 2022.[292]

In these and other returns to source countries, the New York State Antiquities Trafficking Unit, operating within the Manhattan District Attorney's Office and led by Assistant District Attorney Matthew Bogdanos, has played a key role.[293] The Antiquities Trafficking Unit, formally established in 2017 (though it began its operations within the Manhattan District Attorney's Office in 2011),[294] engages extensively in criminal investigations.[295] It has been granted search warrants by the New York courts for cultural items, which in many cases have led to the restitution of objects by museums, art galleries, and collectors without the need

---

[289] *See, e.g.*, Benjamin Sutton, *US Authorities Return 30 Antiquities Recovered During Trafficking Investigations to Cambodia and Indonesia*, THE ART NEWSPAPER, Apr. 26, 2024.

[290] *US Returns Stolen Italian Art Worth $65m in Vow to Put Loot Back "Where It Belongs,"* AP, May 29, 2024.

[291] COMANDO CARABINIERI, TUTELA PATRIMONIO CULTURALE, ATTIVITÀ OPERATIVA 2023 (2024) (It.). *See also* Gareth Harris, *More Stolen Archaeological Treasures Were Returned to Italy from the US*, THE ART NEWSPAPER, Aug. 14, 2023 (reporting on the return of over 200 items, including sixty-five artifacts from the Menil collection in Houston).

[292] *See* Claire Voon, *Authorities In New York Return 14 Looted Artefacts Valued at $2.5m Totally, Including a Black-Figure Hydria by the Renowned Priam Painter*, THE ART NEWSPAPER, Feb. 3, 2023 (describing a series of returns made to Italy, including 142 items in July 2022 and fifty-eight items in September 2022).

[293] Manhattan District Attorney's Office, *Antiquities Trafficking*, https://manhattanda.org/category/antiquities-trafficking/ (last visited Feb. 1, 2025).

[294] *See* Jason Daley, *Manhattan DA Launches First Antiquities Trafficking Unit*, SMITHSONIAN MAG., Dec. 22, 2017; Ariel Sabar, *The Tomb Raiders of the Upper East Side: Inside the Manhattan DA's Antiquities Trafficking Unit*, THE ATLANTIC, Nov. 23. 2021.

[295] *See* Edward Helmore, *The New York DA's Office Fighting to Stop Trade of Looted Antiquities*, THE GUARDIAN, May 30, 2022.

to go through the full process of criminal indictments and convictions.[296] According to a press release issued in September 2024, the Antiquities Trafficking Unit had, up to that point, recovered more than 5,700 antiquities valued at over 450 million dollars and returned more than 4,600 of them to over twenty-five countries.[297]

The legal basis for initiating criminal investigations and obtaining search warrants against current possessors of cultural objects – even in those cases where the Antiquities Trafficking Unit is unable to engage in criminal proceedings against members of smuggling rings involved in cross-border trafficking – derives from New York's Penal Law. Specifically, the offense of criminal possession of stolen property, which is divided into five degrees based on the value of the property (§§165.40–165.54), and the related offense of conspiracy to commit the same crime under Penal Law §105.10(1) have been utilized. Another provision in New York's Penal Law that has been employed by the Antiquities Trafficking Unit is §165.55 (criminal possession of stolen property; presumptions), which provides in subsection (2): "A collateral loan broker *or a person in the business of buying, selling or otherwise dealing in property* who possesses stolen property is presumed to know that such property was stolen if he obtained it *without having ascertained by reasonable inquiry* that the person from whom he obtained it had a legal right to possess it."[298]

This innovative (or "creative") utilization of New York's Penal Law to allow for the opening of numerous criminal investigations against the current possessors of cultural items – including, for that matter, museums or collectors located in New York City but also outside of it – and the application for judicial search warrants and seizure of such items, has relied on three elements.

First, because the offense of criminal possession of stolen property is considered a continuing offense under previous New York case law,[299] this offense does not become time-barred if the possession continues,

---

[296] *See* Sabar, *supra* note 294 (describing cases in which artifacts were returned without the pressing of criminal charges).

[297] Manhattan District Attorney's Office, *D.A. Bragg Announces Return of 14 Antiquities to the People of Türkiye*, Sept. 12, 2024, https://manhattanda.org/d-a-bragg-announces-return-of-14-antiquities-to-the-people-of-turkiye/.

[298] New York Penal Law §165.55(2) (my emphasis). For New York case law that implemented the principle of "presumption of knowledge" under §165.55(2) for other types of property, *see* People v. Von Werne, 41 N.Y.2d 485, 362 N.E.2d 982 (N.Y. App. Div. 1977); People v. Reichbach, 131 A.D.2d 515, 515 N.Y.S.2d 891 (N.Y. App. Div. 1987).

[299] People v. Lawson, 64 Misc. 3d 200, 99 N.Y.S.3d 602 (N.Y. City Crim. Ct. 2019).

even if related criminal offenses – including the original act of theft or cross-border smuggling of the cultural item – are subject to the statute of limitations. This means that museums or collectors who have been in possession of cultural property for decades – until it turns out in retrospect that the item entered the market following its illegal excavation in the source country, or another form of illegal dispossession from its rightful owner – may find themselves potentially implicated by the continuing offense of such wrongful possession.

Second, the application of §165.55(2) of the Penal Code to museums, galleries, collectors, and other professionals dealing with cultural property serves to create, according to the Antiquities Trafficking Unit, a legal presumption of "willful ignorance" against current possessors who failed to actively and diligently probe the provenance of the item prior to its acquisition. This presumption applies in principle to museums that acquired items for millions of dollars. In other words, the interpretation given to §165.55(2) by the Antiquities Trafficking Unit is that possessors of cultural property need to prove they exercised due diligence as a defense against the criminal offense.[300]

Third, the related offense of conspiracy under Penal Law §105.10(1) – specifically conspiracy to commit the offense of criminal possession of stolen property – has been utilized by the Antiquities Trafficking Unit to extend the territorial scope of applications for search warrants and seizures of items possessed by museums or other parties outside of New York State, in cases where a New York-based party, such as an antiquities dealer or an art gallery, has played a key role in the trade of the item prior to its arrival to its current location outside of New York State.

Accordingly, New York courts have granted such out-of-state search warrants for the seizure of cultural objects (including "seizure in place," meaning that the item remains physically at the museum during the interim period of the criminal process).[301] In most cases, this has led to the surrender of objects by the possessors and their restitution without the need to exhaust the criminal proceedings.[302] However, in two recent high-profile cases, both involving out-of-state museums – the Cleveland Museum of Art and the Art Institute of Chicago – the possessors have

---

[300] *See* Sabar, *supra* note 294 (describing how this provision was used to pierce the "ostrich defense" by possessors).

[301] Karen Matthews, *Artworks Believed Stolen During Holocaust Seized from Museums in Three States*, AP, Sept. 14, 2023.

[302] Sabar, *supra* note 294.

legally challenged the proceedings initiated by the Manhattan District Attorney's Office on multiple grounds. Particularly, as shown below in Section 2.3.2.3, it is likely that the resolution of the case involving the Art Institute of Chicago will have broader implications for determining whether the "legal creativity" described above has overreached its legitimate boundaries.

2.3.2.2   Statue of a Draped Male Figure ("Marcus Aurelius")

The first case involves the "seizure in place" of what the New York court described in its search warrant issued in August 2023 as "a headless bronze statue of the Roman emperor Marcus Aurelius ('Marcus Aurelius'), dated c. 180-200 C.E., measuring 76 inches tall, and valued at $20,000,000," which "may be found at the Cleveland Museum of Art" (see Figure 2.3). The court cited reasonable cause to believe that the "object is stolen" and constitutes evidence of the crimes of "Criminal Possession of Stolen Property in the First Degree, Penal Law § 165.54, and Conspiracy to commit the same crime under Penal Law § 105.10(1)."[303]

The search warrant was granted as part of a broader criminal investigation conducted by the HSI and the Antiquities Trafficking Unit, together with law enforcement agencies in Turkey, regarding the "Bubon Bronzes" – a group of bronze statues and other items that had been illegally excavated in the late 1950s and early 1960s from a site in the Asia Minor region, now in the territory of Turkey.[304] During the Roman period, the site, in the ancient city of Bubon, served as a shrine and featured a pantheon of emperors. According to the investigation, many of the illegally excavated items were sold by local villagers to American antiquities dealer Robert Hecht, who trafficked them into the United States, where they were subsequently sold to American collectors and museums.[305]

Prior to the August 2023 search warrant issued against the Cleveland Museum of Art, the Antiquities Trafficking Unit had already seized alleged Bubon items through search warrants from the Metropolitan Museum of Art; the Museum of Greek, Etruscan and Roman Art at Fordham University; the San Antonio Museum of Art; the Princeton University Art

---

[303] Supreme Court of the State of New York, Search Warrant, Aug. 14, 2023 (Justice Ruth Pickholz), https://news.artnet.com/app/news-upload/2023/09/2023-08-14-SW-Cleveland-Bubon-Marcus-Aurelius-W.pdf.

[304] *See* Graham Bowley & Tom Mashberg, *Tracing Treasures of Ancient Rome to a Village That Looted Its Own Heritage*, N.Y. TIMES, Oct. 30, 2023.

[305] *Id.*

Museum; and the Worcester Art Museum in Massachusetts.[306] In these cases, the museums, whether located within or outside of New York, surrendered the items without a legal contest, and some were already returned to Turkey in 2023.[307] In September 2024, other items looted from Bubon and nearby sites were handed back to Turkey.[308]

The Cleveland Museum of Art, which acquired the *Marcus Aurelius* statue (which the museum currently refers to as a "draped male figure," thereby questioning the identity of the person depicted) from an art dealer in 1986, has taken a different approach.[309] In October 2023, the museum submitted a complaint to the U.S. District Court in Ohio against the Manhattan District Attorney, requesting that the federal court (based on the diversity of the parties) issue a declaratory judgment affirming that the museum is the rightful owner of the statue and that the District Attorney's Office has no right to it. The museum also sought an order of replevin for the immediate return of the statue.[310]

The Cleveland Museum of Art argued, inter alia, that the statue (which it refers to in the complaint as "the Philosopher") has been exhibited in the United States and studied for nearly sixty years, including after its acquisition by the museum in 1986.[311] The museum further claimed that Turkey approached it in 2009 with questions about its collection, and the Philosopher in particular, but abandoned its inquiry.[312] Additionally, the museum maintained that there is significant doubt that the statue originates from Bubon;[313] and that, as a matter of legal principle, in two previous cases in which the possessor of an object chose to contest the claim

---

[306] See Tom Mashberg & Graham Bowley, *The Headless Statue of a "Roman Emperor" Is Seized from the Met*, N.Y. TIMES, Mar. 30, 2023 (reporting on the seizure of a Bronze statue from the Metropolitan Museum of Art); Kelsey Ables, *Ancient Roman Bust Seized from U.S. Museum in Trafficking Probe*, THE WASHINGTON POST, Sept. 6, 2023 (reporting on the seizure of a Roman bust from the Worcester Museum in Massachusetts); Tom Mashberg, *Investigators Seize "Marcus Aurelius" Statue from Cleveland Museum*, N.Y. TIMES, Aug. 31, 2023 (also reporting on previous seizures in 2023).

[307] Bowley & Mashberg, *supra* note 304.

[308] Manhattan District Attorney's Office, *supra* note 297.

[309] See Steven Litt, *New York Authorities Order Seizure of Ancient Statue at Cleveland Museum of Art Possibly Connected to Looting, Trafficking of Antiquities in Turkey*, CLEVELAND .COM, Aug. 30, 2023; Karen K. Ho, *Cleveland Museum of Art Sues Manhattan DA's Office Over Seizure of $20 M. Bronze Statue*, ARTNEWS, Oct. 19, 2023.

[310] Cleveland Museum of Art v. Alvin Bragg, Case No. 1:23-cv-02048-CEF, filed Oct. 19, 2023 (U.S.D.C., N.D. Ohio, East. Div.).

[311] *Id*. paras. 6–13.

[312] *Id*. para. 14.

[313] *Id*. paras. 19–28.

Figure 2.3 Statue of a draped male figure ("Marcus Aurelius"). Roman or possibly Greek Hellenistic. c. 150 BCE–CE 200.
Source: Cleveland Museum of Art. Made available under the Creative Commons CC0 1.0 Universal Public Domain Dedication. www.clevelandart.org/art/1986.5.

by the Manhattan District Attorney, "the criminal courts of New York, in different ways, have deferred to courts with civil jurisdiction to determine questions of title,"[314] such that the appropriate forum to resolve the matter is a civil court, rather than a criminal one.

However, in February 2025, the Cleveland Museum of Art agreed to end the court case and surrender the statue to the Manhattan District Attorney's Office. As key to its decision, the museum cited an extensive forensic testing, which included comparing soil samples using soil from within the statue, lead isotope analysis, and 3-D modeling that confirmed the statue was one that had stood in the archaeological site known as Bubon. While the museum maintains its position by which the statue did not depict the emperor Marcus Aurelius but rather a Greek philosopher, it nevertheless accepted the determination by which the statue was illegally excavated from the site in Turkey – where it will eventually head back.[315]

2.3.2.3   *Russian War Prisoner*

Another current case in which the possessor of a cultural item has legally challenged not only the facts surrounding the item's history but also the legitimacy of using criminal proceedings under New York's Penal Law to seize an item long in its possession, involves the 1916 painting *Russian War Prisoner (Russischer Kriegsgefangener – Grigori Kladjishuli)* by the Austrian painter Egon Schiele. The painting was acquired in 1966 by the Art Institute of Chicago.[316]

To understand the background to this legal process, following a claim made in February 2024 by the Manhattan District Attorney's Office,[317] it is essential to consider the broader context of a collection of eighty-one works by Egon Schiele, which were owned, prior to the Nazi rule, by the Jewish-Austrian cabaret artist Fritz Grünbaum. These works have been the subject of multiple cross-border legal proceedings over the past few decades.

Grünbaum, whose ownership of the collection can be traced back to 1928, tried to escape to Czechoslovakia with his wife Elizabeth after the Nazi invasion of Austria on March 12, 1938. However, he was apprehended by the Nazis and subsequently imprisoned in various concentration

---

[314] *Id.* paras. 15–18.
[315] Tom Mashberg & Graham Bowley, *Cleveland Museum to Return Prized Bronze Thought Looted from Turkey*, N.Y. TIMES, Feb. 14, 2025.
[316] *See* text accompanying *infra* notes 331–34.
[317] Torey Akers, *Art Institute of Chicago Accused of Holding onto Nazi-Looted Egon Schiele*, THE ART NEWSPAPER, Mar. 1, 2024.

camps, including Buchenwald and Dachau, until his death in January 1941. In July 1938, while Grünbaum was imprisoned in Dachau, the Nazis forced him to sign a power of attorney in favor of Elizabeth. She was then compelled to permit a Nazi official named Franz Kieslinger to inventory Grünbaum's property, including his art collection, which contained the eighty-one pieces by Schiele. Some time after it was inventoried, Grünbaum's entire art collection was deposited with a Nazi-controlled shipping company and marked for "export," though it appears the collection did not leave Austria during that time. Elizabeth was murdered in a Nazi death camp in 1942.

In 1956, sixty-five pieces by Schiele surfaced at an art gallery in Switzerland, managed by Eberhard Kornfeld. The artworks were put on sale by Kornfeld in September 1956, almost immediately after the time window for claims made in Austria for Nazi-looted art closed. Some of the works included in the 1956 Schiele catalog published by Kornfeld ended up in U.S. museums and private collections.[318]

In 2002, Milos Vavra, a great-nephew of Grünbaum, and Leon Fischer, a second cousin of Elizabeth, were declared by an Austrian court to be the legal heirs of Grünbaum. They pursued legal measures to reclaim the Schiele works located in Austria and the United States.[319] Since their passing, the claims have been managed by the coexecutors of their estate, Timothy Reif and David Frankel.[320]

One such claim, *Bakalar v. Vavra*, was discussed in Section 2.1 in the context of the 2010 decision by the federal Court of Appeals (Second Circuit) to apply New York law, rather than Swiss law, to the case.[321] However, in 2012, the Second Circuit affirmed the decision of the U.S. District Court for the Southern District of New York, which had ruled in favor of David Bakalar – who had purchased the Schiele painting from an art dealer – based on the New York doctrine of laches.[322]

---

[318] For the statement of these facts, *see* Reif v. Nagy, 175 A.D. 3d 107 (N.Y. App. 2019) (hereinafter: "Reif, 2019").

[319] For a report on a 2023 claim filed in a New York court against the Albertina and Leopold museums in Vienna for the recovery of twelve works by Schiele, *see* Catherine Hickley, *Jewish Cabaret Artist's Heirs File Suit for the Return of 12 Works by Schiele*, THE ART NEWSPAPER, Nov. 9, 2023.

[320] *See* Reif, 2019, *supra* note 318, at 113–14.

[321] Bakalar v. Vavra, 619 F.3d 136 (2d Cir. 2010). *See* Section 2.1.2, text accompanying *supra* notes 50–51.

[322] Bakalar v. Vavra, 500 Fed.Appx 6 (2d Cir. 2012), *affirming* Bakalar v. Vavra, 819 F.Supp.2d 293 (S.D.N.Y. 2011).

Grünbaum's heirs were successful in a later civil claim for conversion and replevin, filed in 2015 against the art dealer Richard Nagy, who had purchased two paintings by Schiele in 2013: *Woman Hiding Her Face* (1912) and *Woman in a Black Pinafore* (1913). In its 2018 decision regarding the first painting, the Supreme Court of New York ruled that the claim was timely under both the New York three-year statute of limitations and the provisions of the federal 2016 HEAR Act. The court also determined that the doctrine of laches did not bar the plaintiffs' claim. It granted the plaintiffs' motion for summary judgment on their claims of replevin and conversion, directing Nagy to return the artworks to the plaintiffs.[323] The Appellate Division affirmed this ruling, stressing in its conclusion the importance of the 2016 HEAR Act and agreeing, on the merits, that the plaintiffs had met their prima facie burden that the two artworks belonged to Grünbaum and were not voluntarily relinquished by him.[324]

Alongside the civil claims concerning Grünbaum's collection of Schiele's works, the Manhattan District Attorney's Office has also become involved in the matter by exercising its criminal jurisdiction, based on the offense of criminal possession of stolen property and related doctrines, including the "continuing offense" doctrine analyzed above.[325] The Manhattan District Attorney's Office has seized several of Schiele's works from public and private collections throughout the United States.[326]

In September 2023, the Manhattan District Attorney's Office returned seven Schiele works to Grünbaum's heirs, which had been seized from institutions and collections including the Museum of Modern Art (MoMA), the Morgan Library & Museum in New York, and the collection of Neue Galerie founder Ronald Lauder.[327]

In January 2024, two other museums handed over works by Schiele to Grünbaum's heirs: the Carnegie Museum of Art in Pittsburgh returned the pencil drawing *Portrait of a Man* (1917), and the Allen Memorial Art Museum at Oberlin College in Ohio surrendered the 1911 watercolor

---

[323] Reif v. Nagy, 80 N.Y.S. 3d 629, 61 Misc.3D 319 (N.Y. Sup. Ct. 2018) (hereinafter: "Reif, 2018").

[324] *See* Reif, 2019, *supra* note 318.

[325] *See* text accompanying *supra* notes 298–302.

[326] Tom Mashberg, *Schiele Works Believed to Be Stolen Are Seized from U.S. Museums*, N.Y. Times, Sept. 13, 2023.

[327] Benjamin Sutton, *US Authorities Return Seven Schiele Works to Heirs of Cabaret Performer Murdered by the Nazis*, The Art Newspaper, Sept. 22, 2023.

painting *Girl With Black Hair*.[328] Eight of the nine pieces have since gone
to auction.[329] In July 2024, the Manhattan District Attorney's Office
announced the return of another drawing, *Seated Nude Woman, Front
View (1918)*, to Grünbaum's heirs – this time from the heirs of a collector
who had purchased it in 1961.[330]

One work, however, remains under legal contention: the 1916 watercolor and pencil on paper painting *Russian War Prisoner*, acquired in
1966 by the Art Institute of Chicago. Following the February 2024 criminal claim by the Manhattan District Attorney's Office, the Art Institute of
Chicago responded in April 2024, arguing that the claim should be denied,
as the matter had already been resolved in a civil process by a federal U.S.
district court in favor of the Art Institute of Chicago.[331]

On November 24, 2023, the U.S. District Court for the Southern District
of New York, applying New York State law, held that a civil claim submitted in December 2022 by Grünbaum's heirs against the Art Institute of
Chicago was barred by the New York statute of limitation (noting that
that three-year period began to run when the museum refused a demand
to return the work in 2006); that the case fell under one of the exceptions
to the 2016 HEAR Act such that the Act did not grant the plaintiffs a pro-
longment of the period to submit a claim; and that the 2016 HEAR Act did
not preclude a laches defense, which should be accepted in favor of the
museum in this case.[332] In a subsequent decision on February 28, 2024,
the U.S. District Court dismissed the plaintiffs' motion for consideration
and motion for leave to file an amended complaint, reiterating its decision
that, under the specific circumstances, the claim is untimely under both
federal and state law.[333]

In its April 2024 response to the criminal court claim, the Art Institute
of Chicago also challenged the authority of the Manhattan District
Attorney's Office to act in the matter on other grounds, including its

---

[328] Carlie Porterfield, *Two More Egon Schiele Works Restituted to Heirs of Holocaust Victim Will Head to Auction*, THE ART NEWSPAPER, Jan. 19, 2024.

[329] *See id.*; Benjamin Sutton, *Egon Schiele Works Recently Restituted to Holocaust Victim's Heirs Head to Auction*, THE ART NEWSPAPER, Oct. 5, 2024.

[330] Eileen Kinsella, *Manhattan DA Returns 11th Nazi-Looted Egon Schiele Artwork to Grünbaum's Heirs*, ARTNET.COM, July 26, 2024.

[331] Daniel Grant, *Art Institute of Chicago Argues Nazi Loot Claim to Its Egon Schiele Portrait Lacks "a Single Shred" of Evidence*, THE ART NEWSPAPER, Apr. 25, 2024.

[332] Reif v. Art Institute of Chicago, 23-cv-2443 (JGK), 2023 WL 8167182 (U.S.D.C., S.D. New York, 2023).

[333] Reif. v. Art Institute of Chicago, 23-cv-2442 (JGK), 2023 WL 838431 (U.S.D.C., S.D. New York, 2024).

capacity to seize items located outside of New York State. However, in April 2025, these and other arguments were rejected by the New York court that dealt with the criminal claim. The court reasoned, inter alia, that the painting had been considered "stolen" under New York law ever since it had been involuntarily taken from Grünbaum in 1938; that no subsequent sales can render the purchase legitimate given the New York rule by which "a thief cannot pass good title"; that the Art Institute of Chicago did not make reasonable inquiries into the work's provenance at the time of purchase or at any point thereafter despite the fact that it is considered "a person in the business of buying, selling, or otherwise dealing in property," thus presumed to be in criminal possession of stolen property based on the provisions of §165.55(2) of New York's Penal Code; that New York County had jurisdiction over the matter because the offense of criminal possession of stolen property, which was partly committed in the State of New York (where the sale was made) and consummated in the State of Illinois (where the Art Institute of Chicago is in possession of the work) constitutes an offense under the laws of both of the State of New York and the State of Illinois; that the turnover of the item is not barred by a statute of limitations (because criminal possession of stolen property is considered a continuing offence), the doctrine of laches (because there has been no showing by the possessor of "a change in circumstances that would make it inequitable to grant the relief sought"), or adverse possession (because it is a civil doctrine that generally does not apply in a criminal case); and that a turnover order is the appropriate remedy in this case. The Art Institute of Chicago appealed the decision in May 2025, and an appellate judge issued a stay order, pausing the return of the artwork until the matter is resolved by the New York appellate court.[334] Accordingly, once decided finally, the case is likely to lay out broader jurisprudential principles regarding the legitimate scope of the use of criminal proceedings relying on the "continuing offense" of criminal possession of stolen property, its relation to time limits under civil claims, and the question of the Manhattan District Attorney's Office's authority to act outside the borders of New York State.

---

[334] For the decision of the Supreme Court of New York (which is the first instance in this case), see In re Application for a Turnover Ord. in Rel. to Egon Schiele's Artwork Russian War Prisoner, SMZ-70042-24, 2025 NYLJ LEXIS 1438 (N.Y. Sup. Ct. Apr. 30, 2025). For a report about the appeal submitted by the Art Institute of Chicago and the stay order issued by the appellate judge, see Angelica Villa, *Art Institute of Chicago Appeals Return of Schiele as Legal Battle Deepens*, ARTNEWS, May 7, 2025.

Moreover, this case and others discussed above may also delineate the boundaries for the legitimate use of domestic criminal law when the investigation into the illicit cross-border trafficking of cultural property does not result from a request for bilateral collaboration with law enforcement agencies in another country, or when the potential beneficiary of the criminal process against the current possessor of the cultural item is a private party who is otherwise legally barred from taking action.

2.4   Legalistic Ethical Reasoning for the Return of Cultural Property

The final section of this chapter concisely addresses the influence of the emerging domestic, bilateral, regional, and international body of hard-law norms on claims for the return of cultural property that cannot rely on formal legal proceedings – whether that is because such a claim is time-barred, the plaintiff cannot assume jurisdiction over the defendant, the claimed act of dispossession was not considered illegal at the time it occurred, or any other reason.

The issue of addressing such claims through alternative institutional mechanisms and normative reasoning will be explored in detail in Chapter 6, which examines the work processes and body of norms developed by "restitution committees" established in several European countries to address claims by persons dispossessed of cultural property during the Nazi era. It also considers whether, and how, such mechanisms can be utilized to address claims for return made in other historical contexts.

That said, it is important to highlight within the context of the current chapter that the moral or ethical reasoning that typifies such claims – both in the context of the Holocaust era and in the various stages of "art imperialism," particularly during the colonial era – seems to adopt a line of reasoning that is not entirely detached from jurisprudential principles of hard-law norms.

Accordingly, instead of adopting an all-encompassing moral framework for examining past events – which may lead to an "all-or-nothing" approach" toward a certain historical context[335] – contemporary dispute-resolution mechanisms, public policy instruments, and related sources

---

[335] See CARSTEN STAHN, CONFRONTING COLONIAL OBJECTS: HISTORIES, LEGACIES, AND ACCESS TO CULTURE vi–vii (2023).

appear to lean closer to what I term "legalistic ethical reasoning" for handling and deciding such claims.

This means, inter alia, that questions of wrongfulness, attribution of liability or entitlement, and the choice of appropriate remedies are not detached from jurisprudential principles of legal norms, even if they are applied differently due to substantive, procedural, and evidentiary considerations. Thus, hard-law norms and ethical/moral considerations need not be juxtaposed or divorced from one another, especially whenever such considerations converge to create a body of soft-law norms that seeks to complement – rather than contrast with – hard-law instruments.

The most prominent setting in which moral or ethical principles about cultural property are gradually creating a body of norms with soft-law power, and at least some degree of cross-border coordination, involves the growing efforts to provide restitution or other forms of relief concerning cultural objects wrongfully seized from Jewish persons and other victims of Nazi persecution.

While efforts in this regard date back to the 1943 London Declaration, issued in the midst of the Second World War,[336] and to time-limited laws and institutions set up after the war in the Western-controlled parts of Germany and other jurisdictions that were under Nazi occupation,[337] once these temporary arrangements expired, the issue was largely sidelined by museums and other market actors.[338]

Institutional cross-border efforts to address the issue were relaunched in the mid-1990s. After the fall of the Soviet bloc, U.S. President Bill Clinton tasked the Department of State in 1996 with assembling a group of experts, whose work was coordinated by Under Secretary of Commerce Stuart Eizenstat, appointed as Special Envoy of the Department of State on Property Restitution in Central and Eastern Europe. The results of its Preliminary Study were published in May 1997.[339] While these inquiries originally focused on real estate in Eastern Europe, and then on gold and financial assets located primarily

---

[336] Jacques Schumacher, Nazi-Era Provenance of Museum Collections: A Research Guide 50–52 (2024).

[337] Id. at 52–57.

[338] Id. at 58–59 (describing the "return to normal" among museums and other art experts).

[339] U.S. Department of State, U.S. and Allied Efforts to Recover and Restore Gold and Other Assets Stolen or Hidden by Germany during World War II: Preliminary Study (May 1997), www.govinfo.gov/app/details/GOVPUB-S-PURL-LPS658.

in Swiss financial institutions, the findings of this study also raised awareness of the possibility that looted cultural items may have ended up in American museums.[340]

Following this and other developments in the United States, Britain, and elsewhere, the U.S. Department of State convened an international conference in Washington, D.C., in late 1998, attended by delegates from forty-four countries and thirteen nongovernmental organizations.[341] The conference concluded with a joint statement, the Washington Conference Principles on Nazi-Confiscated Art.[342]

The 1998 Washington Principles were the first of a series of nonbinding instruments on the matter, among them the 2009 Terezin Declaration on Holocaust Era Assets and Related Issues, adopted by forty-seven countries,[343] and the 2024 Best Practices for the Washington Conference Principles on Nazi-Confiscated Art, endorsed by twenty-five countries as of early 2025.[344] These instruments recognize the existing disparity among different countries – as a matter of both public policy and legal rules – in addressing the historical injustice embedded in the mass looting, confiscation, and involuntary transfer of property from their owners, while trying to build a new common ground.

As noted in the Preamble to the 1998 Washington Principles, "[i]n developing a consensus on non-binding principles to assist in resolving issues relating to Nazi-confiscated art, the Conference recognizes that among participating nations there are differing legal systems and that countries act within the context of their own laws."[345]

Considering this disparity, Principle VIII of the 1998 Washington Principles states: "If the pre-War owners of art that is found to have been confiscated by the Nazis and not subsequently restituted, or their heirs, can be identified, steps should be taken expeditiously to achieve a *just and*

---

[340] SCHUMACHER, *supra* note 336, at 59–60.

[341] *Id.* at 60–64.

[342] U.S. Department of State, WASHINGTON CONFERENCE PRINCIPLES ON NAZI-CONFISCATED ART (Dec. 3, 1998), www.state.gov/washington-conference-principles-on-nazi-confiscated-art/ (hereinafter: "1998 Washington Principles").

[343] U.S. Department of State, TEREZIN DECLARATION ON HOLOCAUST ERA ASSETS AND RELATED ISSUES (June 30, 2009), www.state.gov/prague-holocaust-era-assets-conference-terezin-declaration/ (hereinafter: "2009 Terezin Declaration").

[344] U.S. Department of State, BEST PRACTICES FOR THE WASHINGTON CONFERENCE PRINCIPLES ON NAZI-CONFISCATED ART (Mar. 5, 2024), with a list of states endorsing it, www.state.gov/best-practices-for-the-washington-conference-principles-on-nazi-confiscated-art/ (last visited Feb. 1, 2025) (hereinafter: "2024 Best Practices").

[345] 1998 Washington Principles, *supra* note 342, Preamble.

fair solution, recognizing this may vary according to the facts and circumstances surrounding a specific case."[346]

The normative benchmark of a "just and fair solution" is reiterated in the 2009 Terezin Declaration[347] and in the 2024 Best Practices,[348] though it is not defined in much detail in these instruments. This leaves the task of giving concrete substance to this term to each of the countries, while at the same time creating an overarching cross-border principle: that of achieving a "just and fair solution."

As analyzed further in Chapter 3 in the context of provenance research and due diligence, in Chapter 4 in the context of digital databases, and in Chapter 6 in the context of the institutional and normative features of restitution committees set up in certain European countries, the means of bridging existing legal disparities while respecting the sovereignty of states in implementing the joint nonbinding principles lies in practically binding together the two main pillars of these instruments. First, broadly accessible information about the history of possession and ownership of the assets, especially in the period between 1933 and 1945, should be provided. Second, institutional frameworks and substantive criteria should be created in each country to implement the normative benchmark of a "just and fair solution" when the information about the specific cultural object points to what is essentially wrongful dispossession. Such dispossession can be attributed to a victim on the one hand, and a perpetrator on the other, justifying the use of a remedy chosen from a number of options deemed most appropriate for the specific circumstances of the case.

Therefore, even though the resolution of such claims is conducted through alternative mechanisms and processes, and is not formally governed by the same substantive, procedural, and evidentiary rules that ordinarily apply to civil court cases, the ethical and moral reasoning embedded in the "just and fair solution" principle relies on "legalistic" principles of wrongfulness, attribution, and scale of remedies. The soft-law principles emerging in this context are not detached from the gradual development of national and cross-border hard-law norms in the field of cultural property.

---

[346] *Id.* Principle VIII.

[347] 2009 Terezin Declaration, *supra* note 343, Section on "Nazi-Confiscated and Looted Art," §3.

[348] 2024 Best Practices, *supra* note 344, Principle D ("In principle, as set out in the Terezin Declaration, the primary just and fair solution is restitution, among other just and fair solutions").

This approach is demonstrated in Principles B–D of the 2024 Best Practices, which provide:

> B. "Nazi-confiscated" and "Nazi-looted" refer to what was looted, confiscated, sequestered, and spoliated, by the Nazis, the Fascists and their collaborators through various means including but not limited to *theft, coercion, and confiscation*, and on grounds of relinquishment, *as well as forced sales and sales under duress*, during the Holocaust era between 1933-45.
>
> C. Taking into account the specific historical and legal circumstances in each case, the sale of art and cultural property *by a persecuted person* during the Holocaust era between 1933-45 *can be considered equivalent to an involuntary transfer of property based on the circumstances of the sale.*
>
> D. "Just and fair solutions" means just and fair solutions first and foremost for the victims of the Holocaust (Shoah) and other victims of Nazi persecution and for their heirs. In principle, as set out in the Terezin Declaration, *the primary just and fair solution is restitution, among other just and fair solutions.*[349]

Chapter 6 will address in detail the evolution of legalistic ethical reasoning through the work of restitution committees, recent reforms proposed or already implemented for these committees, and the development of what may be considered "soft-law jurisprudence." This jurisprudence, in fact, is embedded in, and should work in synergy with, the various instruments of hard-law norms.

---

[349] *Id.* Principles B–D (my emphasis).

The Evolution of Norms on Due Diligence and Provenance Research

3.1 Prologue: Provenance in Musée du Louvre, the Met, and Kunsthaus Zürich

The Musée du Louvre, one of the world's most celebrated cultural institutions, launched a new open-access database in 2021, which, as of early 2025, features more than 500,000 objects in the museum's collections.[1] Alongside photographs and various details of great interest to art historians, museum professionals, and the global public of art lovers, each entry in the database also includes details known to the museum about the object's provenance – namely, the history of ownership and possession of the object prior to its arrival in the museum.[2] Undertaken by a team of experts at the Louvre, including its eight curatorial departments and the History of the Louvre Department,[3] this extensive provenance research into the Louvre's collection is an unprecedented effort in French museums, and among the most comprehensive provenance research initiatives ever undertaken by any cultural institution in the world.[4]

The purpose of making data about the provenance of cultural objects publicly available extends beyond merely satisfying the curiosity of those interested in historical details. Rather, a primary objective of the provenance research carried out by the Louvre is to reconstruct a chronological chain of ownership and possession for the artifact, identify potential problems in the object's history, and accordingly, enable parties who claim to have been dispossessed of a legitimate interest in the object to come

---

[1] Musée du Louvre, *Collections*, https://collections.louvre.fr/en/ (last visited Feb. 1, 2025).

[2] For the origins of the concepts of "provenance" and "provenience," *see* Patty Gerstenblith, *Provenience and Provenance Intersecting with International Law in the Market for Antiquities*, 45 N.C. J. INT'L L. 457, 461–69 (2020).

[3] Musée du Louvre, *About the Collections Website*, https://collections.louvre.fr/en/page/apropos (last visited Feb. 1, 2025).

[4] Vincent Noce, *Louvre Probes Its Collection for Nazi and Colonial Loot in Massive Provenance Research Project*, THE ART NEWSPAPER, Mar. 26, 2021.

forward.[5] While the issue of digital databases and their implications for cultural property is analyzed in Chapter 4, this chapter addresses the dramatic shifts in law, policy, and markets concerning provenance research and the related duty of "due diligence."

In the context of the Louvre's collections, the current focus on provenance research and the collection practices of cultural institutions emphasizes identifying works that entered the museum after being wrongfully taken from their Jewish owners between 1933 and 1945.[6] The effort to identify such pieces builds upon a series of developments outlined in Chapter 2,[7] and later in this chapter,[8] concerning Nazi-looted cultural property. In the French context specifically, the mandate for such examination stems from a 2013 report issued by the Cultural Affairs Committee of the French Senate, entitled *Looted or Unclear Cultural Work or of Unclear Background and Public Museums: Assessment and Perspectives*.[9] This report called for the adoption of a more proactive approach to provenance research in France, with the purpose of clarifying the history of objects held by museums and devoting special attention to items with indications of past spoliations or other involuntary transfers. The stated goal of this report is to prepare a complete inventory of the archives relating to such items, and to make this information publicly available.[10] The Louvre has accordingly taken up the task of inspecting nearly 14,000 items acquired by the museum between 1933 and 1945 for potential indications of looting or other forms of involuntary transfers, and signed a contract with Sotheby's to collaborate on this endeavor.[11]

In addition to probing the history of the abovementioned works, the Louvre's provenance project also seeks to shed more light on items already identified as having been involuntarily taken from their owners during

---

[5] *Id.*

[6] In the case of France, the majority of the dispossession of Jewish owners took place during the period of the Vichy regime between 1940 and 1944. *See* EMMANUELLE POLACK, LE MARCHÉ DE L'ART SOUS L'OCCUPATION 1940–1944 (2019) (Fr.).

[7] *See* Chapter 2, Section 2.4.

[8] *See infra* Section 3.4.2.

[9] Corinne Bouchoux, *Œuvres culturelles spoliées ou au passé flou et musées publics: bilan et perspectives* (2013), www.senat.fr/fileadmin/Fichiers/amdcom/cult/6P_C_Bouchoux_oeuvres_spoliees_.pdf (Fr.).

[10] *Id.* For a survey of this report, *see* Mélina Wolman, *Restitution of Nazi Looted Art in France: A Historic Law Adopted*, 68 JUSTICE (LEGAL MAGAZINE OF THE INTERNATIONAL ASSOCIATION OF JEWISH LAWYERS AND JURISTS) 33, 37 (2022).

[11] Gareth Harris, *Louvre Teams Up with Sotheby's to Investigate Provenance of Works Bought during the Second World War*, THE ART NEWSPAPER, Jan. 24, 2022.

the Nazi period – those belonging to the category of Musées Nationaux Récupération (National Museums Recovery), or "MNR."[12]

The MNR category refers to works of art that were retrieved from Germany and brought back to France after the Second World War. Originally, this category included about 61,000 works, many of which had been stolen or looted from Jewish families. To date, more than 45,000 works have been returned to their rightful owners. Unclaimed works were sold by the French state, except for 2,143 objects placed under the legal responsibility of the Ministry of Foreign Affairs and entrusted to French national museums, primarily the Louvre, for safekeeping.[13] The key purpose of the provenance research conducted by the Louvre on these MNR items is, therefore, to carry out further research in an effort to identify their rightful owners or beneficiaries. Making such data globally accessible thus serves the goal of promoting restitution in line with the 2013 report.[14]

The Louvre's provenance project is not limited, however, to Nazi-looted art. Another category concerns items in the collection that originate from former French or other colonies.[15] Provenance research into such items and the question of their restitution to their states of origin (i.e., former colonies that have since become independent states) lies at the heart of current policy debates across many governments and cultural institutions, as discussed in Chapter 1,[16] and particularly in the French context, as discussed in Chapter 6.[17] The provenance efforts undertaken by the Louvre illuminate, therefore, a broader shift that is taking place in the field of cultural property – uncovering "black holes" in the history of ownership and possession of cultural items for the purpose of addressing incidents of controversial transfers of items made within and across national borders.

However, not all museums have adopted the same approach. The Metropolitan Museum of Art in New York serves as a prominent example. As noted in Chapter 1 in the context of Egyptian antiquities

---

[12] Musée du Louvre, *National Museums Recovery: MNR Works at the Musée du Louvre*, https://collections.louvre.fr/en/album/1 (last visited Feb. 1, 2025).

[13] The Louvre currently has 1,739 items under this category. *Id.* In addition, as of 2021, the Louvre has checked some two-thirds of the 13,943 works it acquired between 1933 and 1945 for problematic provenance. Noce, *supra* note 4.

[14] Bouchoux, *supra* note 9.

[15] Noce, *supra* note 4.

[16] *See* Chapter 1, Section 1.1.

[17] *See* Chapter 6, Section 6.2.

that had been illegally excavated during the chaos of the Arab Spring and then sold to the Met,[18] and in Chapter 2 regarding Roman-era bronze statues illegally excavated in the site of Bubon in modern-day Turkey,[19] the Met has often found itself entangled in investigations related to the illicit trafficking of cultural property across borders. In several cases, the Manhattan District Attorney's Office has seized items from the Met after being granted search warrants by New York courts.[20] More generally, the Met has faced increasing scrutiny in media reports about its collecting practices, especially in the context of archaeological and ethnographic items; reports indicate that over 1,100 artifacts in its collection are allegedly tied to individuals who have been indicted or convicted for trafficking crimes.[21] Only after facing legal and reputational backlash, as well as a growing number of cases in which it announced it would surrender items from its collection,[22] did the Met decide to form a provenance research team in 2023.[23] In 2024, it hired a prominent expert from Sotheby's to head the team.[24] With more than 1.5 million items in its permanent collection,[25] it remains to be seen how the Met will manage such mass-scale provenance research and whether the results will be made publicly available.

[18] *See* Chapter 1, text accompanying notes 51–53.

[19] *See* Chapter 2, Section 2.3.2.2.

[20] Spenser Woodman et al., *"The Stuff Was Illegally Dug Up:" New York's Met Museum Sees Reputation Erode over Collection Practices*, THE GUARDIAN, Mar. 20, 2023 (noting that "throughout 2022, US authorities seized at least 29 items from the Met's collection – including Greek busts, Egyptian bronzes, and ancient plates, helmets and statues made from gold, bronze and terracotta pillaged from across the Mediterranean and India").

[21] *Id.* (citing an investigation held, as of 2021, by the International Consortium of Investigative Journalism (ICIJ)).

[22] *See, e.g.*, Elena Goukassian, *The Met and Yemeni Government Reach Agreement for Long-Term Display and Care of Two Ancient Sculptures*, THE ART NEWSPAPER, Sept. 21, 2023 (reporting that, while the Met had recognized Yemen's ownership of the two sculptures, the items would remain in New York due to the lingering civil war in the country); Graham Bowley & Tom Mashberg, *The Met Will Return 16 Ancient Treasures Tied to Looting*, N.Y. TIMES, Dec. 15, 2023 (reporting on the return of 16 Khmer-era artworks to Cambodia and Thailand).

[23] Robin Pogrebin & Graham Bowley, *After Seizures, the Met Sets a Plan to Scour Collections for Looted Art*, N.Y. TIMES, May 9, 2023 (reporting that, in 2022, the Met returned forty-five items to a variety of countries).

[24] Benjamin Sutton, *Metropolitan Museum Hires Sotheby's Veteran to Lead Its Provenance Research Team*, THE ART NEWSPAPER, Mar. 22, 2024.

[25] Torey Akers, *Amid Mounting Scrutiny of Its Collection Practices, Metropolitan Museum Will Form Provenance Research Squad*, THE ART NEWSPAPER, May 10, 2023 (reporting that the Met holds over 1.5 million objects).

Some of the problems associated with conducting provenance research for existing collections are illustrated in the case of the Kunsthaus Zürich fine art museum. In October 2021, the museum opened a new wing exhibiting 205 works from the collection of Emil G. Bührle, following a long-term loan agreement signed in 2012 between the museum and the E.G. Bührle Foundation.[26] Bührle, who became the richest man in Switzerland by selling antiaircraft cannons to Germany during the Second World War and who also profited from slave labor in Nazi concentration camps, had amassed his art collection, comprising 633 works, from 1936 until his death in 1956.[27]

According to the Bührle Foundation, out of the 205 works loaned to the museum, 203 were deemed unproblematic: 113 works were classified by the foundation as falling under "Category A" (fully researched, unproblematic provenance) and 90 were classified under "Category B" (not fully researched provenance, but with no indications of problematic connections).[28]

However, following the inauguration of the new wing of the museum and the public criticism surrounding the exhibition of the Bührle collection – stemming both from Bührle's personal history and allegations that many of the artworks had previously belonged to Jewish owners – the canton and the city of Zurich, along with the trustees of Kunsthaus Zürich, asked Raphael Gross, president of the German Historical Museum in Berlin, to compile a report evaluating the provenance research conducted by the Bührle Foundation.[29] In June 2024, Gross published the report, concluding that the provenance research conducted by the Bührle Foundation was inadequate, and holding, inter alia, that "on the matter of previous Jewish ownership, it can be concluded that sixty-two of the 205 works appear to have belonged to previous Jewish owners during the Holocaust."[30] Gross also criticizes the methodology used by the Bührle Foundation, including its use of categories, stating that:

---

[26] Cathrine Hickley, *Bührle Foundation's Provenance Research Is Inadequate, Report Finds,* THE ART NEWSPAPER, June 28, 2024.

[27] *Inquiry Finds "Tainted" Bührle Art Collection Needs Much More Provenance Research,* Swissinfo.ch, July 17, 2024, www.swissinfo.ch/eng/culture/b%C3%BChrles-tainted-art-collection-needs-much-more-provenance-research/83449370 (hereinafter: "Swiss Info").

[28] RAPHAEL GROSS, ÜBERPRÜFUNG DER PROVENIENZFORSCHUNG DER STIFTUNG SAMMLUNG E. G. BÜHRLE (June 26, 2024), 10, www.stadt-zuerich.ch/de/aktuell/publikationen/2024/evaluation-buehrle.html (German, with an executive summary in English and French).

[29] Swiss Info, *supra* note 27.

[30] GROSS, *supra* note 28, at 10.

What is serious is the realization that Category B of the E.G. Bührle Collection Foundation leads to false results in its entirety. In any case, the 90 works that the Foundation has classified in this Category B should therefore be re-examined. This is because the lack of evidence of a problematic change of hands was sufficient for the Foundation to classify them in Category B. As a result, works with particularly incomplete provenance were classified by the Foundation as unproblematic.[31]

To illustrate the inadequacy of the provenance research carried out, Gross examines five works in detail, including Vincent van Gogh's 1885 painting *Head of a Peasant Woman with White Cap* (Figure 3.1), about which he notes:

The fact that the work was offered for auction in 1932 but remained unsold was not acknowledged. At the same time, the fact that the 1932 owner, Gustav Schweitzer, was a Jewish collector did not merit research. He still possessed the work after 1933. This fundamentally changes the perspective compared to previous research. It remains unclear whether *The Head of a Peasant Woman* was taken from Gustav Schweitzer after 1933 because of persecution. The history of the artwork is still so little researched that even the in-depth examination was unable to provide conclusive clarification.[32]

Accordingly, the report recommends that Kunsthaus Zürich: (1) continue provenance research on the Bührle collection; (2) set up a professional committee to develop an examination scheme for Nazi-related confiscations and apply it to both the Kunsthaus's own collection and long-term loans; and (3) facilitate further debate about the Bührle collection.[33] Kunsthaus Zürich, alongside other cultural institutions around the world that have conducted limited, if any, provenance research into their collections, is therefore likely to face a major challenge ahead.[34]

This chapter seeks to highlight the rise of ethical, professional, and legal norms on due diligence and provenance research. It explores how this gradual, albeit incomplete, shift may address – and hopefully redress – disparities among legal systems in identifying, verifying, and enforcing the chain of title for cultural property; the lack of binding international legal

---

[31] *Id.*

[32] *Id.* at 11.

[33] *Id.* at 12.

[34] Following the report, the city and canton of Zurich and the trustees of the Kunsthaus said in a statement that they see it as their duty "to determine appropriate steps as quickly as possible." Swiss Info, *supra* note 27. It should also be noted that in June 2024, two weeks prior to the publication of the report, the Bührle Foundation announced that it would seek settlements with the heirs of previous Jewish owners of five paintings included in the collection. *Id.*

Figure 3.1   Vincent van Gogh, *Head of a Peasant Woman with White Cap* (1885).
Source: Foundation E.G. Bührle Collection. Made available under the Creative
Commons Attribution-Share Alike 4.0 International License. https://creativecommons
.org/licenses/by-sa/4.0.

norms; and the long-standing practices of opacity and lack of accountability in the cultural property market.

Because the scope and aggregate impact of the emerging norms on due
diligence and provenance research extend beyond formal rules that can
be enforced by courts or other governmental or international organs, it
is essential to understand the interplay between the array of hard-law

instruments and the emerging soft-law effects of professional reputation, ethical obligations, and public opinion in requiring different stakeholders to act diligently and engage in provenance research. This chapter analyzes the various features of this process of change.

3.2   Practices of Market Opacity

Chapter 2 highlighted the divergence across legal systems regarding the protection of the chain of title and possession in cultural property and the – at least until recently – limited scope of binding cross-border legal instruments, which pose challenges for cultural property law and policy.

Another key factor that has been detrimental to both domestic and cross-border efforts to protect and enforce the chain of title or posses-sion and, accordingly, to require different market actors to act prudently and investigate an object's provenance prior to any transaction, lies in the long-standing practices of opacity, secrecy, and anonymity in the market for cultural property items.

The motives of the various actors operating in the market to preserve such opacity have been diverse. For artists and their agents, this practice dates back to the earliest days of the art market in the fifteenth and six-teenth centuries, when the sale of art expanded beyond the commission-ing of works by aristocratic or clerical patrons to include wealthy clientele from the European merchant class in Europe.[35] For artists operating from workshops in cities, it may have made sense to conceal the identity of their clients so that they would not be approached by other artists, or to obscure the prices charged to different customers, allowing for price variability.[36]

For sellers operating in the secondary market – namely, collectors sell-ing pieces that they or their ancestors had purchased, preserving their anonymity may have saved them the public embarrassment of having to admit they were in debt.[37] During the eighteenth and nineteenth centu-ries, cash-strapped gentry were able to sell their family collection of art and antiquities to avoid a public declaration of financial insolvency. This prac-tice also allowed buyers to purchase cultural objects without incurring the stigma of having profited from the misfortune of another member of their

---

[35] Graham Bowley, *As Money Launderers Buy Dalís, U.S. Looks at Lifting the Veil on Art Sales,* N.Y. TIMES, June 19, 2021.

[36] *Id.*

[37] SIMON MACKENZIE ET AL., TRAFFICKING CULTURE: NEW DIRECTIONS IN RESEARCHING THE GLOBAL MARKET IN ILLICIT ANTIQUITIES 11 (2020).

social class.[38] This logic is still prevalent today, as sellers often use anonymity to cloak the embarrassment of debt, avoid family conflicts over the sale of assets, or simply maintain their privacy.[39]

On the part of buyers, the desire to preserve anonymity may stem from various reasons, including the exercising of power by concealing from others exactly "what artworks or assets you own,"[40] quietly amassing a collection of works by a particular artist without luring competition in real time, addressing security concerns by trying to prevent theft,[41] or facilitating illicit acts such as money laundering (discussed in detail below).[42]

Practices of opacity have been observed not only by dealers but also by auction houses, which have significantly increased their involvement in facilitating private sales alongside public auctions. This trend was discernible not only in 2020, when private sales by auction houses increased by 36 percent worldwide, in part due to a decline in public auctions caused by the COVID-19 crisis, but also in the following years. Private sales increased by 32 percent in 2021, reaching an estimated 4.1 billion dollars, three billion of which was brokered by the auction houses Christie's and Sotheby's.[43] As noted by Sotheby's in promotional materials for its private sales services, "it's in their nature that most are confidential," with Sotheby's emphasizing its ability to work "discreetly for buyers and sellers."[44]

In some jurisdictions, opacity in the cultural property market is even advanced institutionally by national or local governments, as exemplified by "freeports" – high-security storage facilities exempt from customs duties. These facilities, such as the one operating in Geneva and others in Singapore and Luxemburg,[45] allow artifacts to be sold and purchased without ever leaving the freeport, bypassing the need to report these

---

[38] *Id.*

[39] The ArtSecure Blog, *Sellers at Auctions Can Remain Anonymous* (Dec. 18, 2013), www.artsecure.gr/blog/sellers-at-auctions-can-remain-anonymous.

[40] Helen Holmes, *The Art World "Mystery Buyers" Who Spend Big and Stay Secret*, THE DAILY BEAST, May 14, 2022.

[41] *Id.*

[42] *See* Bowley, *supra* note 35; text accompanying *infra* notes 53–63.

[43] ART BASEL & UBS REPORT, THE ART MARKET 2022 122–23 (2022), www.ubs.com/global/en/our-firm/art/2022/apac-key-findings.html.

[44] Chris Jenkins, Sotheby's View, *How Sotheby's Private Sales Work Discreetly for Buyers and Sellers*, www.artsandcollections.com/how-sothebys-private-sales-work/ (last visited Feb. 1, 2025).

[45] For the modern concept of freeports as "sophisticated store-rooms for valuable collections," *see* Stefan Schwarzkopf & Jessica Inez Backsell, *The Nomos of the Freeport*, 39 EPD: SOCIETY & SPACE 328, 333–35 (2020).

secret transactions to local customs authorities.[46] As noted by the U.S. Department of the Treasury, in the cultural property market "art storage facilities have been identified as 'black boxes,' where items can be stored anonymously and indefinitely."[47]

Practices of opacity, secrecy, and anonymity have obvious implications for the ability of legal systems and relevant stakeholders to detect, enforce, or otherwise remedy problems with the chain of title or other violations of rules pertaining to the ownership, export, or trade of art and antiquities. Detecting the provenance of cultural objects – or otherwise acting prudently in ensuring that a certain item can be exported, sold, or otherwise alienated, by a person or entity authorized to do so, and to an eligible buyer, is a major challenge when opaque market practices prevail. From the illicit excavation of antiquities in source countries and their smuggling across borders by chains of intermediaries to buyers in destination countries – as discussed in Chapter 1[48] – to acts of fraud in the art market designed to conceal theft, embezzlement, or illegal exports of artwork (such as the investigation by the Carabinieri, reported in 2023, into the illicit trade of a painting by Flemish painter Peter Paul Rubens[49]), the inherent problems in the combination of high-value movable items, global markets, and practices of opacity, become evident.

Accordingly, while certain market actors, such as dealers and auction houses, may be internally motivated to act prudently and investigate an object's history – especially when this may mitigate their potential liability to their clients, primarily through contractual warranties,[50] or out of fear of public embarrassment and reputational damage if a transaction is discovered to be dubious or outright illegal – engagement in due diligence

---

[46] Nina dos Santos, *$1B Feud Involving Leonardo's "Salvator Mundi" Reveals Dark Side of the Art World*, CNN, May 30, 2021 (portraying the operation of such freeports).

[47] THE U.S. DEPARTMENT OF THE TREASURY, STUDY OF THE FACILITATION OF MONEY LAUNDERING AND TERROR FINANCE THROUGH THE TRADE IN WORKS OF ART 18 (Feb. 2022), https://home.treasury.gov/system/files/136/Treasury_Study_WoA .pdf (hereinafter: "U.S. DEPT. OF TREASURY").

[48] *See* Chapter 1, Section 1.1.

[49] James Imam, *Italian Police Widen Fraud Investigation after Seizing Rubens Painting from Genoa Exhibition*, THE ART NEWSPAPER, Jan. 4, 2023 (relaying an investigation by the Carabinieri of alleged acts of fraud in which owners of a Rubens painting deliberately "downgraded" it, attributing it to an unknown Flemish artist and decreasing its assessed value to 25,000 euros to enable its illicit export outside of Italy).

[50] *See, e.g.*, Anny Shaw, *The Five Year Warranty on the Salvator Mundi by Leonardo Is about to Run Out – Could the Buyer Have Asked for Their Money Back?* THE ART NEWSPAPER, Nov. 14, 2022; Riah Pryor, *Recent UK High Court Rulings Raise Questions over Dealers' Duty of Care towards Clients*, THE ART NEWSPAPER, Jan. 5, 2023.

practices concerning both the cultural item and the parties to the transaction have traditionally been voluntary.[51] Moreover, such practices have been constrained by countervailing forces, including profit motives, fierce competition, and client demands for secrecy.[52]

One concern about the operation of the market for cultural property, which has led in turn to legislative and other regulatory changes on both the national and supranational levels, with consequent implications for practices of opacity, is that this market may serve as a conduit for money laundering, terrorism financing, and related criminal offenses. As noted in the U.S. Department of the Treasury's 2022 report, the high-value art market and its participants "have certain inherent qualities that make them potentially vulnerable to a range of financial crimes," including the "historically opaque nature of the high-value art market," the "transportability of certain types of artworks, including across international borders," and the "accepted use of third-party intermediaries to purchase, sell, and hold artwork while their clients remain anonymous (i.e., art dealers, advisors, interior designers, shell companies, trusts)."[53] While evidence of the use of archaeological looting to finance terrorism – such as in the case of the Islamic State in Iraq and Syria (ISIS) – is more sporadic,[54] there is a substantial record of cases in which the trade in cultural property has been used for money laundering and related crimes. Examples include the use of artwork as an alternative mode of payment for illicit actions such as bribes; its purchase as a means of hiding illicit income (such as from drug trafficking); or its use as collateral to obscure illicit proceeds.[55]

---

[51] SOTHEBY'S, CODE OF BUSINESS CONDUCT 47 (2021), www.sothebys.com/en/docs/pdf/code-of-conduct-2021.pdf (stating its commitment to conducting due diligence, by which: "Before offering property for sale, we must be satisfied that we have conducted the level of due diligence required to be satisfied that the property we are handling is authentic and that there are no known legal obstacles to selling and passing title").

[52] Holmes, *supra* note 40.

[53] U.S. DEPT. OF TREASURY, *supra* note 47, at 3. *See also* dos Santos, *supra* note 46 (quoting author and filmmaker Ben Lewis, who explains that art masterpieces "often pack high dollar value into a small, portable canvas").

[54] CLOONEY FOUNDATION FOR JUSTICE, CONFLICT ANTIQUITIES: THE NEED FOR PROSECUTING PARTICIPANTS IN THE ILLEGAL ANTIQUITIES TRADE FOR COMPLICITY IN INTERNATIONAL CRIMES AND TERRORISM FINANCING 7–8 (June 8, 2022), https://cfj.org/the-docket-projects/looted-antiquities/need-for-prosecutions/.

[55] U.S. DEPT. OF TREASURY, *supra* note 47, at 22–25. *See also* Gela Pertusini, *Monet Laundering: How Criminal Use Art Transactions*, MODUS, June 22, 2022, https://ww3.rics.org/uk/en/modus/business-and-skills/ethics/monet-laundering--how-criminals-use-art-transactions.html; Bowley, *supra* note 35.

Accordingly, certain governments have taken steps to apply general rules and regulations that impose obligations to engage in anti-money laundering or countering the financing of terrorism ("AML/CFT"). Most prominently, in its 4th and 5th Anti-Money Laundering Directives,[56] the European Commission applied the requirements for adopting a risk-based approach to money laundering and due diligence to the art market. These directives mandate due diligence on buyers, including beneficial owners when art is purchased via intermediaries or other proxies. The current definition of obliged institutions under the 5th Directive includes "persons trading or acting as intermediaries in the trade of works of art, including when this is carried out by art galleries and auction houses, where the value of the transaction or a series of linked transactions amounts to EUR 10 000 or more."[57] The United Kingdom has followed suit, despite leaving the European Union, by adopting the principles of the 5th Directive in its domestic law,[58] requiring relevant institutions to register.[59]

The United States has so far taken a more differential approach. As far as antiquities are concerned, the Anti-Money Laundering Act of 2020 broadened the definition of a "financial institution" to include "a person engaged in the trade of antiquities, including an advisor, consultant, or any other person who engages as a business in the solicitation or the sale of antiquities."[60] This subjects antiquities dealers and their intermediaries to the same AML reporting responsibilities as banks, requiring them to introduce AML/CFT programs.[61] In September 2021, the Financial Crimes

---

[56] See, respectively, Directive 2015/849 of the European Parliament and of the Council of 20 May 2015 on the Prevention of the Use of the Financial System for the Purposes of Money Laundering or Terrorist Financing, Amending Regulation No. 648/2012 of the European Parliament and of the Council, and Repealing Directive 2005/60/EC of the European Parliament and of the Council and Commission Directive 2006/70/EC, 2015 O.J. (L 141) 73; Directive 2018/843 of the European Parliament and of the Council of 30 May 2018 Amending Directive 2015/849 on the Prevention of the Use of the Financial System for the Purposes of Money Laundering or Terrorist Financing, and Amending Directives 2009/138/EC and 2013/36/EU, 2018 O.J. (L 156) 43 (hereinafter: "5th Directive").

[57] 5th Directive, *supra* note 56, art. 1.

[58] The Money Laundering and Terrorist Financing (Amendment) Regulations 2019, No. 1511 (U.K.).

[59] For the impact of these regulations on hundreds of institutions in and outside of the United Kingdom, see Riah Pryor, *Art World Rushes to Conform to UK's Anti-Money Laundering Laws*, THE ART NEWSPAPER, Sept. 3, 2021.

[60] Section 6110 of the Anti-Money Laundering Act (Amending the Bank Secrecy Act) (hereinafter: "AML Act").

[61] See U.S. Department of the Treasury, Financial Crimes Enforcement Network, *The Anti-Money Laundering Act of 2020*, www.fincen.gov/anti-money-laundering-act-2020 (last visited Feb. 1, 2025).

Enforcement Network (FinCEN) in the Department of the Treasury issued an "advance notice of proposed rulemaking" (ANPRM) to solicit public comment on the implementation of Section 6110 of the AML Act regarding the trade in antiquities.[62]

At the same time, anti-money laundering rules do not yet apply to the art market, following the conclusion of the U.S. Treasury's report, which stated that, despite the risks of abuse of the art market by illicit financial actors, "the infrequent use of cash in the high-value art market and preexisting requirements for financial institutions and commercial businesses to report high-value cash transactions … may make the institutional high-value art market a poor vehicle for laundering illicit cash proceeds" – such that the U.S. government should consider alternative types of regulatory or nonregulatory action to AML/CFT measures.[63]

While anti-money laundering rules do provide better information on some aspects of the cultural property market, they do so primarily for the purpose of revealing the identities of buyers or beneficial owners, thereby indirectly deterring some types of illicit transactions. However, these measures do not offer a more general framework for engaging in due diligence and provenance research on cultural objects, as well as for other issues concerning the legitimacy of cultural property markets. As the following sections demonstrate, other factors have contributed to the rise of broader professional, ethical, and legal norms on the duties of due diligence and provenance research. These norms may bridge long-standing disparities in national laws and promote cross-border norms.

3.3 Due Diligence as a Legal, Professional, and Ethical Norm for Cultural Property

This section highlights the increasing role of due diligence as a benchmark for dealing with cultural property and, consequently, the various ways in which obstacles to enforcing the chain of title and possession of cultural objects across national borders may be gradually overcome. These factors include, inter alia, the growing practical effects of both hard-law and soft-law international norms; increasing attention within national legal systems to the specific attributes of cultural objects, as distinct from the

---

[62] Financial Crimes Enforcement Network, *Anti-Money Laundering Regulations for Dealers in Antiquities*, Sept. 24, 2021, 86 F.R. 53021, www.federalregister.gov/documents/2021/09/24/2021-20731/anti-money-laundering-regulations-for-dealers-inantiquities.

[63] U.S. DEPT. OF TREASURY, *supra* note 47, at 21, 30–33.

general category of chattels or goods; and the development of professional and ethical norms that move toward adopting a common framework for due diligence practices.

3.3.1   Due Diligence as a Legal Benchmark: Cross-Border Developments

The concept of "due diligence" is prevalent across several fields of law, but its precise content, as well as the ways in which it can be binding and enforceable, may vary considerably – and this is not by coincidence. Generally, due diligence is defined as "such a measure of prudence, activity, or assiduity, as is properly to be expected from, and ordinarily exercised by, a reasonable and prudent man under the particular circumstances; not measured by any absolute standard, but depending on the relative facts of the special case."[64] Beyond the inherently open-ended nature of the term, due diligence is often perceived as located at the intersection of law, public policy, and morality, such that "due diligence is inevitably a concept which transgresses the confines of the positive, black letter law and opens a window for considerations of ethics and politics."[65]

For example, in the broad context of international law, due diligence emerged as a "state-to-state obligation through arbitral decisions, mixed claims commissions, and diplomatic practice in the late nineteenth and early twentieth century."[66] It was seen as a corollary duty of sovereignty, most prominently in the law of neutrality, the law of aliens, and environmental law. States were required to exercise such diligence "as can reasonably be expected if all circumstances and conditions of the case are taken into consideration."[67] Alongside its binding (albeit vague) application in some contexts, due diligence has been perceived as a voluntary process of risk regulation in other areas of international law, such as anti-corruption and international finance law.[68] In other legal fields, such as corporate or securities law, the term "due diligence" was designed as a legal standard

---

[64] THE LAW DICTIONARY, *Due Diligence*, https://thelawdictionary.org/due-diligence/ (last visited Feb. 1, 2025).

[65] Anne Peters, Heike Krieger & Leonhard Kreuzer, *Due Diligence in the International Legal Order: Dissecting the Leitmotif of Current Accountability Debates, in* DUE DILIGENCE IN THE INTERNATIONAL LEGAL ORDER 1, 2–3 (Anne Peters, Heike Krieger & Leonhard Kreuzer eds., 2021).

[66] *Id.* at 4.

[67] *Id.* at 5 (internal references omitted).

[68] *Id.* at 5–6.

that serves as a potential defense for certain legal actors against criminal or civil liability. For instance, under Section 11 of the U.S. Securities Act of 1933,[69] due diligence is a key component of liability defense, whereas in commercial law the term refers most prominently to a process of risk regulation and caution undertaken by buyers, such as in mergers or acquisitions of business entities.[70]

The term "due diligence" was introduced into the law of cultural property in the 1995 UNIDROIT Convention on Stolen or Illegally Exported Cultural Objects.[71] While, as discussed in Chapter 2, the convention has had limited effectiveness in the traditional sense of formally serving as the basis for returning stolen or illegally excavated artifacts – primarily because most destination or market countries have not yet joined the convention[72] – it has been highly influential in elaborating the legal and ethical standards of behavior required from buyers and possessors of art and antiquities.

In other words, alongside the 1995 UNIDROIT Convention's hard-law impact among its fifty-five member states,[73] its soft-law influence has extended well beyond those jurisdictions, especially in the context of developing a standard of due diligence for dealing with cultural property. This impact is also evident among public and private actors in the United States, Europe, and other market countries, where the convention has served as a source of inspiration for subsequent legal instruments, as shown below.[74]

The importance of the solidifying of the term "due diligence" in the 1995 UNIDROIT Convention should be understood in the context of some of the legal and organizational gaps in the 1970 UNESCO Convention on the Means of Prohibiting and Preventing the Illicit Import, Export and

---

[69] Codified as 15 U.S.C. §77k (2023); *See* William K. Sjostrom Jr., *The Due Diligence Defense under Section 11 of the Securities Act of 1933*, 44 BRANDEIS L.J. 549 (2006). For a comparative analysis of due diligence as a defense to corporate criminal liability for corruption offenses, *see* Bram Meyer, Tessa van Roomen & Eelke Sikkema, *Corporate Criminal Liability for Corruption Offences and the Due Diligence Defence: A Comparison of the Dutch and English Legal Frameworks*, 10 UTRECHT L. REV. 37 (2014).

[70] *See, e.g.*, PETER HOWSON, DUE DILIGENCE: THE CRITICAL STAGE IN MERGERS AND ACQUISITIONS (2003).

[71] UNIDROIT Convention on Stolen or Illegally Exported Cultural Objects, June 24, 1995, 2421 U.N.T.S. 457 (hereinafter: "1995 UNIDROIT Convention").

[72] *See* Chapter 2, Section 2.2.1.

[73] For the list of the current member states of the 1995 UNIDROIT Convention, *see* UNIDROIT, *States Parties*, www.unidroit.org/instruments/cultural-property/1995-convention/status/ (last visited Feb. 1, 2025).

[74] *See infra* Section 3.3.2.

Transfer of Ownership of Cultural Property.[75] As explained in Chapter 2, although the 1970 UNESCO Convention has been accepted or ratified by 147 countries as of early 2025,[76] including key market countries (unlike the 1995 UNIDROIT Convention), its application as a hard-law instrument to allow for the restitution of stolen or illegally excavated items has also been limited, albeit for different reasons.

Under the 1970 UNESCO Convention, the duty of a destination state to return a cultural artifact to the state of origin arises only when the object was stolen from a "museum or a religious or secular public monument or similar institution" and upon the specific request of the state of origin to the destination state, submitted through "diplomatic offices."[77] The 1970 UNESCO Convention thus applies only among states, and does not grant standing to potential nonstate claimants. Moreover, it does not establish substantive rules regarding the conditions under which the buyer or current possessor of an artifact should be compensated for restitution. While Article 7(b)(ii) provides that the "requesting State shall pay just compensation to an innocent purchaser or to a person who has valid title to that property,"[78] it does not specify the standards for identifying the buyer or possessor as an "innocent purchaser," thereby leaving room for cross-border legal ambiguity.

The 1995 UNIDROIT Convention seeks to overcome this legal and institutional gap. With regards to the illegal export of cultural objects, the 1995 UNIDROIT Convention stipulates that a court or other competent authority in the destination state must order the return of the object if the state of origin establishes that the removal of the object from its territory violated the provisions of its domestic law on exporting cultural objects.[79] In such cases, the possessor of the object, who acquired it after its illegal export and "neither knew nor ought reasonably to have known at the time of acquisition that the object had been illegally exported" – thus placing

---

[75] UNSECO Convention on the Means of Prohibiting and Preventing the Illicit Import, Export and Transfer of Ownership of Cultural Property, Nov. 14, 1970, 823 U.N.T.S. 231 (hereinafter: "1970 UNESCO Convention").

[76] For the list of the current member states of the 1970 UNESCO Convention, *see* UNESCO, *Convention on the Means of Prohibiting and Preventing the Illicit Import, Export and Transfer of Ownership of Cultural Property*, www.unesco.org/en/legal-affairs/convention-means-prohibiting-and-preventing-illicit-import-export-and-transfer-ownership-cultural?hub=416#item-2 (last visited Feb. 1, 2025).

[77] 1970 UNESCO Convention, *supra* note 75, arts. 7(b)(i)–(ii).

[78] *Id.* art. 7(b)(ii).

[79] The state of origin should also show that the unauthorized export "significantly impairs" the physical preservation or integrity of the object, preservation of information of a scientific or historical character, or the traditional or ritual use of the object. *Id.* art. 5(3).

the onus of proof on the current possessor – is entitled to "fair and reason-able compensation" from the requesting state.[80]

In the case of a stolen object, which also applies to an object "which has been unlawfully excavated or lawfully excavated but unlawfully retained … when consistent with the law of the State where the excavation took place," its current possessor is required to return it.[81] Article 4(1) states:

> The possessor of a stolen cultural object required to return it shall be enti-tled, at the time of its restitution, to payment of fair and reasonable com-pensation provided that the possessor neither knew nor ought reasonably to have known that the object was stolen and can prove that it exercised *due diligence* when acquiring the object.[82]

The term "due diligence," which does not appear in the 1970 UNESCO Convention, was deliberately chosen as a distinctive benchmark to avoid the ambiguity and legal disparities among national legal systems about the more commonly used legal concept of "good faith."[83] The drafters of the convention decided that defining the concept of "due diligence" would provide a more sophisticated approach to addressing diverging national laws on the protection of bona fide purchasers, facilitating a consistent application of the convention's text and its unique terms.[84]

How can the current possessor of a cultural object meet the burden of proof to demonstrate that they exercised due diligence?[85] To address this, Article 4(4) of the 1995 UNIDROIT Convention sets out a nonexhaustive list of potential indicators, specifying the following parameters:

---

[80] *Id.* art. 6(1). Article 6(2) then provides: "In determining whether the possessor knew or ought reasonably to have known that the cultural object had been illegally exported, regard shall be had to the circumstances of the acquisition, including the absence of an export cer-tificate required under the law of the requesting State."

[81] *Id.* art. 3(1)–(2). For the process leading to the expansion of the concept of a "stolen" item under this convention also to illegally excavated or returned archaeological artifacts, *see* LYNDEL V. PROTT, COMMENTARY ON THE 1995 UNIDROIT CONVENTION ON STOLEN OR ILLEGALLY EXPORTED CULTURAL OBJECTS 52–55 (2nd ed. 2021).

[82] 1970 UNESCO Convention, *supra* note 75, art 4(1) (my emphasis).

[83] Marina Schneider, *The 1995 UNIDROIT Convention: An Indispensable Complement to the 1970 UNESCO Convention and an Inspiration for the 2014/60/EU Directive,* 2016 SANTANDER ART & CULTURE L. REV. 149, 154; *See also* ASPER TAŞDELEN, THE RETURN OF CULTURAL ARTEFACTS: HARD AND SOFT LAW APPROACHES 77–87 (2016); JOHN SPRANKLING, THE INTERNATIONAL LAW OF PROPERTY 55–56 (2014).

[84] Schneider, *supra* note 83, at 154–55.

[85] It should be noted that reversing the burden of proof in this regard, and placing it on the buyer or the possessor, represents a significant departure from the approach taken in the 1970 UNESCO Convention. *See* MARA WANTUCH-THOLE, CULTURAL PROPERTY IN CROSS-BORDER LITIGATION: TURNING RIGHTS INTO CLAIMS 213–14 (2015).

> In determining whether the possessor exercised due diligence, regard shall
> be had to all the circumstances of the acquisition, including the character
> of the parties, the price paid, whether the possessor consulted any reason-
> ably accessible register of stolen cultural objects, and any other relevant
> information and documentation which it could reasonably have obtained,
> and whether the possessor consulted accessible agencies or took any other
> step that a reasonable person would have taken in the circumstances.[86]

Chapter 4 will examine in detail the requirement to consult "any reasonably accessible register of stolen cultural objects," in view of the rapidly growing number of digital databases on cultural property since this
provision was incorporated into the 1995 UNIDROIT Convention.

Alongside such registries or databases, other elements of due diligence
included in Article 4(4) have also been the subject of both legal analysis
and evolving market practices.[87] For example, in considering "the character of the parties," major collectors or cultural institutions may be held
to higher standards in examining the details of the object and the overall
transaction. That said, amateur collectors would also be required to take
reasonable precautions, especially by purchasing items from reputable
dealers who will be prepared to repurchase items they have sold that later
prove to have been stolen, or who offer other warranties that a reasonable buyer can rely on given the nature of the item, the price paid, and the
documentation provided by the seller.[88] Importantly, these requirements
have had an effect on the development of domestic norms on due diligence in certain state parties to the 1995 UNIDROIT Convention, such as
Italy and Greece.[89]

The 1995 UNIDROIT Convention, and its provisions on the duty of due
diligence, served as a source of inspiration for another key supranational
instrument: the 2014 Council Directive on the Return of Cultural Objects
Unlawfully Removed from the Territory of a Member State.[90]

---

[86] 1995 UNIDROIT Convention, *supra* note 71, art. 4(4).

[87] *See* PROTT, *supra* note 81, at 70–77 (analyzing the different components of Article 4(4) of
the 1995 UNIDROIT Convention).

[88] *Id.* at 74.

[89] *See also* Christa Roodt, *Article 4 of the 1995 UNIDROIT Convention: Possessor's Rights and
Claims for Restitution of Cultural Objects, in* THE 1970 UNESCO AND 1995 UNIDROIT
CONVENTIONS ON STOLEN OR ILLEGALLY TRANSFERRED CULTURAL PROPERTY: A
COMMENTARY 561, 571 (Ana Filipa Vrdoljak, Andrzej Jakubowski & Alessandro Chechi
eds., 2024) (pointing, however, to some ambiguities that remain in Italian law on the matter).

[90] Directive 2014/60/EU of the European Parliament and of the Council of 15 May 2014 on
the Return of Cultural Objects Unlawfully Removed from the Territory of a Member State
(Recast), 2014 O.J. (L 159) 1 (hereinafter: "2014 EU Directive").

Providing in Article 3 that "cultural objects which have been unlawfully removed from the territory of a Member State shall be returned in accordance with the procedure and in the circumstances provided for in this Directive," the 2014 EU Directive focuses on interstate claims for the restitution of cultural objects that had been removed from the territory of a Member State in breach of its national provisions or the 2009 Council Regulation on the Export of Cultural Goods.[91] Specifically, concerning the right of the current possessor of the cultural object to compensation from the requesting Member State in the case of restitution, the 2014 EU Directive uses the legal benchmark of requiring the possessor to exercise "due care and attention" in acquiring the object.[92]

While the term "due care and attention" had already been used in the previous European directive on this matter, Council Directive 93/7/EEC,[93] the 1993 Directive did not elaborate on any criteria for identifying "due care and attention." This left the term open to interpretation by the national court with jurisdiction over the claim, thereby perpetuating legal disparities among Member States.[94]

In contrast, the 2014 EU Directive offers a nonexhaustive list of considerations for identifying "due care and attention," taken almost verbatim from the list of criteria used to define the term "due diligence" in Article 4 of the 1995 UNIDROIT Convention in the case of stolen cultural property. Article 10 of the 2014 EU Directive states:

> In determining whether the possessor exercised due care and attention, consideration shall be given to all the circumstances of the acquisition, in particular the documentation on the object's provenance, the authorizations for removal required under the law of the requesting Member State, the character of the parties, the price paid, whether the possessor consulted any accessible register of stolen cultural objects and any relevant information which he could reasonably have obtained, or took any other step which a reasonable person would have taken in the circumstances.[95]

As with the 1995 UNIDROIT Convention, the concept of "due care and attention" has impacted the national legislation of some of the twenty-seven EU Member States, and even beyond, creating a heightened

---

[91] Council Regulation (EC) No. 116/2009 of 18 December 2008 on the Export of Cultural Goods, 2009 O.J. (L 39) 1.

[92] *Id.* art. 10.

[93] Council Directive 93/7/EEC of 15 March 1993 on the Return of Cultural Objects Unlawfully Removed from the Territory of a Member State, 1993 O.J. (L 74) 74.

[94] *See* Schneider, *supra* note 83, at 158.

[95] 2014 EU Directive, *supra* note 90, art. 10, §2.

standard of conduct for various actors dealing with cultural property.[96] The cases of the Netherlands and Switzerland (a non-EU member) are discussed in Section 3.3.2.

The legal norm of "due care and attention" was also embraced by the Nicosia Convention on Offences Relating to Cultural Property,[97] discussed in Chapter 2 in the context of criminal law instruments against the illicit trafficking of cultural property.[98] Article 7 of the Nicosia Convention, entitled "Acquisition," reads:

1. Each Party shall ensure that the acquisition of movable cultural property that has been stolen in accordance with Article 3 of this Convention or has been excavated, imported or exported under circumstances described in Articles 4, 5 or 6 of this Convention constitutes a criminal offence under its domestic law where the person knows of such unlawful provenance.
2. Each Party shall consider taking the necessary measures to ensure that the conduct described in paragraph 1 of the present article constitutes a criminal offence also in the case of a person who should have known of the cultural property's unlawful provenance if he or she had exercised *due care and attention* in acquiring the cultural property.[99]

Therefore, alongside the duty to exercise "due diligence" or "due care and attention" as a condition for receiving compensation when the possessor of cultural property is required to return it under the provisions of the 1995 UNIDROIT Convention or the 2014 EU Directive, respectively, a failure to exercise "due care and attention" may also subject the possessor of an item to criminal liability under domestic laws adopted by member states of the Nicosia Convention.

This bears resemblance to the provision of §165.55(2) of New York's Penal Law (criminal possession of stolen property; presumptions), which has been increasingly utilized by the New York State Antiquities Trafficking Unit, as discussed in Chapter 2.[100] According to this provision, "[a] collateral loan broker or a person in the business of buying, selling or otherwise dealing in property who possesses stolen property is presumed to know that such property was stolen if he obtained it without having

---

[96] *See* Roodt, *supra* note 89, at 571–73.
[97] Council of Europe Convention on Offences Relating to Cultural Property, adopted on May 3, 2017 (Council of Europe Treaty Series (CETS) no. 221) (hereinafter: "Nicosia Convention").
[98] *See* Chapter 2, Section 2.3.1.
[99] Nicosia Convention, *supra* note 97, art. 7 (my emphasis).
[100] *See* Chapter 2, Section 2.3.2.

ascertained *by reasonable inquiry* that the person from whom he obtained it had a legal right to possess it."[101]

Moreover, the duty of a possessor of cultural property to act diligently upon acquiring or otherwise receiving it, as part of the growing body of international legal norms pertaining to cultural property, is also manifested in the 2024 decision of the European Court of Human Rights (ECHR) in the matter of *Getty v. Italy*,[102] analyzed in detail in Chapter 2.[103] The authority of Italian law enforcement agencies to issue a confiscation order, based on Article 174(3) of the Code of the Cultural and Landscape Heritage (CCLH),[104] has been interpreted by Italian courts – and embraced by the ECHR as part of its analysis of the proportionality of this measure – as also applying to possessors who have failed to act diligently in obtaining a cultural item, even if they are not directly liable under domestic criminal law.[105] Accordingly, the ECHR held that, while "the Trust's representatives had a clear duty to take all the steps that could reasonably be expected of them to investigate the Statue's legitimate provenance before purchasing it … they did not carry out a careful and objective assessment of the Statue's provenance."[106]

Therefore, the duty to exercise due diligence (or the closely related concept of "due care and attention") is gradually emerging as a key international legal norm, with implications for both private international law and public international law. Moreover, this international norm is also affecting, directly or indirectly, the evolution of private, administrative, and criminal domestic legal rules.

3.3.2 Due Diligence and the Specific Protection of Cultural Property in National Laws

As discussed in Chapter 2, private law doctrines governing cultural property disputes have traditionally followed the rules that apply to the broader

---

[101] New York Penal Law §165.55(2) (my emphasis).

[102] The J. Paul Getty Trust and Others v. Italy, App. No. 35271/19 (May 2, 2024), https://hudoc.echr.coe.int/eng?i=001-233381 (hereinafter: "Getty v. Italy").

[103] *See* Chapter 2, Section 2.2.3.

[104] Decreto legislativo 22 gennaio 2004, n. 42., G.U Feb. 24, 2004, n. 45 [CCLH] (It.), as amended, www.normattiva.it/uri-res/N2Ls?urn:nir:stato:decreto.legislativo:2004;42. *See* English translation of the 2004 CCLH (without later amendments) at https://whc.unesco.org/document/155711?.

[105] Getty v. Italy, *supra* note 102, at paras. 390, 408–9.

[106] *Id*. paras. 387–88.

category of chattels or goods.[107] This has led, in turn, to a lingering disparity between national legal systems for reasons that had little, if anything, to do with the normative and jurisprudential justifications most relevant to cultural property.

This reality is slowly changing, with more national legal systems introducing specific legal provisions that govern proprietary disputes over cultural property. Moreover, in delineating the respective rights and duties of parties, one can observe the practical influence of the requirements to act diligently, as set out in the 1995 UNIDROIT Convention and later in the 2014 EU Directive.

Consider, for example, Switzerland. It is not a member of the European Union (and therefore not a party to the 2014 EU Directive) and it has not ratified the 1995 UNIDROIT Convention.[108] That said, the Swiss legal system developed statutory and judicial doctrines about the prudence required from sellers, dealers, and buyers in transactions involving cultural property. Since the mid-1990s, these rules have been influenced by the due diligence requirement articulated in the 1995 UNIDROIT Convention, and later by the corresponding "due care and attention" norm established in the 2014 EU Directive.[109]

Thus, in a 1997 decision, the Swiss Federal Court refused an appeal against the decision of a cantonal court to return a painting, proven to have been stolen, to France. The court held that the purchaser, an experienced businessman, bought the painting at a price well below its estimated value, did not inquire about its authenticity or provenance, dealt with persons previously unknown to him, and failed to verify the legality of the painting's import.[110]

In a 2013 decision, the Swiss Federal Court held that a buyer, an art collector, failed to meet the obligation of due diligence in acquiring a painting by Kazimir Malevicz by ignoring a "rumor" that had spread in art market circles suggesting that the painting had been stolen.[111]

---

[107] *See* Chapter 2, Section 2.1.2.
[108] Switzerland signed the convention on June 26, 1996, but has not ratified it since then. *See supra* note 73.
[109] *See* Marc-André Renold, *Legal Obstacles to Claims for the Restitution of Looted Art*, 19 Y.B. PRIV. INT'L L. 247, 259 n.37 (2017/2018) (referring to the 1995 UNIDROIT Convention and the 2014 EU Directive in explaining the characteristics of Swiss law).
[110] For a review of this case, *see* PROTT, *supra* note 81, at 74–75.
[111] A. v. B., ATF 139 III 305, Apr. 18, 2013, Journal des Tribunaux 2015 II 79 (Switz.). For a review of this case, *see* Renold, *supra* note 109, at 259.

The duty of due diligence was codified in the 2003 Swiss Federal Act on the International Transfer of Cultural Property.[112] Under Article 16 of the Act, titled "Duty of Diligence" ("*Sorgfaltspflichten*"), a seller of cultural property may transfer such property only if they "may assume, under the circumstances" that the property "was not stolen, not lost against the will of the owner, and not illegally excavated" or that it was "not illicitly imported."[113] Persons "active in the art trade and auctioning business" are obligated to undertake a number of measures of prudence, including establishing the identity of the supplier or seller, informing their customers about existing import or export regulations, maintaining written records on the acquisition, and providing "all necessary information on fulfilling this duty of diligence" to a specialized entity established under the Act.[114]

The duty of due diligence in dealing with cultural property has also been codified in other legal systems. In the Netherlands, the current Dutch Civil Code[115] explicitly references the provisions of the 1970 UNESCO Convention. In determining whether the current possessor of a cultural artifact "has observed the necessary diligence (prudence) at the acquisition of a cultural object," the court examines all relevant circumstances, including the capacity of the parties, the price paid, whether "the possessor has consulted any reasonably accessible register of stolen cultural property and any other relevant information and documentation that he reasonably could have obtained," and whether the possessor "has taken all other steps which a reasonable person in those circumstances would have taken."[116] The Dutch Civil Code also imposes due diligence duties on traders and auction houses. Thus, a trader is deemed not to have observed the necessary diligence when acquiring a cultural object

---

[112] Bundesgesetz vom 20. Juni 2003 über den internationalen Kulturgütertransfer (Kulturgütertransfergesetz, KGTG), www.fedlex.admin.ch/eli/cc/2005/317/de (hereinafter: "2003 Act" or "KGTG") (Switz.). An unofficial English version of KGTG is available at https://sherloc.unodc.org/cld/uploads/res/document/federal_act_on_international_transfer_of_cultural_property_english_html/ch_actintaltrsfertcultproties2005_engtno_sec9.pdf (last visited Feb. 1, 2025).

[113] *Id*. art. 16(1).

[114] *Id*. art. 16(2). The features and tasks of this specialized body (*Fachstelle*) are set out in Article 18 of KGTG.

[115] Dutch Civil Code, Book 3 (*Burgerlijk Wetboek Boek 3*), https://wetten.overheid.nl/BWBR0005291/2024-11-08 (Neth.). An unofficial English version is available at www.dutchcivillaw.com/civilcodebook033.htm (last visited Feb. 1, 2025).

[116] *Id*. art. 3:87a(1).

if they fail to verify the identity of the seller, obtain proper documen-tation confirming that the seller is competent to dispose of the object, record the details of the transaction, or "consult the registers for stolen cultural property which in the given circumstances in view of the nature of the cultural object are eligible for consultation."[117] Civil liability is also imposed on an auction house that "does not act in conformity with the diligence requirements" pertaining to sellers and traders when dealing with a cultural object.[118]

The Cultural Property Protection Act,[119] enacted in Germany in 2016 (replacing an earlier act from 2007 that had proven to be ineffec-tive),[120] comprehensively addresses the protection of German and inter-national cultural property by establishing rules and procedures for the export and import of cultural artifacts, cross-border claims of return, and dealings within the market.[121] The requirement for due diligence (*Sorgfaltspflichten*) in such dealings is detailed in the 2016 Act, in what is probably the most extensive treatment of this standard in cultural prop-erty legislation.

Section 41 of the 2016 Act sets out general due diligence requirements for anyone placing cultural property on the market, obligating such individuals to verify whether the cultural property has been lost, unlaw-fully imported, or unlawfully excavated.[122] Any such person is required to comply with the affirmative duty to exercise due diligence "if a rea-sonable person might assume" that one of the aforementioned offenses has been committed. Such an assumption is particularly relevant if, dur-ing the previous acquisition of the cultural property, "an extremely low price was demanded without further explanation" or if the previous seller "demanded cash payment for a purchase price exceeding €5,000."[123]

---

[117]   *Id.* art. 3:87a(2).

[118]   *Id.* art. 3:87a(3).

[119]   Cultural Property Protection Act of 31 July 2016, Federal Law Gazette [BGBl] Part I, at 1914 (Gesetz zum Schutz von Kulturgut (Kulturgutschutzgesetz – KGSG)), www.gesetze-im-internet.de/kgsg/ (hereinafter: "2016 Act" or "KGSG") (Ger.). A formal English version of the KGSG is available at www.gesetze-im-internet.de/englisch_kgsg/englisch_kgsg.html.

[120]   For the criticisms against the 2007 Act, and the ways in which such deficiencies were addressed in the 2016 Act, *see* Julia Weiler-Esser, *The New German Act on the Protection of Cultural Property: A Better Protection for Archaeological Heritage in Germany and Abroad*, 18 J. ART CRIME 3 (2017).

[121]   For a review of the key provisions of the 2016 Act, *see* Silvan Nennett-Schaar, *A Prowl through the New German Cultural Property Legislation*, 24 ART ANTIQUITY & L. 349 (2019); Weiler-Esser, *supra* note 120.

[122]   2016 Act, *supra* note 119, §41(1).

[123]   *Id.* §41(2).

Exercising general due diligence also requires verifying "relevant information that can be obtained with reasonable effort" or conducting "any other examination that a reasonable person would carry out under similar circumstances."[124]

Section 42 imposes additional due diligence requirements on "anyone who places cultural property on the market in conducting his business"[125] (namely, professional dealers, auction houses, and so forth) by providing a list of obligations relating to the retrieval and provision of further information, including a duty "to examine the provenance of the cultural property" and determining "whether the cultural property is registered in publicly accessible registers and databases."[126]

While these additional due diligence requirements do not apply to cultural property that "does not constitute archaeological cultural property" and "has a financial value of no more than €2,500,"[127] such an exemption from the additional requirements would not apply to cultural property that has been proven or is presumed to have been taken from its owner during the Nazi era; items originating from a state for which the International Council of Museums (ICOM) has published a red list of endangered cultural property; or to cultural property "that is prohibited by a regulation of the European Union from being imported, exported or placed on the market."[128]

Other legal systems have similarly incorporated the concept of due diligence for cultural property, either by codifying it in national laws or by judicial development of the good-faith requirement.[129] While the specific details of the due diligence concept may vary slightly across this new generation of national lawmaking on cultural property, when taken together with the key role of the 1995 UNIDROIT Convention and the 2014 EU Directive, these legal doctrines do seem to represent an emerging common denominator, with cross-border implications for the handling of cultural property.

---

[124] *Id.* §41(3).

[125] *Id.* §42(1).

[126] *Id.* §§42(1)(3) and 42(1)(6), respectively.

[127] *Id.* §42(3).

[128] *Id.* §44.

[129] *See* Birgit Kurtz, Friederike von Bruhl & Gregor Kleinknecht, *Standards of Care in the Art Market: A Comparative Study on What Is Expected of Buyers, Sellers, and Consignors in the United States, Germany and England*, 21 ART ANTIQUITY & L. 1, 18–20 (2016) (explaining that, under English case law, exercising due diligence, such as by performing a search in a public register of stolen art, has become a key feature for holding that a purchaser of an object acted in "good faith" under the Sales of Goods Act 1979 or the Limitation Act 1980).

3.3.3   Industry Changes: From an "ALR Certificate" to the "Responsible Art Market" Initiative

Alongside the growing prevalence of due diligence as a legal concept, on both the international and national levels, norms requiring actors in the cultural property market to act prudently – with a particular focus on identifying breaches in the chain of title or other acts of theft, embezzlement, coercion, and so forth – are increasingly becoming part of the industry's professional norms.

Although far from complete, and while obviously subject to competing financial and other interests within the market, the simultaneous development of a general duty of due diligence as both a legal norm and a professional standard of behavior is a significant phenomenon.

Following a series of high-profile cases in the 1980s involving stolen artworks that found their way to auction houses and art dealers before reaching museums and collectors, various industry professionals contributed to the foundation of the Art Loss Register (ALR) in 1990.[130] The ALR is a for-profit company that defines itself as "the leading due diligence provider for the art market."[131] It conducts extensive online and offline searches at the request of potential sellers or buyers and maintains the largest digital database of its kind. As of early 2025, it includes over 700,000 items of lost, stolen, and looted art, antiquities, and collectibles (the database is analyzed in more detail in Chapter 4). The search process is designed to "check objects with the ALR database to demonstrate due diligence, to prevent the handling of stolen art and to find out more about an object's history through our in-house Provenance Research team."[132]

At the end of this process, the company issues an "ALR certificate" if the search does not identify any problems.[133] While the ALR certificate has no formal legal status that protects the client from future legal claims, the search process itself can serve the practical purpose of alerting the customer to potential issues in the chain of title. It also attests to the customer's effort to exercise due diligence should a dispute arise later. The search process and the issuance of an ALR certificate have thus emerged as a mechanism for demonstrating due diligence, at least for certain contractual obligations, in addition to serving reputational purposes.[134]

---

[130] Dan Klerman & Anja Shortland, *The Transformation of the Art Market: Law, Norms, and Institutions*, 23 THEORETICAL INQ. L. 219, 229–32 (2022).

[131] *See* the Art Loss Register homepage at www.artloss.com/ (last visited Feb. 1, 2025).

[132] *Id., About Us*, www.artloss.com/about-us/ (last visited Feb. 1, 2025).

[133] *Id., Search*, www.artloss.com/search/ (last visited Feb. 1, 2025).

[134] Klerman & Shortland, *supra* note 130, at 233–37.

Dealers and auction houses have also taken their own steps to engage in a process of due diligence, which may serve both certain contractual and reputational purposes, although this does not grant such entities formal immunity against potential claims by clients or other parties.

For example, in its 2021 Code of Business Conduct, Sotheby's addressed the issue of due diligence by stating generally that "[b]efore offering property for sale, we must be satisfied that we have conducted the level of due diligence required to be satisfied that the property we are handling is authentic and that there are no known legal obstacles to selling and passing title."[135]

Another example of professional norms adopted by market actors in the context of due diligence is that of the art market guidelines adopted by the Responsible Art Market ("RAM") initiative, a nonprofit, cross-market organization established in Geneva in 2015.[136] As part of these guidelines, the RAM published an "Art Transaction Due Diligence Toolkit,"[137] according to which "investigating and obtaining as much information as possible about the parties to the proposed transaction, the artwork and the transaction itself protects art businesses and collectors and helps art businesses manage their reputational and financial risks."[138] The toolkit includes checklists for the various areas of inquiry, such as "client due diligence," "artwork due diligence," and "transaction due diligence," while highlighting potential "red flag situations" for each of these categories.[139]

For example, the toolkit on "artwork due diligence" looks into issues of identification, trade restrictions, ownership, provenance and exhibition history, artwork location and recent movement, and authenticity. It then provides examples of red flag situations, such as if "the seller is reluctant to provide written evidence of the artwork's provenance" or if "the artwork is an archaeological object or part of a monument and its source country … is or has been in recent conflict."[140]

---

[135] SOTHEBY'S, CODE OF BUSINESS CONDUCT 47 (2021), www.sothebys.com/en/docs/pdf/code-of-conduct-2021.pdf.

[136] Responsible Art Market (RAM), *RAM Initiative*, www.responsibleartmarket.org/about-ram/ram-initiative/ (last visited Feb. 1, 2025).

[137] RESPONSIBLE ART MARKET (RAM), ART TRANSACTION DUE DILIGENCE TOOLKIT (2018), http://responsibleartmarket.org/guidelines/art-transaction-due-diligence-toolkit/.

[138] *Id*. at 1.

[139] *Id*. at 2–12.

[140] RESPONSIBLE ART MARKET (RAM), ART TRANSACTION DUE DILIGENCE TOOLKIT – CHECKLISTS, PART 2 (2018), http://responsibleartmarket.org/guidelines/art-transaction-due-diligence-toolkit/.

This type of professional standard-setting is intended to address the incomplete and substandard nature of due diligence inquiries that buyers of cultural property, including cultural institutions, have long settled for. This is exemplified by a 2023 report revealing how the British Museum acquired an Egyptian artifact from a dealer who had previously been convicted in the United States for smuggling antiquities, without conducting a proper inquiry into the item's documentation.[141]

3.3.4   Due Diligence in Cultural Institutions: ICOM's Code of Ethics

Ethical rules have also been adopted by a growing number of market actors, organizations, and institutions, committing themselves to engaging in due diligence even when such practices are not legally required and cannot be practically enforced. For example, University College London published its "cultural property policy," guided, among other things, by the principle that "it has a duty of care to inform and advise staff and students so that they are able to exercise due diligence in the acquisition of cultural property for any purposes, whether for corporate or personal reasons."[142]

On a broader scale, the U.S. Association of Art Museum Directors (AAMD) adopted "Guidelines on the Acquisition of Archaeological Material and Ancient Art."[143] Its statement of principles declares, inter alia, that it is "committed to the exercise of due diligence in the acquisition process, in particular in the research of proposed acquisitions, transparency in the policy applicable to acquisitions generally, and full and prompt disclosure following acquisition."[144]

Most prominently, the Code of Ethics of the ICOM provides minimum standards of professional conduct for museums in 138 countries and territories, thereby reaching many actors beyond the state parties to binding conventions, including those in all major destination

---

[141]   Tariq Tahir, *British Museum Bought Ancient Egyptian Artefact from Convicted Antiquities Smuggler*, THE NATIONAL, Sept. 25, 2023.

[142]   UNIVERSITY COLLEGE LONDON, CULTURAL PROPERTY POLICY (2009), Sect. 3.1, www.ucl.ac.uk/archaeology/sites/archaeology/files/Cultural_Property_Policy_2009.pdf.

[143]   ASSOCIATION OF ART MUSEUM DIRECTORS (AAMD), GUIDELINES ON THE ACQUISITION OF ARCHAEOLOGICAL MATERIAL AND ANCIENT ART (revised ed. 2013), https://aamd.org/object-registry/new-acquisitions-of-archaeological-material-and-works-of-ancient-art/more-info.

[144]   *Id.* §I(D).

states.[145] According to Rule 2.3, which addresses "provenance and due diligence," "[e]very effort must be made before acquisition to ensure that any object … [h]as not been illegally obtained in, or exported from its country of origin or any intermediate country in which it might have been owned legally … Due diligence in this regard should establish the full history of the item since discovery or production."[146]

The glossary accompanying the ICOM Code of Ethics further elaborates on the term "due diligence," defining it as the "requirement that every endeavor is made to establish the facts of a case before deciding a course of action particularly in identifying the source and history of an item offered for acquisition or use before acquiring it."[147] Accordingly, by requiring cultural institutions to study the full history of an item, the ethical duty of due diligence creates a mutually reinforcing effect with legal and professional norms on due diligence. Moreover, by identifying the substantive and time-based scope of due diligence as establishing "the full history of the item since discovery or production," the Code of Ethics ties this duty to the field of provenance research, which is addressed in detail in the following section. Notably, the Code of Ethics is undergoing a review process, scheduled to be concluded by the end of 2025, and it remains to be seen how due diligence and provenance research will be intertwined in the revised version.[148]

As with hard-law international instruments analyzed in previous sections, such as the 1995 UNIDROIT Convention and the 2014 EU Directive, the ICOM Code of Ethics – which can be considered a soft-law international instrument due to its global reach among cultural institutions in 138 countries and territories – has had an impact on domestic law and regulation. One example is the United Kingdom's adoption of the 2003 Dealing in Cultural Objects (Offences) Act,[149] which was influenced by the due diligence requirements set out in the ICOM Code of Ethics.[150]

---

[145] International Council of Museums (ICOM), ICOM Code of Ethics for Museums (June 2017), https://icom.museum/wp-content/uploads/2018/07/ICOM-code-En-web.pdf.

[146] *Id.* rule 2.3.

[147] *Id., Glossary* ("Due Diligence").

[148] ICOM, *Be Part of the Process: Review the ICOM Code of Ethics* (Sept. 4, 2024), https://icom.museum/en/news/join-the-global-webinar-on-the-revision-of-the-icom-code-of-ethics-for-museums/.

[149] Dealing in Cultural Objects (Offences) Act, c. 27 (U.K.).

[150] Carsten Stahn, Confronting Colonial Objects: Histories, Legacies, and Access to Culture 425 n.87 (2023).

3.4   The Changing Role and Scope of Provenance Research

3.4.1   Provenance as Showcasing an Object's "Career Highlights"

The term "provenance," originating from the French verb *provenir* and the Latin verb *provenire* (from *pro-* "forth" + *venire* "come"), was first used in the late eighteenth century to denote "something's origin" in general. It later came to refer more specifically to a "record of ownership of a work of art or an antique, used as a guide to authenticity or quality."[151] This definition "conveys clearly the traditional approach to, and the central and dominant strand of, provenance research that, until relatively recently, was mainly the province of art historians, principally when working in a museum or collection curatorial context."[152]

Alongside the term "provenance," the term "provenience" had also come to be used in the context of tracking the history of objects, with some scholars viewing the two terms as interchangeable and others using the term "provenience" to depict the history of archaeological objects and the term "provenance" for works of (nonarchaeological) fine arts.[153] Anthropologist Rosemary Joyce highlights the use of these terms in determining the authenticity of archaeological objects, representing concepts of place, time, and meaning of an object as it transitions from its original location to its current site.[154] Joyce refers to the term provenience as depicting the fixed point of the item's place of origin, and the concept of provenance as representing the "object's itinerary" as it moves through time and space to reach its present location.[155]

An early example of documenting the provenance of objects, while tying the issue of authenticity to broader societal concepts and the principle of legality, can be found in the recording of King Charles I's art collection following his execution in 1649. This process was ordered by the

---

[151] NEW OXFORD AMERICAN DICTIONARY, "Provenance" and "Provenience" (Angus Stevenson & Christine A. Lindberg eds., 3rd end., 2010).

[152] Arthur Tompkins, *The History and Purposes of Provenance Research, in* PROVENANCE RESEARCH TODAY: PRINCIPLES, PRACTICE, PROBLEMS 16, 16–17 (Arthur Tompkins ed., 2020).

[153] Gerstenblith, *supra* note 2, at 463–64 (2020).

[154] Rosemary A. Joyce, *When Is Authentic? Situating Authenticity in Itineraries of Objects, in* CREATING AUTHENTICITY: AUTHENTICATION PROCESSES IN ETHNOGRAPHIC MUSEUMS 39, 44–48 (Alex Geurds & Laura van Broekhaven eds., 2013).

[155] Rosemary A. Joyce, *From Place to Place: Provenience, Provenance, and Archaeology, in* PROVENANCE: AN ALTERNATE HISTORY OF ART 48, 48–51 (Gail Feigenbaum & Inge Reist eds., 2012).

English Parliament with the aim of selling the collection and using the revenue for public purposes.[156]

As Arthur Tompkins notes, the preparation of the inventory for this sale had two key consequences for the later development of provenance research.[157] First, generating a narrative of an artwork's history became inextricably linked to the artwork's reputation, appreciation, and value. The inventory compelled those responsible for the task not only to record that the artwork was in fact the property of King Charles I (and thus eligible for sale) but also to account for the proceeds of its sale. This involved reporting to Parliament to whom each artwork had been sold and for how much, with the result being that the documentation of these aspects of an artwork's "social life" became indispensable features of its provenance. Second, the act of documenting the "object's itinerary" for the bulk of these artworks – including their entry into King Charles I's royal collection, their dispersal into private hands during the sale, and the retrieval of the majority of them by Charles II after the restoration of the monarchy – laid the groundwork for the creation of a broad and durable art market beyond the scope of this specific collection. Between 1670 and the early 1690s, approximately 35,000 paintings were sold and bought through the emerging London art market, relying on such practices of documentation.[158]

These features of provenance research, and their role in the art market, have persisted in the centuries since. As Jacques Schumacher notes in his review of documentation practices at the Victoria and Albert Museum (V&A) since its establishment in 1852, while curators consistently recorded in their acquisition files the names of individuals or entities from whom they acquired objects, further information about the work's provenance was typically documented only if the object had been in the possession of historically significant figures, such as royals.[159] The traditional role of provenance research was thus to emphasize an artwork's "career highlights" to enhance the reputation of both the artwork and the person or institution currently holding it, as well as to increase the artwork's potential market value. Such instances notwithstanding, gaps in provenance were not regarded as a source of concern.[160]

---

[156] Tompkins, *supra* note 152, at 17.
[157] *Id.* at 18–19.
[158] *Id.*
[159] Jacques Schumacher, *British Museums and Holocaust-Era Provenance Research, in* MUSEUMS AND THE HOLOCAUST 34, 35 (Ruth Redmond-Cooper ed., 2nd ed. 2021).
[160] *Id.* at 35–36.

Beyond the traditional roles of provenance research – boosting professional reputation, fostering the art market, and serving as an object of academic inquiry by archaeologists, art historians, and others – the legal significance of provenance (even if this exact term was not used) began to emerge in the twentieth century. This was especially the case for archaeological or ethnological artifacts, as states – including newly independent states that were former colonies and source territories for antiquities – began enacting state patrimony laws for archaeological items discovered within their territory and controlling the export of cultural objects more broadly.[161] Greece began by introducing such a law as early as 1834 (following its independence in 1821),[162] revising it in 1899,[163] and amending it most recently in 2002.[164] Turkey enacted similar laws in 1906,[165] and Italy followed suit in 1909.[166]

Patty Gerstenblith identifies the ways in which the concepts of provenience and provenance gradually began to carry legal significance.[167] This was not only in the context of domestic law enforcement by states that had enacted such patrimony laws and export controls, but also in the international setting, and specifically following the 1970 UNESCO Convention.

For example, establishing the provenience of an object – meaning the country within its (current) borders where the archaeological object in question was excavated or discovered, as well as the date of its discovery – mattered for determining whether the artifact was subject to the state of origin's patrimony laws over archaeological artifacts. This, in turn, could

---

[161] Gerstenblith, *supra* note 2, at 470–76.

[162] For the legislative history of Greece's patrimony law, *see* Katerina Ampela, *The Parthenon Marbles and Greek Cultural Heritage Law* (Jan. 6, 2022), www.culturalheritagelaw.org/ The-Parthenon-Marbles-and-Greek-Cultural-Heritage-Law.

[163] *See id.*

[164] Law No. 3028/2002, On the Protection of Antiquities and Cultural Heritage in General, Government Gazette A153 (June 28, 2002) (Greece). An English version of this law is available at www.bsa.ac.uk/wp-content/uploads/2018/11/Archaeological-Law-3028-2002.pdf.

[165] Article 4 of the 1906 Decree, issued during the Ottoman Period, stipulates: "All monuments and immovable and movable antiquities situated in or on land and real estate belonging to the Government and to individuals and various communities, the existence of which is known or will hereafter become known, are the property of the Government of the Ottoman Empire. Consequently, the right to discover, preserve, collect and donate to museums the aforementioned belongs to the Government." *See* Republic of Turkey v. Christie's, Inc., No. 17-cv-3086 (AJN), 2021 WL 4060357 (S.D.N.Y. Sept. 7, 2021), at 214–15.

[166] Legge 20 giugno 1909, n. 364, G.U. June 28, 1909, n. 150 (It.), www.gazzettaufficiale.it/eli/ gu/1909/06/28/150/sg/pdf.

[167] Gerstenblith, *supra* note 2, at 476–77.

establish whether it would be governed by reciprocal restrictions, bilateral obligations, or other mechanisms for enforcing export restrictions under the 1970 UNESCO Convention or other cross-border instruments for cultural property.[168]

However, the dynamic aspect of provenance – tracing the object's subsequent movements and dates after its initial discovery, within or across national borders, until it ended up in its current location – may also matter from a legal perspective. This is particularly relevant if the object passed, at some stage, through a transit country, potentially altering its legal status. Such changes can affect legal proceedings in the country where the object is intercepted by law enforcement or where a claimant files a suit to recover the object from its current possessor.

For example, when a country limits the import of cultural artifacts only from certain countries with which it has a bilateral agreement – as is the case with the way in which the United States implements the 1970 UNESCO Convention – the entry of an object from a transit country that does not restrict cross-border movements may have legal consequences. Similarly, customs laws that may define the "country of origin" as either the original place of the object's discovery or as the previous port of entry can affect the object's legal status.[169]

Thus, the concepts of provenience and provenance already carried some legal weight prior to the twenty-first century. That said, their applicability was limited for at least two reasons.

First, even in the context of cultural artifacts governed by patrimony laws or export restrictions, cross-border enforcement under the 1970 UNESCO Convention was practically limited, as explained in Chapter 2, such that many museums, collectors, and other possessors could practically disregard the need to provide proof of provenance prior to 1970, or rely on vague accounts of the object's pre-1970 itinerary without significant scrutiny. Moreover, as shown in Chapter 2, it was not until the twenty-first century that national jurisdictions began enforcing foreign countries' patrimony laws through criminal proceedings or civil cases involving archaeological items that had been illegally excavated, smuggled, and then sold to museums and collectors in other countries. It is only in the current era of more effective cross-border law enforcement that the collection and acquisition practices of museums and collectors have come under legal scrutiny, requiring them to investigate the item's provenance.

---

[168] *Id.* at 477–90.
[169] *Id.* at 490–93.

Second, outside the scope of patrimony laws or export limits, traditional provenance research by cultural institutions and art historians rarely engaged in the reconstructing of an unbroken chain of owners or possessors of cultural objects to identify potential title issues, including in cases of artworks that had changed hands over time. This gap in provenance research only began to shift in the last decade of the twentieth century, in the context of Nazi-era art plunder.[170]

3.4.2   A Paradigm Shift: Addressing Dark Holes in Provenance for Nazi-Looted Art

3.4.2.1   The Road to the Washington Conference and Beyond

A key turning point in the transformation of provenance research from the province of a small group of art historians or archaeologists into a field of inquiry entangled in high-profile political, social, and legal issues can be attributed to the renewed interest during the 1990s in identifying works that had been wrongfully taken from Jewish owners in the period between 1933 and 1945.[171]

In the immediate period following the end of the Second World War, a considerable number of works of art were returned to their original owners or their countries of origin, including through "central collecting points" and a series of regulations adopted by the Allied forces between 1947 and 1949.[172] Additionally, statutory or administrative mechanisms were established to allow Jewish survivors to submit claims, primarily through West Germany's 1953 Federal Compensation Law,[173] with subsequent legislation setting the end of 1969 as the deadline for submitting such claims.[174] After the expiry of these special laws, most potential claims by victims or their heirs became effectively blocked in most relevant jurisdictions owing to statutes of limitations or other legal barriers,

---

[170] Schumacher, *supra* note 159, at 35.

[171] Christoph Zuschlag, Einführung in die Provenienzforschung: Wie die Herkunft von Kulturgut Entschüsselt Wird 13–15 (2022) (Ger.).

[172] For a review of these mechanisms, *see* Olaf S. Ossmann, *25 Years of the Washington Principles on Nazi-Confiscated Art*, 69 Justice 36, 37–38 (Spring 2023).

[173] Bundesgesetz zur Entschädigung für Opfer der nationalsozialistischen Verfolgung (Bundesentschädigungsgesetz – BEG) (Federal Law on Compensation for Victims of National Socialist Persecution) (Sept. 18, 1953), www.gesetze-im-internet.de/beg/BJNR013870953.html (Ger.).

[174] Avraham Weber, *The Federal Republic of Germany's Creation of Compensation Laws for Nazi Wrongdoing*, 69 Justice 29, 30–31 (Spring 2023).

including the good-faith purchaser and acquisitive prescription doctrines in European countries.[175]

While the avenue of civil litigation largely ceased to be effective during this period, a series of events that unfolded during the late 1980s and 1990s spurred governments, international organizations, civil society groups, and other stakeholders to reconsider public policies on cultural property plundered or otherwise illegitimately taken from its owners during the period of the Nazi regime, and to explore what measures could be taken to identify such items and their whereabouts. One catalyst for this renewed interest was the opening of archives following the collapse of the Soviet Union, which revealed the extent of such dispossession in Eastern Europe.[176]

In 1996, U.S. President Bill Clinton commissioned Under Secretary of Commerce Stuart E. Eizenstat to investigate the whereabouts of assets looted by the Nazis, following growing evidence that financial institutions, particularly Swiss banks, had played a role in secretly harboring such assets.

While much of the focus has been on gold, the mandate granted to the commission also extended to other assets.[177] Accordingly, the commission's 1997 study, titled *U.S. and Allied Efforts to Recover and Restore Gold and Other Assets Stolen or Hidden by Germany during World War II*, prepared in collaboration with the U.S. Holocaust Memorial Museum established in 1993, played a pivotal role in raising awareness of the scope of artwork and other tangible assets looted from Jewish owners and not specifically identified.[178] In December 1997, the *New York Times* published a story alleging that the Museum of Modern Art in New York was holding, on loan, a painting by Egon Schiele that had been looted by the Nazis from its Jewish owner.[179] That same year, in Britain, the Holocaust Educational Trust alerted the British Secretary of State for Culture to the possibility that museums in the United Kingdom may also be holding artworks looted under the Nazis.[180]

---

[175] Ossmann, *supra* note 172, at 38; Renold, *supra* note 109, at 258.
[176] Ossmann, *supra* note 172, at 38.
[177] Schumacher, *supra* note 159, at 40–41.
[178] Stuart E. Eizenstat et al., U.S. and Allied Efforts to Recover and Restore Gold and Other Assets Stolen or Hidden by Germany during World War II (May 1997), https://fcit.usf.edu/holocaust/resource/gold/gold.pdf.
[179] Judith H. Dobrzynski, *The Zealous Collector: A Singular Passion for Amassing Art, One Way or Another*, N.Y. Times, Dec. 24, 1997.
[180] Jacques Schumacher, Nazi-Era Provenance of Museum Collections: A Research Guide 60–61 (2024).

As noted in Chapter 2,[181] following these developments the U.S. Department of State convened an international conference in Washington, D.C., in late 1998, attended by delegates from forty-four countries and thirteen nongovernmental organizations.[182] The conference concluded with a joint statement, the Washington Conference Principles on Nazi-Confiscated Art.[183] Among other provisions, Principle VIII of the 1998 Washington Principles called on the different member states to establish "just and fair solutions" for cases involving artworks confiscated by the Nazis and not subsequently restituted, as discussed in Chapter 2. The 1998 Washington Principles also highlighted the importance of provenance research; the first four principles state:

    I. Art that had been confiscated by the Nazis and not subsequently restituted should be identified.

    II. Relevant records and archives should be open and accessible to researchers, in accordance with the guidelines of the International Council on Archives.

    III. Resources and personnel should be made available to facilitate the identification of all art that had been confiscated by the Nazis and not subsequently restituted.

    IV. In establishing that a work of art had been confiscated by the Nazis and not subsequently restituted, *consideration should be given to unavoidable gaps or ambiguities in the provenance in light of the passage of time and the circumstances of the Holocaust era.*[184]

Therefore, the 1998 Washington Principles explicitly refer to the term "provenance" as reconstructing, to the greatest possible extent, the history of ownership and possession of artworks dating back to the Nazi era, and emphasize the need to engage in professional provenance research to achieve this goal.

The key role of provenance research in identifying potential cases of involuntary transfers of cultural property during the Nazi period is also underscored in subsequent cross-border soft-law instruments. The 2009 Terezin Declaration on Holocaust Era Assets and Related Issues,[185]

---

[181] *See* Chapter 2, Section 2.4.

[182] SCHUMACHER, *supra* note 180, at 60–64.

[183] U.S. Department of State, *Washington Conference Principles on Nazi-Confiscated Art* (Dec. 3, 1998), www.state.gov/washington-conference-principles-on-nazi-confiscated-art/ (hereinafter: "1998 Washington Principles").

[184] *Id.* principles I–IV (my emphasis).

[185] U.S. Department of State, *Terezin Declaration on Holocaust Era Assets and Related Issues* (June 30, 2009), www.state.gov/prague-holocaust-era-assets-conference-terezin-declaration/ (hereinafter: "Terezin Declaration").

adopted by forty-seven countries, provides in the section dealing with "Nazi-Confiscated and Looted Art":

> 3. In particular, recognizing that restitution cannot be accomplished without knowledge of potentially looted art and cultural property, we stress the importance for all stakeholders to continue and support intensified systematic provenance research, with due regard to legislation, in both public and private archives, and where relevant to make the results of this research, including ongoing updates, available via the internet, with due regard to privacy rules and regulations.[186]

The 2024 Best Practices for the Washington Conference Principles on Nazi-Confiscated Art, endorsed as of early 2025 by twenty-five countries,[187] establish the following guidelines regarding provenance research:

> G. Governments should encourage provenance research and projects to catalogue, digitize and make available on the internet public and private archives, including dealer records. Public and private collections should be encouraged to publish their inventories.
> H. Provenance researchers should have access to all relevant archives and source documents. Provenance research carried out by public or private bodies should be made publicly available on the internet. Where queries are made, as a matter of fairness current possessors in particular should disclose all documentation related to acquisition and provenance to claimants. Provenance research, particularly regarding potential claims, ideally should be conducted by an independent research body to avoid possible conflicts of interest. Such an independent institution should be granted access to all relevant archives whether public or private.[188]

The next two sections outline the very different paths that Germany and the United States have taken regarding Holocaust-era provenance research. The subsequent section analyzes the establishment of national bodies for such provenance research in Austria, France, and the Netherlands, and the way in which their work is tied to the operation of restitution committees established following the 1998 Washington Principles – an issue discussed in detail in Chapter 6.

---

[186] *Id.*, section on "Nazi-Confiscated and Looted Art," §2.
[187] U.S. Department of State, *Best Practices for the Washington Conference Principles on Nazi-Confiscated Art* (Mar. 5, 2024), www.state.gov/office-of-the-special-envoy-for-holocaust-issues/best-practices-for-the-washington-conference-principles-on-nazi-confiscated-art (hereinafter: "2024 Best Practices").
[188] *Id.* §§G–H.

3.4.2.2   Germany: Government-Funded, Decentralized Research Conducted by Cultural Institutions

In Germany, following the 1998 Washington Principles, the federal government, the states (*Länder*), and the local governments issued a joint declaration in December 1999.[189] Alongside a statement in which the governments committed to "bring their influence to bear in the responsible bodies of the relevant statutory institutions" to restitute Nazi-confiscated property,[190] and a recognition of past efforts undertaken by museums, archives, and libraries to trace Nazi-confiscated art,[191] the 1999 Joint Declaration called for the creation of a website that would provide information about objects identified by public institutions as, or suspected to be, Nazi-looted cultural property. Additionally, the website was envisioned to include a "search list in which every claimant may enter the items he is looking for."[192]

In April 2000, this first-of-its-kind open database, the Lost Art Database (*Lost Art-Datenbank*) was posted online.[193] This database, analyzed in Chapter 4, has been managed by the German Lost Art Foundation (*Deutsches Zentrum Kulturgutverluste*) since 2015.[194] As noted in Chapter 4, the registration of a cultural item in the search list of the Lost Art Database carries major practical implications, effectively rendering the item unmarketable, even if the party making the registry is unable to legally enforce the restitution of the item from its current possessor.[195]

In 2001, the government published the Guidelines (*Handreichung*) for implementing the 1999 Joint Statement, with a revised version published

---

[189] Erklärung der Bundesregierung, der Länder und der kommunalen Spitzenverbände zur Auffindung und zur Rückgabe NS-verfolgungsbedingt entzogenen Kulturgutes, insbesondere aus jüdischem Besitz (14 Dezember 1999) [Joint Declaration by the Federal Government, the Länder (Federal States) and the National Associations of Local Authorities on the Tracing and Return of Nazi-confiscated Art, especially Jewish Property, Dec. 14, 1999] (hereinafter: "1999 Joint Declaration"), https://kulturgutverluste .de/sites/default/files/2023-04/Gemeinsame-Erklaerung.pdf. An informal English translation is available at www.lootedart.com/MFEU4B68721_print;Y.

[190] 1999 Joint Declaration, *supra* note 189, at §I.

[191] *Id.* §II.

[192] *Id.* §III.

[193] German Lost Art Foundation, *About the Lost Art Database*, www.lostart.de/en/ueber-lost-art (last visited Feb. 1, 2025).

[194] German Lost Art Foundation, *History of the Foundation*, https://kulturgutverluste.de/en/foundation/history (last visited Feb. 1, 2025).

[195] *See* Chapter 4, Section 4.2.3.1.

in 2019.[196] Part B of the Guidelines, titled *Checking and Documenting Items Held in Collections – Advice on Identifying Nazi-Confiscated Art*, provides a "casework checklist" as well as contact details and funding information, and states:

> In principle, all public institutions of the Federal Republic of Germany – especially museums, libraries and archives – can apply to the German Lost Art Foundation for project funding. Applications are also accepted from privately owned institutions and private persons who hope to find just and fair solutions through their own research into Nazi-looted art, in line with the Washington Principles (provided there is a public interest in supporting them).[197]

In 2019, the Lost Art Foundation, in collaboration with other German organizations, published a Provenance Research Manual (*Leitfaden Provenienzforschung*) designed "to identify cultural property seized due to persecution during the National Socialist era."[198] The 2019 Manual includes detailed provisions for conducting such research, including "methods of provenance research,"[199] and describes the process by which German cultural institutions engage in provenance research as a "voluntary obligation,"[200] which is financially supported by the German Lost Art Foundation.[201] The 2019 Manual also features an Annex, which includes details about digital databases (addressed in Chapter 4) alongside other resources on art dealers, indexed and partially accessible online.[202]

---

[196] Minister of State for Culture and the Media, *Guidelines for Implementing the Statement by the Federal Government, the Länder and the National Associations of Local Authorities on the Tracing and Return of Nazi-Confiscated Art, Especially Jewish Property, of December 1999* (new ed. 2019), www.beratende-kommission.de/en/grundlagen#s-guidelines (hereinafter: "2019 Guidelines").

[197] *Id.* at 23.

[198] German Lost Art Foundation, *Provenance Research Manual to Identify Cultural Property Seized Due to Persecution During the National Socialist Era* (2019), www.bibliotheksverband.de/sites/default/files/2020-12/Provenance%20Research%20Manual.pdf (hereinafter: "2019 Manual").

[199] *Id.* at 39–76.

[200] *Id.* at 13–22.

[201] The German Lost Art Foundation receives institutional funding from the Federal Government Commissioner for Culture and the Media. German Lost Art Foundation, *Nazi-Looted Cultural Property: Basics & Overview*, https://kulturgutverluste.de/en/contexts/nazi-looted-cultural-property (last visited Feb. 1, 2025).

[202] German Lost Art Foundation, Provenance Research Manual Annex (Jana Kocourek et al. eds, 2019), https://kulturgutverluste.de/sites/default/files/2023-06/Manual-Annex-Download.pdf.

As of early 2025, the Lost Art Foundation has funded over 450 provenance research projects on Nazi-looted cultural property, most conducted by public museums, universities, and libraries.[203] The results of the funded projects are published on the Proveana database, analyzed in Chapter 4.

Importantly, the process of provenance research is carried out by museums on a voluntary basis. While the federal government, through the Lost Art Foundation, provides funding for such requested projects, it does not have the legal authority to require cultural institutions to undertake such research.

Moreover, the various levels of government do not operate their own research bodies dedicated to provenance research. This has had implications for the processing of claims before the German Advisory Commission (*Beratende Kommission*), set up in 2003 based on the 1998 Washington Principles and replaced in 2024 by an arbitration mechanism, as discussed in Chapter 6.[204]

That said, Holocaust-era provenance research has advanced significantly in Germany. The growing professionalism and systematic research of collections to address potential cases of confiscation between 1933 and 1945 have been bolstered by the professional network *Arbeitskreis Provenienzforschung e.V.* (Research Association for Provenance Research), which brings together hundreds of provenance researchers in Germany and beyond.[205] Additionally, some German universities now offer academic degree programs in provenance research.[206]

3.4.2.3   United States: Ad Hoc Provenance Inquiries Following Civil and Criminal Cases

The issue of provenance research has taken a very different path in the United States. As noted in Section 3.1 in the context of the Metropolitan Museum of Art in New York,[207] U.S. museums historically paid little

---

[203] German Lost Art Foundation, *Project Statistics*, https://kulturgutverluste.de/en/projects/project-statistics (last visited Feb. 1, 2025).

[204] *See* Chapter 6, Section 6.1.

[205] Arbeitskreis Provenienzforschung e.V., *About Us*, www.arbeitskreis-provenienzforschung.org/en/about-us/ (last visited Feb. 1, 2025). For a publication marking the organization's 20th anniversary, *see* ENTZUG, TRANSFER, TRANSIT: MENSCHEN, OBJEKTE, ORTE UND EREIGNISSE. 20 JAHRE ARBEITSKREIS PROVENIENZFORSCHUNG E.V. (2024), https://books.ub.uni-heidelberg.de/arthistoricum/catalog/book/1315 (Ger.).

[206] *See, e.g.*, the master's program in provenance research and history of collections offered by the University of Bonn. Universität Bonn, *Master of Arts, Provenienzforschung und Geschicte des Sammelns*, www.uni-bonn.de/de/studium/studienangebot/studiengaenge-a-z/provenienzforschung-und-geschichte-des-sammelns-ma (Ger.) (last visited Feb. 1, 2025).

[207] *See supra* Section 3.1.

attention to verifying the historical chain of title and possession of artifacts prior to acquiring them – particularly during the second half of the twentieth century,[208] a period characterized by fierce competition among museums for the "very best" objects.[209] This was also the case with cultural objects that may have been involuntarily taken from their Jewish owners during the Nazi era.

Thus, although American and British curators and art historians played a key role in identifying, safeguarding, and restituting looted artworks in Germany and its occupied territories in the framework of the Monuments, Fine Arts, and Archives program established in 1943 by the Allies, the U.S.-created Art Looting Investigation Unit, and the central collecting points set up in postwar Germany,[210] they did not apply the provenance research skills they had acquired to their own collections.[211] Rather, the desire to return to "prewar normality" in U.S. and U.K. museums "also extended to the way in which provenance was recorded; no new standards were implemented to account for the dramatic dislocation of cultural property perpetrated by the Nazis."[212]

Even in the aftermath of the 1998 Washington Principles, unlike in Germany, U.S. cultural institutions generally did not come up with systematic plans to engage in provenance research on their collections. Furthermore, U.S. federal, state, and local governments did not offer earmarked funding for provenance research. While the two key associations of U.S. museums, the AAMD and the American Alliance of Museums, issued recommendations in 1998 and 1999, respectively, urging museums to investigate the provenance of their collections to identify potential cases of Nazi-era dispossession,[213] many museums have failed to do so.[214]

---

[208] Graham Bowley, *For U.S. Museums with Looted Art, the Indiana Jones Era Is Over*, N.Y. TIMES, Dec. 13, 2022.

[209] Stephanie M. Lee, *The Little Museum's Big Score*, THE CHRONICLE OF HIGHER EDUCATION, Aug. 23, 2023. *See* discussion of these collection practices in Chapter 1, text accompanying notes 78–79.

[210] SCHUMACHER, *supra* note 180, at 50–56.

[211] *Id.* at 58.

[212] *Id.*

[213] *See*, respectively, Association of Art Museum Directors, *Report of the AAMD Task Force on the Spoliation of Art during the Nazi/World War II Era (1933–1945)* (June 4, 1998), https://cms.aamd.org/sites/default/files/document/Report%20on%20 the%20Spoliation%20of%20Nazi%20Era%20Art.pdf; American Alliance of Museums, *Unlawful Appropriation of Objects during the Nazi Era* (Nov. 1999; amended Apr. 2001), www.aam-us.org/programs/ethics-standards-and-professional-practices/ unlawful-appropriation-of-objects-during-the-nazi-era/.

[214] *See* Nicholas M. O'Donnell, *Nazi-Displaced Art Promotes Understanding but Raises Questions*, 69 JUSTICE 25, 26–27 (Spring 2023).

The change occurred instead through a different process – one of growing awareness of Holocaust-era provenance research that resulted initially from ad hoc inquiries into the history of specific items of cultural property as part of civil court claims and, later, of criminal investigations.

As shown in Chapter 2, the United States is probably the only key jurisdiction in which at least some civil court claims for Holocaust-era involuntary dispossession of cultural property can still be pursued.[215] This is owing to the prevalence of the substantive *nemo dat* principle in property claims, and the relatively lenient statutes of limitations on the submission of such civil claims – particularly after the enactment of the federal Holocaust Expropriated Art Recovery (HEAR) Act of 2016.[216]

Moreover, as noted in Chapter 2, U.S. federal and state authorities (most prominently the New York State Antiquities Trafficking Unit) have been increasingly pursuing criminal proceedings against possessors of cultural items, investigating the provenance of such items to unveil potential offenses of illicit trafficking or criminal possession.[217] Provenance research has thus become an essential part of case-specific fact-finding in such civil and criminal proceedings.

A turning point in the history of professional and public awareness of Holocaust-era provenance research, resulting from a specific legal proceeding – although not one implicating a U.S. museum – was the 2004 U.S. Supreme Court decision in *Republic of Austria v. Altmann*.[218] The decision followed proceedings initiated in a U.S. federal district court by Maria Altmann, the niece and sole surviving heir of Jewish businessman and art patron Ferdinand Bloch-Bauer. Altmann sought to recover six paintings by Gustav Klimt, including two portraits of Ferdinand's wife, Adele Bloch-Bauer, which had been looted by the Nazis and were eventually placed in the Austrian state gallery in Vienna.[219]

---

[215] *See* Chapter 2, Section 2.1.2.

[216] Public Law No. 114-308, 130 Stat. 1524 (hereinafter: "2016 HEAR Act").

[217] *See* Chapter 2, Section 2.3.2.

[218] *Republic of Austria v. Altmann*, 124 S. Ct. 2240 (2004) (hereinafter: "Altmann case").

[219] Altmann initially announced that she would file a lawsuit in Austria to recover the paintings under Austrian law. Because Austrian court costs are proportional to the value of the recovery sought – and in this case, would have totaled several million dollars, an amount far beyond Altmann's means – she requested a waiver. The Austrian court granted this request in part but still would have required Altmann to pay approximately 350,000 U.S. dollars. When the Austrian government appealed against the partial waiver, Altmann voluntarily dismissed her suit and filed a suit in the United States District Court for the Central District of California (her place of residency). *See id.* at 2245.

Altmann asserted jurisdiction under Section 2 of the Foreign Sovereign Immunities Act of 1976 (FSIA),[220] which authorizes federal "civil suits for relief in personam with respect to which the foreign state is not entitled to immunity" under other sections of the FSIA. She further asserted that the Republic of Austria and the gallery were not entitled to immunity under FSIA's "expropriation exception."[221] This exception expressly exempts from sovereign immunity certain cases involving "rights in property taken in violation of international law," provided that the property has a commercial connection to the United States, or that the agency or instrumentality that owns the property is engaged in commercial activity in the United States.[222] The Supreme Court ruled in favor of Altmann, holding that the FSIA has retroactive force to cover past violations of international law in taking property.[223] Accordingly, and because the lower federal courts had determined that the gallery, being state-owned, qualified as an "agency or instrumentality" of Austria, and that the gallery's publishing and advertising activities in the United States amounted to "commercial activity" under the FSIA,[224] the Supreme Court allowed the case to move forward.[225]

Following this ruling, both parties agreed to arbitration in Austria, where the tribunal ultimately ruled in favor of Altmann, relying on the provisions of the 1998 Austrian Federal Act Regarding the Restitution of Artworks from Austrian Federal Museums and Collections.[226] The tribunal ordered the gallery to return the paintings without remuneration to Ms. Altmann as the sole heir of Bloch-Bauer.[227] Upon the return of the paintings, Ms. Altmann sold one of them, *Adele Bloch-Bauer I* (known as *The Woman in Gold*) in a private sale for 135 million dollars, and auctioned the remaining paintings, fetching a total of over 327 million dollars.[228]

Reflecting on the U.S. Supreme Court decision, Donald Burris and Randol Schoenberg, who represented Ms. Altmann, attributed the

---

[220] 28 U.S.C. §1330(a).
[221] 28 U.S.C. §1605(a)(3).
[222] 124 S. Ct. 2240, at 2245–46.
[223] *Id*. at 2252–54.
[224] *Id*. at 2258 (Breyer J., concurring).
[225] *Id*. at 2256 (Stevens, J.).
[226] Federal Law Gazette 1 No. 18111998, Dec. 4, 1998 (Austria).
[227] Arbitral case Maria v. Altmann et al. v. The Republic of Austria (Jan. 15, 2006), https://jusmundi.com/en/document/decision/en-maria-v-altmann-francis-gutmann-trevor-mantle-and-george-bentley-and-dr-nelly-auersperg-v-the-republic-of-austria-award-sunday-15th-january-2006 (Austria).
[228] C. Michaud, *Christie's Stages Record Art Sale*, REUTERS, Jan. 19, 2007.

willingness of U.S. courts to assert jurisdiction in this case to two factors.[229] The first was the fact that, under U.S. law, a thief cannot convey good title to a bona fide purchaser. The second was the "strong public-policy interest" of U.S. governmental institutions in seeking the return of Nazi-looted art.[230] Accordingly, while the Altmann case implicated an Austrian museum, and the decision on the merits of the case – including the provenance of the artworks – was made by an arbitration panel in Austria, the case subsequently had direct implications for U.S. museums and collectors. Heirs of allegedly dispossessed Jewish owners began initiating civil proceedings against U.S. museums and collectors in possession of such works – especially in states like New York, which have relatively lenient statutes of limitations. This trend intensified in the aftermath of the HEAR Act.[231] Consequently, U.S museums and collectors were compelled to account for Nazi-era gaps in the provenance of works in their possession.

A prominent example of U.S. museums and collectors having had to account for major gaps in Holocaust-era provenance involves numerous works by the Austrian painter Egon Schiele, which were owned, prior to the Nazi rule, by the Jewish-Austrian cabaret artist Fritz Grünbaum. As discussed in Chapter 2, in 1956, sixty-five pieces by Schiele surfaced at an art gallery in Switzerland and were put on sale that September, after the expiration of Austria's time window for claims related to Nazi-looted art. Some of the works included in the 1956 Schiele catalog published by the art gallery ended up in U.S. museums and collections.[232]

As detailed in Chapter 2, in 2002, Milos Vavra, a great-nephew of Grünbaum, and Leon Fischer, a second cousin of Elizabeth Grünbaum, were declared by an Austrian court to be the legal heirs of Grünbaum. They pursued legal measures to recover works by Schiele located in Austria and the United States.[233] Since their passing, the claims have been managed by the coexecutors of their estate, Timothy Reif and David Frankel.[234] While

---

[229] D.S. Burris & E.R. Schoenberg, *Reflections on Litigating Holocaust Stolen Art Cases*, 38 VANDERBILDT J. TRANSNAT'L L. 1041 (2005).

[230] *Id.* at 1043.

[231] 2016 HEAR Act, *supra* note 216.

[232] For the statement of these facts, *see* Reif v. Nagy, 175 A.D. 3d 107 (N.Y. App. 2019) (hereinafter: "Reif, 2019").

[233] For a report on a 2023 claim filed in a New York court against the Albertina and Leopold museums in Vienna for the recovery of twelve works by Schiele, *see* Catherine Hickley, *Jewish Cabaret Artist's Heirs File Suit for the Return of 12 Works by Schiele*, THE ART NEWSPAPER, Nov. 9, 2023.

[234] *See* Reif, 2019, *supra* note 232, at 113–14.

one claim, submitted against a private collector and dealer, David Bakalar, was dismissed based on the New York doctrine of laches,[235] the heirs of Grünbaum were successful in a later civil claim filed in 2015 against art dealer Richard Nagy. In this case, Nagy had purchased two Schiele paintings in 2013, and the New York court ruled that the plaintiffs had met their prima facie burden of proving that the artworks belonged to Grünbaum, who did not voluntarily relinquish them.[236]

As was further explored in Chapter 2, alongside the civil claims concerning Grünbaum's collection of Schiele's works, the Manhattan District Attorney's Office has also become involved in the matter by exercising its criminal jurisdiction. It has seized several of Schiele's works from public and private collections throughout the United States, including the Museum of Modern Art (MoMA), the Morgan Library & Museum in New York, the Neue Galerie in New York, the Carnegie Museum of Art in Pittsburgh, and the Allen Memorial Art Museum at Oberlin College in Ohio. One work, however, remains under legal contention: the 1916 watercolor and pencil on paper painting *Russian War Prisoner*, acquired in 1966 by the Art Institute of Chicago. As detailed in Chapter 2, this dispute is under consideration, as of early 2025, by an appellate court in New York.[237]

Interestingly, and likely not coincidentally, in August 2024, the Art Institute of Chicago announced the appointment of art historian Jacques Schumacher, who had previously served as Senior Provenance Research Curator at the V&A in London, as its new Executive Director of Provenance Research. According to the Art Institute, Schumacher will head the provenance team, which was formally established in 2020, and "lead the museum's provenance initiatives across the entire collection, including building on the museum's existing provenance research practice and coordinating this important work among specialists across the museum."[238]

The Art Institute of Chicago thus joins the Metropolitan Museum of New York,[239] as well as a growing number of other U.S. museums, such

---

[235] Bakalar v. Vavra, 500 Fex.Appx 6 (2d Cir. 2012), *affirming* Bakalar v. Vavra, 819 F.Supp.2d 293 (S.D.N.Y. 2011).

[236] *See* Reif, 2019, *supra* note 232.

[237] Art Institute of Chicago, Press Release, *Art Institute of Chicago Appoints Dr. Jacques Schumacher as Executive Director, Provenance Research* (Aug. 6, 2024), https://www.artic.edu/press/press-releases/362/art-institute-of-chicago-appoints-dr-jacques-schuhmacher-as-executive-director-provenance-research.

[238] *Id.*

[239] *See supra* note 24.

as the Museum of Fine Arts in Boston,[240] in establishing a professional department for provenance research. These departments are tasked with investigating the museums' collections, including items that may have provenance gaps for the period of Nazi rule between 1933 and 1945.

Another noteworthy development was introduced in 2022 by the New York State legislature. According to an amendment to New York Education Law Section 233-AA, signed into law in August 2022:

> Every museum which has on display any identifiable works of art known to have been created before nineteen hundred forty-five and which changed hands due to theft, seizure, confiscation, forced sale or other involuntary means in Europe during the Nazi era (nineteen hundred thirty-three – nineteen hundred forty-five) shall, to the extent practicable, prominently place a placard or other signage acknowledging such information along with such display.[241]

While this new law was put in place as a hard-law mechanism in response to the fact that the AAMD and AA guidelines (soft-law mechanisms) were not followed in practice, the New York law also suffers from certain drawbacks and ambiguities that may affect its implementation. As Nicholas O'Donnell notes, "[i]n some ways the law could act as a disincentive to further inquiry, rather than a galvanizing force. After all, the law does not compel investigation, nor does it condemn a lack of knowledge. Arguably, a museum would be safer to cease further research lest that research uncover information that would then have to be disclosed."[242] In this and other respects, U.S. law and policy still lag behind Germany in promoting systematic provenance research.

3.4.2.4   Austria, France, the Netherlands: Central Agencies for Provenance Research

Following up on the 1998 Washington Principles, and in particular Principle XI, by which "[n]ations are encouraged to develop national processes to implement these principles, particularly as they relate to alternative dispute resolution mechanisms for resolving ownership issues,"[243] five European countries established "restitution committees."

---

[240] Museum of Fine Arts Boston, *Provenance Research*, https://mfa.org/collections/provenance (last visited Feb. 1, 2025).

[241] N.Y. Education Law §233-AA (Aug. 19, 2022), www.nysenate.gov/legislation/laws/EDN/233-AA.

[242] O'Donnell, *supra* note 214, at 27.

[243] 1998 Washington Principles, *supra* note 183, Principle XI.

These include Austria, France, Germany, the Netherlands, and the United Kingdom, with Switzerland announcing in late 2023 its plans to set up an independent panel to address both Holocaust-era cases as well as claims in colonial contexts.[244] Chapter 6 will look in detail at the lessons learned from the work of these restitution committees – also in light of the German government's March 2024 decision to replace its Advisory Commission (*Beratende Kommission*) with a binding arbitration mechanism – and how these lessons can help to design mechanisms for other disputes involving cultural property.

This section examines how three of these countries – Austria, France, and the Netherlands – support the work of their restitution committees with national bodies of experts on Holocaust-era provenance research, and how such collaborations may also work across borders.

3.4.2.4.1 Austria The Commission for Provenance Research (*Kommission für Provenienzforschung*) was established in February 1998 by the federal ministry responsible for culture at the time, currently known as the Ministry for Art, Culture, Public Service and Sports (*Bundesministerium Kunst, Kultur, öffentlicher Dienst und Sport*).[245] The commission's task is to investigate Austrian federal museums and collections for objects that were confiscated during the persecution of Jews in the Nazi period and ended up becoming the property of the Republic of Austria. Its investigations cover acquisitions by, or donations to, federal collections from 1933 to the present. Alongside its research coordination offices, the Commission for Provenance Research employs individual provenance researchers, who work directly within federal museums and collections.[246]

The commission prepares case dossiers, which are passed on to the Art Restitution Advisory Board (*Kunstrückgabebeirat*).[247] This board examines the dossiers and issues recommendations to the federal ministry

[244] *See* Catherine Hickley, *Swiss Government Approves Panel to Assess Claims for Art Acquired in Nazi and Colonial Eras*, THE ART NEWSPAPER, Nov. 23, 2023.

[245] Bundesministerium Kunst, Kultur, öffentlicher Dienst und Sport, *Provenance Research and Restitution in the Austrian Federal Collections, Commission for Provenance Research*, https://provenienzforschung.gv.at/en/commission-for-provenance-research/ (last visited Feb. 1, 2025).

[246] *Id.*

[247] Bundesministerium Kunst, Kultur, öffentlicher Dienst und Sport, *Provenance Research and Restitution in the Austrian Federal Collections, Art Restitution Advisory Board*, https://provenienzforschung.gv.at/en/empfehlungen-des-beirats/ (last visited Feb. 1, 2025).

on whether to restitute the object in question. In addition to preparing case dossiers, the commission contributes to fundamental Nazi-related provenance research, for instance by introducing an online Lexicon of Austrian Provenance Research (*Lexikon der österreichischen Provenienzforschung*),[248] whose purpose is to make the "research results accessible" and help "promote international cooperation between researchers, interested parties and victims."[249]

3.4.2.4.2 France The Mission for Research and Restitution of Spoliated Cultural Property between 1933 and 1945 (*la Mission de recherche et de restitution des biens culturels spoliés entre 1933 et 1945*) (M2RS) was created in 2019 by an order of the French minister of culture,[250] following a request by the prime minister to improve the research and restitution of art stolen from Jewish families.[251]

The M2RS is a service of the General Secretariat of the Ministry of Culture (Legal and International Affairs Service), with jurisdiction over "disposals of cultural property in France during the Second World War, whether the property is located or not" in France today, and the "spoliation of cultural property in Europe between 1933 and 1945 when the cultural property that was looted is now in France, particularly in public collections or in the custody of national museums" (MNR).[252] The M2RS has two main objectives:

> Define, coordinate and implement research and restitution policy, and contribute to public and professional awareness;
>
> Study, in conjunction with the cultural institutions concerned, individual cases of spoliation of cultural property, on the initiative of families, cultural institutions or on its own initiative, with a view to achieving a measure of reparation (restitution or compensation).[253]

---

[248] COMMISSION FOR PROVENANCE RESEARCH, LEXICON OF AUSTRIAN PROVENANCE RESEARCH, www.lexikon-provenienzforschung.org/en (last visited Feb. 1, 2025).

[249] Bundesministerium Kunst, Kultur, öffentlicher Dienst und Sport, *Commission for Provenance Research*, *supra* note 245.

[250] Arrêté du 16 avril 2019 portant création de la mission de recherche et de restitution des biens culturels spoliés entre 1933 et 1945, JORF n°0091 du 17 avril 2019 (Fr.), www.legifrance.gouv.fr/jorf/id/JORFTEXT000038383357.

[251] Ministère de la Culture, *Mission de recherche et de restitution des biens culturels spoliés entre 1933 et 1945*, www.culture.gouv.fr/nous-connaitre/organisation-du-ministere/le-secretariat-general/mission-de-recherche-et-de-restitution-des-biens-culturels-spolies-entre-1933-et-1945#:~:text=La%20Mission%20de%20recherche%20et,des%20affaires%20juridiques%20et%20internationales. (Fr.) (last visited Feb. 1, 2025).

[252] *Id.* For the Musées Nationaux Récupération (National Museums Recovery), or "MNR," *see supra* notes 12–14.

[253] Ministère de la Culture, *supra* note 251.

Following the provenance research of individual cases, the M2RS sends the results to the Commission for the Restitution of Property and Compensation of Victims of Anti-Semitic Spoliations (*Commission pour la restitution des biens et l'indemnisation des victimes de spoliations anti-sémites* – CIVS),[254] the French restitution committee. The committee's powers, organizational structure, and deliberative processes were significantly expanded and reformed in early 2024 by a decree of the French minister of culture,[255] as discussed in detail in Chapter 6.

3.4.2.4.3 The Netherlands Established in September 2018, the Expert Centre Restitution (ECR), which is part of the NIOD Institute for War, Holocaust and Genocide Studies in Amsterdam, conducts Holocaust-era provenance research for cultural property.[256] It does so at the request of the Advisory Committee on the Assessment of Restitution Applications for Items of Cultural Value and the Second World War (*De Adviescommissie Restitutieverzoeken Cultuurgoederen en Tweede Wereldoorlog*), the Dutch restitution committee established in 2001[257] for the purpose of assessing individual restitution applications. The ECR may also conduct such provenance research if both the possessor of a cultural object and the party seeking restitution jointly request it (through the Cultural Heritage Agency, which is part of the Ministry of Education, Culture and Science).[258]

In addition to provenance research in the context of individual restitution claims, the ECR also engages in broader research on history, cultural heritage, and art theft – primarily in the context of the persecution of Jews during the Nazi era but also in areas such as colonialism and international heritage politics – by collaborating with museums, archives, universities, and research institutes.[259]

---

[254] Premier Ministre, *Commission for the Restitution of Property and the Compensation of Victims of Anti-semitic Spoliations*, www.civs.gouv.fr/ (last visited Feb. 1, 2025).

[255] Décret n° 2024-11 du 5 janvier 2024 instituant une commission pour la restitution des biens et l'indemnisation des victimes de spoliations antisémites et pris en application des articles L. 115-3, L. 115-4 et L. 451-10-1 du code du patrimoine, JORF n°0004 du 6 janvier 2024 (Fr.), www.legifrance.gouv.fr/jorf/id/JORFTEXT000048865626.

[256] NIOD Institute for War, Holocaust and Genocide Studies, *Expert Centre Restitution*, www.niod.nl/en/research/expert-centre-restitution (last visited Feb. 1, 2025).

[257] Restitutions Committee, *Looted Art and Restitution in the Netherlands: A Historical Overview*, www.restitutiecommissie.nl/en/history/ (last visited Feb. 1, 2025).

[258] Rijkdienst voor het Cultureel Erfgoed, Ministrie van Ondrwijs, Cultuur en Wetenschap, *Cultuurgoederen WOII (1933–1945)*, www.cultureelerfgoed.nl/onderwerpen/cultuur goederen-wo2-1933–1945 (Neth.) (last visited Feb. 1, 2025).

[259] NIOD Institute for War, Holocaust and Genocide Studies, *supra* note 256.

Figure 3.2   Cover page of Newsletter No. 18, Network of European Restitution
Committees on Nazi-Looted Art (Aug. 2024).
Source: By permission of the Spoliation Advisory Panel.

The three central agencies for provenance research also share information and collaborate through the Network of European Restitution
Committees on Nazi-Looted Art, established in 2018 by the restitution
committees in Austria, France, Germany, the Netherlands, and the United
Kingdom.[260]

The network publishes a newsletter[261] that addresses, alongside
the work of restitution committees, various issues related to provenance research (see Figure 3.2). As explained by the then-chairman of
the French restitution committee CIVS in the network's first newsletter, published in March 2019, "[b]ased on the exchange and sharing
of information and know-how, our Network offers a new response to

---

[260] Restitutions Committee, *Network of European Restitution Committees on Nazi-Looted
Art*, www.restitutiecommissie.nl/en/newsletter-network-european-committees/ (last visited Feb. 1, 2025).

[261] *See id.* for a list and digital copies of all newsletters published by the network.

the effectiveness of provenance research and the moral requirement of 'clean museums.'"[262]

As shown below, the professionalization and systematization of Nazi-era provenance research, especially when conducted through central agencies such as those in Austria, France, and the Netherlands, may serve to broaden the scope of legal, professional, and ethical norms on provenance research to other contexts, and involve a growing number of actors in the global cultural property landscape.

3.4.3 Moving beyond Holocaust-Era Research: Colonial and Other Contexts

In early 2024, Germany and France announced that they would jointly allocate approximately 2.1 million euros over a period of three years to further research into the provenance of African heritage objects in the collections of their national museums. This sum is designated to fund research on objects from anywhere in sub-Saharan Africa, although priority is expected to be given to states that were colonized by France and Germany, such as Togo and Cameroon. The provenance research will be led by mixed French and German teams comprising experts from academia and museums.[263]

This joint venture is expected to move forward the systematic provenance research of colonial-era cultural items, which have been the object of increasing cross-border attention in legal, policy, and market contexts, as explored in previous chapters with regard to the Benin Bronzes and beyond.[264]

Alongside the French 2018 Sarr–Savoy report[265] and the 2023 report on "returnability criteria" commissioned by President Emmanuel Macron[266] – which will be surveyed in Chapter 6 – Germany has also

---

[262] Michel Jeannoutot, *Editorial*, 1 NETWORK OF EUR. RESTITUTION COMMITTEES ON NAZI-LOOTED ART 1 (Mar. 2019), www.provenienzforschung.gv.at/wp-content/uploads/Newsletter_Network_Nr-1_2019-03.pdf.

[263] Philip Oltermann, *France and Germany to Research Provenance of African Objects in National Museums*, THE GUARDIAN, Jan. 19, 2024.

[264] *See* Chapter 1, Section 1.1.

[265] FELWINE SARR & BÉNÉDICTE SAVOY, THE RESTITUTION OF AFRICAN CULTURAL HERITAGE. TOWARD A NEW RELATIONAL ETHICS (2018), www.about-africa.de/images/sonstiges/2018/sarr_savoy_en.pdf (hereinafter: "Sarr–Savoy Report").

[266] Jean-Luc Martinez, *Rapport À l'attention de M. le Président de la République, Patrimoine partagé : universalité, restitutions et circulation des oeuvres d'art: Vers une législation et une doctrine françaises sur les "critères de restituabilité" pour les biens culturels* (2023) (Fr.), www.vie-publique.fr/files/rapport/pdf/289235.pdf (hereinafter: "2023 Report").

been increasingly focusing on provenance research of colonial-era collections.

In March 2019, the German federal government, states (*Länder*), and local governments adopted the Framework Principles for Dealing with Collections from Colonial Contexts.[267] In October of that year, the governments decided to establish a "German Contact Point for Collections from Colonial Contexts" to implement one of the priority measures of the Framework Principles.[268]

This contact point aims to serve individuals and institutions from the countries and societies of origin, constituting "the first, central point of contact for all questions concerning collections from colonial contexts in Germany."[269] The German Contact Point will carry out various tasks, including "providing information and advice on collections from colonial context in Germany and related topics" and "collecting, organising, documenting, publishing and evaluating statistically pertinent data and information."[270] The Framework Principles and German Contact Point serve as an anchor for various collaborations between German and African professionals, including the 2022 establishment of the Digital Benin online database, analyzed in Chapter 4.[271]

Other European countries are also promoting provenance research on colonial-era objects in public collections. Dutch museums, such as the National Museum of World Cultures and the Rijksmuseum in Amsterdam, were among the first to introduce provenance research for their colonial-era collections.[272] In 2021, a consortium of nine Dutch museums and research institutes, together with Vrije Universiteit in Amsterdam, launched a 4.5 million euro project – the Pressing Matter program – to develop practical guidelines for museums on colonial

---

[267] Auswärtiges Amt [Federal Foreign Office], *Framework Principles for Dealing with Collections from Colonial Contexts Agreed by the Federal Government Commissioner for Culture and the Media, the Federal Foreign Office Minister of State for International Cultural Policy, the Cultural Affairs Ministers of the Länder and the Municipal Umbrella Organisations* (Mar. 13, 2019), www.auswaertiges-amt.de/blob/2210152/ b2731f8b59210c77c68177cdcd3d03de/190412-stm-m-sammlungsgut-kolonial-kontexten-data.pdf (hereinafter: "Framework Principles").

[268] GERMAN CONTACT POINT FOR COLLECTIONS FROM COLONIAL CONTEXTS, www .cp3c.org/ (last visited Feb. 1, 2025).

[269] *Id.*

[270] *Id.*

[271] *See* Chapter 4, Section 4.1.

[272] Catherine Hickley, *Forging Ahead with Historic Restitution Plans, Dutch Museums Will Launch €4.5m Project to Develop a Practical Guide on Colonial Collections*, THE ART NEWSPAPER, Mar. 10, 2021.

collections.[273] The four-year program is funded primarily by the Dutch National Science Agenda.[274] Efforts to engage in provenance research on colonial-era objects, as part of a growing commitment to restitution to source states in appropriate cases, are also underway in Austria and Switzerland.[275]

Perhaps the most comprehensive initiative to date in consolidating various historical contexts of provenance research into a single framework – and correspondingly, a single digital database – is Proveana, the new research database of the German Lost Art Foundation.[276] This project represents a pivotal development in the global framing of cultural property law, which is the subject of Chapter 4.

Proveana brings together four areas of research: Nazi-looted art, cultural property displaced as a result of war (wartime losses), expropriation of cultural property in the Soviet occupation zone and the GDR (East Germany), and cultural goods and collections from colonial contexts.[277] As outlined in Chapter 4, the Proveana database facilitates searches for people, corporations, events, collections, provenance information, objects, and other documentary sources. It includes the contents of the Lost Art Database and links to additional databases. The primary objective of Proveana is to "support provenance research through documenting historical information, thereby making it more transparent and contributing to the solution of unresolved cases."[278]

Indeed, transparency is probably the term that best typifies this and other recent provenance research initiatives. As Chapter 4 demonstrates in the context of digital databases, transparency is the epitome of a profound change within the realm of cultural property law, policy, and markets. Transparency is arguably the defining feature in the evolution of norms on due diligence and provenance research, marking a significant shift from the early days of secrecy, opacity, and anonymity.

---

[273] Id.
[274] Pressing Matter, *Ownership, Value and the Question of Colonial Heritage in Museums*, https://pressingmatter.nl/ (last visited Feb. 1, 2025).
[275] Catherine Hickley, *Austrian Government to Propose Law on Returning Museum Objects Acquired in a Colonial Context*, THE ART NEWSPAPER, June 20, 2023; Hickley, *supra* note 244 (reporting on Switzerland).
[276] German Lost Art Foundation, *Proveana – Provenance Research Database, Accessible Data for Improved Provenance Research*, www.proveana.de/en/start (last visited Feb. 1, 2025).
[277] Id.
[278] Id.

4

The Transformative Role of Digital Databases

4.1 Digital Benin

In November 2022, a new online database, "Digital Benin," was launched.[1] As of early 2025, it collects information about 5,285 historic Benin objects from 136 museums and other institutions across twenty countries, and places this data for the first time in a single virtual space, accessible and searchable to the public, with a particular eye toward residents in Africa, including younger generations – which explains why this digital database was designed in a mobile-friendly way (see Figure 4.1).[2]

Digital Benin marks a turning point not only for the particular group of assets known as the Benin Bronzes[3] but, more generally, for the future of dealing with the various aspects of cultural property. As noted in a story published about Digital Benin in the *Financial Times*, supporters of this project believe it will fundamentally "change the debate over millions of other contested items, from the British Museum's Parthenon Marbles to human remains acquired across centuries."[4]

While it remains to be seen whether this will indeed be the result of the project, this chapter shows that the use of digital technology for the purpose of collecting information – much of which has been hitherto kept purposefully or practically unknown to the public, or dispersed among multiple sources – processing it, and presenting it in a user-friendly way, already has discernible effects on professional norms, public policy, and legal practice. This chapter seeks to demonstrate that digital databases

---

[1] Digital Benin, *Explore Digital Benin* (created by K. Agbontaen-Eghafona et al.), https://digitalbenin.org/ (last visited Feb. 1, 2025).

[2] Digital Benin, *Documentation, Introduction* (Dr. Anne Luther), https://digitalbenin.org/documentation/introduction (last visited Feb. 1, 2025) (hereinafter: "Luther, Introduction").

[3] *See* Chapter 1, Section 1.1.

[4] Josh Spero & Aanu Adeoye, *The Benin Bronzes and the Road to Restitution*, FINANCIAL TIMES, Nov. 4, 2022.

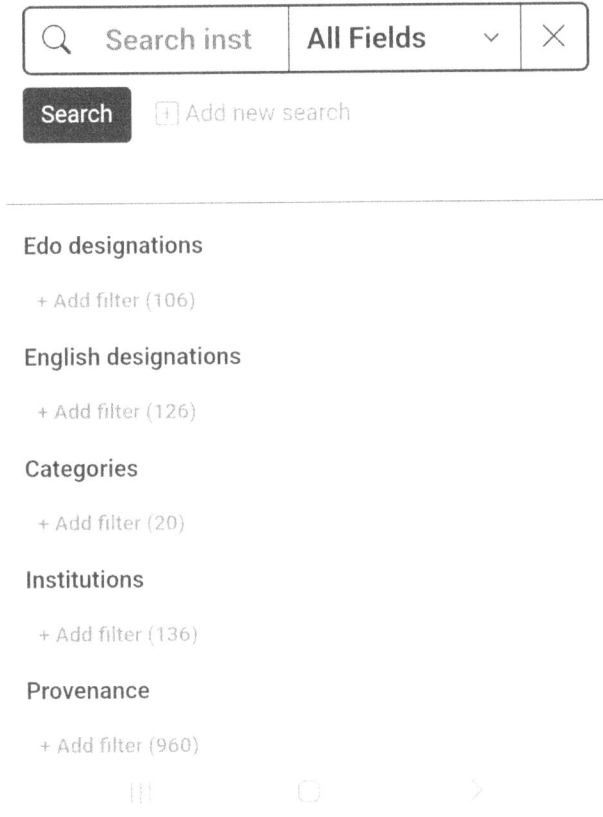

Figure 4.1   Screenshots from the mobile-phone version of the Digital Benin database.
Source: By permission of the Digital Benin project.

Institutions

Study each institutional collection of Benin objects and sort the list of institutions by name, object count and country. Selecting an institution gives access to an introduction page with details about the institution, the collected data and an overview of object groups in the collection. Read more

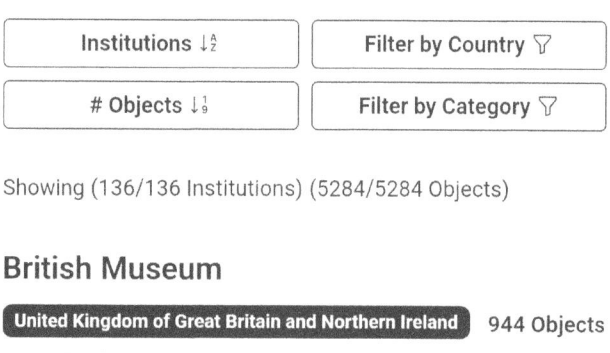

Figure 4.1   cont.

on cultural property can (1) facilitate fact-finding in specific disputes; (2) serve as a professional or even legal benchmark for abiding by "due diligence" and similar norms; (3) enable information-sharing as a basis for "just and fair solutions" in the context of Nazi-looted artifacts, as well as in colonial contexts and other circumstances that address past wrongs; and (4) promote a general value of transparency in a field previously dominated by opacity and secrecy.

Digital Benin was developed within a relatively short period of two years. It is a collaborative effort of principal investigators and other researchers, developers, designers, and data stewards, coordinated by the Museum am Rothenbaum (MARKK) in Hamburg. The Digital Benin project, funded by the German Ernst von Siemens Foundation, also set up offices in Benin City in Nigeria.[5]

The ability to identify the 136 institutions across twenty countries that hold Benin Bronzes and to gather information from them – with many such institutions keeping such information private up until that point – should be credited not only to previous work done by academic researchers and museum professionals but also to the general change of political winds in the global setting about cultural property in general, and the Benin Bronzes in particular, as shown in Chapter 1.[6] The announcement by French president Emmanuel Macron in his 2017 visit to Burkina Faso that he wanted, within five years, "the conditions to be met for the temporary or permanent restitution of African heritage to Africa"[7] – with the French Senate approving in 2020 the return of twenty-seven cultural items to Benin and Senegal[8] – alongside the public debate about the construction of the museum for non-European collections as part of the Humboldt Forum in Berlin,[9] and other developments, paved the way for persuading institutions to provide data about their Benin Bronzes'

---

[5] Luther, Introduction, *supra* note 2.

[6] *See* Chapter 1, Section 1.1.

[7] *See* Spero & Adeoye, *supra* note 4. *See also* Chapter 6, Section 6.2.

[8] *France to Return Artifacts to Benin and Senegal within a Year*, ARTFORUM INT'L, Nov. 5, 2020.

[9] This museum, opened in September 2021, has about 20,000 items on display. It combines the collections of the Museum für Asiatische Kunst (Asian Art Museum) and the Ethnologisches Museum (Ethnological Museum), which have an estimated total of about 500,000 items – many of which were forcibly taken during the colonial expansion. *See* Adrian Murphy, *Opening of Collections at Humboldt Forum Heralds New Era for Museum Provenance*, MUSEUM NEXT, Sept. 23, 2021, www.museumnext.com/article/opening-of-collections-at-humboldt-forum-heralds-new-era-for-museum-provenance/.

holdings.[10] With the exception of items held in private hands,[11] Digital Benin is a comprehensive database.

A key methodological feature of constructing the Digital Benin database – with corresponding substantive implications – is one of preserving "the data structure of each institution by displaying their distinct data setting of information on the platform while giving our users the possibility to search across all datasets."[12] Namely, instead of seeking to standardize the raw data and the way it is expressed and presented, so that it would comprise a single dataset, Digital Benin shows the data (ranging from images and 3D scans to text-based information), as it was received from the 136 institutions, alongside the digitalization of about 1,200 physical catalog cards from the Nigerian national museums in Benin City, Lagos, and Owo.[13] Working with multiple datasets through a metadata-linking process that was conducted inductively and manually (meaning that all the data sent was examined by the project's staff in order to develop connecting categories based on similarities of the values in the respective fields), the examination led to thirty-seven fields that showed similarly across all datasets.[14] All metadata fields that are not linked are still accessible in the "full text search" across the datasets because they are connected by at least one field, the "Object IDs."[15]

The methodologies and work processes employed in the Digital Benin project show that such an endeavor is "repeatable, scalable and global," such that, according to Dr. Anne Luther, an expert in digital humanities and the chief coordinator of the Digital Benin project, with a "budget of 5 million euros, five years, and an ambitious team," one could track "all objects in all institutions."[16]

Moreover, as a matter of guiding future professional norms, public policy, and potentially legal reforms, Digital Benin is also instrumental in reinvigorating the discussion about restitution of colonial-era objects and items from other contexts, which will be explored in detail in Chapter 6.

---

[10] See Spero & Adeoye, *supra* note 4.

[11] Barnaby Phillips, *Can Digital Benin Reconnect Future Nigerians with Their History*, ARTREVIEW, Nov. 16, 2022 (arguing that at least fifteen objects apparently looted in 1897 are in private hands, with some of them owned by descendants of a British officer who took part in the expedition).

[12] Luther, Introduction, *supra* note 2.

[13] *Id.*

[14] *Id.* (detailing the list of thirty-seven fields, ordered under five categories: "Object Information," "Object Production," "Provenance," "Object Context," and "Museum Context").

[15] *Id.*

[16] Spero & Adeoye, *supra* note 4 (interviewing and quoting Dr. Anne Luther).

As discussed in Chapter 1, the forces that drive destination countries, and cultural institutions within them, to restitute objects to source countries – or not to do so – go well beyond formal legal decrees resulting from international conventions, court decisions, or arbitration awards. The changing balance of power among countries, at least in the context of "cultural diplomacy," has led countries and institutions to return artifacts to source countries, heirs of dispossessed persons, or indigenous groups, even in cases where there is no legal cause of action or a formal process of fact-finding that proves the existence of an object-specific wrongdoing. That said, fact-finding matters – even for disputes or other dealings that do not follow a purely legalistic approach.

In fact, much of the reluctance by many museums and other institutions to return items to source countries has been grounded in the assertion that there is no record that clearly establishes the existence of a past wrong related to the specific item (in contrast to a general recognition of historic injustice). Consider, for example, the contention that has been made by Britain that Lord Elgin acted with permission of the Ottoman Empire in taking away the Parthenon Marbles.[17] While refuting (or, rather, validating) such a factual claim may no longer matter from a strict legal sense, getting the facts right does make a difference also in considering political and moral arguments.

The Digital Benin project can lead to a fact-based approach to the Benin Bronzes, and beyond. By undertaking the effort to explore and publish the provenance of each one of the items that ended up in museums and other institutions, the fact-based inquiry not only demonstrates the general value of accessible information about an object's provenance but may also have an impact on public-policy decisions and ethical approaches developed regarding their potential restitution.

Interestingly, current information shows that only 1,427 objects are "directly related in the museum data to the British colonial campaign on Benin," namely, that there is specific evidence that shows that these items were looted by the British army in 1897, and "this implies that there are significant provenance gaps for over three thousand objects in the data

---

[17] For a recent academic study that seeks to refute this British claim, *see* David Rudenstine, *Trophies for the Empire: The Epic Dispute between Greece and England over the Parthenon Sculptures in the British Museum*, 39 CARDOZO ARTS & ENT. L.J. 377, 443–45 (2021) (arguing that the 1816 British Parliamentary Committee that recommended the purchase of Lord Elgin's collection by the British government committed fraud by knowingly altering an Italian document, then central – and still central – to whether the Ottomans granted Elgin permission to take the sculptures).

that museums have provided to date."[18] At the same time, examining the provenance of each one of the items included in the database is instrumental in dealing with contentions, by which some of the Benin Bronzes' items that ended up in the museums may have not originated in the 1897 looting but are rather items that had either circulated in Europe before 1897, commodified or displaced in the years following 1897 (i.e., not as a direct result of the British loot), or were instead produced after 1897.[19]

By examining the specific provenance of each one of the objects, Digital Benin no longer allows museums and other stakeholders to hide behind a general mist of doubt or ignorance, which may correspondingly make a countercase against restitution. While gaps in information will continue to exist, at least regarding the items for which provenance research does not attest specifically to a historic wrongful act, such fact-finding – made publicly accessible via the online database – can and should play a role in considering the policy decisions taken on political or moral grounds.

This is so especially because the range of options for dealing with such past wrongs (while no longer remediable in a strict legal sense) goes beyond either physical restitution or doing nothing.

As noted by Godwin Obaseki, the governor of Edo state, in a 2022 interview, Nigeria does not seek to physically possess every artifact held in foreign museums, because these items serve as "ambassadors" for the country's past that the "rest of the world still needs to know about."[20] At the same time, Nigeria does seek recognition of the underlying ownership of these items, even if this is done mostly to set the record straight, such that it would be understood that "the pieces are owned by the people of Nigeria. It came from the Edo people in Nigeria. That is the basic minimum. Where they're held and kept becomes secondary."[21] Fact-finding done through provenance research, and made available via a digital database, is thus essential for policymaking.

Building on these initial insights from the Digital Benin project, this chapter moves to analyze how the emergence of digital databases on cultural property, and particularly those that can be accessed by parties across national borders for purposes of both data insertion and data

---

[18] Digital Benin, *Documentation, Provenance* (Dr. Felicity Bodenstein), https://digitalbenin.org/documentation/provenance (last visited Feb. 1, 2025) (hereinafter: "Bodenstein, Provenance").

[19] *See id.*

[20] Spero & Adeoye, *supra* note 4 (interviewing Godwin Obaseki, the governor of Edo state). *See also* Chapter 6, Section 6.2.

[21] *Id.*

retrieval, can impact cross-border professional and ethical norms and, consequently, legal norms.

This chapter offers a first-of-its-kind taxonomy of the growing number and scope of coverage of cultural property databases. It then identifies the potential role of such databases in facilitating fact-finding, serving as a benchmark for "due diligence" and similar norms, enabling information-sharing as a basis for crafting ethically driven norms, and promoting the key value of transparency.

4.2   Digitally Accessible Databases on Cultural Property

Recent advances in computing technology, data analysis, and development of digital networks are changing the way that data is collected, stored, and searched – and this has a profound impact on cultural property. While the long-term, systemic impact of digital art or the use of nonfungible tokens and blockchain technology in the field of cultural property remains to be seen,[22] one can already discern a fundamental change that is taking place due to digital databases that are developed and expanded at an accelerated pace by a multitude of private and public entities.[23]

As explained in Chapter 3, alongside the more traditional role of provenance research as an academic and professional enterprise aimed at emphasizing "career highlights" of the artifact, the current focus of information-gathering about the history of the artifact lies in reconstructing the chain of ownership or possession of the item in order to identify potential problems, such as theft, looting, or illegal transition across borders.[24] Provenance thus becomes inherently related to crime detection, enforcement of international and national legal rules on ownership and control over cultural assets, and the duty of due diligence (or similar norms) in buying or otherwise dealing with such artifacts. Some of these databases can and do promote various goals simultaneously.

---

[22] *See, e.g.,* Andrew R. Chow, *NFTs Are Shaking Up the Art World – But They Could Change So Much More,* TIME, Mar. 22, 2021; Gareth Harris & Ben Munster, *Italian Government Plans to Halt Digital Sales of Masterpieces from Its Major Museums,* THE ART NEWSPAPER, July 8, 2022; Dorian Batycka, *From Ordinals to Ownership: Christie's Explores New Frontiers of Blockchain-Based Provenance,* THE ART NEWSPAPER, Oct. 11, 2024.

[23] Jason Sousa & Ariane Moser, *Data and Databases in Provenance Research, in* PROVENANCE RESEARCH TODAY: PRINCIPLES, PRACTICE, PROBLEMS 85, 85–86 (Arthur Tompkins ed., 2020).

[24] Jacques Schumacher, *British Museums and Holocaust-Era Provenance Research, in* MUSEUMS AND THE HOLOCAUST 34, 35 (Ruth Redmond-Cooper ed., 2nd ed., 2021).

While the multitude of such databases do not lend themselves to a neat division into distinct categories, this section offers a general outline of the different types of cultural property databases.

4.2.1   International/National Databases for Crime Detection

The first broad category of digital databases is one that aims to prevent or detect acts of theft, looting, or the illicit transfer of cultural property across borders (i.e., without a valid export license, when this is required by the laws of the state of origin). The most prominent database, which applies generally to different types of cultural property, such as artwork, historical documents, ancient musical instruments, and archaeological artifacts, is INTERPOL's Stolen Works of Art database (operated as part of the "Psyche Project").[25] As of 2025, this database includes over 52,000 items.[26] INTERPOL's database enables national law enforcement agencies and other entities to report cases of theft, looting, and so forth. At the other end, it allows registered users – which are not limited to law enforcement agencies at potential destination states but may also include museums, art dealers, collectors, and all other interested persons – to search INTERPOL's database prior to dealing with a certain cultural artifact. Searching INTERPOL's database is viewed as a standard benchmark in exercising the duty of due diligence or due care when such a norm is required under relevant national or international rules.[27] In 2021, INTERPOL also launched the ID-Art mobile app that enables users to search the database.[28]

In addition to the role of INTERPOL's database in detecting crimes that have already been committed in regard to particularly identified objects, with the purpose of locating and returning such objects – other databases have been developed to alert the key actors in the global market for art and antiquities about the types of cultural objects and places of origin that may be especially prone to cases of theft or illegal trafficking. Thus, the International Council of Museums (ICOM) established the

---

[25] INTERPOL, *Stolen Works of Art Database*, www.interpol.int/en/Crimes/Cultural-heritage-crime/Stolen-Works-of-Art-Database (last visited Feb. 1, 2025).

[26] *Id.*

[27] *See, e.g.*, Birgit Kurtz et al., *Standards of Care in the Art Market: A Comparative Study on What Is Expected of Buyers, Sellers, and Consignors in the United States, Germany and England*, 21 ART ANTIQUITY & L. 1, 18–19 (2016).

[28] INTERPOL, *ID-Art Mobile App*, www.interpol.int/en/Crimes/Cultural-heritage-crime/ID-Art-mobile-app (last visited Feb. 1, 2025).

"Red Lists Database,"[29] which includes various types of "objects at risk" in certain places, such as countries that are in the midst of a military conflict or ones that lack effective law enforcement to prevent looting. These lists are intended also to curb the motivation of organized crime or terrorist groups to engage in the illicit trade of objects for profit-making.[30]

Alongside databases that focus on the cross-border illicit trafficking in cultural property, several countries have developed their own databases as part of their effort to fight illegal activities pertaining to cultural property and, more generally, to protect their national cultural heritage.

In 1969 Italy established the Carabinieri Command for the Protection of Cultural Heritage (*Comando Carabinieri per la Tutela del Patrimonio Culturale* – TPC).[31] Pursuant to a legislative decree from 2004, the TPC established the "TPC Stolen Works of Art Database" (*La Banca Dati dei beni culturali illecitamente sottratti*), which contains details about over 1.2 million stolen cultural artifacts in Italy.[32] Access to the database is available to law enforcement agencies as part of INTERPOL's Psyche Project.[33] The Carabinieri has also started to use artificial intelligence (AI) tools, including a system for the detection of stolen works of art, which uses AI technology to search for objects that are listed for sale online. According to information provided by the Carabinieri, investigations based on such AI technology resulted in the return of over 105,000 objects at a total estimated value of 264 million euros in 2023.[34] Alongside Italy, national law enforcement databases about stolen cultural artifacts exist in Austria, Belgium, the Netherlands, Spain, and other countries.[35]

---

[29] International Council of Museums (ICOM), *Red Lists Database*, https://icom.museum/en/resources/red-lists/ (last visited Feb. 1, 2025).

[30] *See, e.g.*, ICOM, Emergency Red List of Iraqi Antiquities at Risk (2008) (explaining that "cultural heritage in Iraq has suffered seriously as a result of war. Many objects have been looted and stolen from museums and archaeological sites and risk appearing on the market through illicit trafficking").

[31] The Carabinieri Command for the Protection of Cultural Heritage (TPC), *About TPC*, https://tpcweb.carabinieri.it/SitoPubblico/home (last visited Feb. 1, 2025).

[32] TPC, *Search by Data and Images*, https://tpcweb.carabinieri.it/SitoPubblico/home/funzioni/ricerca-dati-immagini (last visited Feb. 1, 2025).

[33] TPC, *Psyche*, https://tpcweb.carabinieri.it/SitoPubblico/home/informazioni/psyche (last visited Feb. 1, 2025).

[34] Carlie Porterfield, *More than 600 Artefacts Worth a Total of €60m Are Repatriated to Italy from the US*, The Art Newspaper, May 31, 2024.

[35] ENSP Team, *Stolen Works of Art Databases for Law Enforcement Agencies at European level*, Netcher Social Platform for Cultural Heritage, Nov. 17, 2020, https://netcher.eu/project-news/stolen-works-of-art-databases-for-law-enforcement-agencies-at-european-level/.

In addition to databases created and maintained by law enforcement agencies, the use of digital databases, and digital technology more generally, to detect stolen cultural items involves other bodies, such as academic institutions and nonprofit organizations.

One such example is the Circulating Artefacts (CircArt) project, launched in April 2018 and completed in February 2021, which brought together law enforcement agencies, cultural organizations and universities in Egypt and Sudan, auction houses, and dealers, and was funded by the British Council and the British government's Department for Digital, Culture, Media and Sport.[36] Aimed to "assist in the fight against the widespread global trade in illegally sourced antiquities, with special focus on those from Egypt and Sudan," CircArt created a digital system that researched more than 50,000 objects advertised on the open market and on social media.[37] At least 15 percent of these researched objects appeared to be traceable to unauthorized excavations that happened after the introduction of state patrimony laws in the relevant source countries.[38]

A different kind of initiative is the Antiquities Trafficking and Heritage Anthropology Research (ATHAR) project, led by independent experts, which monitors groups engaged in transnational trafficking.[39] The ATHAR project is particularly critical of digital platforms, such as Facebook, for not taking enough action to prevent them being used as a channel for illicit trade. Thus, a 2019 study identified ninety-five Facebook groups serving for antiquities trafficking, with a global reach.[40]

Yet another independent digital database, launched in June 2024,[41] is the online Museum of Looted Antiquities, which is a "virtual gallery that collects, displays and studies looted antiquities that have been repatriated since 1950."[42] Because this database presents objects that have already been restituted to source countries, it does not have a direct crime-prevention effect. It seeks to preserve information about objects that is

---

[36] British Museum, *Circulating Artefacts (CircArt)* www.britishmuseum.org/our-work/departments/egypt-and-sudan/circulating-artefacts (last visited Feb. 1, 2025).

[37] *Id.*

[38] *Id.*

[39] ATHAR Project, *About the ATHAR Project*, http://atharproject.org/ (last visited Feb. 1, 2025).

[40] ATHAR Project, *Facebook's Black Market in Antiquities* (2019), http://atharproject.org/report2019/.

[41] Alexandra Bregman, *Jason Felch Launches Museum of Looted Antiquities*, FORBES, July 4, 2024.

[42] Museum of Looted Antiquities (MOLA), *Welcome to the Museum of Looted Antiquities*, https://mola.omeka.net/ (last visited Feb. 1, 2025).

often lost when an item goes back to a source country and serves to collect "unique data about the illicit antiquities trade that is essential to understanding a black market that the United Nations recently recognized as a global security issue."[43]

4.2.2   Private Databases Offering Services for Due Diligence

Alongside the national and international network of databases operated by law enforcement agencies and other entities with the goal of detecting and combating illegal trading in cultural artifacts, a few private companies offer paid services to the different actors in the market for art and antiquities, such as museums, auction houses, and private collectors. Such companies offer market actors search and research services, which are anchored in a digital database, while allowing owners of stolen or missing artifacts to report the theft or loss at no cost, so that these items would be registered on the database. Such databases are therefore based on numerous sources, including those of INTERPOL and national law enforcement agencies, alongside reporting by victims of looting or theft, insurance companies, and other public and private actors.

The world's largest private database of lost, stolen, and looted art, antiquities, and collectibles is that of the Art Loss Register (ALR),[44] which includes over 700,000 items. While services are offered free of charge to law enforcement agencies and nation-states, the ALR offers paid services to potential vendors and purchasers, as well as to other interested parties. At the end of the database search, and other research done, the company issues an "ALR certificate" that details the results of the search.[45] Although such a document has no formal status as such, it can serve the practical purpose of alerting the customer against a potential problem in the chain of title and, accordingly, of attesting to an effort made by the customer to exercise due diligence when a dispute arises later.

That said, concerns have been raised about the potential manipulation of the ALR database by sophisticated illicit actors.[46] For example, by requesting searches for freshly looted items, such as recently illegally excavated antiquities that dealers know will not yet be recorded in the

---

[43] *Id.*

[44] Art Loss Register, *About Us*, www.artloss.com/about-us/ (last visited Feb. 1, 2025).

[45] Art Loss Register, *Search*, www.artloss.com/search/ (last visited Feb. 1, 2025).

[46] Alexandra Tremayne-Pengelly, *Every Act Collector Needs This Database. But Is It Being Manipulated by Thieves?* OBSERVER, Sept. 27, 2022, https://observer.com/2022/09/every-art-collector-needs-this-database-but-is-it-being-manipulated-by-thieves/.

ALR database, some traffickers have been able to obtain certificates stating a specific item was not found in the database of lost or stolen items.[47] Trafficking rings can thus insert the item into the "legitimate" market, claiming it has been cleared by an ALR certificate. This requires the ALR company, as well as dealers, buyers, and other market actors, to be very cautious in, respectively, issuing, or relying on, an ALR certificate for items for which there is no record of provenance.

Another prominent private database is Artive.[48] This too facilitates the reporting of cases of looting or theft for registration on the database, while offering paid services for provenance and due diligence research. However, in 2025 Artive announced that it would discontinue its services.

4.2.3   Theme-Specific Databases: Nazi-Looted Assets and Colonial Contexts

4.2.3.1   The Lost Art Database and Other Holocaust-Era Databases

A prominent setting in which national and international norms pertaining to cultural property have been leading to an extensive flow of information through provenance research and digitally accessible databases concerns the growing effort to provide restitution or compensation for property wrongfully seized between 1933 and 1945 from victims of the Nazi persecution. Beyond provenance research conducted in the context of specific disputes by heirs of victims, museums, or administrative agencies charged with such a task – especially in the European countries that established restitution committees, as discussed in Chapter 6 – digital databases play an important role in facilitating a broader-based compilation and dissemination of information from various sources about potentially looted artifacts. As stated in the 2009 Terezin Declaration, "[i]n particular, recognizing that restitution cannot be accomplished without knowledge of potentially looted art and cultural property, we stress the importance for all stakeholders to continue and support intensified systematic provenance research … and where relevant to make the results of this research, including ongoing updates, available via the internet, with due regard to privacy rules and regulations."[49]

---

[47] Id.

[48] Artive, *Due Diligence and Research*, www.artive.org/database/ (last visited Feb. 1, 2025).

[49] U.S. Department of State, *Terezin Declaration on Holocaust Era Assets and Related Issues* (June 30, 2009), "Nazi Confiscation and Looted Art" §2, www.state.gov/prague-holocaust-era-assets-conference-terezin-declaration/.

Consequently, various databases have been set up by national and supranational agencies. A prominent database is the Lost Art Database (*Lost Art-Datenbank*),[50] which was initially launched by the German government in 2000 and has been operated since its establishment in 2015 by the German Lost Art Foundation (*Deutsches Zentrum Kulturgutverluste*).[51] The Lost Art Database contains "search requests/object reports" in which institutions or individuals ask for current information about objects taken from them during the Nazi era, as well as "found-object reports" that include details about found cultural objects known to have been illegally taken from their owners, alongside reports on other items with an incomplete or uncertain provenance, suggesting the possibility of illegitimate dispossession between 1933 and 1945.[52]

In July 2023, the Federal Court of Justice (*Bundesgerichtshof* – BGH), Germany's highest court of civil and criminal jurisdiction, issued a decision by which the registration of an artwork in the Lost Art Database, if based on true facts, does not constitute an infringement of the property rights of the artwork's current owner/possessor, even if the latter has a valid property right to the item under German law. Accordingly, the BGH rejected a claim by the current owner against the party that registered the historical facts about the item and ruled that this entry should not be removed.[53] While the BGH ruling is formally limited to the Lost Art Database and to the parties to the dispute, its potential implications may extend to other databases in other jurisdictions. The following paragraphs provide a brief overview of the decision, with such a broader perspective in mind.[54]

In 1999, at a London auction, the claimant, Dr. Peiffer, an art collector, bought the painting *Calabrian Coast* (*Kalabrische Küste*), made in 1861 by the German painter Andreas Achenbach. The painting was owned by the Stern Gallery in Düsseldorf from 1931 to 1937. In 1935, Dr. Max Stern was prohibited from continuing to practice his profession by the Reich Chamber of Fine Arts (*Reichskammer der bildenden Künste*), but the order was not initially implemented. In March 1937, Dr. Stern

---

[50] German Lost Art Foundation, *Lost Art Database*, www.lostart.de/en/start (last visited Feb. 1, 2025).

[51] German Lost Art Foundation, *Historical Contexts*, https://kulturgutverluste.de/en (last visited Feb. 1, 2025).

[52] Lost Art Database, *supra* note 50.

[53] BGH – V ZR 112/22, judgment of July 21, 2023, https://openjur.de/u/2473051.html (Ger.) (hereinafter: "*Calabrian Coast* case") (all translations from the judgment are mine).

[54] For a detailed overview of the decision, *see* Pierre Valentin, *Removal of Artworks from the Lost Art Database: The Approach of the German Courts*, 28 ART ANTIQUITY & L. 333 (2023).

sold the painting to a private person from Essen. In September 1937, Dr. Stern was forced to give up his gallery, whereupon he emigrated to Canada via England. His estate is managed by a Canadian foundation of which the defendants are trustees. In June 2016, the Max Stern Restitution Project placed a search notice for the painting on the Lost Art Database website.[55]

The relevant text on the Lost Art Database reads as follows:

Description	Signed and dated over left: A. Achenbach 1861.
Exhibited,	Galerie Stern, Gemälde alter und neuer Meister, 22 Juni-31 August 1935, no. 85, plate 24 (as "Sizilianische Landschaft").
Collection	Galerie-Bestand 1933–1938.
Provenance	Dr. Max Stern, Düsseldorf; 1937 Gottfried Bischoff, Essen; March 23, 1999 Phillips, London, Lot 25 (as "Vessels off a Coast at Sunset").
Published since	29.06.2016.
Contact	Please contact the German Lost Art Foundation.
…	
Search Request	Person Stern, Dr. Max.[56]

The plaintiff was informed of the search notice made by the Max Stern Restitution Project, and that INTERPOL was searching for the painting because it had been reported stolen in Canada.[57]

Importantly, in 1999, when Dr. Peiffer bought the painting through the Phillips auction house, the painting was most likely not published on any other public database. Dr. Peiffer therefore most probably qualifies as a good-faith purchaser under German law, since there is no indication that he knew, or should have known, when acquiring the painting, that it might be subject to a claim. After failing to settle the matter with the Max Stern Restitution Project, Dr. Peiffer submitted a civil claim against the defendants to order the removal of the registration from the Lost Art Database.[58]

The BGH held that the search report of a cultural asset on the website of the Lost Art Database, "which is based on true facts," does not constitute an impairment of ownership within the meaning of Section 1004 §1 of the

---

[55] *Calabrian Coast* case, *supra* note 53, at para. 1.
[56] Lost Art Database, *Search Request | Object Report, Calabrian Coast – Sicilia, Lost Art-ID 533378*, www.lostart.de/en/lost/object/calabrian-coast-sicilia/533378 (last visited Feb. 1, 2025).
[57] *Calabrian Coast* case, *supra* note 53, at para. 4.
[58] Valentin, *supra* note 54, at 332–33.

German Civil Code (BGB),[59] and therefore "does not give rise to any claim by the current owner to request deletion against the person who made the report."[60] The BGH therefore affirmed the holding made by the regional court of appeals in the matter, by which:

> There is no impairment of ownership, because the defendants did not assume ownership of the painting either with the search report in the Lost Art Database or through the search initiated solely outside Germany. According to the principles for the entry and deletion of reports in the Lost Art Database, their search report merely expresses that Dr. Max Stern was previously the owner of the painting and it can be assumed or cannot be ruled out that the painting was taken from him due to Nazi persecution, was moved due to the war or was lost. The plaintiff's current ownership of the painting is not called into question by this.[61]

The BGH then portrayed, however, the practical effects that should emerge from the registry of such a "search request/object report" in the Lost Art Database:

> The Lost Art Database serves to implement the so-called Washington Principles of 1998, which is not binding under international law, on the handling of works of art lost during the Nazi era, as well as the joint declaration of the federal government, states and municipal associations of December 1999 … The purpose of the publication on the Lost Art Database website is to bring together the previous owners or their heirs and the current owners of a cultural asset and to support them in developing a just and fair solution in the spirit of the Washington Principles.[62]

The BGH recognized the fact that the publication of a search notice does indeed limit the marketability of the cultural asset, "which has a detrimental effect on its value,"[63] such that, although the plaintiff is formally the legal owner, his ability to sell the painting is practically nonexistent and, moreover, any prospective buyer would be obliged to engage in increased due diligence under Section 44 of the German Cultural Property

---

[59] According to Section 1004 §1 of the German Civil Code (BGB), "[i]f the ownership is interfered with by means other than removal or retention of possession, the owner may demand that the disturber remove the interference. If there is the concern that further interferences will ensue, the owner may seek a prohibitory injunction." For an official English translation of the BGB, *see* Federal Ministry of Justice, German Civil Code (BGB), www.gesetze-im-internet.de/englisch_bgb/englisch_bgb.html#p4705 (last visited Feb. 1, 2025).

[60] *Calabrian Coast* case, *supra* note 53, syllabus, §2.

[61] *Id.* at para. 7.

[62] *Id.* at paras. 34–35.

[63] *Id.* at para. 44.

Protection Act of 2016.[64] According to Section 44, titled "Increased Due Diligence Requirements Related to the Placing on the Market for Commercial Reasons," such a heightened standard of due diligence would apply, inter alia, for cultural property "if it has been proven or is assumed that this cultural property was taken from its original owner between 30 January 1933 and 8 May 1945 due to National Socialist persecution, unless it was restituted to the original owner or his heirs or they have come to a different final agreement regarding the deprivation."[65] According to the BGH, a search request/object report in the Lost Art Database would normally give rise to such a presumption and, accordingly, to an increased standard of due diligence placed on potential buyers in the market.[66]

However, per the court, the "reduction in the expectation of profit from a sale affects the owner of the cultural asset as a matter of his or her financial interests. These are not protected by the owner's property defense claims under § 1004 Para. 1 BGB."[67] Moreover, the BGH held that "[t]he legitimate interest of previous owners of cultural property or their legal successors, as well as the general public's interest in the provenance of cultural property confiscated as a result of Nazi persecution, outweighs any interest of the current owner in keeping such facts secret, which is usually based solely on economic considerations."[68]

At the same time, the BGH limited the scope of its decision, and left open the consideration of other types of cases in which entries in such databases may be contested by the current owner.

First, the court reasoned that "it is questionable whether an impairment of property rights is to be assumed if untrue market-relevant facts are asserted with regard to the item" and it held, accordingly, that "the question of whether untrue factual statements in relation to an object can constitute an impairment of ownership does not require a final decision here."[69]

Second, the BGH noted that if a cultural property database is run by the government, based on public law provisions, then the inclusion of entries

---

[64] Cultural Property Protection Act of 31 July 2016, Federal Law Gazette [BGBl] Part I, 1914 (Gesetz zum Schutz von Kulturgut (Kulturgutschutzgesetz – KGSG)), www.gesetze-im-internet.de/kgsg/ (hereinafter: "2016 Act" or "KGSG") (Ger.). A formal English version of KGSG is available at www.gesetze-im-internet.de/englisch_kgsg/englisch_kgsg.html.
[65] *Id.* at Section 44, §1.
[66] *Calabrian Coast* case, *supra* note 53, at paras. 45–46.
[67] *Id.* at para. 44.
[68] *Id.* at para. 43.
[69] *Id.* at paras. 44–45.

in the database, and their contents, may be considered "state action" of providing information. Accordingly, a public law claim made before an administrative court could be considered if keeping the record of such a search request/object report "is no longer within the scope of the database's intended purpose and is incompatible with higher-ranking law, in particular fundamental rights."[70] For example, if in the case of such a public law registry the question of legal ownership of the item is already established, and the parties became acquainted with each other (and their respective claims) through the publication of the entry in the database, but the parties have not been able to reach a "just and fair solution" – then the public law purpose of the database may be considered to have exhausted itself, such that an administrative court may weigh whether the entry is still valid as a matter of public law.[71]

However, since the Lost Art Database is currently operated by the German Lost Art Foundation under private law, "it is controversial whether publications in the database are still to be assessed under public law and thus the administrative legal process is open … or whether the civil courts must now decide on legal questions relating to the inclusion of works suspected of being Nazi-looted."[72] Even if the latter holds, the question would arise if and how "public law obligations to which the state is subject in its information activities also affect the foundation operating the database under private law and lead to the foundation being obliged under civil law to delete an entry if the purpose of the database no longer justifies keeping the entry."[73] The BGH held that:

> However, none of this needs to be clarified here. Even if the exceeding of the database's intended purpose by entering a search report relating to a work of art would result in the owner's right to have the data deleted, this could – regardless of whether the claim is of a public or private nature – only be directed against the foundation as the operator of the database, but not against the defendants as the mere initiators of the report, who are merely making use of the database's services … Whether the search report corresponds to the purpose of the database is – as explained – only relevant in the relationship between the plaintiff and the foundation as the operator of the database, but not in the relationship between the plaintiff and the defendants.[74]

---

[70] *Id.* at para. 53.
[71] *Id.*
[72] *Id.* at para. 54.
[73] *Id.*
[74] *Id.*

The *Calabrian Coast* case, and its potential future development under various circumstances or by other national and supranational courts that may have jurisdiction over cultural property databases, will therefore have a paramount effect on these databases' formal and practical weight.

Government-run or -sponsored digital databases have also been constructed for specific collections of items that had been previously identified as wrongfully taken during the Nazi era.

Thus, as shown in Chapter 3, the Louvre's online database also features items that are kept in the museum under the category of Musées Nationaux Récupération (MNR).[75] Information about all MNR items that are kept in France, including in other public museums, is available through the database Rose-Valland (MNR-Jeu de Paume), which is accessible through the Open Heritage Platform website of French National Patrimony (POP: la plateforme ouverte du patrimoine).[76] This database contains a record for each MNR item, and is intended to help heirs of Nazi-era dispossessed owners to identify works and submit to the French government a claim for return.[77]

This is also the case with the Dutch Art Property Collection (*Nederlands Kunstbezit/NK-collectie*), which consists of artwork that was illegally taken during the Nazi era, and then seized and returned to the Dutch government after the war.[78] Items for which the rightful owners or their heirs have not been identified have been placed under the custody of the Cultural Heritage Agency of the Netherlands. Following research done about the works by the Origins Unknown Agency (*Bureau Herkomst Gezocht*), a digital database was set up and is now publicly accessible – with a key purpose of revealing the identity of heirs of deprived owners and enabling restitution to them.[79]

---

[75] *See* Chapter 3, Section 3.1.

[76] Ministère de la Culture, *POP : la plateforme ouverte du patrimoine, Rose-Valland (MNR-Jeu de Paume)*, https://pop.culture.gouv.fr/advanced-search/list/mnr?qb=%5B%7B%22fie ld%22%3A%5B%22INV.keyword%22%5D%2C%22operator%22%3A%22%2A%22%2C% 22value%22%3A%22%22%2C%22combinator%22%3A%22AND%22%2C%22index%22 %3A0%7D%5D (Fr.) (last visited Feb. 1, 2025).

[77] *Id.*

[78] Origins Unknown, *Cultural Goods World War II*, www.herkomstgezocht.nl/origins-unknown (last visited Feb. 1, 2025). *See also* Evelien Campfens, *Bridging the Gap between Ethics and Law: The Dutch Framework for Nazi-Looted Art*, 25 ART ANTIQUITY & L. 1, 4–6 (2020) (describing the postwar organization of recovery and restitution of looted property in the Netherlands).

[79] Cultural Goods World War II, *supra* note 78; Campfens, *supra* note 78, at 12 (explaining that the results of the work done by the Origins Unknown Agency, made publicly available, "formed the basis of a liberal restitution policy for claims to artefacts in the NK collection").

Other databases have been set up by nongovernmental agencies and other organizations working across national borders. The Commission for Looted Art in Europe, which is an international, expert, and non-profit representative body founded in 1999, established lootedart.com, the Central Registry of Information on Looted Cultural Property 1933–1945.[80] This registry includes an "Information Database" containing various types of information and documentation from forty-nine countries, and an "object database" with details coming from over fifteen countries about more than 25,000 cultural objects that were looted, missing, and/or identified.[81]

4.2.3.2   Databases on Colonial Contexts and Beyond

A different context, in which a reconsideration of legal and public policy is closely intertwined with a commitment to provide transparent and accessible information through provenance research and digital databases, is that of collections from colonial contexts. As shown in Section 4.1, a prominent digital database with a colonial context is Digital Benin, which collects information, as of early 2025, about 5,285 historic Benin objects from 136 museums and other institutions across twenty countries – with a substantial part of these items resulting from the 1897 massive loot, by the British army, from the royal palace of the then Kingdom of Benin.[82]

More broadly, as part of adopting a new public policy on artifacts from colonial contexts, some governments become increasingly committed to engage in research about artifacts and collections with colonial contexts and to present any such information in publicly accessible digital databases.

As shown in Chapter 3,[83] in their 2019 joint Framework Principles, the German federal, state, and local governments declared their commitment to "deal with collections from colonial contexts in a responsible manner in close coordination with the respective countries and societies of origin" and, in so doing, to "create the conditions for the return of ... cultural objects from colonial contexts which were appropriated in a way which

---

[80] Commission for Looted Art in Europe, *About Us*, www.lootedartcommission.com/Services (last visited Feb. 1, 2025).
[81] THE CENTRAL REGISTRY OF INFORMATION ON LOOTED CULTURAL PROPERTY 1933–1945, www.lootedart.com/home (last visited Feb. 1, 2025).
[82] *See infra* Section 4.1.
[83] *See* Chapter 3, Section 3.4.3.

is no longer legally and/or ethically justifiable."[84] To facilitate this, the Framework Principles acknowledge the importance of conducting inventories of and digitizing collections from colonial contexts and "call upon cultural heritage institutions and scientific institutions engaged in cultural preservation to present the circumstances surrounding the acquisition" of artifacts from colonial contexts "in a transparent manner."[85]

In 2020, the German federal, state, and local governments established the "German Contact Point for Collections from Colonial Contexts," administered by the Cultural Foundation of the German Federal States (*Kulturstiftung der Länder*).[86] The project is "intended to serve as the first, central point of contact for all questions concerning collections from colonial contexts in Germany," with one of its tasks being that of collecting, organizing, documenting, publishing and evaluating "statistically pertinent data and information."[87]

Consequently, the German Lost Art Foundation established a new research database, titled Proveana, which contains information about assets and collections from colonial contexts as one of its four research areas.[88] The other research areas included in the Proveana database are "cultural goods confiscated as a result of Nazi persecution" (including all data from the Lost Art Database), "cultural goods displaced as a result of war," and "confiscation of cultural goods in the Soviet Occupation Zone and the GDR." The last two research areas therefore extend the reach of publicly funded provenance research and the presentation of information in a digital database beyond Nazi-looted assets and colonial contexts. The category of "cultural goods displaced as a result of war" refers mostly to the confiscation, movement, or relocation of cultural goods because of the Second World War, outside of the context of Nazi loot. It includes, for example, the "confiscation campaigns of the Soviet Trophy

---

[84] Auswärtiges Amt [Federal Foreign Office], *Framework Principles for Dealing with Collections from Colonial Contexts Agreed by the Federal Government Commissioner for Culture and the Media, the Federal Foreign Office Minister of State for International Cultural Policy, the Cultural Affairs Ministers of the Länder and the Municipal Umbrella Organisations* (Mar. 13, 2019), 1–2 www.auswaertiges-amt.de/resource/blob/2210152/b2731f8b59210c77c68177cdcd3d03de/190412-stm-m-sammlungsgut-kolonial-kontext-en-data.pdf.

[85] *Id.* at 4–5.

[86] GERMAN CONTACT POINT FOR COLLECTIONS FROM COLONIAL CONTEXTS, www.cp3c.org/ (last visited Feb. 1, 2025).

[87] *Id.*

[88] German Lost Art Database, *Proveana – Provenance Research Database, Accessible Data for Improved Provenance Research*, www.proveana.de/en/start (last visited Feb. 1, 2025).

Commissions, thefts by individual Allied forces military personnel and relocated museum items which, for various reasons (e.g., territorial shifts after the war), were not returned to their original place when hostilities ceased." The category of "confiscation of cultural goods in the Soviet Occupation Zone and the GDR" covers works of art, cultural property, and collections seized from private individuals by the authorities in the Soviet Occupation Zone (1945–1949) and the German Democratic Republic (1949–1990).[89]

The Proveana database (see Figure 4.2) makes accessible the results of provenance research done by public cultural institutions, private institutions, and individuals, which is funded by the Lost Art Foundation. These results are supplemented by additional information from academic literature, archived documents, and digital offerings, including the contents of the Lost Art Database.[90] Accordingly, the data provided in Proveana is assigned to eight different record types: (1) Persons, groups of persons and corporate bodies; (2) Events; (3) Collections; (4) Physical objects; (5) Provenance attributes; (6) Archived documents; (7) Literature and digital offerings; and (8) Projects.[91]

4.2.4   Academic and Professional Databases for Provenance Research

Digital technology is also having a major impact on the methodology and accessibility of provenance research, documentation, and archiving conducted regularly by academic institutions and professional organizations that deal specifically with cultural artifacts and more generally with cultural heritage. Accordingly, numerous databases and other types of digital resources have been set up over the past few years, including through institutional and cross-border collaborations.

A prominent example is the Getty Provenance Index, which includes the world's largest amalgam of digital records of various items of art-focused information.[92] Established by the Getty Research Institute, the Getty Provenance Index provides access to about 2.5 million items,

---

[89] German Lost Art Database, *Proveana – Provenance Research Database, The Basics of Proveana*, www.proveana.de/en/about-proveana/basics-proveana (last visited Feb. 1, 2025).

[90] *Id.*

[91] *Id.*

[92] Getty Research Institute, *Search the Getty Provenance Index*, www.getty.edu/databases-tools-and-technologies/provenance/ (last visited Feb. 1, 2025).

www.proveana.de

Proveana
Provenance Research Database
German Lost Art Foundation

| Search | **Advanced search** | Map |

All fields ⌄

╋ Add search field

With all words (AND) ⌄

╋ Add search condition

search 🔍

Figure 4.2 Screenshots from the mobile-phone version of the Proveana database. Source: By permission of the German Lost Art Foundation (Deutsches Zentrum Kulturgutverluste).

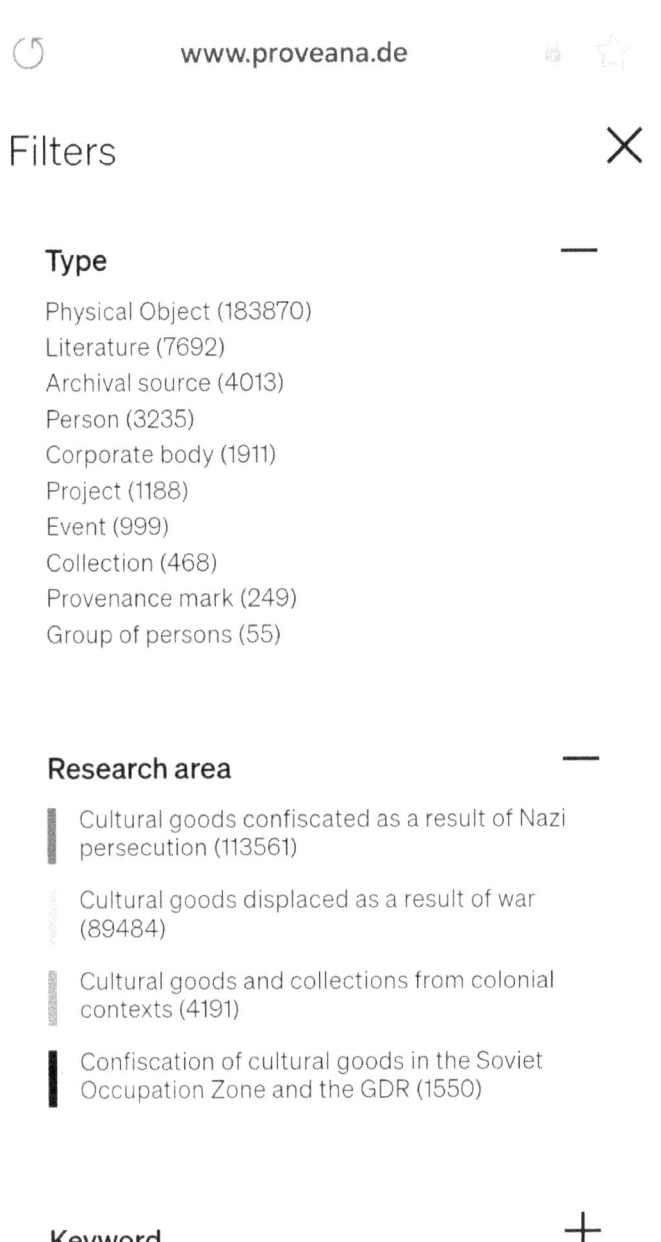

www.proveana.de

Filters   ✕

Type   —

Physical Object (183870)
Literature (7692)
Archival source (4013)
Person (3235)
Corporate body (1911)
Project (1188)
Event (999)
Collection (468)
Provenance mark (249)
Group of persons (55)

Research area   —

Cultural goods confiscated as a result of Nazi persecution (113561)

Cultural goods displaced as a result of war (89484)

Cultural goods and collections from colonial contexts (4191)

Confiscation of cultural goods in the Soviet Occupation Zone and the GDR (1550)

Keyword   +

Figure 4.2   cont.

including archival inventories, sales catalogs, dealer stock books, collectors' files, records of payments to artists, and records from public collections. Among these items are over 1.8 million records of sales catalogs from major cities in Belgium, France, Germany, Britain, the Netherlands, and Scandinavian countries from 1650 to 1945, alongside private contract sales through which collectors were able to acquire artworks during an extended period of exhibition.[93] As such, entries included in the database serve as a key tool for provenance research of cultural objects.

Another key database, which is becoming increasingly accessible online, is that of PHAROS – an international consortium of fourteen European and North American art-historical photo archives, committed to creating a digital research platform allowing for comprehensive consolidated access to photo archive images of cultural artifacts and their associated scholarly documentation (estimated overall at about 25 million records).[94] In addition, a multitude of other databases provide public access to an increasing number of auction catalogs and records, dealer records and archives, photo archives, and so forth.[95]

Finally, museums and other cultural institutions are increasingly digitizing their collections and making them accessible via open databases – and many of these databases provide details about the provenance research done for such collections.

As shown in Chapter 3, in 2021 the Louvre launched an open-access digital database, which features more than 500,000 objects in the museum's collections.[96] Each entry in the database includes details known to the museum about the object's provenance – the result of one of the most extensive provenance research efforts taken on by a cultural institution.[97] Other prominent museums, galleries, and cultural institutions are also moving forward in digitizing their collections, researching the provenance of items, and making this information available via a digital database.

---

[93] Id.

[94] Pharos – The International Consortium of Photo Archives, *About*, http://pharosartresearch.org/about (last visited Feb. 1, 2025).

[95] See *Select Resources*, in PROVENANCE RESEARCH TODAY: PRINCIPLES, PRACTICE, PROBLEMS 194–209 (Arthur Tompkins ed., 2020) (containing a list of such digital resources).

[96] See Chapter 3, Section 3.1; Musée du Louvre, *Collections*, https://collections.louvre.fr/en/ (last visited Feb. 1, 2025).

[97] Vincent Noce, *Louvre Probes Its Collection for Nazi and Colonial Loot in Massive Provenance Research Project*, THE ART NEWSPAPER, Mar. 26, 2021.

Thus, the Victoria and Albert Museum in London has a searchable database of over 1.25 million objects.[98] In May 2021, a new web portal of public numismatic collections was launched, with a consolidated digital database that includes images and data – including provenance information – about more than 90,000 coins held in dozens of German and Austrian public collections.[99] Another type of online registry, which brings together dozens of U.S. museums with collections of archaeological artifacts and ancient art, is the Registry of New Acquisitions of Archaeological Material and Works of Ancient Art, coordinated by the Association of Art Museum Directors (AAMD).[100] Founded in 2008, this registry includes information about recent acquisitions made by museums of archaeological and ancient art items that lack complete provenance after November 1970 (when the 1970 UNESCO Convention was signed). By early 2025, thirty-five museums had posted information in this registry about a total of 2,431 objects.[101]

4.3   Cultural Property Databases as Cross-Border Standard-Setters

The cultural property databases surveyed in the previous section do much more than provide information. Such databases, and particularly those that can be accessed by parties across national borders for purposes of both insertion and retrieval of data, can – and already do – impact ethical and professional norms, and consequently legal norms, pertaining to cultural property. While not aiming at cross-border unity, publicly accessible databases can mitigate certain ill-effects of legal divergence among national legal systems, given the currently limited scope of hard-law international instruments. More broadly, such databases facilitate the establishment of a professional, ethical, and legal common ground among public and private actors located across national borders – without undermining national authority to engage in governing cultural objects. This section highlights some of the ways in which accessible cultural property

---

[98] Victoria and Albert Museum (V&A), *From the Collections*, www.vam.ac.uk/collections?type=featured (last visited Feb. 1, 2025).

[99] Digital Coin Cabinet ikmk.net, *About*, https://ikmk.net/about?lang=en (last visited Feb. 1, 2025).

[100] Association of Art Museum Directors (AAMD), *New Acquisitions of Archaeological Material and Works of Ancient Art*, https://aamd.org/object-registry/new-acquisitions-of-archaeological-material-and-works-of-ancient-art/more-info (last visited Feb. 1, 2025).

[101] *Id.*

databases play a role in setting professional and legal principles that often also have a cross-border effect.

4.3.1   Facilitating Fact-Finding in Specific Disputes

The rapid growth in the number of accessible databases and the scope of their coverage, especially in the case of integrative databases that comprise multiple specific databases coming from various sources and across many territories, may aid parties to specific disputes to gain better access to essential pieces of evidence. The nature of proprietary disputes over cultural property is such that the process of fact-finding is cumbersome and expensive, requiring parties to track documentation going back decades or even centuries.[102] The need of such parties to engage in an item-specific provenance research, with the purpose of presenting admissible pieces of evidence to a court or tribunal that adjudicates a specific despite, may prove prohibitively costly, especially for private parties, such as heirs of dispossessed owners.

Therefore, the digital gathering of data via multiple sources, relating to different points in time and coming from various territories, may substantially lower the costs and other administrative obstacles that parties incur in trying to reconstruct the history of ownership and possession of a cultural object and to provide a comprehensive and reliable evidentiary picture to the court.

Importantly, such relevant data can relate not only to the specific cultural asset that is the object of the dispute but also to other artifacts that were or may have been interrelated to the disputed asset. Thus, for example, evidence about the provenance and chain of possession regarding other artifacts that were part of a collection of an allegedly dispossessed owner may provide at least circumstantial evidence about whether the contested artifact also belonged to this collection, or about the trajectory that other items have followed once taken out of the collection. Similarly, reports such as the "red lists" published by ICOM[103] may identify not only types of items that are prone to illicit trading but also the routes that items may have followed before ending up in the hands of the previous or current possessor, such as a museum, trader, or collector.

---

[102] Ruth Redmond-Cooper & Charlotte Dunn, *Original but Not Enduring Title: Issues of Space and Time, in* MUSEUMS AND THE HOLOCAUST 14, 14 (Ruth Redmond-Cooper ed., 2nd ed. 2021) (pointing to the "undoubted evidential, geographical and time-related difficulties confronting persons seeking to claim the return of artworks looted or otherwise lost during the Nazi era").

[103] *See* Chapter 3, text accompanying notes 127–28.

Thus, while courts and tribunals may apply different rules pertaining to the admissibility of evidence, required standard of proof, etc.[104] – the availability of accessible information that can be derived from cultural property databases increases the probability of identifying relevant pieces of evidence and lowering the cost of gaining access to them in the context of a specific dispute. In so doing, cultural property databases may aid in mitigating disparities across different jurisdictions at least with regard to the practical ability of different litigants and courts to engage in fact-finding.

4.3.2 Database Use as a Benchmark for Due Diligence and Similar Norms

As explained in Chapter 2, national legal rules that address proprietary conflicts between an owner who involuntarily lost control over a tangible asset and a current possessor of the item may exhibit materially different approaches. Some legal systems adhere to the *nemo dat quod non habet* ("he who does not have cannot give") rule – which categorically favors the original owner, subject to certain periods of limitation on submitting claims – while other legal systems protect a bona fide (good faith) possessor, either immediately or after a certain period of time.[105] These divergences may be grounded in long-standing jurisprudential principles or even in more fundamental concerns, such as cultural attributes of a certain society.[106] Yet even across the legal systems that focus on the concept of good faith as a key determinant in deciding the proprietary dispute, the particular legal indicators that attest to the meaning of this term, as well as the way in which these indicators are implemented by courts in particular cases, may substantially diverge. This leads to legal disparity that can prove burdensome in the case of cross-border disputes, including in the specific context of cultural property disputes adjudicated before national courts.[107]

---

[104] *See, e.g.*, Kevin M. Clermont & Emily Sherwin, *A Comparative View of Standards of Proof*, 50 Am. J. Comp. L. 243 (2002) (comparing common law and civil law standards of proof).

[105] *See* Chapter 2, Section 2.1.2.

[106] Giuseppe Dari-Mattiacci & Carmine Guerriero, *Law and Culture: A Theory of Comparative Variation in Bona Fide Purchase Rules*, 35 Oxford J. Legal Stud. 543 (2015) (surveying rules on good-faith acquisitions in 126 jurisdictions and arguing that a "culture of self-reliance" is the key determinant of variations in the doctrine).

[107] Lyndel V. Prott, Commentary on the 1995 UNIDROIT Convention on Stolen or Illegally Exported Cultural Objects 73–75 (2nd ed. 2021).

As shown in Chapters 2 and 3,[108] the drafters of the 1995 UNIDROIT Convention opted not to use the term "good faith" to avoid ambiguity and disparity among national legal systems – and selected, instead, the term "due diligence" as the norm that applies to a possessor who seeks to be compensated when required to return a stolen object that he or she purchased.[109] Similarly, the drafters of the 2014 EU Council Directive (and, previously, Council Directive 93/7/EEC) refrained from the term "good faith" – and defined the norm as one of "due care and attention."[110] Both these instruments offer a similar, nonexhaustive list of factors to examine whether the possessor meets the burden of proving "due diligence" or "due care and attention," respectively. Thus, Article 4(4) of the 1995 UNIDROIT Convention reads:

> In determining whether the possessor exercised due diligence, regard shall be had to all the circumstances of the acquisition, including the character of the parties, the price paid, *whether the possessor consulted any reasonably accessible register of stolen cultural objects*, and any other relevant information and documentation which it could reasonably have obtained, and whether the possessor consulted accessible agencies or took any other step that a reasonable person would have taken in the circumstances.[111]

While the multitude of legal norms applying in different national and cross-border settings pertaining to cultural property (e.g., good faith, due diligence, or due care and attention – and identifying factors for each one of them) may have originally led to legal disparity and even an increased danger of "legal arbitrage" – this chapter suggests that the growing scope

---

[108] *See* Chapter 2, Section 2.2.1; Chapter 3, Section 3.3.1.

[109] Marina Schneider, *The 1995 UNIDROIT Convention: An Indispensable Complement to the 1970 UNESCO Convention and an Inspiration for the 2014/60/EU Directive*, 2016 SANTANDER ART & CULTURE L. REV. 149, 155 (2016).

[110] *See* Chapter 2, Section 2.2.1.

[111] UNIDROIT Convention on Stolen or Illegally Exported Cultural Objects, June 24, 1995, 2421 U.N.T.S. 457, art. 4(4) (hereinafter: "1995 UNIDROIT Convention") (my emphasis). Article 10 of the 2014 EU Directive reads: "In determining whether the possessor exercised due care and attention, consideration shall be given to all the circumstances of the acquisition, in particular the documentation on the object's provenance, the authorizations for removal required under the law of the requesting Member State, the character of the parties, the price paid, *whether the possessor consulted any accessible register of stolen cultural objects and any relevant information which he could reasonably have obtained*, or took any other step which a reasonable person would have taken in the circumstances." Directive 2014/60/EU of the European Parliament and of the Council of 15 May 2014 on the Return of Cultural Objects Unlawfully Removed from the Territory of a Member State (Recast), 2014 O.J. (L 159) 1, art. 10, §2 (my emphasis).

of coverage and improved accessibility of digital databases can gradually change this trend. In other words, the fact that these databases allow for both registration/reporting of data on behalf of dispossessed owners or source countries and the retrieval of data on behalf of dealers or prospective buyers – alongside the broader-based access to provenance research done by state agencies, cultural institutions, and collectors – is likely to make this amalgam of databases the focal point for interpreting and applying the relevant standards across different legal instruments and scenarios.

Thus, for example, as shown in the 2023 decision of Germany's BGH in the *Calabrian Coast* case,[112] a search request/object report in the Lost Art Database – if based on true facts – would give rise to an assumption of a wrongful dispossession of a cultural item between 1933 and 1945, and, accordingly, to an increased standard of due diligence placed on buyers in the market under Section 44 of the German Cultural Property Protection Act of 2016.[113]

Accordingly, although the insertion or retrieval of data may not always be a sufficient condition for proving if one meets the relevant standard of care, it can certainly become a necessary condition. Even more importantly, beyond the context of resolving a specific dispute, the increasing investment in such databases by various types of public and private actors, and, particularly, the growing role of provenance research as an expression of professional and ethical best practice, is likely to generate cross-border norms that may have the effect of approximating different legal terms and preventing certain conflicts.

Moreover, the potential of cultural property databases to become a benchmark for defining and identifying the legal standards of behavior, on the part of the various stakeholders, can also impact other substantive and procedural rules pertaining to cultural property disputes. This is the case, for example, with the implementation of statutes of limitations or other types of time-related rules that govern the rights and duties of parties.

Therefore, to the extent that an auction house, cultural institution, or collector posts the details of a cultural artifact in its possession in an accessible digital database, then such an act can be viewed as creating at least a presumption of knowledge on the part of potential claimants (consider the 1995 UNIDROIT Convention, by which "any claim for restitution shall be brought within a period of three years from the time when the claimant knew the location of the cultural object and the

---

[112] *Calabrian Coast* case, *supra* note 53.
[113] KGSG, *supra* note 64, Sect. 44; *Calabrian Coast* case, *supra* note 53, at paras. 45–46.

identity of its possessor").[114] Conversely, if a claimant can prove that he or she exercised efforts in searching such databases but that such searches did not produce results in identifying a missing object, then such an act can create a presumption against starting to "run the clock" of a limitation period or a doctrine of laches. In this respect as well, digital databases can increasingly serve a role that goes beyond a mere source of information into one of constituting a benchmark for setting professional and legal standards. In so doing, globally accessible digital databases can mitigate legal disparities that result from varieties in legal concepts in national and international legislative instruments and in adjudicative proceedings.

4.3.3   Information-Sharing as a Basis for "Just and Fair Solutions"

Alongside the growing influence of cultural property databases on professional and hard-law rules in various national and supranational settings, such databases may also facilitate collaboration between governments, organizations, and cultural institutions in coming to terms on ethical norms and policy choices.

This is particularly the case with the impact of the comprehensive provenance research, accessible digital databases, and the thick exchange of information between national governments or agencies in settings such as Nazi-looted cultural assets. As shown in Chapters 2 and 6,[115] decisions on whether to return such assets to heirs of dispossessed owners or to the source countries are usually done outside of the regular legal regime (e.g., because limitation periods ran out a long time ago or since there is no formal cause of action). Governments, national agencies, cultural institutions, and individual collectors in possession of such objects are encouraged, however, to reach "just and fair solutions," and digital databases may play a key role in the context. This was explicitly stated by the BGH in its 2023 decision in the *Calabrian Coast* case,[116] according to which:

> The purpose of the publication on the Lost Art Database website is to bring together the previous owners or their heirs and the current owners of a cultural asset and to support them in developing a just and fair solution in the spirit of the Washington Principles.[117]

---

[114] 1995 UNIDROIT Convention, *supra* note 111, art. 3(3).
[115] *See* Chapter 2, Section 2.4.
[116] *Calabrian Coast* case, *supra* note 53.
[117] *Id.* at para. 35.

As further shown in Chapters 3 and 6 in the context of the restitution committees on Nazi-looted art set up in several European countries,[118] the establishment of a "network" attests to the potential of "exchange and sharing of information and know-how" to arrive at some type of a common denominator (even if not unity or harmonization) about the "effectiveness of provenance research and the moral requirement of 'clean museums.'"[119] This means that, in devising "just and fair solutions," restitution committees across these countries will be impacted by the broader set of data compiled by committees and agencies in charge of provenance research located in counterpart countries. This collaborative process, facilitated to a large degree by the Holocaust-era digital databases, could have an impact, in turn, on administrative and political decisions on restitution or compensation in other contexts – without necessarily aspiring for wholesale unity.

4.3.4 Accessible Databases as Promoting a General Value of Transparency

The rapid development of digital databases, which enable multiple parties to both register data and retrieve it, while allowing broad access to them, is instrumental in promoting a much broader value: transparency.

In various proprietary contexts, questions arise as to whether practices of secrecy and opacity are normatively legitimate, or do they lead to illegal consequences, such as tax evasion or money laundering, and damage the interests of parties that are deprived of essential information. Such dilemmas arise, for example, in the context of secret and half-secret trusts, the secret buy-out of corporate shares, or the hiding by purchasers of real estate of their identity via shell companies.[120]

Moreover, a validation of secrecy and opacity can exacerbate cross-border legal disparity. This is the case, for example, when jurisdictions actively engage in tax competition, and in so doing combine low effective tax rates with ensuring financial secrecy for clients, or when sophisticated parties otherwise take advantage of "loopholes" and various forms of legal

---

[118] *See,* respectively, Chapter 3, Section 3.4.3; Chapter 6, Section 6.1.

[119] Michel Jeannoutot, *Editorial,* 1 NETWORK OF EUR. RESTITUTION COMMITTEES ON NAZI-LOOTED ART 1 (Mar. 2019), www.restitutiecommissie.nl/wp-content/uploads/2021/12/Network-Newsletter-no.1-March2019.pdf.

[120] For these various case studies, and the broader debate about secrecy in proprietary contexts, *see* Amnon Lehavi, *Property and Secrecy,* 50 REAL PROP. TR. & EST. L. J. 381 (2016).

arbitrage – such as varieties in reporting duties across legal systems – to extract private financial benefits.[121]

As shown in Chapter 3,[122] the international art market has been particularly typified by practices of secrecy and opacity, such that it is referred to as a "notoriously insular and opaque world."[123] These features go well beyond practices of preserving the identity of buyers and/or sellers in secret – as was the case with the world's highest-ever art transaction: the auctioning off of the painting *Salvator Mundi* to a (then) secret buyer in 2017.[124] Secrecy and opacity may also be aided by various types of "legal competition" and "legal arbitrage," such as when jurisdictions otherwise serving as banking hubs and tax havens, like Switzerland, Luxemburg and Singapore, establish "freeports" – high-security warehouses that store valuable items exempt from usual customs rules, which make them ideal for dealers and collectors that look to transport, store, and view artworks without paying customs.[125]

The same also holds true for trade in antiquities. As exemplified in Chapter 1, illicit trade in archaeological artifacts is often facilitated by a lack of transparency and accountability, which aids looters, smugglers, and illicit traders in moving such artifacts across borders, often via transit countries that may also enable such illicit chains to "whitewash" the title to an object prior to its transfer to dealers or collectors in a destination state.[126] Secrecy and opacity may therefore plague the governance

---

[121] *See, e.g.,* Annelise Riles, *Managing Regulatory Arbitrage: A Conflict of Laws Approach*, 47 CORNELL INT'L L. J. 63, 71 (2014) (distinguishing between two different types of regulatory arbitrage: jurisdictional arbitrage, which is a matter of "profiting from differences in the laws of different jurisdictions," and categorical arbitrage, which involves "profiting from a legal discrepancy between the treatment of two forms of conduct that are functionally the same").

[122] *See* Chapter 3, Section 3.2.

[123] Adrian Horton, *Driven to Abstraction: The Inside Story of a $60m Art Forgery Hoax*, THE GUARDIAN, Aug. 28, 2020.

[124] Oscar Holland, *Rare da Vinci Painting Smashes World Records with $450 Million Sale*, CNN, Nov. 16, 2017. *See also* Chapter 2, Section 2.1.1.

[125] Nina dos Santos, *$1B Feud Involving Leonardo's "Salvator Mundi" Reveals Dark Side of the Art World*, CNN, May 30, 2021; Stefan Schwarzkopf & Jessica Inez Backsell, *The Nomos of the Freeport*, 39 EPD: SOCIETY & SPACE 328, 333–35 (2021).

[126] *See, e.g.,* NORDIC COUNCIL OF MINISTERS, *Illicit Trade in Cultural Artefacts* 44–46 (2017), www.norden.org/en/publication/illicit-trade-cultural-artefacts (identifying "transit countries"); Ruth Schuster, *Vast Cache of Stolen Antiquities Found in Huge Raid in Central Israel*, Haaretz.com, Jan. 5, 2021, www.haaretz.com/archaeology/2021-01-05/ty-article/.premium/vast-cache-of-stolen-antiquities-found-in-central-israel/0000017f-dbcc-df62-a9ff-dfdf91140000 (explaining that, because Israel is one of the few countries

of various cultural artifacts, highlighting problems of cross-border legal disparity. As shown above, to combat these features of the illicit market, one digital database established in 2008 and devoted to antiquities is the Registry of New Acquisitions of Archaeological Material and Works of Ancient Art, coordinated by the AAMD.[127]

The establishment of digital databases and the broad access thereto have the potential of generally tilting the international market for art, antiquities, and collectibles toward more transparency and more accountability. Going beyond the reporting of past cases of theft or looting into a systematic framework of provenance research for items held or controlled by national agencies, cultural institutions, and collectors, digital databases are essential in unveiling the identity of past and present owners or possessors, and how they came to own or control them.

Such digital databases allow for a decentralization of the power embedded in the control over information pertaining to cultural artifacts, and in so doing help to reconsider and reconstruct professional, ethical, and legal norms that would apply both nationally and internationally.[128] As such, cultural property databases not only play a significant role in resolving conflicts over past actions but also serve as a basis for guiding future behavior committed to transparency.

In so doing, the transformative role of digital databases adds a significant component to other dramatic changes that were analyzed in Chapters 1–3, concerning, respectively, cross-border political power, the development of hard-law and soft-law instruments, and the evolution of

---

around the Mediterranean basin that enables traders to obtain a license to sell, then "if one has illegal antiquities and slips them into the inventory of a licensed trader, they're effectively whitewashed. Then one can market them around the world under the guise of artifacts legally traded in Israel"). *See also* Asif Efrat, *A Major Museum Has to Return Another Looted Artifact. Welcome to the Dark Side of the Art World*, THE WASH. POST, Aug. 7, 2017.

[127] *See* text accompanying *supra* notes 100–1.

[128] This book does not address specific problems that may arise in the context of national or supranational legal instruments that deal with the protection of private data, such as the European Union's General Data Protection Regulation (GDPR). Regulation 2016/679 of the European Parliament and of the Council of 27 April 2016 on the Protection of Natural Persons with Regard to the Processing of Personal Data and on the Free Movement of Such Data and Repealing Directive 95/46/EC, 2016 O.J. (L 119) 1. It should be noted, however, that Recital 158 of GDPR empowers Member States to engage in processing personal data for archiving purposes in certain contexts, and more generally requires public and private bodies to "provide access to records of enduring value for general public interest." *Id.* recital 158.

norms on due diligence and provenance research. The role of transparency as a key value for cultural property is discussed further in the next part of the book, which offers a property theory of ownership and custody of cultural objects, and then examines future-looking ethical, professional, and legal mechanisms that could facilitate a new cultural internationalism approach to restitution.

PART II

The Legal Future of Cultural Property

A Normative Blueprint

A Theory of Ownership and Custody of Cultural Objects

This chapter seeks to identify the normative foundations of a theory of ownership and custody of cultural objects. It underscores the unique traits of cultural property as a type of asset, and the implications that this has for delineating a set of rights and duties that may diverge from those that apply to assets such as land, other chattels, intellectual property, and digital assets. Particularly, this chapter aims to lay out the corresponding sets of in rem rights and in rem duties that should apply to museums and other cultural institutions as both proprietors and custodians of cultural objects, by reconsidering the role of "placeness" of such institutions. In particular, a theory of ownership and custody of cultural objects held by cultural institutions should refer to the link between culture and space in considering the mirror-image questions that have been at the center of legal, professional, and public attention, namely: does a cultural institution have an in rem right to appropriate the value components of cultural objects, such as by limiting or prohibiting others from using or reproducing images of items in its collection; and, conversely, does a cultural institution have an in rem duty, as a custodian of culture, to actively make accessible to the public images and other information on items in its collections?

5.1 Introduction: The Cultural Institution as Proprietor and Custodian

What is it exactly that a cultural institution owns when it lawfully holds a cultural object as part of its collections? What is it that such an institution owes, and to whom, as the item's holder? What does it mean to be an owner (or possessor through a loan or trust) of a physical object that attracts visitors, while also being a custodian of the broader cultural values that it embeds? What are the correlative sets of rights and duties of a cultural institution, being both a proprietor and custodian?

As exemplified by the previous chapters, most of the contemporary discussion about the legal, professional, and ethical norms pertaining to cultural institutions, such as museums, focuses on the scope of the duty of such institutions to exercise due diligence prior to acquiring or otherwise gaining possession of a cultural item – such as an archaeological artifact or a work of visual art – and on when a museum should return or restitute such an object when it turns out in retrospect that the circumstances leading to its holding of it were either formally illegal or morally contested.

In contrast, relatively little attention is devoted to reconsidering the normative standing of a cultural institution as a lawful possessor of an object, considering the object's tangible and intangible values. What is the legitimate scope of control and appropriation of value to which a cultural institution is entitled – and what are the value components that should belong, or at least be accessible, to others, and who are they? A local community, other creators, or all of humanity?

This chapter seeks to identify the normative foundations of a theory of ownership and custody of cultural objects. While it cannot address all the conceptual and practical elements that pertain to the rights and duties that a cultural institution would have vis-à-vis other parties and stakeholders, this chapter examines the core legal principles that should guide a cultural institution as a proprietor and custodian of cultural items. It does so as part of the broader effort undertaken in this book to consider the future of cultural property at the interface of law, public policy, and markets, and how this would impact cultural institutions as key actors in this field.

Accordingly, this chapter underscores the unique traits of cultural objects as a type of asset, and the implications for delineating a set of rights and duties that may diverge, at certain points, from those that apply to assets such as land, other chattels, intellectual property, or digital assets. It also considers the fact that other types of actors regularly hold cultural items, such as artists holding their own works, private collectors, galleries, and art dealers, as well as public entities that do not regularly deal with the collection, exhibition, and research of cultural objects. While a property theory would generally do well to abstain from overfragmentation of legal norms according to the identity of a specific actor or right-holder, especially in light of the general structure of property law as embedded in legal interests that have an in rem effect, and operating within the contours of a *numerus clausus* principle,[1] this should not rule out the essentiality of

---

[1] *See infra* Section 5.4.1. The analysis in this chapter is based on my previous work: Amnon Lehavi, *A Property Theory of Ownership and Custody of Cultural Objects*, 57 GEO. WASH. INT'L L. REV. 163 (2025).

introducing a normative blueprint for addressing cultural property held by cultural institutions.

This chapter starts by examining the case study of the current legislative, administrative, and judicial framework in Italy that seeks to grant cultural institutions an essentially eternal right to control the reproduction and use of images of their cultural holdings. It then deals with the redefinition of a "museum" adopted in 2022 by the International Council of Museums (ICOM), and the implications that this may have for the role of cultural institutions as proprietors and custodians. This chapter then seeks to delineate the contours of a property theory of cultural objects and the corresponding sets of in rem rights and in rem duties that should apply to cultural institutions as both proprietors and custodians, by reconsidering the role of "placeness" of cultural institutions and their collections. In so doing, the chapter sheds new light on the tangible/intangible interface of cultural property by dealing not only with the complex link between physical control, intellectual property, and digital representation but also with broader questions of cultural heritage and the sense of belonging and identity that exists across different circles of cultural stakeholders.

5.2 The Italian Case for Eternal Appropriation of Images of Cultural Property

Over the past few decades, Italy has taken a unique path in defining, regulating, and protecting its cultural heritage and, particularly, landscape assets and items of cultural property in the possession of cultural institutions belonging to the state, the regions, and other territorial governments.

As shown below, in addition to a general provision in Article 9 of the Italian constitution,[2] and a detailed treatment of this subject matter in the 2004 Code of the Cultural and Landscape Heritage (hereinafter: "CCLH"),[3] a number of Italian courts have issued decisions that essentially grant cultural institutions an eternal power of control over the reproduction and

---

[2] "The Republic promotes the development of culture and of scientific and technical research. It safeguards natural landscape and the historical and artistic heritage of the Nation." Art. 9 COSTITUZIONE [COST.] (It.). *See* official English translation of the constitution at www.senato.it/documenti/repository/istituzione/costituzione_inglese.pdf.

[3] Decreto legislativo 22 gennaio 2004, n. 42., G.U. Feb. 24, 2004, n. 45 [CCLH] (It.), as amended, www.normattiva.it/uri-res/N2Ls?urn:nir:stato:decreto.legislativo:2004;42. *See* English translation of the 2004 CCLH (without later amendments) at https://whc.unesco.org/document/155711?.

use of images of cultural items in their possession – even if these items are no longer, or were never, protected by copyright.

This position, in conjunction with guidelines originally published in 2023 (and amended since then) by the Italian minister of culture for determining minimum fees to be charged for concessions for the use of places and images of cultural objects (hereinafter: "2023 Guidelines"),[4] places Italy as providing probably the strongest entitlement to its cultural institutions – at least in comparison to other liberal democracies – to control and appropriate the value of cultural objects that are in their possession.

This approach has already drawn much critique, according to which granting such overbroad legal control runs contrary not only to the policies of the European Union but also to the normative virtues of allowing broad access to cultural heritage. Because of Italy's prominence in the field of cultural property, reviewing its law and policy may serve as a starting point for configuring a general theory of ownership and custody of artifacts held by cultural institutions.

Consider, first, the definition of "cultural property" in Article 10 of the CCLH, by which:

1. Cultural property consists in immovable and movable things belonging to the State, the Regions, other territorial government bodies, as well as any other public body and institution, and to private non-profit associations, which possess artistic, historical, archaeological or ethno-anthropological interest.
2. Cultural property also includes:

   a) the collections of museums, picture galleries, art galleries and other exhibition venues of the State, the Regions, other territorial government bodies, as well as any other government body and institute;[5]

   …

Articles 106 to 108 of the CCLH then address the "use of cultural property" as follows:

---

[4] Decreto del Ministro della cultura 11 aprile 2023, rep. n. 161, recante "Linee guida per la determinazione degli importi minimi dei canoni e dei corrispettivi per la concessione d'uso dei beni in consegna agli istituti e luoghi della cultura statali" [2023 Guidelines] (It.), https://cultura.gov.it/comunicato/dm-161-11042023.

[5] CCLH, *supra* note 3, art. 10. Article 10(b) includes within the definition of cultural property "the archives and single documents of the State, the Regions, other territorial government bodies, as well as of any other government body and institute"; and Article 10(c) does the same for "the book collections of libraries of the State, Regions, other territorial government bodies, as well as any other government body and institute." *Id.*

Article 106
Individual Use of Cultural Property

1. The Ministry, the Regions and other territorial government bodies may grant the use of cultural properties – committed to their care – to individual applicants, for purposes which are compatible with their original cultural designation.

   …

Article 107
Instrumental and Temporary Use and Reproduction of Cultural Property

1. The Ministry, the Regions and other territorial government bodies may permit the reproduction as well as the instrumental and temporary use of the cultural properties committed to their care, without prejudice to the provisions in paragraph 2 and those with regard to copyright.

   …

Article 108
Concession Fees, Payment for Reproduction, Security Deposits

1. Concession fees and payments connected to the reproduction of cultural properties are established by the authority to whose care the property is committed, also taking into account:

   a) the nature of the activities to which concession of use refers;

   …

6. The minimum amounts of the fees and payments for use and reproduction of the property shall be established by a provision on the part of the administration granting concession.[6]

   …

Based on the provisions of Article 108 of the CCLH, the Italian minister of culture published the guidelines in April 2023.[7] The Annex (*Allegato*) to the 2023 Guidelines (hereinafter: "2023 Annex") includes detailed rules and lists of fees for the reproduction of cultural property (*riproduzione di beni culturali*) and for the use of spaces (*uso degli spazi*).[8] In the case of cultural property, the amount of fees is based on a few parameters, including the purpose of use, the number and size of digital or physical copies made, the market value of the product for which the reproduction will be used,

---

[6] *Id.* arts. 106–8.
[7] *See* text accompanying *supra* note 4.
[8] Allegato, Linee guida per la determinazione degli importi minimi dei canoni e dei corrispettivi per la concessione d'uso dei beni in consegna agli istituti e luoghi della cultura statali [2023 Annex], 2023 Guidelines, *supra* note 4 (It).

and so forth.[9] Exemptions from fees in the 2023 Annex were very narrow. Thus, while no fee is required for a reproduction of a cultural property requested "for personal use or for the purpose of study,"[10] this exemption did not apply, for example, to the publication of a scholarly work with an academic journal or a book publisher.[11]

The drawing of this line was criticized by, inter alia, persons and associations engaged in academic or scientific research, such as the Italian Association for the Promotion of Open Science (AISA) and the Italian Library Association (AIB).[12] Following this criticism, the minister of culture decided in March 2024 to revise the guidelines (hereinafter: "2024 Guidelines").[13] Accordingly, the amended Annex (*Allegato*; hereinafter: "2024 Annex") to the 2024 Guidelines allows for more exemptions from the need to seek permissions and pay fees, especially in the context of scholarly publications, free publications, and artistic or exhibition catalogues up to 4,000 copies.[14]

Beyond these legislative and administrative provisions, courts in Italy have issued a few decisions over the past few years that establish legal principles that further expand the scope of legal control by cultural institutions over the use and reproduction of cultural property, creating what is effectively an "eternal" right of control in favor of such cultural institutions.[15] Two of these cases have drawn particular attention, both professionally and publicly, not only because of the specific identity of the cultural items at stake but, moreover, because of the development of legal

---

[9] *Id.*

[10] *Id.* at 7, Section A1 ("RIPRODUZIONI SENZA SCOPO DI LUCRO" [reproductions for nonprofit purposes]).

[11] *Id.* at 8–9, Section A2 ("RIPRODUZIONI A SCOPO DI LUCRO" [reproductions for profit purposes]).

[12] Redazione, *Cultural Heritage Photo Fees, Associations Appeal to Minister*, FINESTRE SULL'ARTE, May 9, 2023, www.finestresullarte.info/en/policy/cultural-heritage-photo-fees-associations-appeal-to-minister (It.) For other critiques, such as by archaeologists and other professionals, *see, e.g.*, Daniele Manacorda, *Un Decreto Inopportuno: Appunti di un Archeologo*, 2 AEDON: RIVISTA DI ARTI E DIRITTO ONLINE 225 (2023) (It.).

[13] D.M. 108 21/03/2024, Modifiche al decreto del Ministro della cultura 11 aprile 2023, rep. n. 161, recante "Linee guida per la determinazione degli importi minimi dei canoni e dei corrispettivi per la concessione d'uso dei beni in consegna agli istituti e luoghi della cultura statali" [2024 Guidelines] (It), https://cultura.gov.it/comunicato/26075.

[14] Allegato, Linee guida per la determinazione degli importi minimi dei canoni e dei corrispettivi per la concessione d'uso dei beni in consegna agli istituti e luoghi della cultura del Ministero della cultura [2024 Annex], 2024 Guidelines, *supra* note 13 (It.)

[15] For a review of some of these cases, *see* Elena Varese, Valentina Mazza & Carolina Battistella, *The Reproduction of Cultural Heritage and Artworks in Fashion*, 9 ITALIAN L.J. 289, 306–10 (2023).

principles and corresponding remedies that may have an overarching effect on cultural property.

In November 2022, a civil court in Venice issued a restraining order,[16] requested by the Italian Ministry of Culture and the Italian state museum Gallerie dell'Accademia di Venezia, against Ravensburger, the toy company known for its jigsaw puzzles that feature art masterpieces, following the unlicensed use of the image of Leonardo da Vinci's 1490 drawing known as the *Vitruvian Man* (*Uomo vitruviano*).[17]

The restraining order was granted against both the German parent company and its Italian subsidiary, with the court assuming jurisdiction and applying Italian law – based on the court's reading of Italian rules on private international law on the matter – to the worldwide production of the puzzle. The court also ordered Ravensburger to pay the museum a fee of 1,500 euros for each day in which the puzzle had been manufactured without a license since November 17, 2022.[18]

In its ruling, the Venice court adopted the plaintiffs' position, and tied the provisions of Article 9 of the constitution and Articles 107 to 109 of the CCLH together with Articles 6, 7, and 10 of the Italian Civil Code, which deal with a person's right to control the use of his or her name and image, in order to justify the museum's right to prohibit the unlicensed reproduction and use of images of cultural items in its collections.[19] The court did so without going into a detailed normative or interpretative analysis of how it is that public law provisions about the protection of cultural heritage become embedded with private law rights articulated in the Civil Code about a person's right vis-à-vis other persons to control the

---

[16] Ministero della cultura v. R. A.G., proc. n. 5317/2022, Tribunale Ordinario di Venezia, Sez. II, Ord., Nov. 17, 2022, published in One Legale, 1 (It.) (hereinafter: "*Vitruvian Man* case").

[17] The 1490 drawing studies the proportions of the human body following the ideas of Roman architect Marcus Vitruvius Pollio in his book *De architectura* (c. 15 BCE). The drawing's iconic significance in the history of art and philosophy has been manifested, for example, in it being featured on one-euro coins that were minted in Italy. Giulia Dore, *The Puzzled Tie of Copyright, Cultural Heritage and Public Domain in Italian Law: Is the Vitruvian Man Taking on Unbalanced Proportions?* KLUWER COPYRIGHT BLOG (Apr. 6, 2023), https://copyrightblog.kluweriplaw.com/2023/04/06/the-puzzled-tie-of-copyright-cultural-heritage-and-public-domain-in-italian-law-is-the-vitruvian-man-taking-on-unbalanced-proportions/. This decision was also covered broadly in press reports. *See, e.g.,* Taylor Dafoe, *The Italian Museum That Owns Leonardo's "Vitruvian Man" Has Successfully Sued to Stop Production of a 1,000-Piece Puzzle Based on the Work*, ARTNET NEWS, Mar. 30, 2023.

[18] *Vitruvian Man* case, *supra* note 16, at 6–10, 13.

[19] *Id.* at 11.

use of his or her image.[20] The court simply stated: "Having ascertained the urgency of the precautionary requirements and moving to examine the precautionary instruments as requested by the plaintiffs, the court is of the opinion that the request for an injunction based on Articles 6, 7, and 10 of the Civil Code is well founded."[21]

In so doing, the court not only extended the substantive protection of rights awarded to persons under the said provisions of the Civil Code to cultural institutions that possess cultural items, but it also granted to such parties the right to receive private law remedies – originally designed to protect a person's proprietary rights, including a right of control – over the use of such images.

Moreover, along with its judgment, the court tied the museum's role as custodian (*custode*) of the artwork to its right to control the use of the image of the artwork, that is, whether to allow such use, under what conditions, and to set the fees for granting such a permit – by using terminology that is clearly tied to substantive proprietary protection and entitlement to private law remedies:

> The illicit conduct ascribed to the companies … according to Article 108 of the Cultural Heritage Code essentially consists of the for-profit use and reproduction of the image … in the absence of the consent or authorization of the Administration, who as custodian of the cultural property is the (sole) subject responsible for evaluating the compatibility of the requested use of the image … and who is the owner, exclusively, of the right to economic use of the work, and without paying concession fees and compensation tied to the reproduction of the works.
>
> This illicit conduct, otherwise stated, results in a misappropriation, so to speak, of the company R. [Ravensburger], both abroad and in Italy, of the image – as reproduced – for the purpose of economic/commercial exploitation.[22]

Therefore, the court granted the museum, as possessor and custodian of the *Vitruvian Man*, a strong and exclusive proprietary right, unlimited by time (as opposed to copyright protection) to control the use of the work, including the reproduction of its image. The right itself extends, beyond the administrative or regulatory realm aimed at protecting

---

[20] Dore, *supra* note 17 (arguing that the court "does not address the issue of resorting to the rights of personality with the necessary concern and simply allows it on the grounds that the Galleries are the custodians of the work and only they can assess the compatibility of the use of name and image with the cultural destination of the work").

[21] *Vitruvian Man* case, *supra* note 16, at 13 (my translation).

[22] *Id.* at 8–9.

cultural heritage, to a full-fledged property right embedded in the Civil Code to control uses of the image.

Importantly, in early 2024, a state court in Germany (Landgericht Stuttgart) held that Italian law in the matter did not apply outside of Italy, and that under German law no "right to the image" exists for an artwork that is in the public domain (meaning that is was never, or is no longer, protected by copyright), such that Ravensburger is entitled to sell its jigsaw puzzle in Germany.[23] This ruling therefore exemplifies the broad gap between Italy and other countries, including fellow Member States of the European Union, about the right to appropriate images of cultural property.

The Italian position was further developed in a decision made in April 2023 by a court in Florence in a civil claim for pecuniary and nonpecuniary damages submitted by the Ministry for Cultural Goods and Activities and for Tourism against Condé Nast, the publisher of the magazine *GQ Italia*.[24] The claim followed a reproduction by *GQ Italia* of the image of Michelangelo's *David* and its juxtaposition by lenticular technique on the magazine's cover with a photo of an Italian male model, without permission from Galleria dell'Accademia di Firenze, which holds the sculpture.[25]

The court starts its ruling on the merits of the case by holding as follows:

> Like the right to the image of a person, articulated in Art. 10 of the Civil Code, a right to an image can also arise in reference to cultural property; this right finds its normative basis in an express legislative provision, that is in Articles 107 and 108 of the Legislative Decree No. 42/2004, which constitute rules in direct implementation of Article 9 of the Constitution; Articles 107 and 108 give consigning administrators the power to legitimize, through their consent, the reproduction of cultural property; the Code of Cultural Property includes specific references to the terminology dealing with the right to the image, such as the "decoration" [*decoro*] of cultural property.[26]

---

[23] For the press coverage of this decision, *see* Theresia Blömer, *Rechtsstreit um da-Vinci-Puzzle-Motiv von Ravensburger*, SWR AKTUELL, Apr. 11, 2024 (Ger.); Gian Antonio Stella, *Via alla Vendita del Puzzle dell'Homo Vitruvianus: Nessun Diritto di Immagine All'Accademia di Venezia*, CORRIERE DELLA SERA, Apr. 4, 2024 (It.); Derrick Bryson Taylor, *Da Vinci's Been Dead for 500 Years. Who Gets to Profit from His Work?* N.Y. TIMES, April 10, 2024.

[24] Ministero per i Be. e Le Attività Culturali e per il Turismo v. Edizioni Condé Nast S.P.A., Tribunale Ordinario di Firenze, Sez. II, proc. n. 1207, Apr. 21, 2023, published by DeJure (It.) (hereinafter: "*David* case").

[25] For a critical review of this case, *see* Roberto Caso, *Michelangelo's David and Cultural Heritage Images. The Italian Pseudo-Intellectual Property and the End of Public Domain*, KLUWER COPYRIGHT BLOG (June 15, 2023), https://copyrightblog.kluweriplaw.com/2023/06/15/michelangelos-david-and-cultural-heritage-images-the-italian-pseudo-intellectual-property-and-the-end-of-public-domain/.

[26] *David* case, *supra* note 24, at 7–8 (my translation; internal citations omitted).

The court went on to explain that the right to the image had been expanded in previous case law to include also nonphysical legal persons, such as corporations or associations, as well as mere assets when this has economic significance. This means that the "civil protection of the name and the image, pursuant to Arts. 6, 7, and 10 of the Civil Code can be invoked also … for subjects other than natural persons," such that, in the case of the misappropriation of the use of an asset, "the above protection belongs both to the user of the asset by contract … and to the owner of the right to economic exploitation of the same."[27]

The protection granted by the court to cultural institutions to control the use of the image of cultural property in their collections, based on the provisions of the Civil Code, also carries major legal weight regarding the civil remedies to which the cultural institution is entitled in the case of the unauthorized use or reproduction of the image. This is so because the court established the right of the Galleria dell'Accademia di Firenze to receive compensation from Condé Nast for both pecuniary damages (based on Article 2043 of the Civil Code) and nonpecuniary damages (based on Article 2059 of the Civil Code) caused by the unauthorized use of *David*'s image.[28]

Accordingly, the court set the pecuniary damages at 20,000 euros, based on the annual minimum rates that the Galleria dell'Accademia had published on its website concerning the use of images for advertising purposes (with a specific reference to works by Michelangelo).[29]

As for nonpecuniary damages, the court also established the normative grounding for awarding such damages with regard to the injury caused to the Italian nation and to its individuals, who share "common origins, language, history and culture,"[30] and who are entitled to the protection of their cultural heritage under Article 9 of the constitution, which is referred to specifically in the CCLH, as well as under Article 2 of the constitution, which guarantees the right to individual identity.

Therefore, the nonpecuniary damages paid to Galleria dell'Accademia were intended to reflect, more broadly, the damage caused to the nonpecuniary interests of Italian citizens, "who recognize themselves as belonging to the same nation-state also by virtue of their artistic and cultural heritage."[31] The court reasoned that:

[27] *Id.* at 8.
[28] *Id.* at 4, 8.
[29] *Id.* at 11–12.
[30] *Id.* at 12.
[31] *Id.*

In the present case, the defendant company has seriously damaged these interests since, with the lenticular technique, it has insidiously and maliciously associated the image of David by Michelangelo with that of a [fashion] model, therefore debasing, obscuring, mortifying, humiliating the high symbolic and identity value of the work of art and subjecting it to advertising and editorial promotion purposes. Furthermore ... the defendant company not only failed to ask the Administrator [Galleria dell'Accademia] for consent for purposes of reproduction, but also prevented the body in charge from evaluating the compatibility between the use of David's image and its cultural destination; moreover, it maliciously used the image of David by a method (that of a lenticular paper) that the Director of the Galleria dell'Accademia had already stated and clarified was an alteration of the cultural property that, as such, could not have received authorization.[32]

Considering the scope of this nonpecuniary injury, and the prominent position of Condé Nast as a publisher and social influencer both within and outside of Italy, the court set the amount of the nonpecuniary damages, according to Article 2059 of the Civil Code, at 30,000 euros.[33]

Critics of these recent judgments and of the guidelines published by the Italian minister of culture point, inter alia, to the potential conflict between current Italian law and policy and that of the European Union,[34] and particularly to Article 14 of the 2019 Copyright Directive in the Digital Single Market (CDSM), by which: "Member States shall provide that, when the term of protection of a work of visual art has expired, any material resulting from an act of reproduction of that work is not subject to copyright or related rights, unless the material resulting from that act of reproduction is original in the sense that it is the author's own intellectual creation."[35]

While Italy has effectively circumvented this requirement by subjecting the implementation of the CDSM in amending Italy's copyright law, such that the implementation of the European Directive would not otherwise derogate from the provisions of the Italian CCLH concerning the reproduction of cultural property,[36] Roberto Caso and other

---

[32] *Id.* at 12–13.

[33] *Id.* at 13.

[34] Dore, *supra* note 17.

[35] Directive 2019/790 of the European Parliament and of the Council of 17 April 2019 on Copyright and Related Rights in the Digital Single Market and Amending Directives 96/9/EC and 2001/29/EC, 2019 O.J. (L 130) 92, Art. 14.

[36] Dore, *supra* note 17 ("Italian policymakers felt the urge to provide an explicit derogation for C.b.c. provisions when drafting the domestic transposition of the EU provision, namely Article 32 of the Italian Copyright Act").

commentators point to a more fundamental jurisprudential problem. According to Caso, these recent decisions create a "new form of pseudo-intellectual property (in this case, a pseudo-copyright) that would attribute to the Italian State the power to exclusively control the commercial use of cultural heritage images."[37]

But the implications of this recent legislative, administrative, and judicial framework go even a step further in reconceptualizing the legal standing of Italian cultural institutions as proprietors and custodians of cultural objects. Cultural institutions are endowed with what is essentially an eternal legal power to control not only the physical aspects of the object (e.g., by setting the rules about the exhibition of the object to the public or charging a fee for entry into the museum) but, more broadly, the object's intangible aspects. By limiting the permitted use or reproduction of the image of a cultural object to a narrow set of circumstances in which other parties do not have to seek permission for a specific use or pay a concession fee, the cultural institution becomes an almost omnipotent owner or controller not only of the item itself but also of its intangible value and meaning as a subject of cultural, social, and historical content.

Thus, in property theory terms, a museum that possesses a cultural object becomes a "sovereign,"[38] or the party with the power to "set the agenda" for the asset,[39] enjoying a very broad set of in rem rights, without a corresponding set of duties applying to other parties and the public at large. Whether such an approach should serve as a basis for a property theory of ownership and custody of cultural objects is a question that needs to be considered in a more profound manner.

5.3   Redefining the Museum: Implications for Its Role as Custodian of Culture

In an Extraordinary General Assembly held in Prague on August 24, 2022, ICOM approved a new definition of the term "museum,"[40] which

---

[37] Caso, *supra* note 25. *See also* Roberto Caso, *David, Uomo Vitruviano e Diritto all'Imagine del Bene Culturale, Trib. Firenze 20 aprile 2023 e Trib. Venezia, ord. 17 Novembre 2022,* CXLVIII (n. 7–8) Foro Italiano I 2257 (July–Aug. 2023) (It).

[38] Morris R. Cohen, *Property and Sovereignty,* 13 Cornell L. Q. 8 (1927).

[39] Larissa Katz, *Exclusion and Exclusivity in Property Law,* 58 U. Toronto L.J. 275, 278 (2008) (arguing that "ownership, like sovereignty, relies on a notional hierarchy, in which the owner's authority to set the agenda is supreme, if not absolute, in relation to other individuals").

[40] ICOM, *Museum Definition,* https://icom.museum/en/resources/standards-guidelines/museum-definition/ (last visited Feb. 1, 2025).

has been subsequently incorporated into Article 3, Section 1 of the ICOM Statutes.[41] This change was the result of a process of meetings and consultations coordinated by the ICOM Standing Committee for the Museum Definition (known as "ICOM Define") over a period of eighteen months, from December 2020 to June 2022.[42] The proposed change was approved by an overwhelming majority of over 92 percent at ICOM's General Assembly.[43] It thus reflects a broad consensus among ICOM's approximately 50,000 members, including national committees, cultural institutions, other organizations, and individuals hailing from 138 countries and territories across the world.[44]

The previous definition of a "museum" had read as follows:

> A museum is a non-profit, permanent institution in the service of society and its development, open to the public, which acquires, conserves, researches, communicates and exhibits the tangible and intangible heritage of humanity and its environment for the purposes of education, study and enjoyment.[45]

The definition approved by ICOM's Extraordinary General Assembly in 2022 now reads:

> A museum is a not-for-profit, permanent institution in the service of society that researches, collects, conserves, interprets and exhibits tangible and intangible heritage. Open to the public, accessible and inclusive, museums foster diversity and sustainability. They operate and communicate ethically, professionally and with the participation of communities, offering varied experiences for education, enjoyment, reflection and knowledge sharing.[46]

Reviewing the changes that were made to the definition of a museum, one focal point seems to be the addition of the duty of museums to "operate and communicate ethically, professionally." The duty not only to operate,

---

[41] ICOM Statutes (as amended and adopted by the Extraordinary General Assembly on June 9, 2023), https://icom.museum/wp-content/uploads/2023/07/Statutes_2023_EN.pdf (last visited Feb. 1, 2025).

[42] ICOM, *Extraordinary General Meeting* (Aug. 24, 2022), *Item 2 (Final Report)*, at 3–11, https://icom.museum/wp-content/uploads/2022/07/EN_EGA2022_MuseumDefinition_WDoc_Final-2.pdf.

[43] ICOM, *Museum Definition, supra* note 40.

[44] ICOM, *Become a Member,* https://icom.museum/en/get-involved/become-a-member/ (last visited Feb. 1, 2025).

[45] ICOM, *Extraordinary General Meeting, supra* note 42, at 12.

[46] *Id.* at 13; ICOM, *Museum Definition, supra* note 40; ICOM Statutes, *supra* note 41, art. 3 – Section 1.

but also to "communicate," in such manner, seems to correspond well to the general processes portrayed in Chapters 3 and 4, by which the soft-law, professional, and ethical norms dealing with provenance research, due diligence, and transparency (such as those for setting up and operating digital databases that are accessible to the public) are gradually changing the ways in which cultural institutions are expected to operate on a regular basis.

Another key feature is the redefinition of the identity of the different types of stakeholders with which a cultural institution should engage, and to which it should be held accountable, at least to a certain degree. Thus, while the previous definition referred to "the tangible and intangible heritage of humanity," the current definition uses the term "tangible and intangible heritage" such that the word "humanity" is omitted. At the same time, the new definition requires museums to act "with the participation of communities." What might these changes mean for reconsidering the role of a museum as a proprietor and custodian of cultural objects? Whose interests, besides its own, should a cultural institution promote in fulfilling both these roles?

A point of departure for this query, already referred to in Chapter 1, is John Henry Merryman's depiction of two different ways of thinking about cultural property: "cultural internationalism" versus "cultural nationalism."[47] These competing conceptions have been analyzed in the context of the legitimacy of "universal" or "encyclopedic" museums located in Western countries,[48] in light of growing demands for the return of objects by source nations, including former colonies or territories that had been controlled by Western powers.[49]

As noted in Chapter 1, Merryman sought to anchor the "cultural internationalism" approach in the term "cultural heritage of all mankind" that appears in the Preamble to the 1954 Hague Convention for the Protection of Cultural Property in the Event of Armed Conflict.[50] Adversely, according to Merryman, the "cultural nationalism" approach emphasizes the

---

[47] John Henry Merryman, *Two Ways of Thinking about Cultural Property*, 80 AM. J. INT'L L. 851 (1986).

[48] For the concept of the "universal" or "encyclopedic" museum, whose roots go back to the era of Enlightenment, *see* James Cuno, *View from the Universal Museum, in* IMPERIALISM, ART AND RESTITUTION 15 (John Henry Merryman ed., 2006).

[49] *See* Chapter 1, Section 1.2.

[50] Convention for the Protection of Cultural Property in the Event of Armed Conflict with Regulations for the Execution of the Convention, May 14, 1954, 249 U.N.T.S. 240, Preamble ("Being convinced that damage to cultural property belonging to any people whatsoever means damage to the cultural heritage of all mankind").

interests of states in their "national cultural heritage," an approach supported by more recent international instruments on cultural property,
such as the 1970 UNESCO Convention on the Means of Prohibiting
and Preventing the Illicit Import, Export and Transfer of Ownership of
Cultural Property.[51] This latter approach has gained currency over the past
few decades, such that it was already more dominant by the mid-1980s,[52]
and even more so in the twenty-first century. Accordingly, many source
nations, such as those in Latin America, are engaging in efforts to return
cultural items that are currently located in universal museums and similar cultural institutions in the West as part of an inward-looking political
discourse, driven by an ideology that seeks to "imagine a community of
belonging that the state, as a political organization, claims to embody."[53]

Probably the most prominent clash of these cultural conceptions
is manifested in the nearly 200-year-old British–Greek debate over the
Parthenon Marbles. The two countries have placed themselves at the
forefront of this discourse, with the government of Greece reclaiming
the marbles from the British Museum as part of a broader campaign to
reclaim its sovereignty and control over its history and cultural identity, and the government of Britain currently standing behind the British
Museum as part of its broader view that Britain serves as a proper home
for these world heritage treasures. The claimed proprietary interests of
the British Museum, based also on the argued legitimacy of the Ottoman
letter of permission given to Lord Elgin in 1801, became embedded, in
broader terms, with the initial legitimacy to establish the British Museum
as a world hub of cultural treasures and to keep them in the country, even
with the changing political times.[54]

Thus, the key protagonists of the legal and moral debate about the ownership and possession of the Parthenon Marbles involves – besides the
British Museum itself – two nation-states that promote allegedly different
concepts of "culture" in the service of their (conflicting) national interests.

---

[51] United Nations Educational, Scientific and Cultural Organization (UNESCO), Convention
on the Means of Prohibiting and Preventing the Illicit Import, Export, and Transfer of
Ownership of Cultural Property, Nov. 14, 1970, 823 U.N.T.S. 231, Preamble ("It is incumbent upon every State to protect the cultural property existing within its territory").

[52] Merryman, *supra* note 47, at 846.

[53] PIERRE LOSSON, THE RETURN OF CULTURAL HERITAGE TO LATIN AMERICA:
NATIONALISM, POLICY, AND POLITICS IN COLOMBIA, MEXICO, AND PERU 10–12
(2022).

[54] *See, generally,* ALEXANDER HERMAN, THE PARTHENON MARBLES DISPUTE:
HERITAGE, LAW, POLITICS (2023); CATHERINE TITI, THE PARTHENON MARBLES
AND INTERNATIONAL LAW (2023).

Britain does not seek to altruistically promote an "international" or "global" interest by keeping the Parthenon Marbles in London, but those of the British Museum and itself as a nation-state. Greece, on its part, purports to represent the collective interests of Greek people (past, present, and future) with its demand to recognize its national ownership in the Parthenon Marbles and to take possession of the cultural items by placing them in the Acropolis Museum in Athens.[55]

That said, the new definition of a "museum" by ICOM, alongside other trends that have taken root over the past few decades, seeks to put other types of stakeholders on the map of legitimate interests that should be taken into consideration in thinking about property and custody in the context of cultural objects. These parties may include, on the one hand, subnational or extranational groups, such as indigenous communities, groups of ethnic or religious origin, and even individuals,[56] and on the other a new understanding of a "global audience" that is not represented exclusively by nation-states or formal international organizations such as UNESCO. In a way, the current age of globalization and digitalization may allow us to reconsider concepts of global audience and "global cultural heritage" that are more decentralized in nature. These concepts may reconnect us to notions of museums, culture, and society at large that were developed in early modern times, such as in the 1625 text titled *Musaeum* by Federico Borromeo, founder of the Ambrosiana Gallery in Milan, about the importance of safeguarding art for future generations.[57]

This reconceptualization of the museum is essential for identifying the in rem rights and in rem duties of cultural institutions as proprietors and custodians of cultural objects. While it may define a certain set of rights that a museum may have in charging entry tickets to the museum, making curatorial choices, or appropriating at least part of the value of cultural

---

[55] Andrew Macaskill, Alistair Smout & Renee Maltezou, *Greece, Britain Trade Blame over Cancelled Meeting in Parthenon Marbles Dispute*, REUTERS, Nov. 28, 2023 (reporting on a canceled meeting of the two prime ministers).

[56] Ana Filipa Vrdoljak & Francesco Francioni, *Introduction, in* THE OXFORD HANDBOOK OF INTERNATIONAL CULTURAL HERITAGE LAW 1, 5–9 (Francesco Francioni & Ana Filipa Vrdoljak eds., 2020) (addressing the growing role of nonstate actors such as communities, civil society groups, and corporations in the field of cultural heritage).

[57] Claudia S. Quiñones Vilá, *What's in a Name? Museums in the Post-Digital Age*, 6 SANTANDER ART & CULTURE L. REV. 177, 180 (2020) (citing Giovanni Mazzaferro, *Federico Borromeo, Musaeum. The Ambrosiana Gallery in the Memoirs of Its Founder. Edited by Piero Cigada. With a Commentary by Gianfranco Ravasi. Review by Giovanni Mazzaferro*, LETTERATURA ARTISTICA, CROSS-CULTURAL STUDIES IN ART HISTORY SOURCES (May 4, 2017)).

items and collections in their possession, a new concept of property and custody also requires us to reconsider to whom a museum may have duties as a proprietor of an object and, more broadly, as a custodian of culture.

5.4 Toward a Theory of Proprietary Rights and Duties vis-à-vis Cultural Objects

This section seeks to lay the foundations of a legal theory of the rights and duties of cultural institutions that possess cultural objects as part of their collections, considering these institutions' dual role as both proprietors of cultural objects and custodians of the objects' intangible value to various groups of stakeholders, such as professional circles, communities, and the public at large.

The analysis begins by identifying the fundamental structure of property law as typified by a system of legal entitlements that have an in rem effect (i.e., applicable also vis-à-vis third parties) and that are accordingly governed by a *numerus clausus* ("closed list") principle of recognized proprietary interests in a particular legal system. Notwithstanding these structural traits, this section shows that the substantive content of in rem rights and duties can be designed somewhat differently for various types of objects and for different types of subjects (owners, possessors, or other third parties). It also emphasizes the growing recognition, in both theory and practice, of in rem duties that owners and other holders of proprietary interests in assets may have, alongside their in rem rights. Moving from these general principles to the specific context of cultural objects, this section outlines the main in rem rights and in rem duties that cultural institutions in possession of cultural objects should hold, considering their unique role as both proprietors and custodians.

5.4.1 *Property Law Taxonomy of In Rem Rights and In Rem Duties*

In the early twentieth century, American legal scholar Wesley Hohfeld set out to challenge a long-standing legal dichotomy, dating back to Roman law, of rights in rem (Latin: "against a thing") versus rights in personam ("against a person").[58] Defining and analyzing the different attributes of in personam rights through a delineation of what he termed "jural opposites"

---

[58] Wesley Newcomb Hohfeld, *Fundamental Legal Conceptions as Applied in Judicial Reasoning*, 26 YALE L.J. 710, 720–29 (1917) (hereinafter: "Hohfeld, 1917").

and "jural correlatives" that govern interpersonal legal relationships (such that, for example, one person's right is correlated with a duty imposed on another person), Hohfeld argued that the same typology of jural opposites and jural correlatives applies to in rem rights, except for the large, indefinite number of persons who are bound by such legal relationships.[59] This means that in rem rights, while fundamentally interpersonal in nature just like in personam rights, extend well beyond parties that have a privity of contract between them or another explicit source of interpersonal obligation (such as a duty of care under the law of torts). In other words, interpersonal legal entitlements that are typified as having a proprietary effect, including ownership, lease, and nonpossessory proprietary interests such as a mortgage or a lien, are valid not only vis-à-vis a contractual or similar counterpart but also have a legal effect "good against the world."[60] Moreover, parties to a proprietary dispute are often legal "strangers" that find themselves entangled ex post facto in a clash of competing claims over the same asset: consider the legal contest between a good-faith purchaser of an artwork and a dispossessed original owner (or heirs).

Hohfeld's theory, which was largely analytical-jurisprudential in nature and became identified with the metaphor by which property should be viewed as consisting of a "bundle of rights" that is also applicable to broad categories of third parties,[61] has had a profound influence on subsequent legal theories, including those of authors who sought to advance politically or socially oriented ideas about the justification for a redistribution of wealth through a realignment of interpersonal legal relationships. These broader-based theories cannot be addressed here in detail.[62]

As a structural matter, Hohfeld's reconceptualization of in rem entitlements means that for a system of proprietary entitlements to function well it must consider the broad-based effects of delineating, informing, and enforcing legal interests that apply to broad categories of stakeholders.

---

[59] Wesley Newcomb Hohfeld, *Some Fundamental Legal Conceptions as Applied in Judicial Reasoning*, 23 YALE L.J. 16, 28–32 (1913); Hohfeld, 1917, *supra* note 58, at 710–17.

[60] In the context of property law, this term also follows up on the Latin term *erga omnes*. *See* Jan Felix Hoffmann, *The Proprium of Property Law*, 10 EUR. PROPERTY L.J. 241, 247–51 (2021).

[61] Daniel B. Klein & John Robinson, *Property: A Bundle of Rights? Prologue to the Property Symposium*, 8 ECON. J. WATCH 193, 195 (2011).

[62] AMNON LEHAVI, THE CONSTRUCTION OF PROPERTY: NORMS, INSTITUTIONS, CHALLENGES 26–30 (2013) (discussing "the political version of the bundle of rights" that emerged in the academic literature following Hohfeld's work).

Probably the best example of a currently dominant legal theory that considers such aspects, and actually puts them at the forefront of its theoretical principles, is the "information costs" theory of property, influenced by the law and economics approach and developed in the early twenty-first century by Thomas Merrill and Henry Smith.[63] Setting out to engage in efficient legal design, Merrill and Smith advocate that a key purpose of property is to economize on the legal system's information costs that may accrue ordinarily to multiple types of actors impacted by legal entitlements with an in rem applicability. Property is measured by its ability to "reduce the informational burdens of the owners and non-owners who have to cope with the system."[64] This notion may be allegedly aided by the prevailing legal concept of *numerus clausus*, according to which only limited types of property rights are recognized as such by the legal system, with Merrill and Smith presenting this principle as one of attaining "optimal standardization" in property law.[65]

However, while such general principles are instrumental for a system of legal entitlements with an in rem or third-party applicability to function well, this should not be confused with sticking to a "monochromatic approach" to property, by which the entire world can be explained via a single normative metric. In rem entitlements need not have a single substantive content regardless of the type of asset that is the object of property, or the identity of different subjects (owners and various categories of non-owners). If sufficient clarity, transparency, and publicity of norms can be achieved in articulating certain variations across the system of property for different types of assets or for different categories of stakeholders, property law can maintain its essential structural in rem nature without succumbing to a single substantive blueprint that cannot be normatively defended.

Thus, for example, the "fair use" doctrine in copyright law substantially limits the copyright owner's right to exclude others in a manner that does not exist for other types of intellectual property rights, such as patents, or for other assets, such as land.[66] This doctrinal variation derives from a

---

[63] Thomas W. Merrill & Henry E. Smith, *What Happened to Property in Law and Economics?* 111 YALE L.J. 357, 359 (2001).

[64] Robert C. Ellickson, *Two Cheers for the Bundle-of-Sticks Metaphor, Three Cheers for Merrill and Smith*, 8 ECON. J. WATCH 215, 219 (2011).

[65] Thomas W. Merrill & Henry E. Smith, *Optimal Standardization in the Law of Property: The Numerus Clausus Principle*, 110 YALE L.J. 1 (2001). *See also* BRAM AKKERMANS, THE PRINCIPLE OF NUMERUS CLAUSUS IN EUROPEAN PROPERTY LAW (2008).

[66] *See, e.g.*, Neil Weinstock Netanel, *Making Sense of Fair Use*, 15 LEWIS & CLARK L. REV. 715 (2011).

normative balance between incentivizing creators of innovative and original content and promoting the public interest in allowing nonowners to use such content for certain purposes, such as education – thus distinguishing between different categories of nonowners. Moreover, most types of intellectual property rights, including both copyrights and patents, are time-limited, such that at the end of a set period of protection the underlying asset (the creative work or the technological innovation) becomes part of the public domain and is free for all to use – unlike the case of land, chattels, and other types of objects in which the right of ownership is not time-limited.

The same may hold true for different categories of subjects of property rights (such as owners, holders of other proprietary entitlements, and other persons affected by the asset). In particular, the rules for public ownership may somewhat diverge from those for private ownership, without undermining property law's general structural features. For example, the common law "public trust doctrine," which originated in England and developed in the United States during the nineteenth century – by which the government holds certain types of assets in trust for the public – may place certain limits on the public owner, as compared with private owners of the same kind of asset.[67] At the same time, the rationale by which government holds certain types of assets in trust for its public has also worked to give it increased protection versus certain types of nonowners. Thus, under common law rules originating in England, adverse possession of land does not run against the government.[68] Although this immunity against adverse possession has been somewhat downscaled in the United States, most state courts there still adhere to this rule, reasoning that, because the government holds land in trust for all people, they should not lose it because of the negligence of government officials – thus distinguishing public from private ownership.[69] As shown below, this distinction between different types of subjects may be particularly relevant for cultural institutions that are located along a broad public–private spectrum.

Moreover, any discussion of the in rem nature of property must take into consideration the growing recognition, in theory and practice, of the role of in rem duties alongside in rem rights.

---

[67] *See, generally*, MOLLY SELVIN, THIS TENDER AND DELICATE BUSINESS: THE PUBLIC TRUST DOCTRINE IN AMERICAN LAW AND ECONOMIC POLICY, 1789–920 (1987).

[68] Amnon Lehavi, *Rescaling City Property*, 76 ARK. L. REV. 75, 123–24 (2023).

[69] *Id.* at 103.

While property theory has tended to focus on the normatively desirable scope of in rem rights that an entitlement holder should have regarding an asset, and the corresponding duties that different types of nonowners should have to respect such rights, relatively little discussion has been devoted to the affirmative in rem duties that an entitlement holder may have toward others.

Perhaps not surprisingly, property theories that consider the owner's right to exclude others as the key essential trait of property also see little room for affirmative in rem duties imposed on owners. Thus, according to Merrill and Smith, in rem duties, such as the duty of a landowner to refrain from carrying out a nuisance activity, are very limited in scope and "negative" in nature.[70]

In contrast, legal scholars who advocate a "social-obligation norm in property" or a theory of "property and human flourishing," such as David Lametti,[71] Gregory Alexander,[72] and Joseph Singer,[73] argue that property owners owe certain affirmative duties toward other members of society. Such a social-obligation norm is justified by a broader viewpoint, not necessarily linked to the specific asset, according to which the development of personal human capabilities and the owners' ability to benefit from assets result from their lives in a social setting and the fact that such resources are "internalized from one's culture." This means, in turn, that any person "must be in, belong to, and support a certain kind of society – a society that supports a certain kind of political, social, and moral culture and that maintains a decent background material structure."[74]

A different approach toward in rem duties may take a middle stance, one that goes beyond the narrow scope of negative duties offered by exclusionary theories of property but that is also different from the overbroad scope of progressive property theories that effectively introduce a redistributive element to affirmative in rem duties. A new look at affirmative

---

[70] Thomas W. Merrill & Henry E. Smith, *The Property/Contract Interface*, 101 COLUM. L. REV. 773, 789 (2001).

[71] David Lametti, *The (Virtue) Ethics of Private Property: A Framework and Implications*, in NEW PERSPECTIVES ON PROPERTY LAW: OBLIGATIONS AND RESTITUTION 39, 66 (Alastair Hudson ed., 2003) (arguing that "private property will have to be seen as to be as much about duties and goals as it is about rights").

[72] GREGORY S. ALEXANDER, PROPERTY AND HUMAN FLOURISHING 39–73 (2018) (discussing owners' obligations).

[73] Joseph William Singer, *Democratic Estates: Property Law in a Free and Democratic Society*, 94 CORNELL L. REV. 1009 (2009) (arguing that property owners owe a duty of "attentiveness" toward other members of society).

[74] ALEXANDER, *supra* note 72, at 55.

in rem duties should begin by identifying the various classes of persons or stakeholders that may be impacted by the entitlement holder's modes of control over the asset – especially when such an owner or controller holds significant power over others. This is the case, for example, with patent law, which generally requires patent applicants, as a condition for obtaining a patent, to disclose the content of the invention, such that non-owners, including scientific or professional competitors, would be able to use it once the patent expires. This means that the time-limited in rem right to exclude is balanced by imposing an affirmative in rem duty on the owner of the patent, one which seeks to serve not only the interests of other innovators or manufacturers but also those of the public at large.[75] As the following analysis shows, this concept should be even more robust in the case of cultural items.

5.4.2   Cultural Institutions as Bearers of Proprietary Rights and Duties

5.4.2.1   Preliminary Notes on Subjects and Objects

Prior to delineating the general boundaries of a property theory of in rem rights and in rem duties of cultural institutions vis-à-vis their collections, two preliminary notes are in order: the first is with regard to the taxonomy of subjects (or protagonists) of such rights and duties, and the second pertains to the objects.

First, cultural institutions, and museums in particular, are located along a very broad spectrum of public-to-private modes of ownership and control. At one end of the spectrum are national institutions that are governed by specific statutes and are accordingly subject to relatively strict forms of public control. A prominent example is national museums in the United Kingdom, such as the British Museum, which is governed by the British Museum Act 1963,[76] or the Victoria and Albert Museum, the Science Museum, the Armouries, and the Royal Botanic Gardens, Kew, which are governed by the National Heritage Act 1983.[77] These statutes forbid, inter alia, such museums from deaccessioning cultural objects in their possession, save for narrow exceptions specified in

---

[75] Lisa Larrimore Ouellette, *Do Patents Disclose Useful Information?* 25 HARV. J.L. & TECH. 531 (2012).

[76] British Museum Act 1963 c. 24, as amended (U.K.).

[77] National Heritage Act 1983 c. 47, as amended (U.K.).

the relevant statute.[78] This strong form of government control – including statutory rules on the inalienability of cultural objects in a national collection – exists in other countries as well.[79] More broadly, a large number of cultural institutions around the globe are owned or controlled by national, regional, or local governments, and as such these public institutions rely prominently on public funding and are accordingly subject to public scrutiny and substantial regulation.[80]

Other types of museums, which are governed by nongovernmental charities and other types of nonprofit organizations, are not directly owned by the state but they may nevertheless rely, at least partially, on public funding, or at the least – as is the case with nonprofit private museums in the United States – on a special tax status that incentivizes donations by private benefactors.[81] Then there are entirely private collections, alongside for-profit galleries and other art vendors.

This enormous diversity makes it difficult to define a single set of in rem rights and in rem duties for cultural institutions holding cultural objects, one that also takes into consideration the implications of an institution's specific location along the public–private continuum. However, it seems that one may nevertheless identify the mainstay of what a museum is, as currently defined by ICOM, as a point of departure for establishing at least a basic set of such rights and duties – while leaving room for certain particularities that may derive from rights and duties conferred by specific legal arrangements.

Thus, the definition of a museum as a "non-profit, permanent institution in the service of society and its development, open to the public," one

---

[78] For the potential effect of the Charities Act 2022 c. 6 (U.K.) on the power of national museums to return or restitute cultural items, *see* Alexander Herman, *Museums, Restitution and the New Charities Act*, 27 ART ANTIQUITY & L. 193, 193 (2022) (noting that in October 2022 the "Government stated that before these provisions could come into force it must first seek to fully understand their implications for national museums and other charities").

[79] This is also the case with national museums in France, which are subject to the rule of inalienability of the collections, meaning that for a national museum to restitute or return an object, the French Sensate must enact a special exemption. Hannah McGivern, *French Senate Votes Unanimously for Restitution to Benin and Senegal in "Act of Friendship and Trust,"* THE ART NEWSPAPER, Nov. 5, 2020. *See also* Chapter 6, Section 6.2.

[80] *See* ELINA MOUSTAIRA, ART COLLECTIONS, PRIVATE AND PUBLIC: A COMPARATIVE LEGAL STUDY 59–70 (2015) (discussing the governance, and particularly modes of financing, of museums in Europe that are mostly public).

[81] Amy Lin, *U.S. Senate Questions the Tax Status of Museum*, WIDEWALLS, Nov. 30, 2015 (reporting on letters sent by U.S. Senator Orrin Hatch to several small private museums in the United States, suggesting that "tax-exempt museums should focus on providing a public good and not the art of skirting around the tax code").

that is devoted to the "purposes of education, study and enjoyment,"[82] may create a significant common denominator for most types of public and private cultural institutions in the world, as also reflected in ICOM's broad membership.

Identifying such a common denominator is plausible also because practically all museums, whether public or private, are dependent at least to some extent on potential income deriving from ticket sales, merchandising, and other revenues that are tied to the museum space and to the cultural objects that comprise its collections, such that the assertion of property rights by the museum in the space and cultural objects is instrumental, at least to some degree, to its ability to operate.[83]

As for other subjects (or protagonists), it is important to recall that the current ICOM definition of a museum explicitly introduces the "participation of communities" alongside the operation of museums in the "service of society."[84] More broadly, the contemporary concept of stakeholders of cultural items located in museums and other cultural institutions seeks to include much broader circles, from subnational or extranational groups, such as indigenous communities and groups of ethnic or religious origin, to a new understanding of human society or a "global audience" that is not represented exclusively by nation-states or by international/intergovernmental organizations.[85]

Second, as for the types of objects concerned, it may be useful to rely on the common denominator resulting from definitions in international conventions and similar instruments, such as the one offered in Article 2 of the 1995 UNIDROIT Convention, by which "cultural objects are those which, on religious or secular grounds, are of importance for archaeology, prehistory, history, literature, art or science."[86] Such a definition seems to make clear that, notwithstanding the specific type of cultural institution in possession of an object and the object's market value as may be reflected

---

[82] *See* text accompanying *supra* note 46.
[83] *See, e.g.,* Catherine Hickley, *Berlin's State Museums Raise Ticket Prices as Costs Climb,* THE ART NEWSPAPER, Dec. 14, 2023; Julia Halperin, *The Hangover after the Museum Party: Institutions in the US Are Facing a Funding Crisis,* THE ART NEWSPAPER, Jan. 20, 2024.
[84] *See* text accompanying *supra* note 46.
[85] *See* text accompanying *supra* notes 56–57.
[86] UNIDROIT Convention on Stolen or Illegally Exported Cultural Objects, 24 June 1995, 2421 U.N.T.S. 457, art. 2 (hereinafter: "1995 UNIDROIT Convention"); *See also* Council of Europe, Convention on Offences Relating to Cultural Property (CETS No. 221), May 19, 2017, Ch. 1, art. 2, §2a (referring to items considered "on religious or secular grounds … as being of importance for archaeology, prehistory, ethnology, history, literature, art or science").

in the art market or for purposes of insurance, cultural property also possesses components of value that are attributed to it by various groups of stakeholders, from individuals to local/source communities, to the global public at large. These largely common definitions may, therefore, aid in establishing a joint point of departure for delineating the broad contours of in rem rights and in rem duties concerning cultural objects in the possession of cultural institutions.

5.4.2.2 Proprietary Control over a Physical Item vs. Control over Its Image

As a general principle, any delineation of in rem rights and in rem duties that cultural institutions might have regarding cultural objects should consider both the tangible and intangible features – and respective values – of cultural property, and how these are embedded in the physical and digital spaces occupied by the cultural institution. In considering what aspects of control and appropriation of value should be awarded to cultural institutions, there is special merit in allowing a cultural institution to appropriate the value of a cultural object when, under the relevant circumstances, it is inherently tied to the *space* in which it is exhibited or kept by the institution.

This means, for example, that a museum should be regularly allowed to control physical access to the objects, by establishing opening hours, charging entry fees, and more fundamentally by making curatorial choices about which items to display and how to organize them as part of its collections. In so doing, the cultural institution should protect the integrity of the works and their creators, especially if a moral right (*droit moral*) still exists regarding a certain cultural object.[87] It should also consider the interests of the relevant source community, especially in the context of an ethnographical or archaeological collection. But, at the same time, such parties should not have a formal right of veto over curatorial choices made by the cultural institution in using its space.

The link between a cultural object and the place in which it is physically kept may bear implications also for the potential scope of control that a cultural institution should have over the image of the cultural object. This means that, while basic images and relevant information about each object should be available to the general public as part of the institution's general

---

[87] For the principle of the moral right, and a comparative study of the duration and scope of its protection in different jurisdictions, *see* Cyrill P. Rigamonti, *The Conceptual Transformation of Moral Rights*, 55 AM. J. COMP. L. 67 (2007).

duty as a custodian of culture – while not being a full-fledged trustee or fiduciary formally accountable to a certain group of stakeholders or to humanity at large[88] – the cultural institution should have more power to control value attributes of its collections as such, or of images and other pieces of information about items that are inherently linked to the space in which the cultural object is held.

This point of view may allow us to reconsider the current approach taken in Italy about the use and reproduction of images of cultural property in the possession of public cultural institutions. As Section 5.2 has shown, Italian law and policy currently grants cultural institutions extremely broad powers vis-à-vis third parties in deciding whether to permit the use or reproduction of images of items of cultural property, and if so, what fees to charge – with the ministerial guidelines setting minimum rates, meaning that a specific cultural institution can set the fees at an even higher rate.[89]

The Italian approach can be justly criticized for being overbroad, and particularly for adopting an approach according to which serving as a custodian of cultural property is solely about granting cultural institutions exclusive power of decision-making and entitlement to economic use, but it does not impose any sort of affirmative duty toward third parties (with the exception of the vague duty, identified by the court in *David*'s case, to protect the "Italian people" against alleged injuries to their collective culture by preventing inappropriate uses that may have the effect of "debasing, obscuring, mortifying, humiliating the high symbolic and identity value of the work").[90]

In considering the appropriate scope of in rem rights and in rem duties that cultural institutions should have regarding access to images, and specifically to the reproduction and use thereof, three different questions may be posed: (1) Does a cultural institution have a right to limit, or altogether ban, visitors or other parties from taking photos – or otherwise producing images – of an object located within its premises? (2) Can the cultural institution limit or prohibit the use or reproduction of an already-existing image of the item – whether it was made prior to the item entering the collection of the cultural institution, or at another point in time in which it was already part of it? (3) Does the cultural institution have an affirmative duty to make accessible to the general public images of some or all

---

[88] *See infra* Section 5.4.2.3.
[89] *See* text accompanying *supra* notes 7–14.
[90] *David* case, *supra* note 24, at 11–12.

items in its collections, and, if so, do these have to meet certain minimal standards?

(1) Right of Cultural Institutions to Limit Others from Making Onsite Images or Copies A museum should be generally empowered to set the criteria for the creation of images or reproductions of a cultural item by others inside the museum space, and to settle this also through the contractual terms and conditions applying to visits to the museum. The general norm that has emerged across most of the world's cultural institutions distinguishes between private, noncommercial uses and other types of use, permitting the former and limiting/forbidding the latter.

Thus, according to the "photo and video policy" of the Metropolitan Museum of Art in New York, "photographs and video captured at The Met cannot be published, sold, reproduced, transferred, distributed, or commercially exploited," while allowing for "non-flash photography and video recording for private, non-commercial use, unless otherwise noted."[91] Interestingly, in 2014, Italy enshrined in a legislative decree the legitimacy of taking photos of cultural objects for personal use or study when it does not involve a commercial activity,[92] while defining the term "commercial activity" broadly and placing many other limits,[93] as discussed in Section 5.2.

The ability of cultural institutions to control the ways in which others may make copies or reproductions within the physical premises of the institution is tied to the linkage that a cultural institution is generally entitled to promote between a cultural item and the space in which it is located, as a cultural institution's operation relies on its ability to attract visitors to its physical premises and regulate their behavior while they are visiting. However, as suggested below, this should not release the cultural institution from its general in rem duty, owed to the public at large, to

---

[91] The Metropolitan Museum of Art, *Photo and Video Policy*, www.metmuseum.org/policies/photo-and-video-policy (last visited Feb. 1, 2025).

[92] *See* Chiara Gallo, *The Limits on the Commercial Reproduction of Italian Cultural Heritage: The Application of the Codice dei Beni Culturali e del Paesaggio: From Italian Renaissance Art to New Technologies*, 28 ART ANTIQUITY & L. 299, 309–10 (2023) (referring to Decreto legge 31 maggio 2014, n. 83, Disposizioni urgenti per la tutela del patrimonio culturale, lo sviluppo della cultura e il rilancio del turismo, G.U., May 31, 2014, n. 125; Legge, 29 luglio 2014, n. 106, Conversione, con modificazioni, del decreto-legge 31 May 2014, n. 83, recante disposizioni urgenti per la tutela del patrimonio culturale, lo sviluppo della cultura e il rilancio del turismo, G.U., July 30, 2014, n. 175) (It.).

[93] Gallo, *supra* note 92, at 311–14 (criticizing the overbroad Italian approach of placing limits on use and reproduction of images).

make available images or other digital representations for items that have a broader-based cultural value. The extent of such an affirmative duty placed on the cultural institutions will be discussed below.

Interestingly, although a cultural institution, as owner or lawful possessor of a cultural item, is generally free to make new onsite images and reproductions, or to otherwise commercialize on items in its collections, it may be limited in doing so if the artwork is still under copyright in favor of the artist or an assignee.[94] Accordingly, a museum wishing to enjoy the opportunity to benefit economically from its ownership or lawful possession of a cultural item in its collections would have to reach a contractual agreement with artists or others holding a valid economic copyright.[95] Yet another question – whether a museum making new onsite images or copies would be entitled to limit access to such images, or to charge fees for using them, by arguing that it has copyright in the new photo or another image creation – will be analyzed in subsection (3) as it may coincide with an in rem duty of cultural institutions to make at least some items digitally accessible.

(2)   **Right of Cultural Institutions to Limit Others from Using Existing Images or Copies**   The heart of the debate about the normative legitimacy of Italian law and policy seems to focus on the asserted power of public cultural institutions to block in retrospect the long-standing flow of images, reproductions, and other representations of cultural items that have been part of global culture. These images have served as a source of enjoyment, study, and inspiration, and were truly part of the public domain for decades, centuries, and even beyond (for archaeological items).

Images, reproductions, and other representations of Leonardo da Vinci's 1490 *Vitruvian Man* or Michelangelo's 1501–1504 *David* have been in circulation since their creation – including before entering their current location – and these have helped to shape their prominence in world culture. Accordingly, Ravensburger did not need to go inside the Gallerie dell'Accademia di Venezia to obtain new images of the *Vitruvian Man*, and the same applies to *GQ Italia*, the Galleria dell'Accademia di Firenze,

---

[94] A similar limit may apply if the use or representation made by the museum may infringe on the artist's moral right. *See* Rigamonti, *supra* note 87.

[95] *See, generally,* Association of Art Museums Directors (AAMD), *Guidelines for the Use of Copyrighted Materials and Works of Art by Art Museums* (Oct. 11, 2017), https://cms .aamd.org/sites/default/files/document/Guidelines%20for%20the%20Use%20of%20 Copyrighted%20Materials.pdf.

and images of *David*. Granting a cultural institution absolute control, with a decades/centuries-long retrospective effect, over the circulation of noncopyrighted cultural images and representations, cannot be defended.

That said, what should be the dividing line for a legitimate appropriation of value and control that a cultural institution should have over tangible and intangible features of a cultural item, especially if the museum may have spent a considerable amount of money purchasing the piece, and is continuously investing its resources in preserving and presenting the cultural object?

Such a dividing line – even if it is not always clear-cut – can be drawn between a standalone image of a cultural item (with a history that can be chronologically and conceptually separated from its current location) and tangible or intangible features that connect the cultural item to its current location in a cultural institution, and to the latter's reputation as a cultural hub.

Consider the following hypothetical example: A commercial company wishes to publish a book titled *The Treasures of the Louvre*. The book includes already-existing images of cultural items that are part of the Louvre's collections, including images made before a certain item entered the collections of the Louvre. The book does not include exterior or interior images of the Louvre Palace itself. Such a book links, however, the standalone items to a broader physical and conceptual context, establishing the item's connection to the museum's space and its history.

I argue that in such a case the Louvre would have a normative claim against an entirely unauthorized collection of images that relies on the reputation and allure of the cultural institution and its exhibition spaces. While the exact scope of the legal power that the Louvre should have over the production of such a book, and of the respective legal remedies that it should be entitled to, would have to be determined on a case-by-case basis, the normative standing of the Louvre could be grounded in the law of unjust enrichment (which exists in certain variations across different legal systems). This point will be discussed in further detail in Section 5.4.2.3.

(3) Duty of Cultural Institutions to Make Copies and Records of Cultural Items Accessible   Alongside the (limited) in rem rights of cultural institutions to control the making by others of copies, images, and other representations of cultural items in their collections, these institutions' dual role as both proprietors and custodians of cultural objects should be viewed as placing on them an affirmative in rem duty to make publicly available images and basic records of such items.

While this in rem duty should also be limited, and is not aimed at preventing cultural institutions from financially benefiting from holding
such items, including through the commercialization of items by selling
physical and digital products that serve as mementos from visiting the
museum space and its collections, they have an affirmative role to serve
as conduits of cultural information that will continue to enrich world culture and its various stakeholders.

Chapters 3 and 4 addressed the growing ethical, professional, and
legal duties of cultural institutions to engage in provenance research of
their collections, prior to and after acquiring them, and to make available
digital databases that would allow others to become familiar with such
records – and, if necessary, to contest them – in order to identify and verify the history of such items.

But the duty of museums and similar institutions as custodians of culture
should go beyond identifying potential problems in the chain of title and
possession. While cultural institutions should not be viewed as full-fledged
trustees or fiduciaries that are not supposed to serve their own interests
in managing the assets of others,[96] the role of cultural institutions as custodians of culture does make them accountable to society in other ways.
Alongside the legitimacy of the nation-states in which such institutions are
located to place certain limits on the proprietary rights of cultural institutions, such as rules on inalienability or export control, which are intended
to protect the cultural interests of national societies, cultural institutions
also have a broader duty – even if much more limited in scope – to the
global audience at large, as is the case with the general duty of nation-states
themselves toward the global audience, discussed in Chapter 1. Therefore,
requiring cultural institutions to allow human society to enjoy the free
flow of images, reproductions, and other representations of past cultural
treasures forms part of the broader concept of the "new cultural internationalism" promoted in this book – one that recognizes the legitimate proprietary and financial interests of different actors in the cultural world but
also promotes the free flow of knowledge and inspiration.

To facilitate the key role of cultural institutions as custodians of culture, tasked with promoting human creativity, inspiration, and the for-
mation and reformation of individual and collective identity, museums
and similar institutions should be affirmatively required to offer a

---

[96] See, generally, LIONEL SMITH, THE LAW OF LOYALTY (2023) (identifying the core of the
duty of loyalty owed by trustees and other formal fiduciaries as one of "acting for others"
while abstaining from a self-serving use of power).

window into the treasures from the past in their care. Again, this should not be read as an unbounded duty to satisfy every wish that others may have. A museum can make available low-resolution images of its inventory that would be of sufficient quality to allow others to learn and appreciate cultural items. At the same time, museums can reserve the right to make new high-resolution images of artifacts on site and to merchandise them, or to otherwise charge others for using truly creative images, especially when such images or reproductions tie the item to the space in which it is located.

This latter point is linked to recent case law about the ability of a cultural institution to claim copyright – and, accordingly, to restrict access – to images that it makes of items in its collection. In a 2023 decision by the Court of Appeal in England and Wales (U.K.) in the matter of *THJ Systems Ltd. v. Sheridan*,[97] given in the context of the copyrightability of graphic images created by software designed to display financial information about the performance of options in capital markets, the court analyzed the features of "originality" required to grant copyright protection to artistic works, according to Section 1(1)(a) of the Copyright, Designs and Patents Act 1988. The court held that:

> [S]ection 1(1)(a) of the 1988 Act must, so far as possible, be interpreted in accordance with Article 2(a) of European Parliament and Council Directive 2001/29/EC of 22 May 2001 on the harmonisation of certain aspects of copyright and related rights in the information society ("the Information Society Directive") as interpreted prior to 31 December 2020 by the Court of Justice of the European Union.[98]

Referring to such case law by the ECJ, Lord Justice Arnold explained:

> The Court of Justice has elaborated upon the requirement that the work be its author's own intellectual creation in a number of subsequent judgments. What is required is that the author was able to express their creative abilities in the production of the work by making free and creative choices so as to stamp the work created with their personal touch … This criterion is not satisfied where the content of the work is dictated by technical considerations, rules or other constraints which leave no room for creative freedom.[99]

These legal criteria set out by the Court of Appeal have echoed across the art world, with a report in *The Art Newspaper* suggesting that this decision

---

[97] THJ Systems Ltd. v. Sheridan [2023] EWHC Civ. 1354 (U.K.).
[98] *Id.* para. 15. (L.J. Arnold).
[99] *Id.* para. 16 (internal citations omitted).

heralds the end of U.K. museums "charging fees to reproduce historic art-works" and that the ruling "suggests that museums have been mis-selling 'image licenses.'"[100] On closer inspection, however, some types of images and reproductions, especially those that feature a cultural item – or a group of items – within the physical surroundings inside the space of the cultural institution, or alongside an explanatory text posted next to it, can still be seen as "original" or "creative," and thus worthy of copyright protection.[101]

A more intricate case concerns efforts (and costs) taken by cultural institutions to produce high-quality digital images, such as when "images need to be digitally modified or retouched to remove blemishes, or other-wise enhanced, allowing for creative choices."[102] While it is highly doubt-ful whether a merely "retouched" image can be considered "creative" and allow the museum to limit access of it, the recognition of potential creativity, the significant costs incurred by museums in producing and maintaining their image archives, and the unique aspects of documen-ting a cultural item located within the space of its exhibition may serve in creating legal dividing lines. This means that, alongside the general duty of cultural institutions as custodians to make accessible standard images and supporting information about cultural items in their collection for the benefit of a global audience, cultural institutions as proprietors should be entitled to enjoy the reputational and commercial benefits of space-specific or otherwise creative image-making and documentation.

5.4.2.3   Other Rights or Duties – And the Limits of Unjust Enrichment

The dual role of cultural institutions as both proprietors and custodians of cultural items and collections may implicate yet other types of in rem rights and in rem duties that go beyond the use of images or reproduc-tions of cultural items and their commercialization. Regarding in rem duties, cultural institutions – especially those that are publicly owned or financially supported – should be seen as having a general duty to pre-serve and protect the items in their collections. Thus, the staggering infor-mation revealed in 2023 about the years-long theft by "museum insiders" of over 1,500 artifacts from the British Museum shocked the art world,

---

[100] Bendor Grosvenor, *Court of Appeal Ruling Will Prevent UK Museums from Charging Reproduction Fees – At Last*, THE ART NEWSPAPER, Dec. 29, 2023.

[101] *See* Steve Schlackman, *How Can Museums Copyright the Works of Old Masters?* ART BUS. J., July 15, 2021.

[102] *See* Sarah Barker, *Can UK Museums Still Charge for Images of Artwork?* APOLLO MAGAZINE, Jan. 19, 2024.

and was described by one UNESCO expert as "probably the worst case so far ... No one expects that to happen in a museum."[103]

Moreover, the British Museum's failure to detect the theft was considered a breach – certainly a professional breach, but also one with legal implications – of the institution's role as a custodian of culture. In an editorial in *The Times*, the prominent British newspaper asserted that "the British Museum must swiftly account for the loss of treasures from its holding and repair the damage to its reputation as a global cultural custodian,"[104] with yet other commentators decrying the failure of the British Museum to perform its duties as a "historic crisis of custodianship."[105] The implications of this professional breach of duty also crossed national borders. The government of Nigeria announced it would make a new claim for the Benin Bronzes housed in the British Museum.[106] While such a claim is not based on enforceable legal grounds, this case does highlight the general duty to protect artifacts and the cross-border range of parties that may be impacted.

What about other types of in rem rights? More specifically, what are the value components of cultural objects that a cultural institution should be entitled to appropriate, at least partly, by asserting its double role as proprietor and custodian of cultural items that are part of its collections?

Recall the hypothetical example, discussed in Section 5.4.2.2(2) above, by which a commercial company wishes to publish a book titled *The Treasures of the Louvre*, which would include existing and noncopyrighted images of cultural objects that are part of the collections of the Louvre. Even if such an action would not involve unauthorized entry into the Louvre Palace for the purpose of taking images within the museum's space, one can nevertheless make the case that, since the book would rely on the inherent connection between the cultural items and their location in the Louvre, disregarding the interests of the Louvre may be considered

---

[103] Tom Seymour, *"More than 1500" Artefacts Were Stolen from British Museum, Internal Investigation Reportedly Reveals*, THE ART NEWSPAPER, Aug. 22, 2023 (quoting Christos Tsirogiannis, an antiquities-trafficking expert, who heads the Working Group Illicit Antiquities Trafficking of the UNESCO Chair on Threats to Cultural Heritage).

[104] Editorial, *Absent Antiquities*, THE TIMES, Aug. 23, 2023.

[105] Catherine Titi, *With 2,000 Missing Objects, the British Museum Faces a Historic Crisis of Custodianship – But This Case Is Far from Unique*, THE CONVERSATION, Sept. 6, 2023, https://theconversation.com/missing-objects-leave-british-museum-facing-historic-crisis-of-custodianship-but-case-is-far-from-unique-212755.

[106] Gareth Harris, *Nigeria Doubles Down on Restitution Demands Following British Museum Thefts*, THE ART NEWSPAPER, Aug. 25, 2023.

unjust, even if the creators of such a book would not be committing a clear legal wrong (unlike in the case of Italy).

At the same time, and while the legal line-drawing between legitimate and illegitimate claims that would be made by cultural institutions in these types of cases would be far from clear-cut, I argue that at least some cases of others taking advantage of the reputation and respective selling power of a museum and its collections could be viewed as unjust, or as a type of misappropriation of value that should have been attributed, at least in some part, to the cultural institution itself.

The legal hook for such potential claims by cultural institutions against misappropriation in relevant cases can be that of the law of unjust enrichment, also known as the law of restitution.[107]

The law of unjust enrichment, which is recognized in various forms across legal jurisdictions, serves essentially to provide just or equitable solutions where more established legal doctrines do not easily apply. It is accordingly typified by a general degree of flexibility and judicial discretion.[108] While in some cases the law of unjust enrichment or restitution is used mostly on the remedial level to properly address the full economic consequences resulting from legal wrongdoing, in other cases the law of unjust enrichment can create a self-standing cause of action even in the absence of a legal wrong under established doctrines.

Courts will tend to recognize such a cause of action when three conditions are met: first, a benefit or enrichment accruing to the defendant; second, the enrichment being perceived by the court under the circumstances as "unjust"; and, third, the enrichment being at the expense of another.[109] Although by its nature the doctrine of unjust enrichment does not abide by clearly preset rules, and is often criticized for this,[110] its normative standing can be appealing for resolving complex situations and for delineating legal fields in constant progress.

I suggest that the law of unjust enrichment could, within appropriate limits, serve to consider and delineate the scope of in rem rights and in

---

[107] See, e.g., RESTATEMENT (THIRD) OF RESTITUTION AND UNJUST ENRICHMENT §1 (AM. LAW INST. 2010).

[108] See Emily Sherwin, *Restitution and Equity: An Analysis of the Principle of Unjust Enrichment*, 79 TEX. L. REV. 2083, 2106–12 (2001).

[109] Maytal Gilboa, Yotam Kaplan & Roee Sarel, *Climate Change as Unjust Enrichment*, 112 GEO. L.J. 1139 (2024).

[110] See, e.g., Mark P. Gergen, *What Renders Enrichment Unjust*, 79 TEX. L. REV. 1927, 1947 (2001) (arguing that a "strong objection to defining a precept of law in such broad terms is that it does almost no normative work").

rem duties of cultural institutions in a rapidly changing technological, commercial, and global environment – especially in light of the prospects and challenges resulting from the use of digital technology as a conduit for disseminating culture.

As noted above, in considering the boundaries of in rem rights and in rem duties of cultural institutions, and the respective rights and duties of other categories of parties, museums and similar institutions should have a particularly strong normative claim for the value attributes of cultural items that are linked to their being part of a collection and the space in which they are displayed.

Therefore, the current Italian approach, surveyed in Section 5.2, against free access to images or the making of reproductions of any individual item that is currently in the possession of public cultural institutions, should be rejected as overbroad and even self-defeating for the purpose of preserving and promoting human culture. At the same time, cultural institutions should be entitled to enjoy value components that are linked to the creation of a collection and to the corresponding efforts – both intellectual and material – of building, maintaining, and nurturing spaces of culture. This is because the "placeness" of cultural institutions continues to be a key feature,[111] not only as a matter of physical presence but also as a concept of curation and creation that deserves legal recognition.[112] The dividing lines could be developed over time by soft-law rules, such as professional guidelines and best practices and, more formally, by case law or specific legislation.

5.5 Concluding Observations

Cultural institutions face growing challenges in fulfilling their dual role as proprietors and custodians of cultural items. While continuing to serve as powerful hubs of culture, museums and similar institutions must presently address the complex sets of relations between physical objects and their digital representations, between tangible and intangible values of

---

[111] *See, generally,* Sophie Forgan, *Building the Museum: Knowledge, Conflict, and the Power of Place,* 96(4) FOCUS – ISIS 572 (2005); MUSEUMS & PLACE (Kerstin Smeds & Ann Davis eds., 2019); Kai Yin & William Nitzky, *Openness and Fluidity of Place: A Practical Dilemma for Ecomuseums in China,* 74 MUSEUM INT'L 30 (2022).

[112] For a detailed discussion of the current and future challenges – but also the lingering power – of museums in an era of digital technology, societal developments (both within and across national borders), and their ever-growing financial constraints, *see* GRAHAM BLACK, TRANSFORMING MUSEUMS IN THE TWENTY-FIRST CENTURY (2011).

cultural objects, and between various stakeholders of culture and heritage located within and across national borders.

More broadly, far from the practically omnipotent position that universal museums and similar institutions held during the colonial era, and up until the latter part of the twentieth century, cultural institutions currently need to come to terms with the changing ethical, professional, and legal norms – from the initial phase of acquiring or otherwise gaining possession of cultural items, through the management and control of such items once they become part of the institution's collection, and up until their potential deaccessioning. At the same time, whether publicly or privately owned, cultural institutions are also required to act in a financially prudent manner – and, in so doing, to take (legitimate) advantage of the economic and reputational values of being owners or otherwise lawful possessors of objects that are of intellectual, historical, and symbolic significance to various groups and categories of stakeholders located around the globe.

Allowing cultural institutions to move forward in dealing with such challenges, while considering the potential interests of the various categories of stakeholders and interested parties – from physical visitors to artists, art market professionals, commercial corporations, local communities, nation-states, and up to decentralized, global audiences for culture and heritage – calls for the articulation of a normative theory of ownership and custody of cultural objects. While such a theory should not be limited to museums and other cultural institutions, the need for delineating at least a basic set of in rem rights and in rem duties concerning the control, management, and use of cultural objects seems particularly pressing for these types of bodies.

This chapter has sought to take the first steps in promoting such a theory of ownership and custody, taking into consideration the changing landscape of art, culture, and heritage in the twenty-first century and beyond. It argues that any delineation of in rem rights and in rem duties of cultural institutions with regard to cultural objects should address both their tangible and intangible features, and how these aspects are embedded in the physical and digital spaces occupied by the cultural institution. In considering what aspects of control and appropriation of value stemming from cultural objects should be awarded to cultural institutions as lawful possessors and custodians of such objects, there is special merit in allowing such institutions to appropriate the value attributes of objects that are inherently tied to the *space* in which they are exhibited or kept.

While this criterion for establishing the set of in rem rights and in rem duties in cultural property seems almost evident for defining the legitimate scope of control over physical access to objects, or of curatorial decisions made within an institution's physical premises, this chapter suggests that the link between culture and space should also play a key role when it comes to the nonphysical aspects of cultural objects. In particular, a property theory of ownership and custody of cultural objects held by cultural institutions should refer to the link between culture and space in considering the mirror-image questions that have been at the center of legal, professional, and public attention, namely: does a cultural institution have an in rem right to appropriate the value components of cultural objects, such as by limiting or prohibiting others from using or reproducing images of items in its collection; and, conversely, does a cultural institution have an in rem duty, as a custodian of culture, to actively make accessible to the public images and other information on items in its collections? Such a property theory should serve as a benchmark for national and cross-border law and policy.

Restitution for an Era of New Cultural Internationalism

Chapter 5 offered a normative model for delineating the broad scope of in rem rights and in rem duties of cultural institutions and other holders of cultural objects, whenever their underlying ownership and/or right of possession in the object is not contested, either legally or ethically. This chapter seeks to construct a future-looking theoretical framework for dealing with cultural objects for which questions of past illegality and/or illegitimacy arise but for which a potential claimant – whether an individual, a community, or a source nation – is unable to pursue formal legal proceedings against the current possessor, and the relevant law enforcement agencies are similarly unable to pursue criminal, administrative, or public law proceedings. In other words, this chapter seeks to identify normative principles for dealing with the issue of "restitution" (broadly defined to include any type of remedy or solution that addresses such a troubled past) that operates outside the realm of hard-law norms and institutions. The analysis is premised on two fundamental considerations.

First, pursuant to the analysis offered in Chapter 2 regarding the nature of "legalistic ethical reasoning," this chapter identifies the principles of "soft-law jurisprudence" that emerged in bilateral negotiations and alternative dispute resolution processes in the context of Nazi-looted cultural property, and shows how these principles are not detached from legal or legal-like reasoning. In particular, it focuses on three aspects that seem to prove dominant in such legalistic ethical reasoning, namely wrongfulness, attribution, and scale of remedies. It suggests that these parameters may be influenced by the specific category of past events or historical violations of the chain of title, for example by distinguishing between individual and collective victims of dispossession.

Second, any normative discussion of restitution should consider the broader framework promoted in this book: the concept of "new cultural internationalism." As explained in Chapter 1, this concept seeks to facilitate collaboration between countries, cultural institutions, and other actors – including those located in both source countries and destination countries – while providing the various stakeholders a "safety net" that fosters better-balanced bargaining power, mutual trust, and prospects for long-term cooperation in designing a legal future for governing past treasures. In turn, such an approach may also view potential claimants, such as source nations demanding the return of artifacts taken from them many decades or centuries ago, as bearing certain duties as global custodians of such cultural artifacts, even if their claim for restitution is based on the object's local/territorial origin or significance. In other words, a normative design of restitution for an era of new cultural internationalism must consider the rights and duties of all relevant stakeholders.

Section 6.1 of this chapter examines the key aspects of the institutional/ procedural and normative principles of the restitution committees established in certain European countries to develop and implement "just and fair solutions" to address Holocaust-era wrongful dispossessions, including recent changes in such committees and other mechanisms. Section 6.2 considers whether "just and fair solutions" can be devised for other contexts and, if so, how legalistic ethical reasoning could be adapted for such settings. It focuses on the case study of France and its complex approach to the restitution of colonial-era objects to African source countries. Section 6.3 examines the various remedial mechanisms that are in operation, or that can be developed, to apply such normative principles to broader contexts of addressing past wrongs. Section 6.4 addresses the role of a normative blueprint, aligned with the concept of new cultural internationalism, in moving toward the convergence of law, policy, and markets for cultural property.

6.1 Lessons from the Restitution Practices for Nazi-Looted Assets

The Preamble to the 1998 Washington Conference Principles on Nazi-Confiscated Art states: "In developing a consensus on non-binding principles to assist in resolving issues relating to Nazi-confiscated art, the Conference recognizes that among participating nations there are differing legal systems and that countries act within the context of their own laws."[1]

Principle XIII articulates the key substantive provision for dealing with Nazi-looted art: "If the pre-War owners of art that is found to have been confiscated by the Nazis and not subsequently restituted, or their heirs,

---

[1] U.S. Department of State, *Washington Conference Principles on Nazi-Confiscated Art*, Preamble (Dec. 3, 1998), www.state.gov/washington-conference-principles-on-nazi-confiscated-art/ (hereinafter: "1998 Washington Principles").

can be identified, steps should be taken expeditiously to achieve a *just and fair solution*, recognizing this may vary according to the facts and circumstances surrounding a specific case."[2]

Principles X and XI address the proposed structure of domestic institutions and processes:

> X. Commissions or other bodies established to identify art that was confiscated by the Nazis and to assist in addressing ownership issues should have a balanced membership.
> XI. Nations are encouraged to develop national processes to implement these principles, particularly as they relate to alternative dispute resolution mechanisms for resolving ownership issues.[3]

Following the 1998 Washington Principles, five European countries – Austria,[4] France,[5] Germany,[6] the Netherlands,[7] and the United Kingdom[8] – established restitution committees. While differing substantially from

---

[2] *Id.* principle XIII (my emphasis).

[3] *Id.* principles X–XI.

[4] Bundesministerium Kunst, Kultur, öffentlicher Dienst und Sport, *Art Restitution Advisory Board* (*Kunstrückgabebeirat*), https://provenienzforschung.gv.at/en/empfehlungen-des-beirats/ (last visited Feb. 1, 2025) (hereinafter: "Austrian Advisory Board").

[5] Premier Ministre, Commission for the Restitution of Property and Compensation of Victims of Anti-Semitic Spoliations (*Commission pour la restitution des biens et l'indemnisation des victimes de spoliations antisémites*), www.civs.gouv.fr/ (last visited Feb. 1, 2025) (hereinafter: "CIVS"). The powers, organizational structure, and deliberative processes of the CIVS were significantly extended and reformed in early 2024 by a decree of the French minister of culture. Décret n° 2024–11 du 5 janvier 2024 instituant une commission pour la restitution des biens et l'indemnisation des victimes de spoliations antisémites et pris en application des articles L. 115-3, L. 115-4 et L. 451-10-1 du code du patrimoine, JORF n°0004 du 6 janvier 2024, www.legifrance.gouv.fr/jorf/id/JORFTEXT000048865626. These reforms include the expansion of the authority of the CIVS to address cultural property that was looted outside of France between 1933 and 1945, prior to entering France (whereas the original mandate of the CIVS referred only to cases of dispossessions that occurred inside France during the Nazi regime). *See* Network of European Restitution Committees on Nazi-Looted Art, *Changes at the Commission for the Compensation of Victims of Spoliation (CIVS), Newsletter no. 18* (Aug. 2024), www.restitutiecommissie.nl/wp-content/uploads/2024/08/Network-Newsletter-no.18-August2024.pdf, at 5.

[6] Advisory Commission on the Return of Cultural Property Seized as a Result of Nazi Persecution, especially Jewish Property (*Beratende Kommission im Zusammenhang mit der Rückgabe NS-verfolgungsbedingt entzogenen Kulturguts, insbesondere aus jüdischem Besitz*), www.beratende-kommission.de/en (last visited Feb. 1, 2025) (hereinafter: "German Advisory Commission").

[7] Advisory Committee on the Assessment of Restitution Applications for Items of Cultural Value and the Second World War (Restitutions Committee) (*De Adviescommissie Restitutieverzoeken Cultuurgoederen en Tweede Wereldoorlog*), www.restitutiecommissie.nl/en/ (last visited Feb. 1, 2025) (hereinafter: "Dutch Restitution Committee").

[8] Gov.UK, Spoliation Advisory Panel, www.gov.uk/government/groups/spoliation-advisory-panel (last visited Feb. 1, 2025) (hereinafter: "Spoliation Advisory Panel").

one another in numerous aspects,[9] in 2018 the five committees formed the Network of European Restitution Committees on Nazi-Looted Art,[10] which serves as a joint platform to exchange information about the committees, provenance research, and related issues.[11]

In March 2024, the German federal commissioner for culture and the media, Claudia Roth, announced that the German Advisory Commission (*Beratende Kommission*) would be replaced by a system of binding arbitration.[12] The German Advisory Commission was dissolved at a meeting held in May 2024.[13] In October 2024, the German Federal Ministry of Culture (BKM), the *Länder* (states), and the National Association of Municipal Organizations presented an initial outline of the new arbitration framework, to be developed in collaboration with two representative Jewish organizations: the Central Council of Jews in Germany (*Zentralrat der Juden in Deutschland*) and the Claims Conference on Jewish Material Claims against Germany ("Claims Conference").[14]

The arbitration framework will initially be based on an intergovernmental administrative agreement (*Verwaltungsabkommen*), which would also secure the preliminary commitment of public museums and collections in Germany to engage in binding arbitration proceedings.[15]

---

[9] *See* text accompanying *infra* note 23.

[10] Restitutions Committee, *Network of European Restitution Committees on Nazi-Looted Art*, www.restitutiecommissie.nl/en/newsletter-network-european-committees/ (last visited Feb. 1, 2025).

[11] *See* Chapter 3, Section 3.4.2.4.

[12] Kulturminister Konferenz, *Beratende Kommission: Entscheidende Weichen für Reform gestellt*, Mar. 13, 2024, www.kmk.org/aktuelles/artikelansicht/beratende-kommission-entscheidende-weichen-fuer-reform-gestellt.html (Ger). *See also* Catherine Hickley, *Germany to Replace Nazi-Loot Advisory Panel with Binding Arbitration*, THE ART NEWSPAPER, Mar. 16, 2024.

[13] Patrick Bahners & Andreas Kilb, *Zur Stärkung der Stellung der Opfer*, FRANKFURTER ALLGEMEINE ZEITUNG, Sept. 5, 2024 (Ger.) (conducting an interview with Matthias Weller).

[14] *See* Kulturminister Konferenz, *Bund, Länder und kommunale Spitzenverbände verbessern Restitutionspraxis in Deutschland und stärken die Einbindung der Opfer und ihrer Nachfahren*, Oct. 9, 2024, www.kmk.org/presse/pressearchiv/mitteilung/kulturpolitisches-spitzengespraech0.html (Ger.); Zentralrat der Juden, *Neuregelung der Restitution von NS-Raubkunst*, Oct. 9, 2024, www.zentralratderjuden.de/aktuelle-meldung/artikel/news/neuregelung-der-restitution-von-ns-raubkunst/ (Ger.); Claims Conference, *After Nearly 80 Years, A Significant Step Is Achieved Towards an Art Restitution Law in Germany for Holocaust Survivors and Heirs*, Oct. 9, 2024, www.claims con.org/restitution-law/.

[15] Kulturminister Konferenz, *supra* note 14. In March 2025, the federal government, the sixteen states, and three representative associations of German municipalities

At a later stage, the German government may also promote federal parliamentary legislation (*Restitutionsgesetz*), which could prove instrumental in systematically carving out legal exceptions to general principles, such as statutes of limitations and acquisitive prescription.[16]

Switzerland is in the process of establishing an advisory commission. According to a decision made by the Swiss federal government in November 2023,[17] the proposed commission will issue nonbinding opinions in disputes referred to it by the Swiss Ministry of Culture. This commission could address any object currently located in Switzerland or that changed hands in Switzerland during the Nazi era.[18]

A key research project on the work of European restitution committees is the *Restatement of Restitution Rules for Nazi Confiscated Art: Eine vergleichende Bestandsaufnahme* (*A Comparative Assessment*) (hereinafter: "Restatement" or "RRR").[19] The Restatement research project ran from April 2019 to September 2024 at the Rheinische Friedrich Wilhelm University Bonn, under the academic direction of its lead author, Matthias Weller. The Restatement, written in German[20] and translated into English,[21] examines how the restitution of Nazi-looted art was implemented over the twenty-five-year period following the 1998 Washington Principles in the abovementioned six countries: Austria, Germany, the Netherlands, France, the United Kingdom, and Switzerland (where the implementation of the 1998 Washington Principles has thus far relied on

concluded an intrafederal agreement to set up an arbitration tribunal for Nazi-looted art. *See* Kulturminister Konferenz, *Verwaltungsabkommen zur Einrichtung einer Schiedsgerichtsbarkeit NS-Raubgut unterzeichnet*, March 26, 2023, www.kmk.org/aktuelles/artikelansicht/verwaltungsabkommen-zur-einrichtung-einer-schiedsgerichtsbarkeit-ns-raubgut-unterzeichnet.html (Ger.).

[16] Claims Conference, *supra* note 14 (noting that "a restitution law remains the goal. Only on the grounds of a federal law comprehensive justice and legal certainty can be achieved").

[17] Schweizerische Eidgenossenschaft (Swiss Confederation), Verordnung über die unabhängige Kommission für historisch belastetes Kulturerbe (VUKBK), Nov. 22, 2023 (Switz.), www.newsd.admin.ch/newsd/message/attachments/84302.pdf.

[18] Catherine Hickley, *Swiss Government Approves Panel to Assess Claims for Art Acquired in Nazi and Colonial Eras*, THE ART NEWSPAPER, Nov. 23, 2023.

[19] Universität Bonn, Fachbereich Rechtswissenschaft, Prof. Dr. Weller, *Research Project: Restatement of Restitution Rules for Nazi Confiscated Art*, www.jura.uni-bonn.de/professur-prof-dr-weller/research-project-restatement-of-restitution-rules-for-nazi-confiscated-art (last visited Feb. 1, 2025).

[20] The German version of the text (RRR – Deutschsprachige Fassung), is available at https://uni-bonn.sciebo.de/s/VJuHhtnA52DyPtE (hereinafter: "RRR, German").

[21] The English version of the text (preliminary draft translation, dated Sept. 4, 2024), is available at https://uni-bonn.sciebo.de/s/VJuHhtnA52DyPtE (hereinafter: "RRR, English").

voluntary negotiations),[22] while considering the numerous divergences between the various jurisdictions.[23]

The Restatement was able to gather information, through primary and secondary sources, about over 1,300 cases handled by restitution committees and other alternative mechanisms, such as arbitration and negotiations. These include over 600 cases from Germany, nearly 400 from Austria, approximately 170 from the Netherlands, 150 from France, 20 from the United Kingdom, and nearly 30 from Switzerland.[24]

At the heart of the Restatement lies a comparative and subsequently integrative consideration and articulation of eight recurring groups of substantive questions that emerge in addressing claims for restitution for Nazi-era dispossession of cultural property, namely: (1) subject matter covered, (2) ownership, (3) claimant, (4) respondent, (5) attribution, (6) defining a fair and equitable solution, (7) asset protection, and (8) protection of cultural property.[25]

In so doing, the Restatement engages in what may be seen as the "soft-law jurisprudence" that has emerged across the six jurisdictions, seeking to distill the common denominators (and differences) evident in each of these substantive issues. Each of the eight articles of the Restatement begins by defining a "black letter rule," that is, the text of the rule derived from the analysis of practices across the six jurisdictions. Each rule serves as an "abstract statement reflecting the current state of practice in a particular area."[26] The statement of each such rule is followed by a detailed commentary and respective country reports.[27]

Two of the articles of the Restatement – Article 5 on "attribution" and Article 6 on "defining a fair and equitable solution" – form the core of this research project.[28] These articles shed broader light on the three prongs of the abovementioned "legalistic ethical reasoning" for addressing the troubled past of cultural items: wrongfulness, attribution, and scale of remedies.

---

[22] *Id. Introduction*, at 30–31.
[23] These differences relate, inter alia, to the legal basis under which the restitution committee was established, the scope of coverage of cultural items that are within the mandate of the committee, whether one of the parties is able to initiate proceedings unilaterally, and the operative effects of the committee's opinion. *Id. Introduction*, at 17–32.
[24] *Id. Introduction*, at 8.
[25] For an overview of these eight topics, which are then addressed separately in Articles 1–8 of the Restatement, *see id. Introduction*, at 9–14.
[26] *Id.*
[27] *Id. Introduction*, at 16–17.
[28] *Id. Article 5 RRR – Attribution*, at 2; *Article 6 RRR – Just and Fair Solutions*, at 1.

The following paragraphs analyze these key features of the soft-law jurisprudence that emerged concerning Nazi-looted art, with the purpose of addressing, in the next sections of this chapter, the prospects of devising principles for just and fair solutions, mutatis mutandis, in other contexts.

Article 5, on attribution, addresses the normative principles designed by restitution committees to draw the lines for determining whether a loss of cultural property should be seen as resulting from the Nazi regime, for the purpose of defining an object as "Nazi-confiscated art" – the term used in the Preamble to the 1998 Washington Principles but not further articulated within them.[29] The 2009 Terezin Declaration goes a step further, by establishing that "every effort be made to rectify the consequences of wrongful property seizures, such as confiscations, forced sales and sales under duress of property."[30] In so doing, the Terezin Declaration considers losses that resulted from the Nazi regime to be wrongful and, moreover, identifies categories of wrongful losses that go beyond a narrow interpretation of "confiscation" (i.e., direct state seizure of assets without compensation) to include "forced sales" and "sales under duress," two terms that require further articulation.

The concept of attribution, which emerged in certain varieties and terminologies used across the six jurisdictions, extends beyond mere "causality" to require "a sufficiently close connection between National Socialist rule and the loss."[31] The underlying concept of attribution is thus not essentially different from the hard-law normative framework of distinguishing between mere "cause-in-fact" and "proximate cause" or "legal cause,"[32] such that the assignment of liability in torts and other fields applies only to the latter categories of causation (by showing, for example, that a certain party had a concrete "duty of care" toward another party, and that this duty had been breached).[33]

In the context of Nazi-confiscated art, the requirement of attribution – the demonstration that a person's property loss is "directly related" and has a "sufficiently close" causal connection to the Nazi regime

---

[29] 1998 Washington Principles, *supra* note 1, Preamble.

[30] U.S. Department of State, *Terezin Declaration on Holocaust Era Assets and Related Issues* (June 30, 2009) §2, www.state.gov/prague-holocaust-era-assets-conference-terezin-declaration/ (hereinafter: "2009 Terezin Declaration").

[31] RRR, English, *supra* note 21, *Article 5 RRR – Attribution*, at 1.

[32] *Id. Article 5 RRR – Attribution*, at 12 n.29.

[33] TIMON HUGHES-DAVIS & NATHAN TAMBLYN, TORT LAW 33–36 (2020) (analyzing English case law, which requires "proximity," "foreseeability," and a "fair, just and reasonable" basis for placing a legally binding duty in tort law).

(as per the Dutch model, with functionally similar terms used else-where)[34] – is meant to identify the cases in which the change of ownership of the item was truly involuntary.[35]

Moreover, as the Restatement notes, "assigning attribution also draws attention to the perpetrator's responsibility and thus helps demonstrate the involuntary nature of the loss from the victim's perspective."[36] The requirement for attribution thus helps to identify the concrete wrongdo-ing inflicted upon a specific victim by the actions of an overarching perpe-trator, the Nazi regime.

For example, in a binding opinion issued on May 27, 2024, the Dutch Restitution Committee advised the Amsterdam City Council to resti-tute the painting *Odalisque* by Henri Matisse, which had been held by the Stedelijk Museum Amsterdam since 1941, to the legal successors of Albert and Marie Stern.[37] Following an investigation conducted by the Commission for Looted Art in Europe and assessed by the Expert Centre Restitution (ECR), the committee concluded that it is "highly likely that the painting came from the collection of the Jewish couple Albert and Marie Stern."[38] Moreover, according to the Dutch Restitution Committee, it has also "become sufficiently plausible that the couple lost possession of the painting as a result of circumstances directly connected with the Nazi regime," thus establishing the causation between Nazi rule and the loss.[39]

The Restatement distinguishes between three categories of Nazi-era loss of cultural property: "seizure by state authorities," "seizure by private parties," and "loss occasioned by the injured party's own actions." The lat-ter category addresses whether a sale by the owner during the Nazi era was in fact "forced" or executed "under duress," to use the terminology of the Terezin Declaration.

According to the Restatement, the key rule developed by restitution committees and related mechanisms for the first two categories is that "the loss should be attributed to Nazi rule unless the seizure in the specific

---

[34] RRR, English, *supra* note 21, *Article 5 RRR – Attribution*, at 12–17.

[35] *Id. Article 5 RRR – Attribution*, at 16.

[36] *Id. Article 5 RRR – Attribution*, at 17.

[37] Restitution Committee, Binding Opinion regarding Albert Stern/Amsterdam City Council (Stedelijk Museum), Report no.: RC 3.202, May 27, 2024, www.restitutiecommissie.nl/en/recommendation/albert-stern/ (Neth.).

[38] *Id.* Summary binding opinion.

[39] *Id. See also* Lilian Palmer, *Netherlands Restitutions Committee Issues Opinion on Matisse Painting*, THE INSTITUTE OF ART & LAW, July 29, 2024, https://ial.uk.com/netherlands-restitutions-committee-issues-opinion-on-matisse-painting/.

form it took would also have occurred without Nazi rule" (as opposed, for example, to a tax lien or insolvency procedures unrelated to Nazi rule).[40] The examination of attribution is more complex for sales or other actions taken by the injured party. To show that such actions "were sufficiently involuntary," the committee will consider the specific circumstances that may point toward attribution (e.g., if "the transaction occurred at a point in time where there was already pressure caused by systematic persecution") or challenge attribution (e.g., "if the primary cause for the injured party's actions were financial difficulties which predated Nazi rule").[41]

Article 6 of the Restitution deals with "just and fair solutions," namely the type of remedy awarded or recommended by the restitution committee, or agreed to by the parties, when the claimant has been able to demonstrate the various elements of a Nazi-era involuntary loss of a cultural item.

As is the case with the concept of attribution, the term "just and fair solution" (which is the core of the 1998 Washington Principles) – though anchored in moral or ethical considerations – is not detached from jurisprudential principles or "legalistic ethical reasoning." Accordingly, the practice that has developed among restitution committees regarding a "just and fair solution" in specific cases shares considerable similarities with judicial processes in considering a scale of remedies.[42]

The Restatement highlights two overarching principles that have guided the various restitution committees in selecting options along the scale of remedies: proportionality and equality.

The principle of proportionality (prominent in law, especially in the context of public law)[43] holds that, in the context of rectifying involuntary losses of cultural property due to Nazi rule, "'weaker' injustices should result in correspondingly 'weaker' reactions ('solutions' or 'remedies'), while greater injustices should result in correspondingly stronger reactions."[44] This means, for example, that in deciding whether to adopt

---

[40] RRR, English, *supra* note 21, *Article 5 RRR – Attribution*, at 22–34.

[41] *Id., Article 5 RRR – Attribution*, at 34–54. A particularly contested category in the context of sales under duress is that of "fugitive property" (*Fluchtgut*), which refers to cultural property sold by the owner in a "safe country" but for which the claimant argues that "the sale was directly based on lingering effects of persecution, which must result in a restriction of liberty which resembles that caused by the previous persecution." *Id.* at 47–53.

[42] *Id. Article 6 RRR – Just and Fair Solutions*, at 1–2.

[43] *See, e.g.,* AHARON BARAK, PROPORTIONALITY: CONSTITUTIONAL RIGHTS AND THEIR LIMITATIONS (2012).

[44] RRR, English, *supra* note 21, *Article 6 RRR – Just and Fair Solutions*, at 3–4.

a "strong" remedy – typically, the physical restitution of the object from the current possessor to the victims/heirs – and a "weaker" one, such as "changing provenance information" about the item while allowing the current possessor to retain the object, the restitution committee will examine the extent of the historical injustice caused to the victim.[45]

However, unlike the type of "fair balance" of interests that is featured in the hard-law jurisprudence on the principle of proportionality (as exemplified in Chapter 2 concerning the decision of the European Court of Human Rights in the case of *Getty v. Italy*),[46] the proportionality test for evaluating the scope of historic injustice caused to an owner of cultural property during the Nazi era is not balanced against the interests of the current possessor if the latter is a state holder. This means that a state holder cannot claim the defense of bona fide acquisition and that its current curatorial interests in the item will not be considered. At the same time, the extent of "emotional relationship" that a current claimant – namely, the heir/s of the dispossessed owner – may have with the item will also not be considered.[47] The proportionality test is thus focused on measuring the gravity of the past events to design the "proportionate" solution.

In contrast, when the "just and fair solution" is based on direct negotiation, mediation, or other amicable processes, the parties may be flexible in weighing all of these interests to devise a solution.

This difference also affects the application of another key principle developed in the soft-law jurisprudence on Nazi-looted assets, that of equality, by which "essentially identical cases should be decided the same way."[48] While abiding by this principle may be more feasible for jurisdictions – such as Austria, France, and the Netherlands – in which the practice of dispute resolution is more centralized, with most cases decided by the restitution committee – it is less so in other jurisdictions.[49]

---

[45] *Id. Article 6 RRR – Just and Fair Solutions*, at 9–14. It should be noted that another type of remedy considered by restitution committees is that of monetary compensation. However, it is rarely employed by restitution committees (as opposed to bilateral negotiations or other types of settlement, as shown below), and is practically considered only when the cultural item itself is now lost, or if the transfer of an item from a state collection is otherwise limited by law, as was the case in France until 2023.

[46] The J. Paul Getty Trust and Others v. Italy, App. No. 35271/19 (May 2, 2024), https://hudoc.echr.coe.int/eng?i=001-233381. *See* Chapter 2, Section 2.2.3.

[47] RRR, English, *supra* note 21, *Article 6 RRR – Just and Fair Solutions*, at 14–22.

[48] *Id. Article 6 RRR – Just and Fair Solutions*, at 5.

[49] *Id.*

In Germany, for example, the practice of achieving a "just and fair solution" operates under a subsidiarity principle, by which the claimant and the respondent should first endeavor to reach a solution bilaterally. Only if these efforts fail is the matter referred to the Advisory Commission. Accordingly, while the Advisory Commission has issued only twenty-four decisions throughout its tenure, the authors of the Restatement have been able to identify and review over 600 bilateral resolutions (which are not centrally recorded, and were therefore generally unavailable to other parties).[50]

This fragmentation in the decision-making process and the general lack of transparency, at least during the period of bilateral negotiations, have resulted in a variety of agreed solutions. These solutions do take into account the interests of multiple stakeholders, including the current possessor, in crafting specific amicable resolutions. This has also meant that alongside restitution or, alternatively, "changing provenance information," agreements may comprise financial settlements or other interim or "creative" solutions that go beyond assessing the gravity of the past events.

In 2021, the Alte Nazionalgalerie in Berlin reached an agreement to restitute and buy back the painting *A Square in La Roche-Guyon* (1867) by Camille Pissarro. The heirs of Armand Dorville, a Jewish lawyer, were forced to auction the painting in France in 1942 and were denied access to the proceeds of the sale. Under the agreement, the painting will remain on display at the Alte Nazionalgalerie, which has held the item since 1961, when it was purchased at a London art gallery.[51]

In previous cases, the option of restitution-and-repurchase was occasionally suggested by the Advisory Commission.[52] This remedy differs from straightforward compensation, at least in the expressive sense, by recognizing that the wrong can only be rectified by a legitimate (re) purchase.[53]

In 2024, Berlin's Brücke-Museum reached a financial settlement with the heirs of Victor Wallerstein, a Jewish art historian and art dealer. Wallerstein fled Nazi Germany to Italy, where he was forced to sell much of his collection to make a living prior to his death in 1944. This included

---

[50] *Id.* Introduction, at 19.
[51] Catherine Hickley, *Berlin Museum Restitutes – and Then Buys Back – Nazi-Looted Pissarro Painting*, THE ART NEWSPAPER, Oct. 18, 2021.
[52] RRR, English, *supra* note 21, *Article 6 RRR – Just and Fair Solutions*, at 10–11.
[53] *See, generally*, Cass R. Sunstein, *On the Expressive Function of Law*, 144 U. PA. L. REV. 2021 (1996).

Figure 6.1 Ernst Ludwig Kirchner, *Erich Heckel and Otto Mueller Playing Chess* (1913). Source: By permission of Brücke-Museum. Photo: Nick Ash, Berlin.

the 1940 sale of Ernst Ludwig Kirchner's painting *Erich Heckel and Otto Mueller Playing Chess* (1913) (Figure 6.1).[54]

The parties agreed to keep the amount of the settlement confidential but it is known that the German federal government, the Berlin senate, the Cultural Foundation of the Federal States, and the Ernst von Siemens Art Foundation all contributed to the settlement.[55] As a complementary measure, in the fall of 2024, the Brücke-Museum held an exhibition titled *Biographies of Modern Art: Collectors and Their Works*, which presented eight Jewish collectors, among them Wallerstein, whose works are on display at the museum and who had been the victims of Nazi persecution.

---

[54] Catherine Hickley, *Berlin's Brücke Museum Settles with the Heirs of a Jewish Collector on Kirchner Painting*, THE ART NEWSPAPER, June 4, 2024.
[55] *Id.*

Kirchner's painting was prominently featured in the exhibition.[56] Anne Webber, cochair of the Commission of Looted Art in Europe, noted: "For the heirs, the fair and just solution of this restitution claim represents an acknowledgment of the pain, terror and tragedy to which the innocent Wallerstein family was subjected. It is also a recognition of the cultural contribution that Victor Wallerstein and his siblings made to the arts and society in Germany."[57]

Financial arrangements or other interim or "creative" solutions have also become more prevalent in bilateral agreements reached in other jurisdictions that have endorsed the 1998 Washington Principles but which did not establish institutional mechanisms such as restitution committees.

In 2024, the Allentown Art Museum in Pennsylvania reached an agreement with the heirs of German Jewish judge and art collector Henry Bromberg, who was forced to sell his collection in order to flee Germany in 1938 by paying the punitive *Reichsfluchtsteuer* (flight tax). Among the artworks sold was the painting *Portrait of George the Bearded, Duke of Saxony* (c. 1534), currently attributed to Lucas Cranach the Elder and his workshop (Figure 6.2). The Allentown Art Museum acquired the painting from an art gallery in New York in 1961. According to the agreement between the parties, the painting will be auctioned by Christie's in New York, with the parties sharing the proceeds of the sale.[58]

Prior to relinquishing possession, the Allentown Art Museum held a special exhibition in the fall of 2024, titled *Art in the Nazi Period: Two Paintings' Trajectories*, which featured the story of the Cranach painting alongside that of Dutch painter Adriaen van Ostade's *Village Lawyer* (1655).[59]

Therefore, while the specific financial arrangement reached by the Allentown Art Museum differs from those reached by the Alte Nazionalgalerie and Brücke-Museum, all three museums have specifically acknowledged, by holding exhibitions in line with a contemporary curatorial policy, the broader context of Nazi-looted cultural property and the role of museums in rectifying past wrongs.

---

[56] Brücke-Museum, *Exhibitions, Biographies of Modern Art: Collectors and Their Works*, www.bruecke-museum.de/en/programm/ausstellungen/1973/biographies-of-modern-art-collectors-and-their-works (last visited Feb. 1, 2025).

[57] Hickley, *supra* note 54 (quoting Anne Webber).

[58] Catherine Hickley, *Cranach Portrait Will Be Sold in Accord between Pennsylvania Museum and Jewish Heirs*, THE ART NEWSPAPER, Aug. 26, 2024.

[59] Allentown Art Museum, *Exhibitions, Art in the Nazi Period: Two Paintings' Trajectories*, www.allentownartmuseum.org/exhibitions/art-in-the-nazi-period-two-paintings-trajectories/ (last visited Feb. 1, 2025).

Figure 6.2 Lucas Cranach the Elder and workshop, *Portrait of George the Bearded, Duke of Saxony* (c. 1534).
Source: By permission of Allentown Art Museum, purchase: Charles Ulrick and Josephine Bay Paul Foundation, 1961 (1961.5).

Put differently, while the soft-law jurisprudence of restitution committees, as identified by the Restatement, focuses on the scope and nature
of the historic injustices caused during the Nazi period to craft a "proportionate" remedy – without formally considering the current curatorial
and financial interests of current possessors[60] – it seems that direct settlements between the parties do practically incorporate a broader range of
interests, including those of the cultural institutions.

More generally, bargaining in the shadow of the soft-law jurisprudence
of restitution committees on the principles of a just and fair solution
grants the heirs of dispossessed owners a tentative "safety net," offering
better-balanced bargaining power, and often promoting amicable settlements with current possessors.[61] While in some cases this soft-law jurisprudence may lead museums to unequivocally return items or engage in
full-blown legal battles, as illustrated in Chapter 2 in the context of the
Manhattan District Attorney's investigations of Nazi-looted assets,[62] in
other cases parties may devise other solutions that they consider "just
and fair."

6.2   "Just and Fair Solutions" in Other Contexts? France
and Colonial-Era Objects

What lessons can be drawn from the soft-law jurisprudence and bilateral negotiation dynamics surrounding Nazi-era dispossessions for other
contexts that concern the troubled past of cultural property, particularly
when the current conflict extends across borders?

Can the type of legalistic ethical reasoning that followed the 1998
Washington Principles' framework of a "just and fair solution" offer a
way forward for decades- or centuries-old disputes that remain unresolved despite the changing winds of cross-border politics discussed in
Chapter 1? Specifically, could a form of soft-law jurisprudence emerge for
colonial-era objects, or for other items taken across borders through the
use of force (and not covered by binding international instruments) or
opportunism, as was likely the case with the Parthenon Marbles?

---

[60] *See* text accompanying *supra* notes 43–47.
[61] For the concept of "bargaining in the shadow of the law," namely how the benchmark
of formal legal rules and doctrines is crucial for the way in which parties may work to
reach private, specifically tailored settlements, *see* Robert Cooter, Stephen Marks & Robert
Mnookin, *Bargaining in the Shadow of the Law: A Testable Model of Strategic Behavior*, 11 J.
LEGAL STUD. 225 (1982).
[62] *See* Chapter 2, Section 2.3.2.

Obviously, one key distinction from the context of Nazi-era dispossessions is that the alleged victims of such past actions were not individuals with legally valid private property rights but, typically, local communities, ethnic groups, or other collective entities that might not have had a recognized, enforceable legal interest when the object was taken out of its territory of origin.

This underlying difference has significant implications for both the normative basis of such claims as well as for the institutional and procedural mechanisms that could be designed to address them.

A normative analysis based on legalistic ethical reasoning and, specifically, the concepts of wrongfulness, attribution, and scale of remedies, requires an intricate, intergenerational analysis of both past and present collective entities and the lingering effect that a past wrongful act has, if any, on the current collective entity making the claim. Unlike the process of identifying a private law line of succession on the part of the claimant, determining the affiliation, and accordingly, the attribution of a claimed current interest to an alleged past injustice is often more contestable when a current collective entity seeks to step into the shoes of a past collective entity. This complexity may also reflect the often far-from-straightforward ties between the past collective entity that allegedly committed the past wrongful act and the entity currently in possession of the cultural object, be it a public or private cultural institution, a collector, or any other possessor. The nature of the collective claim also has a bearing on the scale of remedies that should be available for such a normative framework, and particularly, interim solutions beyond physical restitution or no remedy at all.

At the same time, following the analysis in Chapter 5 regarding the duties that cultural institutions should have as global custodians of cultural objects (meaning, inter alia, that they should allow human society some form of access to images or reproductions of cultural items in their possession), source countries or societies should also be viewed, to an even greater extent, as such global custodians.

This suggests that the normative case for requiring restitution when made by a collective entity would be stronger when the purpose of such restitution is not "isolationist" but rather aligns with the concept of new cultural internationalism – a framework that promotes broad access to cultural items.

From an institutional and procedural perspective, a key lesson that can be learned from the case of Nazi-era dispossession for other contexts, such as the colonial era, concerns fact-finding.

In particular, the work of restitution committees in Austria, France, and the Netherlands seems to have proven effective (both in the sense of dealing with a considerable number of cases and in their ability to develop significant soft-law jurisprudence) owing to the establishment of three national-level expert bodies for provenance research that engage in fact-finding for specific cases: the Austrian Commission for Provenance Research (*Kommission für Provenienzforschung*),[63] the French Mission for Research and Restitution of Spoliated Cultural Property between 1933 and 1945 (*la Mission de recherche et de restitution des biens culturels spoliés entre 1933 et 1945*) (M2RS), created in 2019,[64] and the Dutch ECR, established in 2018,[65] whose roles and work processes in dealing with Nazi-looted items were analyzed in Chapter 3.[66]

In the context of colonial-era objects or other claims made by current collective entities for past wrongs allegedly committed against their collective predecessors, with the focus being on a wrong committed by another past collective entity, such as a colonial power, there seems be special merit – also from an institutional and procedural perspective – in forming bilateral (or in other cases, multilateral) expert committees to collaborate on fact-finding for specific claims. While internal disputes are likely to arise, a permanent body of experts engaged in fact-finding, professionally accountable to both collective entities and also to broader groups of stakeholders, could pave a way forward for the consequent stage of decision-making (which could be also based on the establishment of a bilateral or multilateral dispute resolution or advisory entity).

As noted in Chapter 3, in early 2024, Germany and France announced that they would jointly spend approximately 2.1 million euros to further research the provenance of African heritage objects in the collections of their national museums, with priority expected to be given

---

[63] Bundesministerium Kunst, Kultur, öffentlicher Dienst und Sport, *Provenance Research and Restitution in the Austrian Federal Collections, Commission for Provenance Research*, https://provenienzforschung.gv.at/en/commission-for-provenance-research/ (last visited Feb. 1, 2025).

[64] Ministère de la Culture, *Mission de recherche et de restitution des biens culturels spoliés entre 1933 et 1945*, www.culture.gouv.fr/nous-connaitre/organisation-du-ministere/le-secretariat-general/mission-de-recherche-et-de-restitution-des-biens-culturels-spolies-entre-1933-et-1945#:~:text=La%20Mission%20de%20recherche%20et,des%20affaires%20juridiques%20et%20internationales (last visited Feb. 1, 2025) (Fr.).

[65] NIOD Institute for War, Holocaust and Genocide Studies, *Expert Centre Restitution*, www.niod.nl/en/research/expert-centre-restitution (last visited Feb. 1, 2025).

[66] *See* Chapter 3, Section 3.4.2.4.

to territories that were colonized by France and Germany, such as present-day Togo and Cameroon. The research will be led by mixed French and German teams from the fields of academia and museums.[67] This initiative clearly signals a significant step forward. That said, a fact-finding process focused on studying specific cases with the purpose of resolving disputes amicably – while creating a broader foundation for the development of soft-law jurisprudence based on the above principles of legalistic ethical reasoning – would benefit from the involvement of experts from both the relevant source nations and destination nations. Such collaboration is exemplified by the German–African project of Digital Benin.[68]

France and its public collections of colonial-era objects serve as a key example of the possibility of engaging in a "legalistic" ethical approach to develop a normative framework for restitution, through a graduated approach to wrongfulness, attribution, and the scale of remedies. Accordingly, current developments in law, policy, and markets concerning colonial-era objects may also attest to potential procedures for fact-finding and categorizing past actions, while also acknowledging the obstacles to implementing such a new normative approach.

A starting point for this approach can be attributed to the speech delivered by French president Emmanuel Macron in November 2017 at the University of Ouagadougou in Burkina Faso, according to which:

> African heritage cannot solely exist in private collections and European museums. African heritage must be showcased in Paris but also in Dakar, Lagos and Cotonou; this will be one of my priorities. Within five years I want the conditions to exist for temporary or permanent returns of African heritage to Africa.[69]

Following this declaration, President Macron commissioned two scholars, Felwine Sarr and Bénédicte Savoy, to study the issue of the possession of African cultural objects in state-owned museums in France. Their report, published in 2018 and titled *The Restitution of African Cultural Heritage. Toward a New Relational Ethics* (*Rapport sur la restitution du*

---

[67] Philip Oltermann, *France and Germany to Research Provenance of African Objects in National Museums*, THE GUARDIAN, Jan. 19, 2024. *See* Chapter 3, Section 3.4.3.

[68] *See* Chapter 4, Section 4.1.

[69] Élysée, *Emmanuel Macron's Speech at the University of Ouagadougou*, Nov. 28, 2017 (official translation into English), www.elysee.fr/en/emmanuel-macron/2017/11/28/emmanuel-macrons-speech-at-the-university-of-ouagadougou. *See also* Josh Spero & Aanu Adeoye, *The Benin Bronzes and the Road to Restitution*, FINANCIAL TIMES, Nov. 4, 2022 (quoting from President Macron's speech as a milestone in the "road to restitution").

patrimoine culturel africain. Vers une nouvelle éthique relationnelle),[70] offers a first-of-its-kind general taxonomy of about 90,000 objects in French public collections that originate from sub-Saharan Africa – 70,000 of which are currently housed in the Musée du quai Branly – Jacques Chirac in Paris. The report categorizes these items based on the specific circumstances under which these items were taken from Africa.[71]

Drawing on numerous sources, and while obviously not being able to reach a definite conclusion for each one of the items, the Sarr–Savoy Report classifies the objects into broad groups according to the "historical forms of dispossession" under which they entered the collections.[72]

The categorization of such historical circumstances consequently informs the public policy recommendations proposed in the report for each category. For instance, for items that were taken as spoils of war by French forces (and then either sold or "gifted" to French museums),[73] the report recommends "respond[ing] favorably and grant[ing] restitutions concerning objects seized within the military contexts described above, in spite of the specific juridical statute concerning military trophies obtained before the adoption in 1899 of the first Hague Convention codifying the laws of war" (i.e., recognizing that such spoils were not banned by international law before that year).[74]

A similar approach is applied to items that were taken during the "explanatory missions" and "scientific raids" that took place especially after the extraction of such cultural heritage became professionalized in the first decades of the twentieth century with the establishment of the academic field of ethnology.[75] The report recommends "to respond favorably and grant restitutions concerning objects collected in Africa during these types of 'scientific expeditions,' unless there is explicit evidence or information witnessing to the full consent on the part of the owners or initial guardians of the objects at the moment when the objects were separated from them."[76] Here too, fact-finding is crucial for the suggested policy-oriented and ethical approach to restitution.

---

[70] Felwine Sarr & Bénédicte Savoy, The Restitution of African Cultural Heritage. Toward a New Relational Ethics (2018), official English version, www.about-africa.de/images/sonstiges/2018/sarr_savoy_en.pdf (hereinafter: "Sarr–Savoy Report").

[71] *Id.* at 44–46.

[72] *Id.* at 49–50.

[73] *Id.* at 50–53.

[74] *Id.* at 54.

[75] *Id.* at 54–56.

[76] *Id.* at 56–57.

The same approach holds true for other categories, such as "gifts from private collectors" (for which the report calls for restitution unless there is evidence of "consent on behalf of the original seller"),[77] or, conversely, for items that were acquired after the independence of former colonies – for which the report recommends restitution only for items "proven to be acquired through illicit trafficking," namely in violation of export laws adopted by the source countries.[78]

The "new relational ethics" approach advocated in the Sarr–Savoy Report can be also depicted as a "legalistic" ethical approach, in the sense that it categorizes the acquisition of cultural items from Africa to France along a spectrum, based primarily on the degree of wrongfulness of the act and its attribution to a perpetrator and, correspondingly, to a victim.

In so doing, the new relational ethics approach looks practically at the fundamental principles used to determine legal liability, by examining whether an act should be considered tortious or whether an alleged contract should be invalidated owing to coercion, duress, asymmetry of information, and so forth – even if the exact same substantive, procedural, and evidentiary rules that govern civil court proceedings are not applied. Not all instances of acquisition during the colonial period or immediately thereafter are equivalent. Some can be directly attributed to the illegitimate exploitation of unequal power – whether physical power or bargaining power – while others are less wrongful.

The fact-finding and normative tools employed in the context of the Sarr–Savoy Report are not detached from key jurisprudential principles. This connection also informs the choice of an appropriate remedy, based on the level of wrongfulness and scope of attribution.

Accordingly, the law approved at the end of 2020 by the French Senate to return twenty-seven colonial-era objects from French public museums to Benin and Senegal,[79] carved out as a specific exception to the legislative

---

[77] *Id.* at 58–59.

[78] *Id.* at 59–61.

[79] Loi n° 2020–1673 du 24 décembre 2020 relative à la restitution de biens culturels à la République du Bénin et à la République du Sénégal [Law concerning the restitution of cultural property to the Republic of Benin and the Republic of Senegal], www.legifrance .gouv.fr/jorf/id/JORFTEXT000042738023 (Fr.). *See also* Hannah McGivern, *French Senate Votes Unanimously for Restitution to Benin and Senegal in "Act of Friendship and Trust,"* THE ART NEWSPAPER, Nov. 5, 2020; *France to Return Artifacts to Benin and Senegal within a Year,* ARTFORUM INT'L, Nov. 5, 2020; Xavier Perrot, *Colonial Booty and Its Restitution – Current Developments and New Perspectives for French Legislation in This Field,* 8 SANTANDER ART & CULTURE L. REV. 295 (2022) (describing the tense legislative process).

principle of inalienability of state patrimony,[80] was passed primarily for a case that falls within the "spoils of war" category identified in the Sarr–Savoy Report – namely, twenty-six royal artifacts looted by force in 1892 by French troops from the palace of Abomey in present-day Benin.[81]

The degree of "illegality" and "illegitimacy" of past actions that had taken place during the colonial period, as representing a "legalistic" ethical approach, is even more evident in the 2023 report commissioned by President Macron from the former Louvre director Jean-Luc Martinez, appointed to serve as a special ambassador for international cooperation in cultural affairs.[82]

The 2023 Report, which outlines nine normative criteria for French legislation and doctrine on "returnability criteria" for cultural property, identifies two alternative criteria for returnability concerning the way in which the cultural property was acquired: "illegality" and "illegitimacy":

> **Criterion No. 4:** The illegal nature of the acquisition
> The criterion of illegality must be assessed in light of the laws applicable in France and/or in the territory of origin at the time of acquisition. This criterion also applies to works extracted from clandestine excavations.
>
> …
>
> **Criterion No. 5:** The illegitimate nature of the acquisition
> This criterion refers to the nature or status of the person responsible for the acquisition and the context in which it took place. This poses the question of whether the person who sold or transferred a work was the legitimate owner (the procedure for acquisitions of French public collections today requires verification of the seller's or donor's legitimate ownership of the item).[83]

---

[80] *See* text accompanying *infra* note 87.

[81] In addition, France returned to Senegal the sword of El Hadj Omar Tall, a prominent resistance leader against the French colonial regime. Emery Patrick Effiboley, *Repatriation of the Regalia of the Danxomé Kingdom to the Republic of Benin – From the Demand of Restitution to the Celebration of the Return and Beyond*, Opinio Juris, Apr. 19, 2024. https://opiniojuris.org/2024/04/19/symposium-on-confronting-colonial-objects-repatriation-of-the-regalia-of-the-danxome-kingdom-to-the-republic-of-benin-from-the-demand-of-restitution-to-the-celebration-of-the-return-and-beyond/.

[82] Jean-Luc Martinez, *Rapport À l'attention de M. le Président de la République, Patrimoine partagé : universalité, restitutions et circulation des oeuvres d'art: Vers une législation et une doctrine françaises sur les "critères de restituabilité" pour les biens culturels* (2023), www.vie-publique.fr/files/rapport/pdf/289235.pdf (Fr.) (hereinafter: "2023 Report").

[83] *Id.* at 55–56. The report notes that "concerning these two criteria, the particular case of military property 'spoils of war' is treated separately, because international law expressly provides for the conditions under which it is possible to seize them (Art. 53 of the Hague Convention of 1907)." *Id.* at 56 (my translation).

These two criteria are therefore closely associated with legal concepts. The first criterion, illegality, concerns actions that had been considered illegal at the time they were taken but where the victim of the wrongful act is unable to pursue formal legal measures for a variety of reasons, including the expiry of time limits on submitting claims, lack of jurisdiction, the application of the doctrine of a good-faith purchase or acquisitive prescription, and so forth. The second criterion, illegitimacy, deals with past actions that were not considered illegal at the time of acquisition, but would be considered so – or at least as professionally or ethically wrong – by today's standards. This refers primarily to the duties of exercising due diligence when acquiring cultural objects and actively researching the provenance of the items – two contemporary norms explored in Chapter 3.

Accordingly, the criteria set out in the 2023 Report, which, if implemented, will result in new legislation or policy instruments in France, rely on what is essentially a "legalistic" ethical reasoning, addressing wrongfulness, attribution, and remedies. It remains to be seen how the recommendations of the 2023 Report (which were met with mixed responses),[84] and particularly the criteria of "illegality" and "illegitimacy," will be implemented by the French government.

Notably, the issue of "returnability criteria" for cultural property would be inherently related to a draft bill that was discussed by the French legislature – but set aside in 2024 following the opinion of the Conseil d'Etat[85] – regarding the creation of a legislative general exception to the principle of inalienability of state patrimony for colonial-era objects, rather than relying on ad hoc legislation for specific items, as was done in 2020 for the return of the twenty-seven objects.[86]

---

[84] Vincent Noce, *France's Long-Awaited Restitution Policy Is Finally Here*, THE ART NEWSPAPER, Apr. 26, 2023; Roxana Azimi, *In France, Restitution of African Artifacts Is Subject to Conditions*, LE MONDE (Eng.), May 5, 2023.

[85] Roxana Azimi, *Le Conseil d'Etat relève un frein aux restitutions d'oeuvres d'art acquises par la France dans des conditions abusives*, LE MONDE, Mar. 26, 2024 (Fr.). This delay has been met with harsh criticism among those advocating the return of cultural property to Africa. *See, e.g.,* Michel Guerrin, *France Is Pathetically Putting the Brakes on the Restitution of Art to Africa Which Is Inevitable*, LE MONDE (Eng.), Apr. 28, 2024; Babatunde E. Adebiyi, Fatima Fall Niang & Alain Godonou, *Restitution of African Cultural Heritage: "The Postponement of the Promised Law Is a Shock to Us,"* LE MONDE (Eng.), May 1, 2024.

[86] *See* text accompanying *supra* notes 79–81.

At the outset, Article 451-5 of the Cultural Heritage Code (*Code du Patrimoine*) establishes the principle of inalienability of objects contained in the collections of French national museums.[87]

In 2023, the French legislature approved two amendments that provide a general exception to the principle of inalienability in the Cultural Heritage Code for items returned in the contexts of cultural items looted during the Nazi period between 1933 and 1945,[88] and of human remains.[89] These amendments allow items falling within these two categories to be returned to dispossessed persons or their heirs, or to source countries, respectively, without the need for ad hoc legislation.[90]

---

[87] Code du Patrimoine, Livre IV: Musées, Titre V: Collections des Musées de France, Chapitre 1er: Statut des collections, L. arts. 451–55, www.legifrance.gouv.fr/codes/section_lc/LEGITEXT000006074236/LEGISCTA000006159948/. A similar provision, applying to state property held by local governments, is legislated in Article 3111-1 of the Code général de la propriété des personnes publiques (General Code of Property of Public Bodies). *See* Corinne Hershkovitch, *Restitution of Nazi-Looted Art: The French Law of 2022*, 27 ART ANTIQUITY & LAW 13, 13 n.2 (2022).

[88] Loi n° 2023–650 du 22 juillet 2023 relative à la restitution des biens culturels ayant fait l'objet de spoliations dans le contexte des persécutions antisémites perpétrées entre 1933 et 1945 [Law concerning the restitution of cultural property that was the subject of spoliation in the context of anti-Semitic persecutions perpetrated between 1933 and 1945], www.legifrance.gouv.fr/jorf/id/JORFTEXT000047874541 (Fr,). This law amends the Code du Patrimoine by adding Article 451-10-1, which reads: "By way of derogation from article L. 451-10, property from the collections of museums in France belonging to nonprofit private law legal entities, acquired by donations and bequests or with the assistance of the State or a local authority and having been the subject of dispossession between January 30, 1933, and May 8, 1945, in the context of the anti-Semitic persecutions perpetrated by Nazi Germany, by the authorities of the territories which occupied, controlled or influenced, and by the French State between July 10, 1940, and August 24, 1944, may be returned to their owner or his beneficiaries, after opinion of the commission mentioned in article L. 115- 3 and approval of the administrative authority. The High Council of Museums of France is informed in advance. By mutual agreement, the private nonprofit legal entity and the owner or his beneficiaries may agree on terms of reparation for the spoliation other than restitution of the property" (my translation).

[89] Loi n° 2023-1251 du 26 décembre 2023 relative à la restitution de restes humains appartenant aux collections publiques [Law concerning the restitution of human remains that are part of public collections], www.legifrance.gouv.fr/jorf/id/JORFTEXT000048668800 (Fr.).

[90] It should be noted, in the context of Nazi-looted cultural property, that prior to the legislation containing the general-exception law referred to in *supra* note 88, the French legislature enacted a specific law in February 2022 to enable the return of fifteen works to the heirs of victims of Nazi persecution. Loi n° 2022–218 du 21 février 2022 relative à la restitution ou la remise de certains biens culturels aux ayants droit de leurs propriétaires victimes de persécutions antisémites [Law concerning the restitution or return of certain cultural items to the heirs of the owners who were victims of anti-Semitic persecution], www.legifrance.gouv.fr/jorf/id/JORFTEXT000045197692 (Fr.). *See* Hershkovitch, *supra* note 87.

The abovementioned draft bill sought to create a third category of colonial-era objects to be granted a general exception from the principle of inalienability of public collections. However, as noted, the Conseil d'Etat advised the French Parliament not to move forward with the draft bill, citing the lack of a "compelling reason" (*motif impérieux*) or "superior general interest" (*intérêt général supérieur*) to justify contravening the principle of inalienability. The Conseil d'Etat argued that these conditions were not met in the draft bill, which only mentions the "conduct of international relations and cultural cooperation" (*la conduite des relations internationales et la coopération culturelle*).[91]

It remains to be seen whether and how the recommendations of the 2023 Report will be implemented, and how these would be integrated with legislation or other hard-law instruments that would enable the return of colonial-era cultural objects located in public collections in contravention of the principle of inalienability enshrined in the French Cultural Heritage Code. It seems, however, that the key to establishing a new policy on the matter would rely on reorienting the general-scope ethical or political reasoning of the "conduct of international relations and cultural cooperation" into a more "legalistic" mode of reasoning – one tied to the criteria of "illegality" and "illegitimacy" of past actions. The key to consolidating a new policy, in which questions of law, history, markets, and ethics are intertwined, lies in engaging systematically in fact-finding, while delineating a normative spectrum of the wrongfulness of the appropriation of cultural objects, attributing past actions to their perpetrators and assessing their implications for individual or collective victims, and selecting the remedy that is deemed most appropriate under the specific circumstances.

6.3 Reconsidering Remedial Mechanisms for Collective Claims

Constructing a scale of remedies that adheres to legalistic ethical reasoning, and also promotes a broader concept of new cultural internationalism, may prove particularly challenging in dealing with cultural property claims made by a current collective identity – such as an indigenous community or source country – when addressing the troubled past of a cultural object.

The content of an amicable agreement reached between the heirs of a dispossessed individual and a current possessor of a cultural item, or of a decision made by a body established to craft a "just and fair solution"

---

[91] *See* Azimi, *supra* note 85; Guerrin, *supra* note 85.

between such parties, would have few extracontractual limits. The situation would be different, however, when the parties involved are collective entities governed by public law and policy in their respective jurisdictions, or by other constraints on contractual arrangements.

This would be the case, for example, when a claim for restitution is made by a source country to retrieve what it considers to be a "national treasure," and as a result, once the claim is accepted, the item becomes subject to the concept of inalienability under the national code of patrimony. Such a state of events would limit the parties' ability to reach the type of "restitution-and-repurchase" remedy agreed upon in 2021 between the Alte Nazionalgalerie in Berlin and the heirs of Armand Dorville in the case of Camille Pissarro's *A Square in La Roche-Guyon*.[92] These and other differences between private claims for the restitution of cultural property once privately owned and collective claims call for a reconsideration of remedial mechanisms in the latter context.

6.3.1   Restitution and Long-Term Loans

An alternative mechanism that could be adopted for collective claims, which considers the curatorial interests of the current possessor while recognizing the overarching patrimonial interest of the source country, is that of restitution followed by a long-term loan back to the current possessor. Correspondingly, if the problem lies in the fact that the item is currently held in a state museum of a country that prohibits the deaccessioning of state collections, the item could be physically transferred to the source country under a temporary/permanent loan agreement.

As Carsten Stahn notes, such arrangements have become quite prevalent in the context of colonial-era objects.[93] For example, in 2002, France and Nigeria reached an agreement by which France would recognize Nigeria's ownership of three Nok and Sokoto sculptures that had been illegally exported from Nigeria and acquired in 1998 from a private dealer for the Musée du quai Branly – Jacques Chirac. In return, the sculptures would remain in France on a twenty-five-year loan.[94]

---

[92]   *See* text accompanying *supra* note 51.

[93]   CARSTEN STAHN, CONFRONTING COLONIAL OBJECTS: HISTORIES, LEGACIES, AND ACCESS TO CULTURE 495–501 (2023) (additionally discussing other types of "mutually beneficial return agreements" and forms of circulation or mobility).

[94]   Arthemis, Art-Law Centre University of Geneva, *Cases, Three Nok and Sokoto Sculptures – Nigeria and France*, https://plone.unige.ch/art-adr/cases-affaires/three-nok-and-sokoto-sculptures-2013-nigeria-and-france (last visited Feb. 1, 2025).

Such loan agreements may have additional benefits beyond bypassing legal constraints. As shown in Chapter 1, in the context of the growing number of restitution agreements concerning the Benin Bronzes between Western countries and the Nigerian government and/or the Oba of Benin Kingdom, in many cases some of the items remain in Western cultural institutions.[95]

Godwin Obaseki, the governor of Edo state, noted in a 2022 interview that, while recognizing the underlying ownership of the Benin artifacts is the key goal for Nigerians, maintaining possession and display of some of the items in other countries may serve its own purposes. According to Obaseki, Nigeria does not seek physical possession of every artifact being held in foreign museums because these items serve as "ambassadors," given that the "rest of the world still needs to know about the Benin works."[96] Such an arrangement also serves a practical purpose for the interim period until exhibition spaces are fully established in Nigeria.[97]

6.3.2 Digital Restitution

A different type of remedy that is increasingly discussed in the context of claims made by collective entities, including source countries but also indigenous communities and other nonstate groups, is that of digital restitution. The rapidly increasing process of digitalization of museum artifacts, including various forms of virtually recording, processing, and reconstructing the different spatial dimensions of such items, has instigated a broad discussion about the interface between the control and possession of the physical items – such as archaeological artifacts or artworks for which copyright no longer exists – and the entitlements to their "digital twins" or other reproductions,[98] as discussed in Chapter 5 in the context of their appropriation by museums.

Digitalization may also affect remedies. In a few cases, Western institutions have already collaborated with groups and other actors in source

---

[95] *See* Chapter 1, Section 1.1.

[96] Josh Spero & Aanu Adeoye, *The Benin Bronzes and the Road to Restitution*, FINANCIAL TIMES, Nov. 4, 2022.

[97] Alex Marshall, *Who Owns the Benin Bronzes? The Answer Just Got More Complicated*, N.Y. TIMES, June 4, 2023.

[98] *See, generally,* Pınar Oruç & Uma Suthersanen, *Intellectual Property and Cultural Heritage Issues for Museums of Archaeological Materials, in* RESEARCH HANDBOOK ON INTELLECTUAL PROPERTY AND CULTURAL HERITAGE 392, 407–11 (Irini Stamatoudi ed., 2022).

countries to transfer, or at least share, entitlements embedded in such digital recreations of cultural items. One such instance of "digital repatriation" is the result of a collaboration between the People's Palace Projects (sponsored by Queen Mary University of London) and the British-supported foundation Arte Factum, by which scanned reproductions of caves and village environments within the Brazilian Xingu communities were digitally recreated, virtually materialized, and digitally repatriated to the indigenous communities.[99]

The 2018 Sarr–Savoy Report, discussed in Section 6.2, calls for a systematic incorporation of "digital sharing" within the menu of remedial mechanisms designed for colonial-era objects:

> A large number of photographic, cinematographic, or sound documents concerning African societies once held by former colonial administrations have recently been part of intensive campaigns for digitization projects … Within the framework of the project of restitutions, these digitized objects must be made part of a radical practice of sharing, including how one rethinks the politics of image rights use. Given the large number of French institutions concerned and the difficulty that a foreign public has for navigating through these museums, we recommend the creation of a single portal providing access to this precious documentation in the form of a platform that would be *open access*.[100]

Alongside the critique voiced against this recommendation of the Sarr–Savoy Report, arguing that the very concept of digitalization as a replacement to physical restitution may "render all cultural heritage that has a digital surrogate a lesser form of heritage" and diminish the value of objects to the detriment of indigenous communities and other groups in source territories,[101] the concept of open access also disregards another interim option – the possibility that the current possessor (i.e., a national museum in the destination country) and the source nation or community would have joint proprietary control over the digital reproduction of the item, allowing both parties to generate revenue by granting certain types of access or use to third parties.

---

[99] *Id.* at 410 n.81. For further details on this project, *see* People's Palace Projects, *Kamukuwaká: Recreating an Ancient Indigenous Cultural Site in Full Size*, https://peoplespalaceprojects .org.uk/en/projects/the-sacred-cave-of-kamukuwaka/ (last visited Feb. 1, 2025).

[100] Sarr–Savoy Report, *supra* note 70, at 67.

[101] Lucas Lixinski, *Digital Heritage Surrogates, Decolonization, and International Law: Restitution, Control and the Creation of Value as Reparations and Emancipation*, 6 SANTANDER ART & CULTURE L. REV. 65, 80 (2020).

As discussed at length in Chapter 5, a normative model of ownership and custody of cultural objects could distinguish between basic forms of digital access, which should be available to the global audience as part of the possessor's duty as a global custodian of culture, and more high-input forms of reproduction, or those that inherently tie the item to the space where it is located, which could serve as a legitimate source of revenue through merchandizing, licensing, and so forth.

The same holds true, with even greater force, for a situation in which an object is digitally reproduced for the purpose of digital restitution, in the form and manner agreed upon between the source community and the current possessor, and such a digital reproduction may also hold value for others.

The door should be left open, as a matter of principle, for a digital restitution model that endows certain exclusive or proprietary rights to the parties to the agreement vis-à-vis other parties. Unlike the Sarr–Savoy model's suggestion, third-party access to a "digital twin"[102] need not be all-inclusive. Moreover, as a normative matter, in the case of such a digital recreation and restitution, both the current possessor and the source community could argue for an inherent link between the cultural item and the *place* where it is located, or has originated from, as a basis for proprietary entitlement.

The concept of digital restitution, without necessarily committing in advance to unrestrained open access, can be considered as part of the future trajectory of the Digital Benin project, discussed in Chapter 4.[103] While, as noted by art historian Felicity Bodenstein, who leads the provenance section of Digital Benin, in order to alleviate potential tension with the various institutions, "[w]e had to reassure them that they remained owners of their data, we weren't asking for digital restitution, images, rights and things like that,"[104] the question of ownership of the digital data, and its potential restitution to the source country, is being raised by at least some of the African counterparts involved in the project.[105]

---

[102] Compare Xiaomin Zhang, Lemin Zhang & Ako Ullah, *Digital Twin Technology and Wisdom Museum from the Perspective of Artificial Intelligence*, in APPLICATION OF INTELLIGENT SYSTEMS IN MULTI-MODAL INFORMATION ANALYTICS: THE 4TH INTERNATIONAL CONFERENCE ON MULTI-MODAL INFORMATION ANALYTICS (ICCMIA 2022), Vol. 1, 674–82 (Vijayan Sugumaran, A.G. Sreedevi & Zheng Xu eds., 2022).

[103] *See* Chapter 4, Section 4.1.

[104] Spero & Adeoye, *supra* note 96 (quoting Felicity Bodenstein).

[105] *Id.* (interviewing Onyekachi Wambu, executive director of Afford – the African Foundation for Development).

This option has also been raised explicitly by the project's leaders. According to Dr. Anne Luther, the chief coordinator of Digital Benin: "We organised the storing of data received from the museums in a way that would make a digital restitution process possible in the future, which would conclude the transfer of ownership of digital materials currently stored by the institutions about the Benin holdings."[106] While it remains to be seen whether the 136 institutions, or at least some of them, will agree to some form of digital restitution or the sharing of rights to digital products, the very existence of a consolidated digital database makes this option a practical one, regardless of the entirely different issue of physical restitution. Accordingly, the framework of the Digital Benin project opens the door to remedial mechanisms for collective claims that would be based on digital reproduction and restitution, entailing both intangible and material value to the parties, while conforming to their duties as global custodians in an era of "new cultural internationalism."

6.3.3 Introducing the Cross-Border Trust

As noted in Chapter 1, in the context of what is the probably the most prominent lingering cross-border dispute over cultural property, that of the Parthenon Marbles, in a 2022 interview the British Museum's deputy director called for the establishment of a "Parthenon partnership" to resolve the conflict.[107]

While this specific dispute has not yet been resolved, the concept of "partnership" or similar terms have surfaced in other contexts. For instance, in 2022, the Smithsonian Institution published the "Smithsonian Shared Stewardship and Ethical Returns Statement of Values and Principles."[108] However, the term "shared stewardship" is not defined in elaborate terms and does not outline an organizational or legal blueprint for implementing this notion. The document settles

---

[106] Digital Benin, *Documentation, Introduction* (Dr. Anne Luther), https://digitalbenin.org/documentation/introduction (last visited Feb. 1, 2025).

[107] Sarah Bexter & Liam Kelly, *Elgin Marbles: "Partnership" Raises Hope of Deal for First Return to Greece in 200 Years*, THE SUNDAY TIMES, July 30, 2022; Naomi Clarke, *British Museum Executive Calls for "Parthenon Partnership" over Elgin Marbles*, INDEPENDENT, July 31, 2022.

[108] Smithsonian Ethical Returns Working Group, *Smithsonian Shared Stewardship and Ethical Returns Statement of Values and Principles* (Apr. 29, 2022), https://ncp.si.edu/sites/default/files/files/Ethical%20Return%20Docs/shared-stewardship-and-ethical-returns-values-and-principles_4.29.2022.pdf.

for a relatively broad set of principles, stating: "We recognize the benefit of community representation in Smithsonian collections, the value of sharing less widely known or appreciated histories, and our role as collaborative custodians of cultural and historical legacies deserving honor and respect."[109]

Despite calls from commentators advocating for the creation of "special councils or commissions" to provide communities in source territories with a voice in management and a share in the benefits accruing to cultural institutions,[110] no such systematic model is currently in operation.

This should probably not come as a surprise. Recognizing the contemporaneous interests of different groups of stakeholders in a cultural item and, even more so, in a collection of items (which hold special value as a collection and should therefore not be partitioned – consider, again, a potential resolution to the current fragmentation of the Parthenon Marbles between the Acropolis Museum and the British Museum) – while allowing for an effective administration that could overcome differences of opinion and potential deadlocks can prove to be a burdensome task.

Aside from the need to come up with a tentative decision-making structure that would be both fair to multiple stakeholders and efficient in providing for collective action,[111] questions of costs also feature prominently in facilitating models of long-term "shared stewardship" or "partnership." On the one hand, the costs, in terms of both capital expenditures and human labor, of setting up and maintaining a standalone organizational structure to govern a single cultural item may be prohibitive, making such an approach unrealistic as a model of restitution-through-shared-stewardship for each such item. On the other hand, the challenge of establishing a "blanket" costewardship structure to govern an entire collection of items whenever there is a genuine curatorial interest in preventing a full-fledged partitioning of items could also be significant.

In property theory terms, the joint governance of cultural items for the contemporaneous benefit of various stakeholders – such as a public museum in possession of such items (thereby representing both the public interests of its home jurisdiction and its own institutional interests)

---

[109] Id.
[110] See STAHN, supra note 93, at 497; Charity Gates, Who Owns African Art? Envisioning a Legal Framework for the Restitution of African Cultural Heritage, 3 INT'L COMP., POLICY & ETHICS L. REV. 1131, 1159–62 (2020).
[111] For the concept of "collective action" in the context of asset governance, see generally ELINOR OSTROM, GOVERNING THE COMMONS: THE EVOLUTION OF INSTITUTIONS FOR COLLECTIVE ACTION (James E. Alt & Douglass C. North eds., 1990).

and a source nation or community – may encounter both "commons" and "anticommons" problems in governing cultural items.[112]

This section argues that trust law can offer an institutional alternative.[113] It would rely on the long-standing law and practice that governs the fiduciary administration of assets by a trustee in favor of multiple beneficiaries, while extending current doctrine that focuses on the multibeneficiary intergenerational trust to contemporaneous cobeneficiaries, including collective entities.[114] In this way, a cross-border trust can also serve as a key remedial mechanism for restitution.

Prior to engaging concretely in the potential outline of a cross-border trust in the context of mechanisms for restitution, especially following a claim made by a source nation or community, it is worth considering the manner in which institutional mechanisms may be essential for dealing with multiple stakeholders. This is particularly relevant whenever artworks, archaeological artifacts, or other cultural property assets hold particular value as part of a collection or are otherwise substantively interconnected, necessitating coordinated decision-making for the group of assets. Trust or trust-like mechanisms could alleviate at least some collective action problems.

Consider, for example, the types of collective action problems that multiple heirs of an artist may come across. To start with, even in cases where artistic or other valuable objects can be divided or partitioned among the various heirs, the coowners would have to agree on the value of the various

---

[112] The problem of "commons," as articulated by Garret Hardin in *The Tragedy of the Commons*, 162 Sci. 1243 (1968) and subsequent literature, highlights the ways in which an institutional regime, under which each person has a liberty to use a common-pool resource as he or she deems fit but no right to prevent others from doing the same, will likely result in the overuse of, underinvestment in, and inevitable depletion of the resource. On the other end of the scale, under the "anticommons" theory, the overfragmentation of private property rights in assets can lead to inefficient and unjust results, such as the undersupply of biomedical innovation due to exclusive patents over fragments of knowledge. *See* MICHAEL HELLER, THE GRIDLOCK ECONOMY: HOW TOO MUCH OWNERSHIP WRECKS MARKETS, STOPS INNOVATION, AND COSTS LIVES (2008). This theory has not remained uncontested. *See* Richard A. Epstein, *Heller's Gridlock Economy in Perspective: Why There Is Too Little, Not Too Much Private Property*, 53 ARIZ. L. REV. 51 (2011).

[113] Amnon Lehavi, *The Law of Trusts and Collective Action: A New Approach to Property Deadlocks*, 89 U. CIN. L. REV. 388, 431 (2021) (explaining that "trust law offers a new institutional approach for dealing with property deadlocks among multiple stakeholders whenever the partition of the asset or estate among the stakeholders is either impracticable or otherwise suboptimal for the group").

[114] *Id.*

items and the specific allocation of assets for each coheir. For instance, the five coheirs of Pablo Picasso, who died intestate in 1973, leaving behind approximately 45,000 works, endured six years of bitter negotiations, at an overall cost of 30 million dollars, before reaching a settlement on the division of the estate.[115] Interestingly, the division of Picasso's works also involved the French government, which agreed to accept works of art in lieu of estate taxes.[116]

However, in addition to the potential division of the physical works among coheirs, other assets related to the estate cannot be partitioned and therefore require continuous mutual governance. In the case of Picasso, his son Claude Picasso, who had been named the legal administrator of Picasso's estate by a French court, created the Picasso Administration in 1996.[117] This organization acts for and on behalf of "Succession Picasso" or "Indivision Picasso" (*indivision* being a form of joint ownership under French law).[118] The Picasso Administration manages the assets that remain indivisible: rights to Picasso's reproductions and exhibitions; the issuance of merchandizing licenses for the use of Picasso's name, image, autograph, and so on; responsibility for the authentication of Picasso's work, while combating misattributions, forgeries, and so forth; and other issues relating to the management of Picasso's estate as a whole, including his legacy and reputation.[119]

The Picasso Administration, operating as an administrative trust-like entity for the benefit of the heirs as a group, is therefore an essential tool for collectively managing the indivisible components of Picasso's estate, while also streamlining the occasional reassembly of the divided parts of the estate, such as when Picasso's physical works are loaned for the purpose of a retrospective exhibition.[120]

How can such mechanisms be adapted for "shared stewardship" or "shared custody" of a substantial collection of objects, especially when the collection is held in one country by one or more public museums, and a

---

[115] Milton Esterow, *The Battle for Picasso's Multi-Billion-Dollar Empire*, VANITY FAIR, Mar. 7, 2016.

[116] These works included "203 paintings, 158 sculptures, 88 ceramics, nearly 1,500 drawings, more than 1,600 prints, and 33 sketchbooks." *Id.* This transfer to the French government formed the core collection of the Picasso Museum in Paris. *Id.*

[117] *See* Picasso Administration, *Rights*, http://picasso.fr/en/rights (last visited Feb. 1, 2025).

[118] The legal status of *indivision* is governed by the provisions of Articles 815-1 and 1873 of the French Civil Code.

[119] Esterow, *supra* note 115; Sara Hamdan, *Lawsuits, Forgeries and Family Feuds: The Afterlives of Famous Artists*, CNN, Mar. 31, 2017.

[120] *See* Picasso Administration, *Rights*, supra note 117.

source country or community makes a claim for recognizing its proprietary interests in a collection taken from its territory in a contested manner?

One possible way to govern such assets could be the establishment of a cross-border trust, managed by joint trustees from the country of origin and the country of the object's current location or, alternatively, by a third-party trustee (or group of trustees) acceptable to both parties. The underlying goals and purposes of the trust would be defined in the deed of trust signed by the parties while empowering the trustee to make decisions in the interests of the cobeneficiaries.

Under this model, the trustee would be bound by the long-standing rules and practices that have emerged in trust law, most prominently in Anglo-American legal systems but also in continental law ones, by which the trustee is bound by the duty of loyalty, duty of care, duty to inform and account, and so on.[121]

Moreover, the duty of impartiality was developed in trust law to cover situations in which the trust has two or more beneficiaries or purposes – whether such purposes are private, charitable, or mixed. It applies whether the beneficiaries' interests or purposes are successive or concurrent.[122]

This doctrine features most prominently in the context of an intergenerational or otherwise successive trust, such as when one person (e.g., a surviving spouse) is designated as a life beneficiary and another person (e.g., the testator's and/or the beneficiary's child), known as the remainder beneficiary, receives a future interest to be materialized upon the death of the life beneficiary.[123] In multibeneficiary trusts, the trustee is required to give due regard to the interests of the diverse beneficial interests created by the terms of the trust and to act impartially in regard to investing, protecting, and distributing the estate, and in performing all administrative functions. In consulting and communicating with beneficiaries, the

---

[121] Lehavi, *supra* note 113, at 413–16.

[122] RESTATEMENT (THIRD) OF TRUSTS, Reporter's Notes on §79, cmts. a, b (2007).

[123] Such trusts are often crafted such that the life beneficiary is entitled to "income" from the trust's assets, while the remainder beneficiary is entitled to the trust's "principal" or "capital." In such a case, the classification of a certain return as either income or capital decides which of the beneficiaries will be entitled to it. More fundamentally, such a split between current and future beneficiaries of the trust leads to potential conflicts or preferences with regard to the types of investment and management choices that the trustee has to make, such as whether to look for short- or long-term gains, or to replace assets not prone to appreciation. In the case of multiple present beneficiaries, the parties may diverge in their needs, tax positions, level of risk tolerance, etc. A similar set of differences may also apply to multiple future beneficiaries. *Id.* at General Comments.

trustee is further required to proceed in a manner that fairly reflects the diversity of their concerns and beneficial interests. The duty of impartiality further forbids the trustee from being influenced by personal favoritism or animosity toward individual beneficiaries, or from ignoring their interests due to oversight or neglect.[124]

Obviously, adapting the private law, multibeneficiary trust model to an institutional mechanism that incorporates both state and nonstate actors located across national borders as cobeneficiaries, while transferring formal title to the collection – or at least strong legal powers of control and decision-making to a trustee (or group of trustees) – will encounter multiple challenges. The cross-border parties would have to agree not only on the details of the internal structure of the trust and its overarching goals but on the identity of the trustee(s), the applicable law that would apply to the trust, and which court (or other dispute resolution mechanism) would have jurisdiction to adjudicate potential conflicts.

Additional complications may arise. A transfer of formal title or a functionally equivalent set of control and decision-making rights from a state or public museum to a trustee could come into potential conflict with rules of inalienability that exist in some national patrimony laws.[125]

That said, trust and trust-like mechanisms have proven effective in addressing collective action problems involving both public and private parties, including those located across borders. The general flexibility of trusts, alongside their long-standing mechanisms for separating between legal and beneficial ownership while ensuring that trustees abide by their duties to beneficiaries,[126] has demonstrated its efficacy in other cross-border contexts involving both public and private parties.

An example is the World Bank's Trust Funds (TFs) program.[127] TFs are a "financing arrangement set up with contributions from one or more development partners," including countries and sovereign wealth funds as well as other parties located across national borders, which "allow the Bank to mobilize and direct concessional resources to strategic

---

124 *Id.* at Reporter's Notes on §79 cmt. b.
125 *See* the example of France, discussed above in the text accompanying *supra* notes 87–91.
126 *See* Robert H. Sitkoff, *Trust Law as Fiduciary Governance Plus Asset Portioning, in* THE WORLDS OF THE TRUST 428–53 (Lionel Smith ed., 2013) (explaining that, in addition to the trust's internal governance matters, which address the powers and duties of the trustee and the corresponding rights of the beneficiary, trust law is also typified by "asset portioning" – the separation between the trust's property and the trustee's personal assets).
127 World Bank Group, *Trust Funds and Partnerships*, www.worldbank.org/en/programs/trust-funds-and-programs (last visited Feb. 1, 2025).

development priorities and to mobilize the resources and capabilities of other development actors through partnership programs."[128] Such programs advance national, regional, or global goals, such as climate change adaptation and mitigation, pandemic prevention and preparedness, energy access, food and nutrition security, enabling digitalization, and so forth.[129] According to the World Bank, "more than 150 donors partner with the World Bank through trust funds. Most are sovereign entities. Others include multinational agencies, foundations, non-governmental organizations (NGOs), and private organizations."[130] The World Bank serves as the trustee in allocating the funds contributed by the public and private partners located across borders, such that "in administering a trust fund and holding the trust fund resources, the World Bank acts in a fiduciary capacity in accordance only with the provisions of the agreement concerning the trust fund."[131]

A cross-border trust could serve as a potential organizational and legal structure to facilitate the shared stewardship of collections of cultural items affiliated with state and nonstate entities across borders, including in source territories and destination countries where cultural institutions have been long-term custodians of these items. A bilateral cross-border trust could be created, for example, between Germany and Nigeria as an umbrella organization to oversee the governance of the collections of Benin Bronzes housed in German public museums.[132] Similar bilateral cross-border trusts could be created for other dyads of countries in the context of colonial-era items, such as in the case of France and its former colonies in Africa.[133] Outside the colonial context, the bilateral trust structure could also be applied to other dyads of countries where a substantial number of objects have illicitly moved between countries over time.

In some cases, international bodies and organizations such as UNIDROIT or UNESCO could serve as intermediaries or partners within such a trust, or even as the trustee itself. Obviously, many more

---

[128] *Id.*
[129] World Bank, 2023 Trust Fund Annual Report: Addressing Global Challenges (2023), at 1, https://documents1.worldbank.org/curated/en/099625012182377211/pdf/IDU0e4629bd5007e30433f0b0b507fab8443db8a.pdf.
[130] World Bank Group, Partnering with the World Bank Through Trust Funds and Umbrella 2.0 Programs (2023), at 3, https://thedocs.worldbank.org/en/doc/85936e023f875cd12c3d14ce844b6b33-0060072023/original/Partnering-with-the-World-Bank-through-Trust-Funds-and-Umbrella-2-Oct-2023.pdf.
[131] *Id.* at 2.
[132] *See* Chapter 1, Section 1.1.
[133] *See supra* Section 6.2.

details would have to be worked out for such a cross-border trust to become an operational alternative remedial mechanism to wholesale cross-border physical restitution. That said, the cross-border trust could prove essential for enabling remedial mechanisms that allow for the exhibition, preservation, circulation, and financial management of such shared collections.

6.4   Coda: Toward Convergence of Law, Policy, and Markets for Cultural Property

Whereas in the past cultural objects were removed from source territories through the use of force, opportunism, or dealings that were largely typified by an imbalance of power working against the local/national entity that held the object, source countries and communities are now in a better position to secure the preservation of their cultural heritage through a variety of means.

The rapidly evolving landscape of hard-law and soft-law mechanisms, described in this book, provides a safety net that allows countries, communities, and cultural institutions to collaborate with each other, without the constant fear of being exploited or having to make a binary choice between national "isolationism" – for example, by adopting a strict ban on all exports of cultural items – or simply yielding to the forces of the international market for art and antiquities. This does not mean that no cultural objects will ever be offered in the market and sold to the highest bidder but, rather, that that the combination of hard-law and soft-law mechanisms can provide solutions for certain categories or specific items that are contested and could thus hinder cross-border collaboration. Creating an institutional infrastructure for cross-border collaboration requires the establishment of both backward-looking mechanisms for the resolution of past conflicts no longer governed by formal legal rules, as well as a forward-looking construction of legal, professional, and ethical tools. Moreover, creating a system that seeks to advance the concept of new cultural internationalism also calls for the streamlining of real-time law enforcement measures against illicit trafficking, as well as the consolidation of concepts of due diligence, provenance research, and other professional norms that would apply to both public and private parties across borders.

To facilitate this vision of new cultural internationalism – one that recognizes the importance of place, origin, and historical context but also views countries, communities, and cultural institutions in both source countries and destination countries as global custodians of culture – legal, professional, and ethical mechanisms should offer a broad spectrum of arrangements, such as those based on the circulation of objects via loans or various modes of partnerships and joint custody, supported by national and cross-border provisions on export/import controls, patrimony laws, and so forth. These collaborative models should be complemented by organizational and technological solutions, such as digital databases and other forms of information-sharing, which help to create a true sense of transparency and accountability.

More broadly, the drivers of change described in this book can help pave the way for a new normative agenda to guide the field of cultural property in the twenty-first century. This book presents a normative blueprint for designing the legal future of cultural property, while constantly considering the interface between legally binding norms and soft-law instruments, professional norms, ethical considerations, and other forces that impact the actions of the different stakeholders.

This book has shown how the combination of hard-law mechanisms with professional and ethical norms that are gradually maturing toward soft-law jurisprudence can bring about the convergence of law, policy, and markets for cultural property without imposing top-down uniformity. Various mechanisms are already at work, and should be further developed, to address the cross-border governance of cultural items – recognizing that at least certain aspects of law and regulation will continue to diverge among different jurisdictions – with the goal of allowing countries, cultural institutions, and other actors to engage in cross-border collaboration. The convergence of law, policy, and markets for cultural property does not call for wholesale unity, but rather, for cooperative efforts to adopt the normative agenda of new cultural internationalism.

INDEX

For EU product safety concerns, contact us at Calle de José Abascal, 56–1°,
28003 Madrid, Spain or eugpsr@cambridge.org.

www.ingramcontent.com/pod-product-compliance
Ingram Content Group UK Ltd
Pitfield, Milton Keynes, MK11 3LW, UK
UKHW020454240426
470322UK00016B/337